She Is Everywhere!

Tanit, African—Semitic Goddess
by Monica Sjoo

She Is Everywhere!

An anthology of writing in womanist/ feminist spirituality

gathered by Lucia Chiavola Birnbaum, Ph.D.

Matomah Alesha, Laura Amazzone, M.A., Gian Banchero, Anne Bouie, Ph.D., Louisa Calio, Angeleen Campra, Ph.D., Janine Canan, M.D., Susan Carter, Ph.D., Jennifer Colby, Ph.D., Max Dashú, Patti Davis, M.A., M.F.A., Leslene della Madre, Vivian Deziak Hahn, M.A., Latonia Dixon, Naomi Doumbia, Ph.D., Ida Dunson, M.A., Pamela Eakins, Ph.D., May Elawar, MA, Chickie Farella, Tricia Grame, Ph.D., Deborah Grenn Ph.D., Hera Hagstoz, M.A., Kalli Halvorson, M.A., Miri Hunter Haruach, Ph.D, Necia Harkless, Ph.D., Jean Harris, Mara Keller, Ph.D., Velia Kroupa, M.A., Lorraine Macchello, Jodi MacMillan, Diana Marto, Shiloh McCloud, Sandy Miranda, M.A., Mary Beth Moser, M.A., Aikya Param, MA, Delphyne Platner, Ph.D., Dorotea Reyna, M.A., Marguerite Rigoglioso, M.A., Deborah Rose, M.A., Mary Saracino, Elizabeth Shillington, Ph.D., Anya Silverman, M.A., Susan Sopcak, M.A., Elisabeth Sikie, Monica Sjoo, Luisah Teish, Ph.D., Karen Villanueva, M.A., Mari Ziolkowski, Ph. D

iUniverse, Inc.

New York Lincoln Shanghai

She Is Everywhere!
An anthology of writing in womanist/feminist spirituality

2436 Sacramento Street
Berkeley, Ca. 94702
510.883.0600
www.belladonna.ws

iUniverse books may be ordered through booksellers or by contacting:

iUniverse
2021 Pine Lake Road, Suite 100
Lincoln, NE 68512
www.iuniverse.com
1-800-Authors (1-800-288-4677)

ISBN: 0-595-34034-2

Printed in the United States of America

to her

"By venerating Her I am able to salute the divinity in all women and myself."

—Luisah Teish

"A goddess perspective in the world will do whatever is needed to promote a life of dignity, creativity, renewal and resilience."

—Matomah Alesha

"Perhaps the Divine Mother is calling Her prodigal children back home to her waiting arms. Perhaps She is reminding us that there is much in the unseen that our modern world gravely needs. Grace. Compassion. The belief in the power of love to conquer injustice and evil."

—Mary Saracino

"If women's stories were viewed as worthy of record, how might this have altered the course of history?"

—Delphyne Platner

"We live in difficult, increasingly decadent, wildly populous and turbulent times. May we maintain our courage and grow all the more, spreading the light of consciousness and love in a renaissance of the beautiful, caring, all powerful Feminine."

—Janine Canan

"We are at the brink of new age which will be defined by new concepts in science, religion, and the reclamation of the values of the Dark Mother."

—Necia Harkless

"Although the evidence for the concept of sacred female generative energy is widespread and abundant and can be traced back 50,000 years, it has largely been ignored or denied in the relatively recent process of re-imagining divinity as exclusively male."

—Angeleen Campra

"The symbolic language on jewelry is endless, yet a reverent expression for nature can be found on pieces from around the globe. If one looks closely enough, one will see that the Creatrix of Life and Death, the Great Goddess, Mother of the Universe, has been a predominant influence on the sacred art of adornment from earliest times."

—Laura Amazzone

"From the birthplace of humanity where the beginning seeds of life first germinated and developed, beats her steady pulse, in the heart of her bosom, the heartbeat of the Dark Mother."

—Naomi Doumbia

"The more women's voices I heard; the more I came to see the Sacred Feminine as immanent; the more I saw women who seemed to be filled with joy even in the midst of adverse circumstances..."

—Deborah Grenn

"A legion of poets have been called to spirit, leaving what is now an unprecedented number of poems addressing the Great Goddess in her many forms..."

—Louisa Calio

"In my micro-geography, she is everywhere: in a sweat lodge in Indian Canyon, or in the Guadalupe chapel in San Juan Bautista, in a field of blue corn in Aromas protected with corn dollies, or in the Rodriquez Street Laundry in Watsonville…"

—Jennifer Colby

"It's a particularly powerful experience when one's spiritual path, academic pursuits, and ethnic explorations all converge, as they do for me in my research on Italian stregoneria/witchcraft. Discovering the hidden shamanic and goddess-centered culture operating in Sicily and Italy for thousands of years has connected me with my ancestors and provided strength and guidance for my continuing work as both a scholar and a priestess."

—Marguerite Rigoglioso

"When cultural traditions are interpreted from the standpoint of woman hermeneutics, then what was hidden becomes clear."

—Miri Hunter Haruach

"By recognizing that dark female images of the divine have long been honored, we can begin to rethink the meaning of darkness and reclaim its power."

—Mary Beth Moser

"Reclaiming the mother, proudly reclaiming, at last I give birth to myself."

—Susan Carter

"The energy of all human beings began with her bloodline."

—Ida Dunson

"The creation of the Goddess is a world in motion. Her body is the cone: the effulgent point from which all life flows."

—Vivian Deziak Hahn

"We all come from the Dark Mother…attune to her mysteries and you will know that the enlightened do greatly shine, and her darkness is, indeed, *radiant.*"

—Pamela Eakins

"In bringing memories of Her to the surface, I feel reborn, reconnected to the Earth, reunited with my Great Mother."

—Sandy Miranda

"Mother is understanding and intelligence. She is intuition. She is the cup, the Holy Grail."

—Karen Villanueva

"Perhaps the memory of the dark mother through her image as the black stone in Mecca would usher the world into a new era of peace, harmony and religious tolerance."

—May Elawar

"The Great Goddess of prehistory, and by proxy of the land, has evolved and struggled and has had her rituals eclipsed by the modern cult of Christ, and yet still maintained a hold, albeit a subliminal one, on the people of Spain."

—Hera Hagstoz

"...images of Mary throughout Spain reinforced the belief that she is everywhere."

—Velia Kroupa

"Students of women's spirituality are typically taught that patriarchy was cosmologically consolidated with the help of sky gods. However, it seems to me that under patriarchy, the heavens were simply appropriated by male deities, and the female deities were, at best, confined to earth. My work in women's spirituality is therefore dedicated to the principle that heaven and earth are fully female, fully male, and most importantly, fully beyond both."

—Kalli Halvorson

"...I was utterly surprised to discover that the Catholic Church, the religion of my childhood, holds a treasure trove of clues about other times, older times, when women held positions of power as spiritual leaders and teachers."

—Deborah Rose

"The discovery of Her has brought an improved sense of balance into my personal and professional relationships."

—Chickie Farella

"Although little has been written about it, Guatemala is an example of a country where Mary's presence can be seen and felt everywhere."

—Elizabeth Shillington

"Reclaiming, adopting, and internalizing the Crone as a positive image is a way for older women to empower themselves."

—Anya Silverman

"I know that this life force is all there is and it is enough, I call this life force goddess."

—Susan Sopcak

"With this remembering, I am grateful for all that is inside of me. I am grateful, and love fiercely, my body's intelligence, my mind's unquenchable passion to understand the Self, and my inherent, unbreakable link to that which is both divine and feminine."

—Elizabeth Sikie

"I honor [Magdalene] as a vehicle of the divine feminine manifest on the earth plane, priestess, teacher, semi-divine yogini. I honor her as co-redemptrix, initiator and soul-mate to Christ. And I honor her as doorway to the Dark Mother, she who holds all the paradox of the world within Her."

—Mari Ziolkowski

"My life is dedicated to HER. I am aware that I am updating mythology by embodying her teachings in sacred ceremonies and in sacred art."

—Diana Marto

"Traveling to lands and sacred sites where evidence of the Goddess is irrefutable gives me a new spark and added hope…Sardinia herself *is* the Great Mother."

—Leslene della Madre

"It happens after you die. Your body they make into fertilizer but the nishome or spirit that lives inside of you, it's always around, like electricity, they can switch us on and off."

—Jean Harris

Why is the Goddess so important? There is no panacea for all our modern ailments, yet to many, the Goddess symbolizes our best hope for a viable, sustainable future. This is because she represents an antidote to the imbalances between the sexes, humans and other species, the rich and poor, diffferent races, cultures and religions, war and peace.

—Mara Lynn Keller

"I believe the dark goddess teaches us fearlessness."

—Anne Bouie

Contents

List of Illustrations

Creation Song by Shiloh McCloud Prints and greeting cards are available of the front cover image at www.colorofwoman.com. A portion of the proceeds will go towards the next She is Everywhere, Vol. II. (front cover)

Female Series, Female Fusion © 2000 by Tricia Grame (18" x 11" x 13" clay, plaster, cement, acrylic, steel and wood) (back cover)

Note on Style for *She is everywhere!*

This anthology is written by womanists and/or feminists who live, for the most part, in northern California, historical bellwether region of the United States, where we vote left of the violent patriarchal center, and subaltern cultures green everywhere.

Contributors to this anthology are close to the path-breaking scholarly programs in Women's Spirituality at California Institute of Integral Studies and New College in San Francisco. Many of us are also close to women's spirituality resource centers and sanctuaries like Belladonna in Berkeley—where Jodi MacMillan, Laura Amazzone and Andrew Fitzpatrick have helped to see to publication of volumes in the series *She is everywhere! Dark mother rising!*

In the first years of the new millennium—as the dominant polity of the United States wreaks war on the dark and the poor in Iraq as well as in the U. S.—we resist paradigms of the dominant culture based on violence and hierarchy, just as we nonviolently resist war and injustice.

As part of the vast and vibrant network of women's cultures across the world, we consider the what and where of womanist and feminist movements too multi-faceted to be categorized. Subsumed to our major value of equality (documented by geneticists and archeologists in the datum that we are one human race and that the human race began in Africa) we appreciate cultural differences, yet the center of this anthology is suggested in that a variety of participants responded to calls for papers for volumes entitled *She is everywhere!* and *Dark mother rising!*

Contributions to this anthology are "unedited" in the sense that nobody modified anyone's vision, an open-endedness that also extends to style. For example, my own style of downcasing (see Note on Style in *Dark Mother*) reflects my dislike for capitalization; as a historian I consider capitals a custom that perpetuates the hierarchy of nation states and dominant cultures in the modern era. Please note: my ideas about style were not imposed on others in this anthology.

People who like patriarchal definitions and consistency will have to look elsewhere. Participants in this anthology reject the dominant culture's foreshortening of history to the relatively recent epoch of violent patriarchy; in this sense we may be considered *"traditional"* in looking to prehistory as well as to history for possibilities. Against a contemporary backdrop of patriarchal violence, we may be considered *"radical"* in that we consider our nonviolent resistance to injustice and war part of our scholarship as responsible intellectuals.

More *"scholarly,"* perhaps, than contemporary purveyors of masculinist epistemologies, we acknowledge (in the best understanding of science) that the variable of perception conditions all knowledge; and consider that, far from being a flaw, empathy can open the scholar to deeper knowledge. We can also be *insouciant,* for example in reclaiming the first meanings of words like "witch" whose original meaning was wise woman. Or "matriarchy" whose original meaning, before patriarchal distortion, referred to women in the beginning, a woman-centeredness evident in my own research documenting signs of veneration of a dark mother as early as 70,000 BCE in the pubic V and color ochre red of the rock art of central and south Africa.

In my view we can be considered *seers and seekers* who remember our oldest mother, a black woman of Africa, as well as look forward to a new world formed by her values. Some of us think of ourselves as *midwives* helping give birth to a new time when justice with compassion, equality, and transformation—like the *"she"* in our title—are everywhere.

Lucia Chiavola Birnbaum.
Berkeley,
January 17, 2005, Martin Luther King, Jr. Day

Preface

by Lucia Birnbaum, Ph.D.

She is everywhere
Her gifts and wisdom
Known by children, frogs, poppies, olive and banyan trees

She is also in these pages, part of a great warming cloak woven by
    everyone
As we spiral—backward and forward—
To an ancient/new way of living together in
Joy and justice.

—Anonymous

I like to regard my relationship to this anthology with the name some of my students call me, *Strega-Nonna*. Strega, the italian word for witch, suggests my identification with women persecuted throughout the ages for expressing their beliefs. Nonna refers to grandmothers (or godmothers) inspiring/helping/ teaching to bring out the truth everyone has within.

This anthology emerged from the research and realization that she is, indeed, everywhere, that the presence of the ultimately african dark mother (for downcasing, see my "note on style" in *Dark mother*) and her values, are ubiquitous and expressed in a multitude of ways. We hope that this collection of essays will stimulate others to gather their own samplers of the variety and richness of research and other work that comes from knowing that she is everywhere.

In my case, I came to know her ubiquitous presence by writing *Liberazione della donna. Feminism in Italy* (Wesleyan University Press, 1986, 1988), another book, *Black Madonnas of Italy* (Northeastern University Press, 1993; Palomar Editrice, 1997, iUniverse 2000), and then *Dark mother. african origins and godmothers (iUniverse 2001, Media Mediterranea 2004).* The premises of *Dark mother* inform my life and work: modern humans began their journey on this planet 100,000 BCE in central and south Africa; after 50,000 BCE african migrants took signs of their veneration of the dark mother (pubic V, color ochre red) to the caves and cliffs of all continents; the earliest sanctuary we know was created by africans at Mount Sinai (Har Karkom) in 40,000 BCE. Her signs, images, and stories have persisted throughout the epoch of patriarchy to the present, when her values—justice with compassion, equality, and transformation—offer hope in movements of ecology and sustainability, against war, against imperialism—for a harmonious, egalitarian, and peaceful world.

Influenced by italian feminists, I meant this anthology to be "unedited" in the sense that nobody modified anybody's vision. Our "editorial committees" were made up of whoever showed up at announced meetings. At these meetings Angeleen Campra's editorial expertise and Jodi MacMillan's womanagerial talents rose to the surface. Nurtured by Belladonna (http://www.belladonna.ws), Jodi's extraordinary sanctuary/gathering place/resource center in Berkeley, the many skills of Laura Amazzone, and the computer genius of Andrew Fitzpatrick, this anthology has weathered dry as well as moist seasons in its journey to the publisher.

Like other significant endeavors this is an unfinished book because we are overwhelmed by the feeling nobody can capture in one place: the remarkable phenomenon that is today called "women's spirituality." This is a first volume in a continuing project. We are passing on the cloak to Luisah Teish to "edit" (using whatever word she chooses) the next volume, entitled, *Dark mother rising.* Both *She is everywhere!* and *Dark mother rising* may be considered volumes in an ongoing *Darkmother* series nurtured by Belladonna in Berkeley.

The dark mother eludes categories. I have tried to put these pieces in a logical pattern, but like the figure of Guadalupe who refused to stay on the computer page with other black madonnas when we were editing *Dark mother*—Guadalupe is, after all, the matrona of all the Americas—I have done what I do when I sew a quilt. I put the pieces on the floor, arranged, and rearranged them, and put them where it seemed to me they fit. The dark mother originated in Africa, but she is claimed on all continents, where africans migrated, so that one overall pattern of this sampler is that there are many ways of knowing. I was trained as a historian whose perspectives, and methodologies, have been deepened and widened ever since I began my journey to knowing her in 1969 (See my essay, "Dark wheat and red poppies.")

The hypothesis of the african dark mother and suppressed knowledge about her may be the most fruitful research hypothesis of our time. Angeleen Campra's piece begins this volume, suggesting a new way of looking at time. Naomi Doumbia evokes the "African Goddess: Mother of Shadow And Light." Against the backdrop of the african origins of humans in harmonious woman-centered societies the deteriorated condition of contemporary women is poignantly suggested by Luisah Teish; african chief and african american ritualist in "the stained glass whore." Ida Dunson's "Chemistry of Life—DNA" points to the contradiction. Matomah Alesha suggests what the dark mother means to an african/american woman. African origins as they have become blended with subsequent traditions are analyzed in Deborah Grenn's piece on the lemba of Africa and jewish/american women, as well as in May Elawar's essay on the black stone of islamic Mecca.

After publication of *Black madonnas* and *Dark mother*, we have been deepening what we know with more research on site, taking students on research tours to Sicily, Spain, Sardinia. In 2006, we hope to go back to Africa. In early March 2003 we went to Spain looking for the dark mother and her values—justice with compassion, equality, and transformation—as the U.S. launched a pre-emptive bloody war in Iraq. See poem by Janine Canan and essays by Hera Hagstoz, M.A., Vivian Deziak, and Karen Villanueva.

Many ways of knowing the dark mother are suggested in the pieces by Latonia Dixon, Velia Kroupa, Elizabeth Shillington, Jennifer Colby, Kalli Rose Halvorson, Deborah Rose, Necia Harkless, Mary Beth Moser, Leslene della Madre, Max Dashu, Anya Silverman, Anne Bouie, Dorotea Reyna, Pamela Eakins and Jean Harris.

Everywhere is felt in the essays by Mary Saracino, Susan Sopcak, Susan Carter, Laura Amazzone, Elisabeth Sikie, Mara Keller, Diane Marto and Mari Pat Ziolkowski. Everydayness is honored by Sandy Miranda, Marguerite Rigoglioso, and Delphyne Platner.

The bond between contemporary women's spirituality and our grandmothers' lives is implicit in pieces by Lorraine Macchello and Gian Banchero. Chickie Farella looks at family dynamics in a womanly way, that is, with compassion. Louisa Calio finds "revelation" in contemporary women's writings. Pamela Eakins points us to the tarot, deep source of submerged knowledge.

The volume ends with reconciliation suggested in Miri Hunter's essay.

Lucia Chiavola Birnbaum,
Berkeley
November 2004

She Is Everywhere...And Always Has Been

Angeleen Campra, Ph.D.

They say she is veiled
and a mystery. That is
one way of looking.
Another
is that she is where
she always has been, exactly in place,
and it is we,
we who are mystified,
we who are veiled
and without faces.

—Judy Grahn, *Queen of Wands* (1982)

Introduction

Divinity as female is the subject of this essay. Specifically, I will address deity as divine generative force, as that which brings forth life and which illustrates an understanding of the world as a place that fosters and nurtures life and the interconnectedness of all things.[1] I will show that this concept of sacred female generative energy is firmly established within our historical Judaic and Christian theological traditions.[2] Although the evidence for this is widespread and abundant and can be traced back 50,000 years, [3] it has largely been

1

ignored or denied in the relatively recent process of re-imagining divinity as exclusively male.[4]

In fact, the process of setting male deities over female deities as the source of generativity appears to have begun only about 4000 years ago, with the appearance of male creator deities in Egypt and Sumer.[5] As the Chronology on the following pages shows, about that same time, coming out of the polytheism of the Sumerian-Mesopotamian region, the Hebrew patriarchs developed their monotheistic concept of the deity Yahweh, and identification with this image of the divine has been sustained to the present within Judaism. Almost 1300 years later, that is, c. 2700 years ago, the Greek Olympian pantheon emerged with Zeus and other male deities placed in a superior position to that of the earlier Gaia, Hera, and other archaic female deities. And during the past 1600–1700 years, the western Christological perspective was solidified and has gained significant dominance. These Yahweh-, Olympian-, and Christ-centric worldviews are indeed recent when compared to evidence of female deities that go back continuously for 50,000 years or more.

In order to see beyond this current perspective, we must identify the biases within the accepted Greco-Roman interpretation of history with its emphasis on a limited, selected historical context, and look to what preceded it. This is no easy task when our culturally sanctioned worldview is like water to fish in that it is difficult to see what we take for granted. What has surrounded us for so long, what we have wrapped around our stories for such a long time we no longer think of it as a part of our stories, becoming something we do not think of at all. Instead, it becomes something we accept as "what is." In order to think and see beyond what has long been accepted as "givens," we must critically examine the historical record—archeological, iconographic, and textual—to see what has been included and what has been left out of this limiting definition of history. Our contemporary culture looks back mainly to the era of Classical Greece, only 2500 years ago, or when we stretch our imaginations, as far back as the era of the Hebrew patriarchs, c. 4000 years ago. Mainstream contemporary Euro-centric culture has been reluctant to acknowledge our connection to Mesopotamia[6] or to Africa,[7] in spite of the evidence that corroborates those connections.

I encountered the restrictiveness of this abbreviated sense of history during my research on Hochma/Sophia of the Wisdom literature of the Hebrew Bible, the Valentinian Christian Gnostic origin story, and the Gnostic hymn, *The Thunder: Perfect Mind*, which encompass an approximate period from c. 500 B.C.E. to c. 350 C.E. I was perplexed by what I discovered in the story of

Hochma/Sophia, which clearly incorporates evidence of an understanding of the necessity and presence of female divine energy, an acknowledgment of this potent force as the unacknowledged ground from which the then-current patriarchal worldviews sprang. Basically, I came to understand that in rewriting our origin stories to support those patriarchal and male-exclusive monotheistic perspectives, we were unable to write the female divine out of the story, even as we re-named, redefined, and co-opted that vital energy in favor of male divine.[8]

Iconographic evidence of female deity can be traced back to the Upper Paleolithic Era, c. 50,000 B.C.E. The historic record presents abundant representations of human concepts of divinity expressed through nature images, such as sea, earth, and vegetation deities; animal images, such as fish, birds, and snakes; and human female images. A characteristic which commonly connects these ancient, diverse images is generativity,[9] the ability to manifest or bring forth life. In contrast, it is only during a relatively short period—approximately 4000 years—that dominant western culture has chosen to focus its attention on, and invest with superior status, the concept of an exclusively male anthropomorphized deity. My point is not the superiority of female images, but rather their enduring significance for 46,000 years until the relatively late collapse of that ancient understanding of generative power as located in nature and expressed as sacred female, into the more limiting image of sacred male. In this process, the nature-centered locus of generativity was further constricted into a human-centered concept of creativity. Unfortunately, when humans attempt to understand and define divine generative force or deity exclusively in anthropomorphic and gendered terms, the result necessarily limits our concept of and relationship with that reality and, ultimately, with ourselves.

About the Chronology

As I conducted my research on Sophia and on the female divine, I found it necessary to compile a table to help hold the historical data[10] in chronological order. This task, with its pragmatic beginnings, evolved into a useful tool that helped me see the expanded context of human images of the divine.

Historical dating is problematic on a number of levels, including the fact that much of our historical record is iconographic, contained within objects and images, and these artifacts are not always given equal weight when compared to texts. Because we are a text-oriented culture, we tend to regard the time before writing as "pre-history," a definition which prejudices that earlier time and the artifacts it produced as "primitive." We give greater value and weight to the written record, despite the advancement in techniques such as radiocarbon dating and dendrochronology, and despite the fact that our written record was often dictated by the "winners" in any struggle of competing worldviews and usually is partial at best.

Also, in compiling dates, we cannot avoid the institutionalized western Christian bias that is embedded in our current calendar system. The selection of the birth of Jesus to represent "The Year One," the beginning of counted time as most of the world relates to it today, is at the very least arbitrary and Christian-centric. It privileges and establishes as normative the western Christian worldview and history over all cultures from all times and all geographic regions. While the convention of B.C.E./C.E. (Before the Christian or Common Era/Christian or Common Era) represents an improvement upon B.C./A.D. (Before Christ/Anno Domini), it still reinforces the deeply embedded bias of the system.

For the purpose of encouraging an expanded perception of history, I also include the dating system suggested by Merlin Stone.[11] Any date contemporary humans assign to the "beginning" of history will always be arbitrary, but Stone offers an effective and important improvement. She suggests a dating system that begins with the development of agriculture, an event of great significance to a much larger segment of world population when compared to the putative birth date of one individual. Another advantage to Stone's system is that the beginning of rain-fed agriculture[12] is already accepted as the beginning of the Neolithic Era. In this system, the year 8001 B.C.E. becomes the year 1 A.D.A. (After the Development of Agriculture) and the year 2004 of the Christian calendar becomes the year 10,004 A.D.A. of a calendar with a longer view of history. This acknowledgment of a longer and more substantial history provides us with a way to rethink our human story and reclaim the significance of those more ancient historical pieces. It also invites us to become more aware of the distorted perception we hold of a past that so privileges only the last 2000 years of our history.

For an example of this distortion, we have only to look at any given year. If this year were known as 10,004 rather than 2004, it would bestow greater (positive) value on those 8000 years before the birth of Jesus, which are currently described in negative numbers in the Christian calendar. The A.D.A. system pays greater respect to a wider tableau of history and the events which actually formed us. Socio-political assumptions and attitudes are set by much less significant facts than these. Our assumptions and attitudes, acknowledged or not, lead us to study certain things and not others, and allow us to see certain things and prevent us from seeing others. That some years are positive (connoting more weight or value) and others are negative (connoting less weight or value), that counting begins with an event that is significant in the lives of only a small portion of the global population, are examples of unacknowledged assumptions and attitudes which have significant impact in our world.

A Chronology of Divine Image in the West With the Inclusion of Key Cultural Shifts		
	Before the Christian or Common Era	B.C.E.
Paleolithic – Modern Era	**Wide geographic diffusion of similar signs associated with sacred female generativity** pubic V's, chevrons, meanders, nets, tri-lines, red ochre color for childbirth and menstrual blood	Paleolithic – Modern Era
	Har Karkom, oldest known religious sanctuary, suggests female deity, site of Mt. Sinai, on African migration route	c.40,000
	Great Mother of Willendorf, limestone statue, Austria	c.30–25,000
	Great Mother of Laussel, rock carving, Dordogne, France	c.25–20,000
	Great Mother of Dolni Vestonice, clay & bone, Moravia	c.24,000
	Great Mother of Lespugue, mammoth ivory statue, France	c.23,000
A.D.A.	After the Development of Agriculture (Calendar system suggested by Merlin Stone.)	(B.C.E. continues)
1	The development of rain-fed agriculture, as well as domestication of animals, pottery, village living	c.8001 Early Neolithic
c.2000+	**Fish, Bird, Snake, Pregnant Vegetation Deities**, Old Europe, Crete, Near and Middle East, Egypt	c.6000+
c.2000	**Mater Magna** of Phrygia in Anatolia, also known as All-Mother, **Cybele.** The cult of Cybele and her son/lover, Attis, wove through many lands and flourished into Imperial Rome. Her most important shrines are known and honored today as Black Madonna or Marian sites	c.6000
c.2700	Pictographic script with strong similarities to Cypro-Minoan Linear A script, thought to be sacred script for ritual use, Old Europe	c.5300
c.3000	**Inanna** emerges from an established Sumerian pantheon as granddaughter of earlier generative deities and her story incorporates death, resurrection, and rebirth	c.5000
c.3600– 5000	Agrarian, matristic Old Europe invaded by 3 waves of diverse patriarchal Proto-Indo-European pastoralists from northern steppes: c.4400–4300, 3500, 3000. Weapons of war not among grave goods before c.4500–4300 B.C.E. No evidence of hilltop fortifications	c.4400–3000

c.4000	**Isis** of Egypt emerges from earlier nature deities. Isis, her brother/lover Osiris, and their son, Horus, form an early trinity. Like Cybele, Isis maintains a strong presence in many lands, and she was worshipped over 3000 years, until early centuries C.E. Enduring ties connect her to Sophia, Black Madonnas, and Mary	c.4000
c.4200–5500	**Great Goddesses of Malta**, statues, megaliths, temples	c.3800–2500
c.4900	Writing in Sumer, cuneiform on clay tablets. In next few centuries, also developed in Egypt, Anatolia, and Canaan	c.3100
c.5000	Irrigated agriculture appears in Sumer	c.3000
c.5000	Evidence in Sumer of fortified cities, a change from earlier settlement patterns of open villages	c.3000
c.5000	Abraham's ancestors are nomads in Mesopotamia	c.3000
c.5400	Glorification of war in Mesopotamia portrayed in the Royal Standard of Ur, depicting a military victory and celebration banquet.	c.2600
5630–5684	Enheduanna, Priestess of Inanna, first known author. She celebrated the regenerative cycle in nature.	c. 2370–2316
c.5650	Sargon, Enheduanna's father, King of Akkad, united North & South Mesopotamia. Transitions both worlds by claiming a divine mother to legitimate his kingship. His childhood story identical to Moses of the bible	c.2350
c.6000	The first images of male creator deities appear in Egypt and Sumer	c.2000
c.6150	Abraham in Canaan	c.1850
c.6250	The Patriarchs in Egypt	c.1750
c.6550	**Demeter & Persephone** - Eleusinian Mysteries	c.1450
c.6750	The Exodus from Egypt	c.1250
c.6750–7100	*Wisdom of Amenemope*, Egypt. Early written text of already ancient sayings. Basis for oldest section of Hebrew Proverbs	c.1250–1100
6990–7030	King David of Judah and Israel	1010–970
c.7000	The *Enuma Elish*, The Babylonian Creation Myth - battle of Tiamat and Marduk and the Flood story. Oldest known written copy, based on a more ancient Sumerian story	c.1000
c.7020	Earliest written collection of ancient Hebrew stories and oral traditions, incorporated into Pentateuch - 5 books of Torah - Genesis, Exodus, Leviticus, Numbers, Deuteronomy. "J" text for Yahweh – southern kingdom of Judah. Genesis 2&3 (Adam from "soil", Eve from Adam's rib)	c.980
7030–7069	King Solomon, associated with *Song of Songs*	970–931

c.7150	Greek Homeric epic poems	c.850
c.7280	Fall of the northern kingdom of Israel to Assyria. Lost tribes of Israel. From this point forward we speak of "Judaism"	c.720
c.7280	Second written collection incorporated into Pentateuch. "E" text for Elohim (God) — northern kingdom of Israel. Genesis 1 ("God created man in the image of himself . . . male and female he created them")	c.720
c.7300	Hesiod's Theogony - Homer's & Hesiod's works synthesized the older local Greek city deities into the Olympian Pantheon	c.700
7403	Siege of Jerusalem by Nebuchadnezzar - deportation of Jewish upper classes to Babylonia begins	597
7414	Sack of Jerusalem and destruction of the Temple - more deportations to Babylonia	586
7461	Cyrus, King of Medes and Persians, captures Babylonia	539
7462	Cyrus frees the Jewish people from their captivity in Babylonia - approximately 1/3 return to Palestine	538
7480	Temple rebuilt at Jerusalem	520
c.7500–7600	Books of Job, Proverbs, Ecclesiastes or Qoheleth, Song of Songs. Written to address postexilic circumstances. **HOCHMA/SOPHIA** personified in these texts	c.500–400
7520–7677	Classical Age of Greece – including the time of Pericles, Socrates, Plato. up to the death of Alexander the Great, when the Hellenistic Age begins	480–323
c.7550	Final and definitive form of Pentateuch "P" text for Priestly source, reworking of the "J" & "E" texts	c.450
7670	Palestine dominated by Greece	330
7700–7800	Palestine dominated by Egypt	300–200
c.7750–8250	Apocalyptic Jewish movements flourish	c.250 B.C.E.–250 C.E.
7800–7833	Palestine dominated by Syria	200–167
c.7810-7820	Ben Sira (Ecclesiasticus) **HOCHMA/SOPHIA**	c.190–180
c.7900–8100	Probable Gnostic beginnings, most likely in Syria or Palestine **SOPHIA**	c.100 B.C.E.–100 C.E.
7963	Palestine and Syria dominated by Rome	63
c.7950	Book of Wisdom of Solomon **SOPHIA**	c.50

	Christian Era or Common Era	C.E.
8001	Jesus' birth declared (Historical dating c.4-6)	1
c.8030-8070	Early Christian sources — Oral traditions - eye-witness, aphorisms, wisdom sayings, miracle stories, and parables	c.30–70
c.8050-8060	—Paul's undisputed letters are the earliest writings to survive intact - 1Th, 1&2Cor, Ph, Phm, Ga, Rm	c.50–60
c.8050-8070	—Q Sayings - oral traditions and testimonies	c.50–70
c.8030-8200?	Jesus understood as messenger and incarnation of **Sophia** in early Jesus movement	c.30–200?
c.8030?	Philo of Alexandria, a Hellenized Jewish philosopher, begins the transferal of attributes from **Sophia** to Logos, which, over several centuries, were re-directed to Christ	c.30?
8066–8070	Jewish revolt against Rome	66–70
8070	Second Temple and Jerusalem destroyed by Romans	70
c. 8070	Gospel of Mark, in Greek, probably southern Syria. Need for written material for consistency of message and consolidation of the young, fluid Jesus movement	c.70
c.8080-8090	Gospels - Matthew, most probably from Antioch; Luke, probably Greece; John, probably Ephesus	c.80-90
c.8100-8175	Valentinus (and other Gnostic writers) **SOPHIA**	c.100–175
c.8130-8200	Irenaeus, Bishop of Lyon. early "Church Father" and opponent of "heresies;" his contemporaries include: Ignatius, Polycarp, Justin, Tertullian, Hippolytus	c.130–200
c.8150-8400	Christology gradually established as doctrine	c.150–400
8313	Emperor Constantine converted to Christianity, brings Roman imperial structure as overlay on the religion	313
8326 & 8333	Constantine's edicts suppress Gnostic sects	326 & 333
8389	Suppression, after 2000 years, of Eleusinian Mysteries along with other 'pagan' rites by Theodosius of Rome.	389
c.8400	Banned Gnostic texts buried in clay jars in Nag Hammadi, Egypt	c.400
8431	**Mary** decreed Mother of God, Council of Ephesus	431
8432–8440	Santa **Maria** Maggiore Church built on major Cybele site in Rome	432–440
8451	**Mary** decreed *Aeiparthenos*, 'Ever-Virgin', Council of Chalcedon	451
c.9000-9300	Resurgence of female divine images: devotion to Black Madonnas, **Sophia**, Sapienzia, Shekinah	c.1000-1300 Middle Ages
9854	Immaculate Conception of **Mary** added to Roman Catholic dogma	1854
9945	The Gnostic texts buried at Nag Hammadi 1500 years earlier are discovered, translated, and studied	1945
9950	Assumption of **Mary** added to Roman Catholic dogma	1950

Patterns within the Chronology

The chronological table above presents an abbreviated and admittedly selective sketch of western history, particularly as it relates to our concepts of sacrality. However, it is useful in helping us better identify evident historical patterns that have influenced the story and continue to influence our lives. An expanded view of history and geography invites an investigation of wider textual and iconographic evidence to trace our western concept of female divine, which is vital to our cultural and individual sense of wholeness.

The chronology shows the representation of divine generative energy as female from the Early Paleolithic Era through the Neolithic Era, into the Bronze Age, and—despite the rise of patriarchy and its redefinitions of divinity and authority—into the present. There is a shift in iconography from female to male images of the divine, representing a shift in the larger story and alerting us to times of change and transition. It shows another shift in culture, a transition to institutionalized conflict noted in the archaeological record when the grave goods of ancient Sumer[13] and Old Europe[14] began to show evidence of weapons of war and an elevated male status. About the same time, the story of Sargon of Akkad illustrates another transition between these two worldviews by his claim of right to kingship through his claimed status as son and favored one of the influential female deity, Inanna. It shows centuries of warfare and struggle, with repeated episodes of domination for the people who gave the Judaic, Christian, and Islamic world its scriptural canons which are accepted as the basis for both religious and secular worldviews in the West today. It shows the earlier counterparts of a number of ideas and stories that are central to those canons, thus demonstrating the interconnection of the ancient Middle East with the Near East, Africa, Asia Minor, Old Europe and the Mediterranean area. And it shows a continuous thread of sacrality represented by female deities.

I purposefully use a title for this essay and open it with a poem that anthropomorphize deity as an honoring of "She" in order to remind and reconnect us to the thousands of years in which divine generativity was identified and celebrated in nature images and female form. While I believe any image is inadequate to fully represent the mystery of divinity, at the same time, I am aware of the power contained within a culture's image of divinity and how it is used to define and legitimate authority and social norms. Our ability to conceive an inclusive concept of divinity—one that is both female and male, or, alternately, one that is not gendered and is source and container of all life—relates to our ability to establish and maintain social structures which promote the well-being of all humanity and nature and which are not corrupted by a distorted definition or exercise of power and authority. This concept of inclusive divinity has been resisted or denied by a dominant culture that benefits from a literal rather than metaphoric understanding of divinity as male and does not often enough engage the idea that humans and divinity co-create each other.[15]

Notes

1 For an early discussion of the concept of one universal Great Mother, see Edwin O. James, *The Cult of the Mother Goddess* (London, Thames and Hudson, 1959). For a more recent overview discussion and a helpful bibliography on the subject, see Asphodel P. Long, *The One or the Many—the Great Goddess Revisited* (1996) http://www.asphodel-long.com 1st link: List of Works, 2nd link: The Works in Chronological Order. Accessed 9/12/03.

2 Growing up as a Christian American of European descent, the concept of female deity was absent from the catechism and religious history I was taught as a child. As a Catholic, I did have a strong image of Mary to look to, but her humanness and her lack of divine status was carefully and pointedly inculcated. It was through my adult study of other cultures and world religions, particularly those of India and Africa, that I was introduced to deeply established ancient concepts of female divinity. Eventually, I was drawn to Sophia of the Gnostic texts because, located as she was within the early beginnings of my own cultural traditions, she represented a clear placeholder for these ancient deities. [Gnosticism emerged out of apocalyptic Judaism and grew alongside the early Christ cult, which, with the imperial backing of Constantine's Rome in the mid 3rd century, eventually developed into what we know as Christianity today. In the process, the Gnostics were declared heretics and their teachings were suppressed. See Kurt Rudolph, *Gnosis: The Nature and History of an Ancient Religion* (Edinburgh, T. and T. Clark, 1984); Birger A. Pearson, *Gnosticism, Judaism, and Egyptian Christianity*, (Minneapolis, Fortress, 1990); Pheme Perkins, *Gnosticism and The New Testament*, (Minneapolis, Fortress, 1993); Bentley Layton, *The Gnostic Scriptures: A New Translation with Annotations and Introductions*, (New York, Doubleday, 1987)]

3 See Marija Gimbutas, *The Language of the Goddess* (San Francisco, Harper Collins, 1989); Elinor W. Gadon, *The Once and Future Goddess* (San Francisco, Harper Collins, 1989); and Emmanuel Anati, *The Mountain of God: Har Karkom* (New York, Rizzoli, 1986).

4 I believe a culture's symbols affect the ordinary, daily circumstances of that culture. A symbol of an exclusively male representation of divinity, with its cultural translation of superior status of and privilege for elite males, prevails in our current western Euro-American hierarchically dualistic worldview. Because this symbol of male divinity and its cultural translation have been in place for several millennia—only a short blip in our long human history—they are accepted as "natural," as "reality," as historically determined. See the works of Mary Daly, Elisabeth Schussler Fiorenza, Rosemary Radford Ruether, and Elizabeth A. Johnson.

5 We are indebted to the research of historian Gerda Lerner for *The Creation of Patriarchy* (New York, Oxford University Press, 1986), in which she traced the particulars of the story of the Ancient Near East and situated the emergence of a patriarchal perspective firmly within history, thus challenging the deterministic view that patriarchy was a fixed aspect of human nature. The work of mythologists and analytical psychologists Anne Baring and Jules Cashford, *The Myth of the Goddess: Evolution of an Image* (London, Arkana/Penguin Books, 1991), synthesized archaeological, iconographic, and textual sources, and described a rich body of evidence of female divine symbols from a variety of regions and over a broad expanse of time. These important contributions help contextualize and expand our understanding of our human relationship to the perspective of divine energy as generative.

6 Sherrill V. Nilson reminds us of one important exception to our cultural disconnect from Mesopotamia. The Epic of Gilgamesh, discovered only 150 years ago, is widely used today "to illustrate the rejection of the female deity and the rise of the ego-centric, self-reflective unitary male and the god made in his image as the beginnings of western civilization" (personal communication, September 2003). For a different interpretation of this myth, see Sherrill V. Nilson, *Gilgamesh in Relationship: A Feminist, Kleinian Hermeneutic of the Contemporary Epic* (Doctoral Dissertation, California Institute of Integral Studies, 2001, UMI 9992393).

7 For a discussion of the African genesis of humans and the several waves of population movement along ancient migratory routes that have been re-confirmed through modern DNA evidence, as well as the oldest known religious sanctuary which suggests a female deity, and the many ancient female deities that have been venerated along those same migration routes out of Africa, see Lucia Chiavola Birnbaum, Ph.D., *dark mother: african origins and godmothers* (San Jose, CA, iUniverse, 2001).

8 In Genesis 2:7, "Yahweh God shaped man from the soil of the ground and blew the breath of life into his nostrils, and man became a living being." The sacred generative power of Earth apparently could not be written out of the story, but here we see it made invisible through re-naming. Earth becomes soil or dust and through this metaphor, female generativity is subsumed into male creativity. Likewise, we see the same usurpation in the Greek story of Zeus birthing Athena from his forehead, thus claiming procreative power for himself, and as with Yahweh, by extension to human males. The part of the story that contemporary culture has forgotten is Zeus' swallowing of Metis as she was about to give birth. Here the female generative element is literally swallowed and digested until it reappears in another form. For further discussion see Angeleen Campra, Ph.D., *Sophia, Divine Generative Force: A Gnostic Representation of Divine Image,* (Doctoral Dissertation, California institute of Integral Studies, 2002, UMI 3034813).

9 Drawing from the work of Eric Neumann on the connection between early female deities and Mother Earth, Vermaseren states: "Her divine authority did not reside in her power to command, but in her mysterious gift of being able continually to create new beings." Maarten J. Vermaseren, *Cybele and Attis: The Myth and the Cult* (London, Thames & Hudson 1977:9)

10 This data is drawn from numerous sources, including the multi-volume *Cambridge Ancient History*. For a complete list, see Campra, Ph.D., *Sophia, Divine Generative Force*. In addition to references cited in other notes, chief sources include: *The New Jerusalem Bible, Reader's Ed.* (New York, Doubleday, 1990); Dennis Duling and Norman Perrin, *The New Testament: Proclamation and Parenesis, Myth and History, 3rd Ed.* (Fort Worth, TX,

Harcourt Brace, 1994); Elinor Gadon, *Once and Future Goddess*; Baring and Cashford, *Myth of the Goddess*; Eahr A. Joan, *Regenesis: A Mother-line Archive of Feminist Spirituality* (masters thesis, California Institute of Integral Studies, 2000, UMI 1398189); Gimbutas, *Language of the Goddess*; Gimbutas, *Civilization of the Goddess.*

11 Merlin Stone, *Ancient Mirrors of Womanhood, Rev. Ed.* (Boston, Beacon, 1990)

12 There is an important distinction regarding agriculture that must be noted. Rain-fed agriculture supported the beginnings of village life, in small groupings and still semi-nomadic in some areas, and a culture deeply connected to and dependent upon nature, thus imaging divinity through nature-based representations. In Sumer 5,000 years later, irrigated agriculture resulted in larger, more dependable harvests, which led to larger populations, surplus, storage and defense of goods, kingship, and human-centered representations of divinity. See Harriet Crawford, *Sumer and the Sumerians* (Cambridge, Cambridge University Press, 1991). For an examination of two different worldviews in competition during the transition to irrigation, see Rita A. Casey, *Inanna and Enki in Sumer: An Ancient Conflict Revisited* (Doctoral Dissertation, California Institute of Integral Studies, 1998, UMI 9904977).

13 Thorkild Jacobsen, *The Treasures of Darkness: A History of Mesopotamian Religion* (New Haven, CT, Yale University Press, 1976).

14 Marija Gimbutas, *The Goddesses and Gods of old Europe: Myths and Cult Images* (Berkeley, University of California Press, 1982).

15 I am deeply indebted to Rita Casey, Eahr Joan, Deborah Grenn Ph.D., and Sherrill Nilson for their conversations, contributions, and edits, all of which have enriched this essay.

Heavenly Freedom

Matomah Alesha

I was an ardent Christian as a child. It was not that I knew this religion very well but what I did know at the tender age of 10 created so much enthusiasm and inspiration. I did everything to win favor and to fit in as a believer. My brother and I attended Sunday school. Our routine at the times was to go to Sunday school then afterwards to Sunday service. For the most part I participated but every now and again my brother or myself were found nodding ungracefully during sermon. And like most kids we sometimes retained our offering money, using it instead to buy candies and sweets once the church closed.

My brother and I attended Bible camp in the summer for kids and it exemplifies some of the best experiences I had as a young person. But with all this, I somehow fell out with Christianity and even today I am not quite sure why. I got the impression generally that I could not go to heaven. I thought that heaven was only for men, for Jewish men in particular. That is the impression I got so young. I did not know much but I did know for sure…I was not male or Jewish. At the time I did not question it because I didn't know how. And how could a young mind really philosophically engage it or research it with any maturity. Discovering it in my bible study class, I thought to myself this is how it is. I felt great dismay and sadness all at the same time. Today it would be similar to being employed by a big corporation and finally learning after some honest effort that all upper management was, for reasons one could not control, off limits to my aspirations. No one looked like me in upper management so it was a lie to think honest effort and study would change my position. I was just churning my heels, sacrificing all earthly temptations, and developing moral character only to remain outside the ultimate prize. I cease buying into cultivating purity. I gave up thinking about sin and winning favor. This heaven was not for me…it was not something real or attainable.

Today it seems nebulous, even mystical, at least to me. But the only reason I was a Christian was to attain this place of wonders called heaven. Something told me at the time that this is not the plan in this organization…there is no moving up in this organization. I resigned myself, these important things have already been decided and there is no other place for me to go. This realization in Bible school one beautiful Sunday started my soul to wander. I begin to drift, falling ever so disimpassioned and estranged from Christianity. It was rather painful at the time to know that I was in an institution where I would remain at entry level indefinitely. In later years to learn at how women were treated and positioned outside of the leadership and theological history of Christianity only reinforced it. The soul wound was cutting, sever and bloody. This started my inquiring and journeying to find something that would meet my needs for spiritual accomplishment and fulfillment. It never was a question for me if God exists. I just felt in my soul a need and desire for a rich tradition that would allow me to fully explore and to express my abilities in whatever capacity I chose.

Heaven at the time was like this wonderful, extraordinary place. I dreamed of heaven, walking and being in heaven. It was such a beautiful place. Heaven is a place of light, freedom, love and comfort…a place where people could be themselves and also be their very best. My personal mythology of heaven and the attainment of this existential condition is what motivated me to be involved with Christianity and over the years has been the underlying reason behind my search for the black Mother. It was the reason behind my desire to ride in space ships and my personal admiration of people like Mae Jemison and Ammachi (divine Mother) who for reasons obvious and not so…touched the infinite sky of heaven. In Ammachi's case, she embodied the very best of heaven. Today it's not the plaster walls and pearly gates of a Christianized projection, but a land of milk and honey, a blue Nile with sandstone pyramids, an eternal garden filled with the fountains of youth and holy grails of immense wonder. Today for me it's a black Virgin, wondrous and glorious in her abundance, compassion and love.

I did not encounter the black Mother immediately, although in hindsight I believe She was always there. I searched first many philosophical and alternative health approaches. I went through a period of self-help, psychotherapy and [12] step meetings reviewing the painful rumblings of my upbringing. From there I discovered feminism which led me to womanism…and the dissecting of the world and history from a woman's perspective. With womanism I encountered slowly the hidden culture and beliefs of women's culture and the divine Mother. While reading the thoughts and insights of women, the true history of the Christian church emerged. This history, so successful repressed in the school system yet vast in its influence was heart-breaking and painful. It finally made sense why I did not fit in…it was also regrettable that any chance of going back to the church in the state of ignorant bliss I was accustomed to was impossible. It also shined a suspicious light on adults and institutions who for some reason did not get around to teaching this aspect of world history in my studies. At the time I felt betrayed and misdirected. It felt very disheartening to wonder about the honesty and intent of adults around you. No doubt I felt confused, angry and sad.

From there, the larger body of feminism connected me to environmental, lesbian/gay and native dialoguing of people. Ultimately the most remarkable piece of evidence would be found in the images that I created one afternoon while at home. I have discovered that some of the more invaluable but hidden aspects of Goddess can be discovered in the random acts of inspirational art. This is how She is understood and lives through acts of pure creativity and imagination. One day I was sketching and I created three images. One image was of a woman embedded in a tree; the other image was an image of women metaphorically shaped like flowers and their bodies were jammed into a vase like a bunch of weeping, deranged lilies…the last image is hard to explain. It showed two gorgon creatures with wings. I am not sure what type of creatures they are but these creatures no doubt come from the same place as the previous images. When I was talking to a male friend studying Jungian psychology…he illuminated me to the archetypical symbolism that was found in these images. The third image again he had no explanation for, after some study it appears to me to be something very old and fundamental to a native African world-view.

My parents were not faithful to any spiritual lineage and San Francisco at the time turned out to be a very fertile place for philosophical inquiry. There are limitless resources for investigating new and alternatives ways of living and seeing the world. I took advantage of this rich environment seeking out opportunities to engage people and to participate in events that celebrated the Goddess.

When I eventually met the divine black Mother and grew with her beliefs and concepts, one thing that I found remarkable is the level of freedom I had. I have never felt such freedom in any major religion. Their laws, regulations and traditions felt so restraining compared to the horizon opening feeling of the black Mother. The three aspects of the divine black Mother most freeing for me are—(1) ability to view one's inner truth as sacred doctrine (2) the desolution of antagonistic opposites into a third possibility, and (3) the promotion of different forms of social organization in this post-historical world.

In my experiences of Christianity (Baptist), one is taught to be like Jesus…to mimic him in every sense. We all know that no one can really be like him but the devout Christian tries nonetheless to develop in every way to mirror the spiritual, emotional accomplishments of their Master. Having a role model is very important in spiritual growth…one needs to see this and know that this is possible. Usually a spiritually accomplished person shows the way and creates a path to achieve the same results as the enlightened one. Although the Christ ideal is fairly inaccessible to most people, everyone continues to work to emulate His attributes. But with the black Mother these things are remarkably different. Growing into a goddess-based, personal belief system, I feel that being my authentic self and referring to my truth and experiences in the most honest and sincere way becomes the model not only of divinity but ideal humanity. I am no longer a cookie-cutter mirror of a great leader but in my core a perfect example for myself and others to rely on something that is both universal and also incredibly intimate. In relying on this Truth which is found in all, universal and unique, the body which is an extension of this center is also part of the big sacred story. Together one comes to know and cultivate one's inner Truth which is the real doctrine of the black Mother for me. This has allowed me to embrace my many-dimensional, ancestral self and to cease pursuing ideals which in many cases were impossible.

Being your natural self and being validated at the same time is simply paradise. Freedom in the black Mother can be found in the reconciling of dualing aspects. These is one important aspect of Her life-centered paradigm. In Western society which relies in part on the traditions of the Judeo-Christian religion is full of many dualing opposites that have created a legacy more of intellectual and philosophical frustration then understanding. Both dualing concepts have diverged into their own camps and when the discussion is invoked, these old antagonistic opposites emerge anew albeit with the old angles and the old evidence.

People are more concerned with dominating and directing the discourse then cultivating any insight or elements relevant to people's lives. Many dualistic philosophical discussions appear this way to me. For instance, evolution or creation, nature or nurture, individual rights or communal concerns, women's needs or the needs of the child, etc. It has gotten so bad that many ideas are no longer discussed because the level of intimidation and passion is so unreasonable that no one wants to participate. It becomes an agenda and other ways of knowing are suppressed. Within the consciousness of the black Mother for me, there is no more war between opposites. These opposites melt away into a third possibility or they are transcended into another yet inspiring and engaging dialogue. The black Mother promotes solutions for She is interested in the continuation of people both in their physicality and their increased quality of soul life. She is life and Her concern is life. She is cosmic creation, imagination, regeneration and transformation, qualities that are lacking in some institutions in America. It is not to say that the theology and history of the black Mother does not have dualism. I could never assert this knowing how important the divine twins are in many ancient belief systems. She however does create a balance, harmony and neutralizing effect conceptually that does not create some of the deep-rooted pain and angst now experienced in the West. Like a child with its mother, the divine Mother psychically creates an absence of pain because there are no inner struggles or polarization in the world of Western culture. After many years of seeking freedom in civil rights, political activism, academic discussions of gender and philosophy, the black Mother is the next and final frontier. She is closure for me because She is myself...the ultimate place of freedom. This feels so freeing to know this and to rely on something that can create and reimagine a renewed world with new possibilities, new priorities.

A Goddess perspective on the world will do whatever is needed to promote a life of dignity, creativity, renewal and resilience. Like any mother, the black Mother is guardian of the generations, the cyclic movement and growing of souls and people. With this She is most relaxed with new ideas that will allow this to be done even more efficiently and organically. There is no formula for people to relate and organize. This is very attractive to people who need more freedom, diversity and expression in their lives and how they relate to people. The black Goddess has the greatest possibility for people organizing and relating. In an ethnic based community, transgendered, sacred monogamy, loosely organized friends, and even communal adoption includes people as well as animals, plants and organic objects. The type of diversity explored and practiced is not like any other religion. It allows people to create what they need and to seek what will create happiness and peace for them. With nearly 500 names uncovered in my research of the black Mother...it has the greatest ability to address the multitudes and their diverse spiritual, communal and individual needs.

The divine Mother is remarkable and my experiences and understanding of Her is still quite premature. But so far I love having the power to decide how to live, grow, heal and experience my world. I love defining my gender, my womanhood, my rituals, my ancestral legacy, my time and space. Who would have dreamed that after centuries of forced indoctrination and enslavement by major religions and the candy coated, sedative illusions of capitalism that one would encounter in the wee hours something that allows us truly so much liberty, so much unity, so much bliss. Just when you think all has been done, tried, experienced and exhausted, She emerges new and vibrant unfolding like a new universe; very few traditional beliefs or religions have this. Hopefully as more people love to appreciate and incorporate aspects of the black Mother, they will experience this freedom too and be encouraged to not only to share it but to keep its special elements alive, rich, and renewed.

I am still interested in heaven, only this time it does not seem so far away, so fantastic like an utopian dream suspended above natural law. This heaven is very near and real inside me and its most accessible. This heaven, paradise on earth is the eternal waters of the divine Mother who is peace, love and blissful happiness.

African Goddess: Mother of Shadow & Light

Naomi Doumbia, Ph.D.

In the dark, luminous sky of the African night, amidst the howling whistle of the hot Sahel, resounds the steady rhythm of an ancient pulse, the heartbeat of the Motherland. In reverence to Divine Mother, the village elders dance their feet into her firm lap, as the rattle of their gourds chant through the thick bush, and the fresh scent of an abundant harvest fills their humming breath. This subtle, sacred tempo carries with it time immemorial when within the dark, barren womb of the universe echoes the first sound of creation: 'Yo.' Vibrating throughout the cosmos, this First Principle enacts a whirlwind of thought, spiraling through empty space and fashioning life through three phases. In the beginning, the world abounds without expression, ideas proliferate without form, and people exist without bodies. This initial stage is an unfertilized egg, full of potential, not yet developed.

With the first breath of Divine inspiration surfaces naked mother earth. Upon her fertile womb, Spirit manifests as a grain, woman's feeding tool. From this grain sprouts a tree, the *balanza* tree (*acacia albida*), her sacred instrument. But this long, sturdy wood does not stay erect. The tall beam soon withers, and tumbles to the ground. As it lies upon her naked body, it secretes its own saliva and an additional substance, a mildew, between them. From this cosmic union is born a soul, the first soul, affectionately known as *Muso Koroni Kundye,* or "ancient woman spirit with a white head." In a word: *crone.*

In the spirit of the Motherland, where elders are respected and valued for their wisdom and abiding connection with the ancestors, crone reigns supreme. To be old is to be all knowing and all-powerful. To be woman, in the fertility-based, Goddess-venerating culture of the Mande peoples of West Africa,[1] is to possess the attributes of the Divine: creator and destroyer.

With an unbridled enthusiasm, *Muso Koroni* single-handedly plants vegetables, creates animals and engenders human beings. She breathes life into every pebble, every grain, and every living substance, becoming the source of all vital principles. As she is originator of thoughts, inspiration and procreation, her elemental manifestation is air. As activity, transformation and power, she is fire and her name is *Nyalé*. As these elements, she creates, incites and consumes. Accordingly she is bold, wild and extravagant. She represents the abundance, the proliferation, and the ultimate destruction of all things.

As the source of all energy, *Muso Koroni* is the embodiment of activity and the mistress of passion, secrecy and desire. Her taste for touch, sound, smell, and form arouse our own yearnings, aches and hunger, all of which intrinsically yield to a restlessness and haste. In her determined excitement to conduct the brilliant, symphonic orchestra of the cosmic song, cacophony, disharmony and confusion arise. Without these qualities, the world does not exist. The apparent duality of creation inherently imposes the laws of attraction and repulsion, proliferation and decay, light and shadow.

As the queen of magic, she oversees the workings of spells, charms, potions and remedies. Her children are privy to these powers and manipulations of nature manifest, but their own extravagant tastes, like their mothers, can result in misunderstanding, treachery and malice. As *Muso Koroni* is the author of creation, she is accordingly the originator of chaos, an essential ingredient for the regeneration and evolution of life. She pervades in secret, lurks in the shadows, and works her magic in the deep recesses of our souls. She is the source of all knowledge, all ideas, that ever were, have been, or will be. She breathes the spark of life into our bodies, stirs our passions, and defeats our wills.

Through our worship of this Goddess of life and death, creation and destruction, we learn to integrate our own darkness, rather than dichotomize it. Through our love of the Mother, we come to love ourselves without splintering off our own shadow; instead, we embrace it with tenderness and truth. We discover how to face our own mortality with fearlessness and grace, and move through the cycles of change with a courage that teaches us through our suffering, and not in spite of it, the qualities of faith, compassion and wisdom. We become better for facing the worst in ourselves, through an appreciation of our Goddess of darkness and light. We are made whole through an understanding of her complex workings. We are stretched, challenged and strengthened by uncertainty, disorder and perplexity all of which *Muso Koroni* authors as the judicious, but stern mother who confers on us hard lessons, disciplining with a firmness that only a wise and truly caring mother ca. When we have lost our way, she is there is to lead us, shining her luminous light to guide our steps. As the Divine embodiment of air and fire, she will blow us senseless without reprieve, should we stray. Play with danger, and her fire will scald. Depending on our own life choices, her bright flame can illuminate or burn. Surrender to her, and bask in the warmth of her hearth, and the fresh, cool ambiance of her comfort.

This Crone of crones is summoned to generate the fecundity of land, beseeched for the quick ripening of grains, called upon during pangs of labor, and implored to offer strength to newborns. Her children honor her at the base of trees with offerings of *shea butter* and kola nuts.[2] Devotees burn *shea butter* in lanterns carved in her image, to invoke her spirit. Millet, a staple grain of West Africa, is one of *Muso Koroni's* choice offerings. Her children are mindful not to allow millet to drop frivolously upon the earth, as this is a sign of careless disregard for their sustenance. Elders dance in joyful praise to *Muso Koroni* at harvest time.

Muso Koroni, Goddess of life and death, is ever feared, respected, honored and loved: Grandmother to all, Mother of all mothers. Although she is absent for the second phase of creation, she remains as her personifications of air, wind and fire. Before *Muso Koroni* temporarily departs, she replants her Supreme fertilizer, the *balanza* tree, also known as *Pembélé*, back into Mother earth where it takes root and thrives once again. The *Pembélé*, once offered eternal youth to mortals, but eventually this pro-generator also became the source of death, and reverence was instead bequeathed upon *Faro*, the spirit of water.

At the beginning of her origination, *Muso Koroni's* double, or shadow, is entrusted to *Faro*, as well as *Ndomayiri*, the spirit of the earth responsible for restraint and stability. *Faro* may be perceived as the shadow of *Muso Koroni* herself, providing the quality of equilibrium to the earth, a characteristic that is not inherent in *Muso Koroni's* conscious constitution. Through the medium of water, *Faro* literally and figuratively reflects the heavens, and all of her activities to her earthly creatures. *Faro* perpetuates life because she preserves in water the double of all existence. *Ndomayiri* and *Faro* are in complementary union, as is the relationship between earth and water. Earth cups water in the palms of her hands, replenishing her dry palate through abundant rivers and seas.

Faro arises from her bed in the deep crevices of the river's bottom, visiting us through watery vapor, showering us with rain, streaking the sky with colorful rainbows, communicating to us through thunder, and punishing our infringements of taboos with lightening. Devotees offer up sacrifice, primarily at the Niger River, to this Divinity of the waters who is consistently depicted as a mermaid, with breasts, long hair, and a fish tail.[3] Many of her children along the coasts of Africa have been graced with her stunning and peaceful presence.[4]

As *Faro* was born of the vaporous breath of Spirit from a bubble of its saliva, while pronouncing the words of creation, *Faro* represents the word, the word which connects all things—the means by which the world comes to reflect upon and express itself. *Faro* completes the Divine's work by organizing it, maintaining balance and giving it eternal life. *Faro* is both the act of creation and the image of the created world, where Spirit is revealed. Hence, in Mande languages, the word for *both* river and mother, *ba*, is the same. The Mande say that *Faro* is neither the beginning nor the end, but the center.

Nyalé and *Faro* also engage their own symbiotic relationship. While *Nyalé* plants ideas in the human mind, *Faro* makes them perceptible. Together, *Nyalé* and *Faro* are the originators of Mother Earth, who finds her masculine representative or earthly spokesman in *Ndomayiri* (literally, shaman of the trees), the heavenly blacksmith. *Ndomayiri* is the healer supreme and lord of remedies. Earthly blacksmiths emulate the characteristics of *Ndomayiri*, whom they identify as their original ancestor. *Ndomayiri* is fire as well, the element most utilized by the blacksmith to construct his sacred tools. The Mande are not amiss to attribute to the male energy healing properties, nor are they blind to the profound necessity in their cosmology of the Divine Feminine embracing her masculine side. *Ndomayiri* is *Nyalé's* consort providing woman with her iron, her utensils, tools and ritual objects by which she may feed her children, stir her cauldron, enact her rituals and conduct her ceremonies. *Ndomayiri* is the conductor of *Nyalé's* fiery passion. At the smith's sacred forge, where he smelts his iron ore in the procreative furnace, women come during his meditations to receive healings and pray for fertility. In the symbolic imagination of mystical Africa, *Ndomayiri*, shaman of the trees, is the sturdy, inflexible, consistent principle, which takes root in Mother Earth. The two are enjoined, offering the ground upon which we step, and the trees by which we nourish, heal and shelter ourselves. In a sense, *Ndomayiri* is the earth's witch, her ritual conductor, overseeing her ceremonies to honor her existence.

In the third phase of creation, *Ndomayiri* maintains a prominent role, as human societies are formed and social existence reigns. *Muso Koroni* resumes her activity as *Nyalé*, after her absence from the second phase, and once again represents energy, impetus, mystery, and the taste for all human desire. She is exaltation and enthusiasm in mental activities as well as in manual skills and labor. *Ndomayiri* controls the extravagance all human beings would otherwise indulge; he guarantees tradition. But this control to maintain social life is not an ideal; it is rather a necessity to which human beings must adapt. Were *Nyalé* to completely disappear, all activity and animation would cease. Were her power without boundaries, creation would disintegrate. *Faro* surfaces to represent the balance of the workings of both *Nyalé* and *Ndomayiri*.

In short, Mande tradition comfortably honors the Divine Mother without dismissing, neglecting or denigrating her masculine partner. She is at once One and All and, at the same time, in secure and mutual relationship with her companion and co-creator. Goddess is adored through her representation of all elements, while her male counterpart complements. She swims through the sea as *Faro*, blows as the wind and shines as fire in *Muso Koroni*, and brings the peace that comes with rest in the maternal bosom as mother earth, affectionately named *Lennaya*. At the same time, the male principle is at once acknowledged in *Ndomayiri* as earth and fire. *Teliko*, born of *Faro*, is a divinity of air most commonly manifest as a whirlwind. Today when a whirlwind passes, it is a sign of disruption and the standard response is to raise one's left pinkie towards it for it to depart peacefully. Accordingly, in the world of the Mande, where paradox is comfortably embraced, all of the manifestations of the Divine are essentially inseparable and work as one. The tension that lay within this contradiction is where, for the Mande, the truth rests its mysterious though knowable spirit.

Representing the universal sign of the Goddess is the symbol of the chevron, or pubic V, prominent in Mande cosmology. The chevron signifies speech and hearing, *Faro* and *Muso Koroni's* creations. A dual chevron, in the shape of an 'M,' represents the cosmic travels of *Muso Koroni* and *Faro*, as well as the path of Venus, *Muso Koroni's* star. The X or two opposing chevrons, are powerful fertility symbols. The omnipotent circle, round womb, symbolizes fertility, rain, water as well as *Muso Koroni's* tears. The diamond stands for the four directions of space, the cosmic waters and procreation. All of these sacred symbols may serve as ingredients for offerings, amulets or rituals.

Many of the symbols that were once cherished in honor of Goddess, and came to represent evil or darkness, also remain sacred in the Goddess tradition of Mande culture. The revered snake is a symbol of *Muso Koroni*. The python's head specifically represents divinity. To pass along the valuable skill of agriculture to human beings, *Muso Koroni* mates with the cobra, and gives birth to the *Chi Wara*, a half-man, half-animal spirit. Again, she embodies at once, the tameness of nature, and the activities of the wild. Goddess of nature's wild, and the wilderness of the human heart, *Muso Koroni* integrates these seeming dualities into an integral whole.

Black panthers and leopards are also her primary manifestations, and she scratches young women with her claws to bring about their menstruation. Black, the symbol of beauty in Africa, the color of rain clouds and rich soil, honors the fertility *Muso Koroni* engenders. She is darkness and all that darkness hides, contains, breeds and eventually manifests.

Carvings of *Muso Koroni* are easily identifiable by their elaborate coiffure hairstyle, decoration of cowrie shells[5] and sometimes beaded necklace and coils of red thread and white cord, representing her invention of jewelry. She may also adorn her forehead with the engraving of a python head, and lines of scarification on her head and cheeks. Ceremonies of scarification and circumcision all trace their origination to *Muso Koroni*.

Faro's earthly symbols and representations also participate in the universal language of the Goddess. The crocodile carries out *Faro's* will, as well as collects her offerings, while the swallow is her messenger. The water iguana is an avatar of *Faro* and represents fertility, fortune and protection against harmful magic. Tortoises, gazelles, goats and beautiful, seductive women are *Faro's* other popular manifestations.

Faro's favorite offerings are any white objects (the color of water), pieces of copper, like the color of her tail, and red, wild tomatoes, which women consume or offer up for fertility. Tomatoes represent blood, and there is a close link between blood and water in Mande cosmology, both representing the fluids of life.

Twins are *Faro's* children, the spirit who reflects, like a mirror, the shadow or double of creation. Naming ceremonies for twins are performed on the river's bed, where the children are bathed, their heads shaved, and their hair thrown back to *Faro* as an offering. The father offers a special prayer to the twins on bended knees, requesting their special protection to the family. The twins' altar consists of two calabash, and a piece of the twins' umbilical cord bound around the center. The altar is hung above the outside entrance of the home, on high, so as not to make contact with the earth, water or fire, which reduces its vital force, or *nyama*. The altars are given early sacrifices before and after the rainy season, and during all of the major rites of passage of the twins' lives. Standard offerings consist of white kola nuts, two balls of millet and millet beer, and two white chickens. The father pours the blood of the chickens and the alcoholic libations over the umbilical cord on the altar. The existence of the twin's altar allows any twin, or their mother, to handle a scorpion, the twin's protective creature, without being stung. Scorpions also sting those who attempt to harm the twins.

For the outsider to African traditions, the segregation of the roles of men and women do not allow for a comprehensive understanding of the true position of high esteem woman holds. In Africa, woman is the earthly representative of this Divine Feminine and is treated accordingly. Mande traditionalist proverbs, song and story best reflect her representation as Supreme Mother. The Mande teach their children *"All that one has one owes once to one's father, and twice to one's mother."* The rhythms of the *jembe* drum beat *denbadon* (lit. child—mother—dance) during popular festivities to show reverence to mother. Young girls dance the *sorsoner* rhythm in the full moonlight to show respect for their mothers.

Many of the cultural restrictions and taboos around fertility, motherhood and woman's role in the community are actually based on a deep reverence for woman, rather than attempts to confine or denigrate her. Ritual taboos during a woman's menstruation are prevalent on the African continent, and easily misinterpreted if not understood within their profound context. As the Mande recognize that fertility and motherhood are sacred, they honor the consecrated nature of menstruation, and understand the need for ritual regulation to contain and affirm its power. This sacred fluid is replete with the life-force energy, *nyama*, and possesses the ability to override or disempower any ritual object or ceremony. A woman's time of menstruation is her divine offering to Goddess and she appropriately keeps a distance from other ritual activities during this period.

Although it is true that motherhood is highly valued in traditional African culture, the Mande acknowledge that women who receive the calling of healing or divination are often unable to produce children. These powerful women have another kind of role in the community with a great opportunity to "mother" and nurture with their mystical gifts and insights.

A father is not allowed to enter the birth-room where his children are born, as birthing is the sacred process bestowed to woman. Nonetheless, the Mande assert that the father has his own special bond with his child, as the child receives both parents' *nyama*. A father may loosen his belt during the mother's pregnancy to help establish his connection with the child, mother and the pregnancy. Sometimes during the mother's labor, the father will wrap his belt loosely around the mother's waist as an offering of his own *nyama* and support for the child's entry into the world. The pains that a mother feels during her labor, the father may feel as well through the connection of his belt. After the birth of the child, family and friends will sing a song to the mother that she may continue to hear for the months ahead:

> Thank you to our children's mothers
> Thank you to our children's mothers
> Thank you to all of our mothers
> Thank you to all of our mothers
> They are those who are blessed
> They are those who care for us
> It is not easy
> It is not easy to bring forth life

In the Mande world, children who share the same breast-milk, even if only once, share the same blood. The Mande view them as siblings who must abide by the same rules and never marry. Those who are nurtured from the same breast, men and women alike, will sometimes refer to each other as "breast-milk," acknowledging the deep bond that results from sharing this sacred, life-giving substance.

This honoring of mother continues throughout a child's life. Many rites of passage afford children the opportunity to sing their affections to their mothers. After the childhood initiation, children sing to their mothers in appreciation for their love and support.

> Thank you to all my mothers
> Thank you to all my mothers
> Thank you to all my mothers who are blessed
> Thank you for all the things you do for us, bring to us and give to us
> Morning and nighttime
> Respect for you

There is no crying and no sadness

Only appreciation for all the things you do for us, bring to us and
give to us.

Even in the manly realm of hunting, the Divine Feminine is acknowledged
and worshipped. The hunters invoke *Sanènè* and *Kontron*, feminine and masculine spirits respectively who together, represent the balanced forces of
nature. These spirits offer protection to the hunter in the dangerous wilderness. The hunter tells many stories of the two spirits whose relationship
changes from mother and son, sister and brother to wife and husband. Hunters often construct altars to these spirits in the bush where they pour libations
and offer up millet and kola nuts. Hunters sometimes place the written names
of these divinities inside their charms for protection and prosperous hunting.

In Mande culture, women share with the hunter the sacred garment of life.
Women design and produce the protective garment, known as mud cloth, by
staining pieces of cotton with herbal leaves and bark and designing sacred
symbols on the fabric with mud. The whole process is long and demanding
and imbues the clothing with potent levels of *nyama*. Women also wear mud-
cloth during prominent times in their lives, including the periods after the
birth of a first child, the time when a woman first moves to her husband's village, after menopause and at her burial. Women share the powerful act of
shedding blood (or the notable cessation of it) during these times with the
hunter who also sheds a great amount of blood during the hunts. The *nyama*
of the cloth and its symbolism serve as protection and empowerment for
women and hunters.

In short, in the African village, where gender roles are clearly defined,
woman is esteemed as mother, craftswoman, gardener, harvester, herbalist,
diviner and shaman. Through her abilities to create, nurture and heal woman
expresses her complete devotion to the Divine Mother. Children of the Goddess worship her through her many forms as crone and mermaid, venerate her
through her primary manifestations of air, fire, earth and water and most sig-
nificantly, acknowledge her in all her aspects of creation. Daily her children
invoke her name across the terrain of her bosom, lap and back, in the canals
and rivers of her sweat, blood and tears, around her global womb, and on her
rich, dark fertile soil. From the birthplace of humanity where the beginning
seeds of life first germinated and developed, beats her steady pulse, in the
heart of her bosom, the heartbeat of the Dark Mother.

Notes

1 Mande is a large West African language family and homeland, covering the regions of Mali, Gambia, Guinea, Guinea Bissau, Burkina Faso, Ivory Coast, Senegal, and parts of Liberia, Mauritania and Sierra Leone.

2 *Shea butter* oil is both consumed and used as a healing product throughout Africa. It comes from the nut of a sweet, edible fruit and is harvested by the women. *Kola nuts* are edible nuts that serve as medicine, offerings, gifts, and divination aids.

3 Most scholars refer to this apparently androgynous spirit *Faro* as a he, while at once acknowledging that the primary depictions of *Faro* are of a mermaid. It is important to note, too, that in Mande languages pronouns are gender neutral.

4 Throughout Yorubaland, this popular water Goddess is known as *Mami Wata*.

5 Cowries are ocean shells, formerly used as currency, that resemble female genitalia and represent fertility and fortune throughout Africa.

Works Cited

Bâ, Amadou Hampaté. *Aspects de la civilisation africaine: personne, culture, religion.* Paris: Présence africaine, 1972.

Bailleul, Pere Charles. *Dictionnaire Francais-Bambara.* Bamako, Mali: Editions Donniya, 1998.

Birnbaum, Ph.D., Lucia Chiavola. *dark mother: african origins and godmothers.* San Jose, CA: Authors Choice Press, 2001.

Charry, Eric. *Mande Music: Traditional and Modern Music of the Maninka and Mandinka of Western Africa.* Chicago: The University of Chicago Press, 2000.

Cissé, Youssouf. "Notes sur les sociétés de chasseurs Malinké." *Journal de la Société des Africanistes.* 34(2): 175–226, 1964.

Diallo, Yaya and Mitchell Hall. *The Healing Drum: African Wisdom Teachings.* Rochester, Vermont: Destiny Books, 1989.

Doumbia, Adama and Naomi. *The Way of the Elders: West African Spirituality & Tradition.* St. Paul, Minnesota: Llewellyn Worldwide, 2004.

Gleason, Judith. *Oya: In Praise of an African Goddess.* New York, New York: HarperCollins, 1992.

Griaule, M. and G. Dieterlen. *The Pale Fox.* Chino Valley, Arizona: Continuum Foundation, 1986.

Hale, Thomas A. *Griots and Griottes: Masters of Words and Music.* Bloomington and Indianapolis: Indiana University Press, 1998.

Imperato, Pascal James. *Buffoons, Queens and Wooden Horsemen.* New York: Kilima House Pub., 1983

Imperato, Pascal James. *Legends, Sorcerers, and Enchanted Lizards: Door Locks of the Bamana of Mali.* New York: Africana Pub., 2001.

McNaughton, Patrick R. *The Mande Blacksmiths: Knowledge, Power and Art in West Africa.* Bloomington and Indianapolis: Indiana University Press, 1988.

Paques, Viviana. *Les Bambara*. Paris: Presses Universitaires de France, 1954.

Suso, Bamba and Banna Kanute. *Sunjata: Gambian Versions of the Mande Epic*. New York, New York: Penguin Books, 1974 and 1999.

Zahan, Dominique. *The Bambara*. Leiden: E. J. Brill, 1974. The Stained Glass

The Stained Glass Whore and Other Virgins

Luisah Teish, Ph.D.

Today, like many other days, I will gaze into a glass of water to help a woman find her voice, express her creativity, or free her spirit.

Today, like many other days I will wash away the salty tears of a woman who has been sexually, physically or emotionally abused. Today I will wrap myself in white cloth, adorn myself with beads, and dance in undulating rhythms to honor my Goddess. For 22 years I have had the privilege of being an Iyal'orisha (Mother of the Spirits), a priestess of Oshun, the West African Goddess of Love, Art, and Sensuality. By venerating Her I am able to salute the divinity in all women and in myself.

This privilege comes at the price of having endured the rigors of initiation; having studied the tradition under a host of elders from Africa to Oakland; and having healed myself from the ravages of the Madonna-Whore Complex. For many years I was a "Recovering Catholic."

During my adolescent years I was required by a deathbed promise my mother made to her father, to become Catholic. I went to catechism and mass every morning; I worked in the rectory and the convent; I waxed the statues in the church and sang in the choir. I did all of this for free. According to the church I was a "Roman Catholic" and I should do all this for the LOVE OF MARY.

But in reality I was a "Louisiana Catholic." The term bespeaks a form of worship that consists mostly of original (African and Indian) shamanistic and magical practices, which, under the oppression of slavery, were overlaid with a devotion to Mary and the saints. According to church history, Black people had been enslaved because we were "savages" who needed Christian conversion. I went to Catholic school and learned that there were two important women in the stories of the Christian bible: Eve and Mary.

I was introduced to Eve through the Creation story, which seemed a little crazy to me. I tried to imagine the scene. Two white people in a place somewhere near Africa walking around naked with nothing to do. (Unemployment was their first problem as far as I was concerned because I had been taught that an idle mind is "the devil's workshop.") So here comes the devil in the form of a talking snake. I grew up in the Bayous and learned to run from snakes at an early age. The story always insinuated that a slimy old snake talked and dumb Eve didn't run. Because she listened to the snake she was guilty of something, and that something had everything to do with all other women and me.

My adolescent mind couldn't analyze the symbolism in that myth so I tried to dismiss the story as so much rigmarole and go on about my business. I was willing to leave her alone but Eve would not let me alone. As the years passed, her name kept coming up. And it always came up as the reason why I had to do something I didn't want to do, or couldn't do something I wanted to do.

Overcoming Eve:

Because of Eve I had to: Bleed every month, stop having fun, be a temptation, cover my body, go to church and try to wipe out my "Original Sin", get ruined (molested), marry some man and obey him, remain a virgin until I was married, marry in white, imitate Jesus, hate Jezebel, cry a lot, be humble and poor, honor the pope, eat fish on Friday, go to confession, hate sex but do it anyway, get pregnant and do hard labor, cook, clean, and work by the "sweat of my brow: have all my children christened, take a saint's name, beat my chest three times at mass, not talk back, and pray real hard not to go to hell

All this condemning stuff was coming from that book of folktales called "the Bible," and its author was God, an old jealous white man with a beard and a bunch of naked angels around him.

I spent many years of my life trying to get this Old Man God to explain his program to me, but he never said anything I could understand or appreciate. All I knew at the time was that my woman's body was supposed to be the downfall of all of creation. It was my fault that men had to be born, to suffer, and to die.

But adolescence is a time of longing to belong so I tried to be a "good Catholic girl." I was told in no uncertain terms that in order to "Overcome

Eve" I had to be like the Virgin Mary in every way. I donned a blue mantle and became a "child of Mary." But what an assignment that was!

The Perfect Woman:

Mary was a purely miraculous woman. She was powerful! She seemed to travel all over the world appearing to children everywhere. She answered the petitions of the poor and the sick and people held brightly colored processions in her honor all during the year. My favorite Mary was "Our Lady of Perpetual Help" who was regarded as a Mother who never turned her back on you. I thought She was great. In my attempts to be like her I became everybody's little helper (the Eldest daughter syndrome) at home, at school and especially at church. I became a maid for the church. I ironed habits in the convent, and swept floors in the rectory. But my most important job was waxing the statues in the church. At least the saints appreciated my efforts because they smiled, rolled their eyes and paid some attention to my candlelight petitions.

But this servitude was not enough because Mary was a pure white woman. Not only did she have a baby without having sex or labor but her baby belonged to *God*. On top of that she found a man who took care of it even though it wasn't his Baby. We were told that Joseph was a perfect gentleman about the whole thing.

What I learned from all this was that I had a choice I could be a beautiful *virgin-mother* like Mary and enter the gates of heaven or I could be a dumb *whore-wife* like Eve and be condemned to a living hell. It took me years to comprehend that this pull between Eve and Mary manifest in the Madonna-Whore complex. And it took the examples of Lilith, Ishtar, Isis and Oshun to liberate myself from it.

The Madonna-Whore Complex:

In my experience as a spiritual counselor and ritualist, I have dealt with women who suffer from varying degrees of the *"Madonna-Whore Complex."* It is a psycho-spiritual contradiction that has had great impact on women's imaginations, self-image, life choices, and actions.

The word *'whore'* carries an incredible amount of power, most of it negatively directed toward women. Ministers condemn women from the pulpit, and Rap artists degrade their sisters with this word. Innocent little girls have been accused of instigating incest; and women have been murdered by serial killers trying to rid the world of whores. Women may be regarded as whores irrespective of their age, their race, their income, or their conduct. So what does it really mean?

Today the word *whore* conjures up images of an over-painted, under-dressed, disease-ridden junkie woman hailing cars on street corners, turning back alley tricks for chump change which is paid to an abusive pimp. The term "Call Girl" is used to describe a more privileged woman who caters to politicians, celebrities, and the military and big businessmen. "Sex industry workers" is the politically correct term to describe pornography performers; and a person may employ a "sex surrogate" in therapeutic counseling. The term "housewife" describes a woman who provides sex, children, and maintenance services for a sexual partner. All of these relationships imply an exchange of money for sexual services. Apparently no one can escape being seen by someone as some kind of whore.

Virgins Today:

In today's culture we have several kinds of virgins. We have the young unmarried girl who has had no sexual contact, who has not been *"deflowered."* The Virgin Bride in our marriage ceremony wears white for purity and carries a large bouquet of fresh flowers.

We have nuns, those women who have chosen to become *"brides of Christ."* They live in convents (similar to a temple or harem chamber), and in some orders still wear veils. (In former times temple prostitutes wore veils.) Most, but not all, nuns are physical virgins.

Then we have the secular woman who has simply chosen to remain sexually inactive. This culture refers to her as a "spinster" (one who spins thread, like the Goddess Ariadne), or an "old maid", an old woman who remains a girl (with no sexual contact). Although these terms whore and virgin define woman's sexual activity in relationship to penetration of the hymen by men, I do not regard sexually active lesbians as physical virgins.

As a Catholic I was told that any sin (especially any sexual act) I thought/fantasized about committing had to be confessed as if I had committed it. So I learned that no matter how well I behaved it was not possible ever to be truly virginal. This is crazy making at its best.

Virgin or Whore

At this point in our discussion I want to make it clear that I am neither condemning/nor condoning prostitution in any of its forms.

Women are born into this life under varying circumstances and encounter a wide range of experiences that flow into their Self-Image. Nevertheless every woman must make her own choices and experience the consequences. But it is important to know that we have more than just a few ancestral biographies and mythic models to feed our imagination. And we must have the power and the processes to transform our inherited images into contemporary reality. When we analyze the stories we can understand our inheritance; when we study the symbols we can enrich our Imaginations, and when we act upon this enrichment, through rituals and rites we can enjoy a healthier life and leave a richer inheritance for the coming generations. This is not only the right, but also the responsibility, of woman. This is where I function as an Iyanifa, a Mother of Destiny, a counselor and priestess.

Counseling the Complex:

As I describe my experiences counseling women with the Madonna Whore complex, I invite you to breathe deeply and keep a few things in mind:

> A.) You may feel angry and insulted that I'm saying these things. This is a good sign that you (or someone close to you) are trapped in the described complex.
>
> B.) You may find that none of it applies to you. I imagine that there are many women who are perfect. Or they are imperfect, but completely happy with themselves. But I don't know these women. I usually encounter women when they are seeking information and processes to make life-altering changes. I am made aware of the underlying problems and it is my job as priestess to facilitate their transformation.
>
> If you have healed yourself from this complex, I applaud you, and encourage you to share your healing process with other women (especially me). If you've never experienced any aspect of this complex, then I'd like a ticket to the planet you grew up on.
>
> C.) You recognize the condition, are struggling to overcome it and want advice that will increase the possibilities of success. Here's the good news: This article is written for you sister.

I think that most of us will see a bit of ourselves in the descriptions that follow. As you read these descriptions do not become dismayed. Healing is a process not a product and growing is an adventure. Say to yourself "better late than never, and better now than ever." Chant it like a mantra. So let's take a look at who we've been.

1. She Who is Ever Virgin:

She Who Is *Ever Virgin* represses her sexual energy and power in an effort to remain Virgin. She never challenges the status quo; she never allows herself to even imagine anything beyond the role prescribed for her by society. She changes only into what is popular (whether in the larger culture or her subculture). She never grows up into an independent woman.

I've met this woman at the baby clinic, on the TV talk shows, in church and in the university.

She may have spent all her creative energy raising children. If raising children fulfills her that's fine. But I often find that the woman who totally dedicated herself to motherhood really wanted to be an artist. Sometimes she postpones her own desire until the children are "all grown", only to find that she is too tired or too set in her ways to make a significant change when the nest becomes empty.

For example: Momma Routine, a woman in her early sixties came to my Creativity workshop. She complained of boredom, lethargy, and bouts of depression. She thought she was losing her mind.

As the workshop progressed we played with clay and crayons, music and dance, body painting and storytelling. Although Ruti enjoyed each activity she ended each with a "yeah but..." followed by something that said she couldn't possibly do this at home. I questioned her about conditions in her home. She had a four-bedroom house, her children were all "grown and gone", and her husband was preoccupied with his own affairs. When I persisted in questioning her about her desires, she "confessed" that she had a "childish desire" to paint, but that she had nowhere to do it. Again I pressed her by asking why she didn't just buy some supplies and start slapping some paint around. Her response shocked me. Momma Ruti told me that she had no place to paint because her house was so "well appointed." This woman had spent her whole life struggling to make her home look like something in Good Housekeeping magazine, and she had accomplished this in spite of the mess children make naturally. Now she was enslaved by that accomplishment. I gave her the assignment to go home, choose a room that was no longer functional and to tear the room up. I told her to take the furniture out, lift the carpet, tape newsprint paper to the walls, open the window, and sit on the floor and finger paint like a child. It took a while to convince her that it was all right for a grown woman to behave like this. She cried, she got the message, and then she laughed. This was a liberating moment for her.

2. The Most Holy Virgin:

The Most Holy Virgin can be found "sitting in the church." If she is a woman who is truly called to ministry then we have the Mother of Wisdom and Compassion in our midst, and we are fortunate to be in her presence. I am privileged to know such women.

But the Most Holy Virgin who causes concern is the one who thinks that the church is the only acceptable (safe?) place for her to have a social life. She sits, like a hen, in church all day, every day, for every reason imaginable. Sometimes she struts, and then she uses the church as a place to hold her own private fashion show. She will be seen wearing the most lavish hats, wigs, shoes, and jewels, and she will find a way to let the congregation know just how much she put in the offering basket.

Sunday. She may also stand in church as a member of the "good sisters power caucus." They will make a holy career of adamantly condemning women who behave differently from themselves. Often this little band of angels becomes the "sex police" of the church. It's their job to make sure that every woman properly represses her sexual desires.

However, this woman can be found sneaking in the back door of the abortion clinic sometimes, secretly disposing of the child conceived by the holy "ghost" in the back room of the minister's study. To some extent she has bought into both the Eve and the Mary myth. She assumes that all women are the evil Eve, and that it's her job to keep them straight. If she could forgive herself and other women for not being "perfect", we could all rejoice. It is the Mary myth that leads her, ("holier than thou") to the minister's study for redemption. This woman needs to develop a balanced relationship between sexuality and spirituality. She needs a Goddess she can dance with. I serve this woman when she has to have somebody to talk to who can keep her secret.

3. The Crowned Virgin:

The Crowned Virgin can be seen in the university woman who studies, and studies, and studies, and studies. When the crowned virgin is truly educated, (that is, allowed to draw wisdom from within) we are blessed with "Eve, the creative genius" who will challenge outworn ideas and bring fresh insights. I respect and love these sisters.

But most often she is not educated, she is indoctrinated. Her reward comes from being able to recite what others have said while suppressing her original thoughts. Instead of biting the apple (or the fig) she swallows pills, lives "from the neck up", and has no intimate life. Or she may have spent a lifetime in therapy addressing her already overdressed brain while neglecting her body and questioning whether or not she has a spirit. She has spent a lot of time and money but still does not feel whole.

I meet this woman in classes and workshops all the time. Then my job is to prove that she has intuition that is as valid as intellect. This woman needs to regard her dreams not only as psychological paper shredders but also as spirit messages that can be used to guide and direct the flow of her life.

4. The Unholy Whores:

Unholy Whores is a term I use to describe women who over identify with masculine domination. Some of them admit that they are catering to male domination while others imagine that they are competing with it or rebelling against it. In any event masculine power remains relevant to their self-image and they remain embroiled in a reactionary relationship to it.

These women may be actual prostitutes who cater to the taste of customers. As I've said before this woman's dilemma includes danger, disease, and self-esteem problems.

Some prostitutes, especially the porn models, claim that they fully enjoy their work and are empowered by it. If this is true then we have a rare specimen of the Sacred Harlot. All she needs is a temple and a Cultural Revolution to re-sacralize her position.

But, the woman who lands at my door seeking healing has been abused, feels alone, and is full of self-disgust. She wants out and she needs help making the transition to a life of her own. Sometimes I have to accompany the sister to the drug detox center or the mental hospital as part of her ritual.

For example: Collette, the reptile, described herself as a detached cold-blooded, street hooker. She felt she was exercising "power over" the "tricks" who paid her for sex without affection. She thought the money she took from men made her somehow equal to them. She bragged that she made more money in one night than most working women made in a week. But Collette's money didn't do her much good because she spent most of it on cocaine so she could continue not to feel anything. She assumed that both detachment and violence were "a natural part" of sex, so she simply raised the price for "freaks." One night Collette was gang raped and tortured by four men (drag queens in fact) in a van! Her bloody bruises, burns, and razor cuts were medically treated, followed by an AIDS test. It was my job, to help her heal her spirit.

Upon examination I found that this woman had deep-seated self-image problems. In fact, she believed in the curse of Eve and was, unknowingly, acting out the worse of the Lilith myth. It took years for her to overcome the drug habit and to view her sexuality differently. It took many years to cleanse "the curse" from her psyche.

5. The Holy Whore:

The Holy Whore may be a wife whose primary function is to fulfill the will of the person who "pays the cost to be the boss." Her license and ceremony has given her social approval, and birthing has given her some recognition of female power, but only minimally. She develops the habit of self-sacrifice, complains of feeling unappreciated, and concludes by attempting to manipulate family members into manifesting her (supposedly) non-existent Will. This woman often neglects her body, has no time of her own, and fears her imagination. Sometimes I meet her at the battered women's shelter. She wants to learn how to be a whole person while remaining connected to her family.

6. The Star Studded Whore:

The Star Studded Whore may be found in the glamour professions, in modeling and in Hollywood. Occasionally we are fortunate enough to see a true glamour, a woman whose beauty really reflects the light shining from within. But the Hollywood Whore is a flasher rather than a shiner. Carefully wrapped in the fur of endangered species, she peels the animal's skin down at the neck to expose silicon breasts or rolls it up to hide plastic surgery skin seams. She is caught in a life and death struggle much like the animals she wears around her neck. She struggles to fight cellulite, to lose weight, and to avoid laugh lines that become wrinkles (those ungodly things?) with age. Since she must grow old or die young, this woman is caught in a battle that she cannot win. And she may have a love-hate relationship with the mirror. Sometimes I meet her, retching violently in the ladies room. This woman needs Ishtar to show her the true meaning of everlasting beauty.

7. The Stained Glass Whore:

The Stained Glass Whore can be found in the Corporate World, wearing a pin-striped suit, drawing a large salary, and finding acceptance as an honorary male. In order to fulfill this role she must leave all that is "feminine" at the door when she enters the office. She must learn to suppress her feelings (lest she be accused of PMS) as well as a man; and she must learn to oppress those beneath her even more in order to earn his status. She cannot really be a part of the "old boy system" because she will never be accepted into the boy's locker room where the real business deals go down. So she becomes the neutered, "overseer in the red blazer." I meet her hovering just below the glass ceiling, which is stained with the sweat and blood of those who have bounced off it before.

Once in a while she comes to a "women's workshop" but the very fact that she is there must be kept secret. She may have fine clothes, a private spa, and a luxury car; but she is a slave to other people's image and expectations of her. She competes habitually and finds little or no satisfaction in the work she has done. Sometimes there is a nagging guilt over the consequences of her actions. When given a safe space these hard-nosed competitors (predators?) break down easily, longing for real acceptance and a sense of community. If only she could embrace the power of Isis, then she could take her place on the throne and "feminize" (spelled h-u-m-a-n-i-z-e) the workplace. The few rare birds who have done this are an endangered species.

But even the woman who does not buy into any of the identities listed above can still be tricked. Some women become what I call:

8. The Isolated Amazon:

The Isolated Amazon is heavily armored. With sword and shield in hand she blindly wages war against everything and everybody including God, Nature, and herself. Hers is a struggle against pain and anger. She is so angry at the pain she's suffered that she determines not to be anything recognizable as Virgin, Whore. or whatever. So she struggles to be…what? Nothing! because the whole damn world is tainted. Since the whole world is tainted the best she can do is to destroy…what? Every goddamn thing that crosses her path. Especially her stupidass dreams. I first met this woman in the mirror.

Example: One day I looked in the mirror, and I was angry at what I saw. I saw somebody who had become whatever it took to prove that I was not "a dizzy rib." I'd thrown myself into the arms of men, who were totally incapable of loving me, to prove that I was "hot." I worked harder than the average man to prove that I was "strong", and sacrificed my emotions on the altar of my intellect, in order to prove that I was "smart." And I endeavored to "chew bullets" in order to prove that I was "brave."

One day I looked out the window of my second floor apartment and the grass was blowing in the wind. Angrily I decided that the wind was blowing the wrong way; and that it was being done just to spite me. I flew into a rage! When I tried to articulate my anger and disappointment to my "female friends" (who proved themselves to be a pack of blood-sucking predators) I was abandoned by them for not being "woman enough" to handle everything alone. I realized that I needed help to confront myself and change my condition.

Three older women, whom I will call Blessing, Gravity, and Spice, stepped in and served as Wise Mothers for me. Under their guidance I was encouraged to do a thorough examination of my life.

Blessings asked me to look at what I had inherited, and to separate my ancestral blessings from the ancestral curses. I realized that I was blessed with an inherited predisposition for the Performing Arts. Most of my family members are singers, musicians, writers, and storytellers. Unfortunately those who don't perform professionally create a lot of drama in their personal lives. I also inherited a fierce independence and a hair-trigger temper. I did a lot of work on tempering my fire.

Gravity asked me to weigh the effects of societal factors such as racism and economic oppression against problems that arose from poor judgment. I could easily name a dozen ways in which being Black, a woman, and from the south had threatened my life, impeded my progress, and denied me hard-earned rewards. It was more difficult to get clarity around the times I had befriended enemies, diminished my own achievements, or acted on half-baked decisions.

And Spice admonished me to develop a sense of humor, to find joy in daily miracles, and to give myself pleasurable experiences in regular doses. I learned to laugh in the face of my enemies, to be awestruck by sunsets and calla lilies, and to drink in the beauty of the unusual.

At first I fought these Mothers, "tooth and nail"; but they persisted. Then I realized that they were the messengers of the Goddesses Yemonja, Oya, and Oshun. It was then that I laid down my armor and let the healing occur. I took the raw materials of my life and re-formed my self-image by embracing the mythology of a primal spirituality and by changing my personal mythology. I created a ritual of Reformation and Self-Acceptance.

I invite you to find the time and a safe space to examine your past, to release it. I know from experience that changing her personal mythology can change a woman's life. This article was written to encourage you to begin creating a new life.

Chemistry of Life

Ida Dunson, M.A.

DNA: de-ox-y-ri-bo-n-cle-ic acid genes
I've often thought it really means—
DNA: DENIAL OF NEGROES 'N' AMERICA
Cross my heart and hope to die
Our founding fathers told a gross "Constitutional" lie.
In Article1, Section 2, Paragraph 3
They said our African Ancestors
Were three-fifths of a Human Being
To justify that diabolical slave trade scheme.
Mathematically impossible!
The European's African American Holocaust scheme.

The trafficking and selling of fellow humans by the score
From the west coast of Africa, to the Caribbean and New World
    shores.
In the dark holds of ships like sardines in a can,
With a moving ship they were taken to another land.
The women quiet, as their DNA blood flowed,
Men moaning, their ancestor's prayers bestowed.
African women, raped, unable to say 'no'
Reaped this awful fate, most demeaning blow

By colonial governors, soldiers and traders of European nations.
Creating this European African American Bastardization.

In America, female slaves were forced to breed
Without regard to religion or creed.
No husbands required, no fathers desired.
Only a commodity of future slaves
Greedily used, then sent to their graves.

This continuing saga of the founding of our land.
That European African American Holocaust Plan.

The founding fathers gave lip service
To a moral and democratic philosophy
Created a split-mind schizoid personality
In All Americans' Ethnic Geneaology
Unaware of their own pathology.

It was State Constitutions and Higher Education Codes
That perpetuated 'Negro" inferiority in secular and parochial
    Modes
In hidden agendas, amendments, acts and clauses,
Mental and physical disabilities with Emotional causes,
Robbed their identities, completing collective amnesia
So most could accept their slave status seizure.

DNA, DENIAL OF NEGROES IN AMERICA
New findings are proving with massive hysteria,
What a "BOOMERANG" THE SCIENTIFIC COMMUNITY
    CAUSED!
The discovery of fossil bones of an African humanoid.
'Lucy' (sung by the Beatles) they knew would cause some heat.
About the radiation technique, and they didn't miss a beat.
HER DNA, de-ox-y-bo-nu-cle-ic acid gene, the life force kind.
The Energy of all Human Beings, began with her blood line.

SO—BE—AWARE!!!
We are all descendants of what happened there,
When you hear the term, "Constitutional Law,"
Legal, but a deceitful humanitarian flaw!
As it applies to our African American Society.
It's still loaded with prejudice and vile hypocrisy
Set up during slavery, Amendment XIV, declared
Punishment for big and little crimes—none were spared.
From runaway slaves to: racial profiling, banks redlining, and
    many other things.
The powerless underclass. The truth loudly rings.
Universities and college regents are setting the time
For proponents of Admissions to create "White Collar Crime."

How Women Construct And Are Formed By Spirit: She Who Is Everywhere In Women's Voices, Kol Isha, Maipfi A Vhafumakadzi

Deborah J. Grenn, Ph.D.

"She is Creator of the Universe, and of Mankind...
She is the Creator Woman"

—Meshack Raphalalani, Venda artist describing his sculpture, 2001

I dedicate this article, an excerpt from my dissertation, to Rita Kolb Grenn, Hanna Eule, Verena La Mar Grenn & their mothers and to the Kolb, Berlstein, Mathivha, Sabath, Gruenbaum, Silberstein, Lawler and Scott ancestors.

"The Shekhinah[1] is considered an alternative way of thinking about God in the orthodox community...not the major way of thinking about God...but not heresy at all. It's right there in the tradition."

—Blu Greenberg, co-founder, Jewish Orthodox Feminist Alliance, interview, 2001

"He created me in his image so he's inside, within me."

—Hanna Motenda, translator at Hamangilasi village, 2001

"...Spirit lives everywhere. In Mother Earth...in all of Nature and in the stars and the moon...inside each and every sentient being."

—Anya Silverman, educator and ritualist, interview, 2002

My dissertation, "For She Is A Tree of Life: Shared Roots Connecting Women To Deity" was an organic[2] theological inquiry into cultural and religious identities, beliefs and practices among South African Lemba and European-American Jewish women. I tried not to enter the inquiry with a set hypothesis that I would seek to prove. Yet despite my best efforts to remain impartial—a mindset I know to be flawed, since "objectivity" cannot exist in social science research—I could not and cannot help looking for woman in the Divine and divinity in woman wherever I go; I find myself constantly watching for her, in text, icon, spoken language and symbol.

While the notion of God as both Mother and Father is a widespread cosmology throughout much of Africa, I received either no response or negative responses to the idea of a female deity from most of the women I interviewed in South Africa.[3]

In contrast, when I told Venda artist Meshack Raphalalani that those believing in a feminist spirituality sometimes speak of the earth as the body of the Goddess, his response was an enthusiastic "Oh, yes, yes!!!" (Raphalalani, personal communication, 2001).

Eight thousand miles away in northern California, when I asked about the possibility of a female deity, educator Patti Moskovitz said to me: "If we believe God is in and over everything...if you think of God in a womanly way...we're in the womb of God. We are *part* of God.[4] We're in a protected place, even though the world feels frightening to us at times" (Moskovitz, interview, 2001).

The more women's voices I heard, the more I saw the Sacred Feminine as immanent; the more I saw women who seemed to be filled with joy even in the midst of the most adverse circumstances, the more I was able to view even the most mundane daily activities—cooking, cleaning, sewing and sweeping—as sacred.

How God is Constructed

I worked in the field in South Africa with a Lemba co-researcher, Dr. L. Rudo Mathivha of Johannesburg and the Northern Province, an area about

thirty miles from the Zimbabwe border. When we sat with the women at
Hamangilasi, we asked one of the interpreters, Hanna Motenda about the
women's concept of God.

> HM: He's a creator. He's a king who's holding our lives. "If I am sick, it's
> for the Lord, and if I'm living, it's all for God."
> DG: You mean it's…we're serving God?
> HM: We're serving God.
> DG: In Jewish mysticism…the belief is that God can only be realized
> through us. It's similar. In women's spirituality, we also believe that God
> is in each of us…
> I asked Rudo, who often interpreted for the women speaking Tshivenda
> in the villages I visited, how the women felt about that. In other words, do
> the women imagine God as an external in Nature or in Heaven, or as
> present in ourselves as well?
> HM:…ourselves. God is in us. They say God is everywhere. Even in
> Nature, when we look at anything, we see God.
> DG:…in themselves?
> HM: "He created me in his image so he's inside, within me."
> Because there are a number of cultures and religions in which Snake is
> revered as deity, and because the snake is mythologically symbolic of
> rebirth, renewal, growth and transformation I was curious about the
> meanings of the python within Venda mythology and art. I wanted to
> know how this might carry over into Lemba cosmology, and so I raised
> the question with the women at Shayandima:
> DG: Is there any mythology about the snake, the python that you can tell
> me?
> RM: They say if you meet a python and it slithers away it usually means
> you're going to hear bad news…

Rudo asked the women whether they thought the python has some supernatural powers, and told me, "They don't think it's got supernatural properties
but they believe that its fat has healing properties, especially for burns."
Ntshabeni was curious about why I would ask a question about the python.
Rudo added, "They want to know what your concept is, regarding the python,
and also what your concept about God is."

I told them I had read in Venda mythology, about the python in Lake Fun-
dudzi—a legendary creature assigned magical powers from bringing rain to

fertility—and I know that Snake is thought of as god by many people—in the Yoruba religion, for instance.

In writing about the female side of the universe in Igbo cosmology, Sabine Jell-Bahlsen writes, "Chi-Ukwu is the creator who bestows life force, death and rebirth. This force can manifest itself through the royal python...prominent in classic African art, the snake, particularly the python and her consorts symbolize creation, procreation, and death" (in Olupona, 2000, 40.) The snake is also a symbol of the Sacred Feminine in many other cultures; in psychology and religion it is often seen as representative of rebirth, transformation and renewal, I said. As such it is also tied to menstruation[5].

> RM: She says it doesn't happen to them, they don't believe that.
> DG: What does she say, it's superstition...? Rudo answered, laughing, "She says it's rubbish!"

The women's reaction was in stark contrast to Professor Mathivha's response when I asked whether the snake played a role in Lemba origin stories or mythology, as it did for the Venda. He simply said, "No [it's not in the mythology]—it is part of ourselves."

Meshack Raphalalani showed me one of his larger-than-life size sculptures, carved of a beautiful piece of two-toned wood in which a young initiate stands, empty calabash on her head and a python wrapped around her ankles climbing towards her belly. He said, as if stating the obvious, "Everything is done by the womb." His sculptures make clear a positive link between woman and snake, between the python, sexuality and conception; they illustrate the sacred importance of snake as a symbol of fertility and creation in the python dance that is part of the Venda *domba* initiatory puberty rite. The young girls who participate in this rite form a dance line in the shape of a snake, in a ceremony which also is performed to bring rain to nourish the Earth and her fruits.

At Shayandima, Rudo said the women didn't think the snake does anything—"except for that one bit, that it might be bad luck." Rudo noted, "They say the Shangaan[6] people believe that the snake is a type of god. But she said that [people who] believe that the snake is a sign of renewal and rebirth and has supernatural powers do not know God and that's why they believe that."

> DG: For me they are not in conflict. For me the snake is part of nature...And God is still very present for me...

I took the women's last statement as indicative of either strong Christian beliefs or of the fact that they may have been suspicious of my motives, even though I had come to them through Professor Mathivha, a respected Lemba elder, and his daughter. Perhaps they suspected I was testing their Christian—or Jewish—beliefs. Perhaps any other reaction was too much to hope for after their experience of living in an apartheid regime constructed and supported by many people who looked like me.

To my great amusement, some of the people I met, including an Afrikaner art dealer, seemed to think I might have missionary intentions. I noticed Ntshabeni staring at both me and the camera at one point, and found myself wondering if she thought I was a heathen, or whether she was simply deciding how much to tell me. I continued, "God does not just live in heaven for me, but is here, in our heart. We are taught that you are made in God's image." Ntshabeni began to smile by then and kept looking at me. "So then for us God has to have male and female characteristics."

Nourishment and Essence of the Tree—Women's Spiritual Authority

Ibase
Ibase O
Iba baba
Iba yeye
Ibase

Respect to the power of the Spirit
Respect to the Spirit with emotion
Respect to Father Sky
Respect to Sweet Mother Earth
Respect to all in between

—Yoruba prayer, quoted by Ifa chief Luisah Teish
(Teish, personal communication, 2001)[7]

As I began to examine women's relationships with God I also found myself wanting to locate women's spiritual power among both the Lemba and U.S. Jewish women. Although I knew many of the women might define power differently than I did—and my own definition has expanded in the course of this project—I noticed this power in a number of unexpected places. I found it in women's conversation and writing, in their creation of prayers and ritual, in our ability to imagine possibilities not considered attainable by the last generation, in the functions women daily carry out for their families and community. I see spiritual power in the role certain Lemba women play in praying to the ancestors and in the formation of European-American Jewish women's prayer groups worldwide. These activities are rarely accompanied by a self-proclaimed declaration of authority, but the women's spiritual power is nonetheless clear to me and others who witness their acts, often performed in quiet ways that redefine power.

Indeed, self-authorization is something I have grappled with since the day I participated in my first non-Jewish ritual. The standard Jewish rituals, those I had grown up with, were easy to perform, even during those years when I found them largely empty. Once I began to view the texts as unbearably patriarchal and exclusionary, it became more difficult to celebrate rituals such as the Passover *seder*. I started coming to the dinner table armed with cutting-edge texts but no tambourine, ready to defend myself and all women. As I learned more about the possible role of Miriam, Moses' sister, as a priestess leading the Jews out of Egypt and across the Red Sea, singing and playing the timbrel or tambourine, sitting at the Passover table became easier.

It was a great relief, after approaching the holiday with some dread for several years, as if it were a battleground on which I would need to take on a range of threats to my freedom. I never felt able to explain to my family these perceived threats to my historical, intellectual, social and spiritual health as a woman. For those years when I dreaded the dinner, the advent of the orange on the *seder* plate—a metaphor for the inclusion of lesbian and heterosexual women on the *bimah* or pulpit—and putting out spices or a special cup of wine for Miriam were little consolation, unable to suffice as place holders for the millions of women who had been ignored, controlled, or subjugated over the last 3,000 years.

Not until I became heavily involved in feminist/Goddess spirituality in practice and belief was I able to bring myself back with real engagement to observing Jewish holidays with my family. It took the study of women's spirituality to fully waken me to the prevalence of patriarchal, male, woman-excluding language in Temple liturgy, both songs and prayers. Now I was able to label and contextualize what I had felt before on a subliminal level, although the effects of the language had manifested long before in making me feel like an outsider. Little wonder, then, that I could not begin to claim my own spiritual power during those years.

Women's spiritual and/or political power and authority is a necessary tool for women's growth and wholeness. The need is great for women to claim agency and develop their own abilities in this regard, or to recognize and acknowledge other women's potential to fulfill these leadership roles. One can see evidence of this leadership in:

> the efforts of the Women of the Wall, a courageous group which for nearly fifteen years has sought equal rights for women to pray at the Wailing Wall in Jerusalem;

> women leading other women in prayer groups, comprising many configurations from a beer and snuff ritual to the ancestors to praying at a conference gathering;

> in beer making, a religious-social function which may only be filled by those young girls to whom the task is designated—requisite to any family feast—for certain occasions;

> the presence of women on the dais at a Lemba Cultural Association conference;

> the very fact that a group such as the Jewish Orthodox Feminist Alliance (JOFA) was conceived, and in the efforts it has made over the past decade to improve women's lives in the areas of marriage and divorce, education and fuller religious participation;

> the wrapping of *tefillin* by several young women at a recent JOFA conference (just watching them do this practice electrified me; having never expected to see a woman perform such a male-dominated ritual painted a future filled with the promise of more open doors for all our daughters.)

> the ground markings in a village compound signifying the occurrence of a ritual led by women celebrating a new birth;

> the discussions of the Women's Tefilla Network, a group of mostly observant Jewish women who discuss *halakhic*, or legal, and social issues online, often reporting on how women are making change in their religious institutions;

> the role the *makadzi* or highest-ranking woman plays in her community in South Africa; the leadership of public and private rituals, including

Rosh Chodesh groups (started by Arlene Agus and others in the '70s), or New Moon groups and a new Easter mass celebrating Mary (created by Mari Pat Ziolkowski and Marguerite Rigoglioso);

in the creation of new liturgy by Marcia Falk in her *Book of Blessings*, by Rabbi Leah Novick and Rabbi Lynn Gottlieb; and in the writing of new feminist *haggadot* for Passover;

the new ways of creating spiritual community constructed by Mildred Sabath and *Madrikha* Lucie Brandon; and

in the creation of new language and new images to represent Spirit, spirit, divinity and immanence, holiness and the sacred, elements which have been important in the development of my own spiritual practice and theology.

Women's spiritual power is also alive in the ceremonies in which young women are initiated into both menarche and marriage among the Lemba, and in the Jewish *bat mitzvah* coming of age ceremony among European-American women. The application of red ochre by the Lemba at various times in women's lifecycles—as a means of protection, celebration[8], or for fertility—also reflects a spiritual power women have had since ancient times. The application of henna to mark Jewish holidays and for protection, celebration and fertility among Sephardic Jews continues to be prevalent.

Several of the women I spoke with during the course of my doctoral research played down or did not seem aware of their own role as change agents, and I suspect would vehemently deny having any spiritual authority. Yet they serve as powerful role models for their contemporaries and the women who will follow them.

Anya Silverman (Silverman 1999)[9], a colleague who received her MA in Women's Spirituality from New College of California[10], once noted, "It hit me when I started the Women's Spirituality graduate program, early on, that I was doing this work for my mother as well as myself." (Silverman, personal communication, 2002) I asked Anya one day:

DG: Can you tell me anything about women's roles as spiritual leaders, in ancient times and now?

AS: I know there were [women] spiritual leaders in ancient times and that there are women rabbis now. And that we're being spiritual leaders. I guess we're all spiritual leaders, if we have masters degrees in Women's Spirituality!

Anya does give herself credit as a leader and role model for other women. She also credited me with such leadership before I credited myself. As I continued teaching other women, creating and leading rituals, I finally began to understand that I empowered both them and myself in the process.

I explored and eventually owned my spiritual leadership in various communities, which manifested most prominently through the establishment of my Lilith Institute and the formation of Voice of the Spirit/*Kol Ha-Ruach* women's spirituality/study groups. I took Judaism into non-Jewish communities and feminist spirituality and a consciousness regarding Goddess traditions into the Jewish world. Bringing Lilith to consciousness, co-creating a Spiritual Culture class with Luisah Teish (Teish 2002); presenting a Lilith workshop at a Sufi camp were all part of this process. Claiming my leadership allowed me to conduct a healing circle for the environment at an Earth Day community event, to write liturgy and to gather women of many traditions for a Summer Solstice celebration at a Jewish Community Center, despite much hesitation. I had occasional thoughts of becoming clergy, yet wanted more than entering the rabbinate to fulfill the duties of a *kohenet*[11], a priestess, although the definition of this role met in some quarters with great skepticism, including my own. How could I give myself that much spiritual authority, would my leadership be well-received, would the appellation be understood? What were the duties in the 1st Century of a priestess? How could I hope to know? Even without the answer—which no one yet has—could I re-imagine and construct the function to meet 21st Century needs? If the role could be reconstructed, was I the person to define it? I, who spoke no Hebrew, felt that even to attempt such a thing would be so fraudulent I never even tried.

Even though I had started my own institute, created and led rituals, instead of trusting my own knowing, my own experience, I could not feel agency here. Even as I gave teachings, offered comfort, put together events that empowered women and created community, for several years this did not change. Even as I organized drumming circles when I began to recognize drumming as prayer; taught women's spirituality classes, did healing and other invocations, delivered wedding blessings, created and led meditations and visualizations for groups of Jewish women, taught youth in conscious acts of role modeling, published a book which served as the basis for my teaching, I never felt entitled or confident enough to name myself *kohenet*.

How Women Construct And Are Formed By Spirit: She Who Is Everywhere
In Women's Voices, Kol Isha, Maipfi A Vhafumakadzi

55

After struggling with the idea for a while, I found myself most comfortable when one of my teachers, Yoruban elder Luisah Teish (Teish 2002) suggested the term 'feminist priestess' to describe what I was doing. This made the most sense to me because in many ways I could envision feminism as a religion of sorts. Indeed, it had become the central core of my life and thought, after being suppressed for a 20-year period.

Though I had occasionally contemplated becoming a rabbi, and also briefly considered initiation into other traditions, I was never convinced that I could adopt any pre-conceived, prescribed dogma to the degree required. All seemed to present severe limitations which would have curtailed my freedom of thought and practice, I felt at the time. In the case of the rabbinate, there was still the problem of an overwhelmingly patriarchal liturgy, worldview[12] and internal political structure. I was far more interested in continuing to create and practice my own independent, unboundaried style of worship and religious ritual: a combination of prayer, liturgy, invocation, meditation, music and movement, as it arose from my own sense of immanence. The Lilith Institute's Summer Solstice in 2000 was billed as "A celebration of lifeforce, sacred sexuality and embodied spirituality."

Female Divinity In Action

Tali Rosenblatt, a young orthodox Jewish woman who did research at Barnard, is adding to the body of knowledge on the subject of women and prayer, and I believe empowers other women just by virtue of doing the study. In looking at 1000 years of Jewish life through literature, Tali studied Chava Weissler's work, *Voices of the Matriarchs* (Weissler 1999) a study of old Yiddish *tkhines* and decided to compare the Yiddish *tkhines* being used in a contemporary context by Chassidic women, used by Eastern European women who did not speak Hebrew in the fifteenth through nineteenth centuries. Tali and others had assumed that "contemporary women who knew Hebrew should no longer be using the *tkhines* but still were" so she looked for the reason. She found that women believed these personal prayers spoke to who they were more than the traditional male liturgy—which most said in addition to the *tkhines*. She also found a wide range in what the women defined as prayer. (Rosenblatt, personal communication, 2001.)

On the subject of *tkhines* which women say in the *mikvah*, a Jewish ritual bath and a rite which many Jewish women see only as an oppressive patriarchal imposition onto women's lives, Patti Moskovitz, who teaches Judaic studies and leads women in personal and religious lifecycle rituals had this to say: "The *tkhines* women wrote; the blessings men wrote. A *tkhine* comes specifically from women, with *kavanah*[13], they come spontaneously, they are said out of women's own inner feelings...The rabbis formulated the prayers [known as] blessings...these are structured, not spontaneous. They are *kevah*, fixed or set. The women's wishes and prayers are subjective...the *tkhine* comes from a woman's own yearning and what she brings to the *mikvah*. The *b'rakhot*[14]are what the mikvah brings, gives to you. The *tkhinot*...come from deep out of women...The language is clear to me.

"It's like a marriage; you're joining the two...that which is set and that which is spontaneous, the union of both of them. Some of the most powerful moments I've spent in Judaism are in the *mikvah*." (Moskovitz, personal communication, 2002)

The fact that women most likely wrote the prayers which I suspect contain the most intense meaning in the context of the experience, did not surprise me. Nor did the fact that until recently men had largely been credited with writing the corpus of prayers known as *tkhines*.

Patti Moskovitz, whom I experience as an accomplished writer and highly respected Jewish educator, clearly has spiritual authority and yet always defers to more formal "experts" despite the fact that she is extremely knowledgeable in her own right, on a variety of subjects pertaining to Judaism, its language and history.

Where is the Sacred Feminine?

When people mentioned to me during this research that the Shekhinah lives within Judaism, or that contemporary U.S. Jewish women are respected for their knowledge, for holding their families together or for their communal contributions I often took it with a grain of salt because of my awareness of the patriarchy that also still lives within Judaism.

When I mentioned the possibility of a female deity, reactions from South Africa to the U.S. ranged from shock to suspicion to amusement among many of the respondents[15]. The Lemba women talked about God only as male, saying that they are in his service, that they are here to do God's will, and how He can protect them. Does this affect whether the women hold their own work and lives as sacred?

Throughout much of Africa God is imaged as having both male and female attributes, leading me to think that such beliefs may well exist in the Northern

Province. It showed among the Venda but not the Lemba people I met. I wondered whether belief in God as Mother was buried deep beneath layers of Christianization and Western colonization, possibly hidden from their view and definitely hidden from mine. God's name, *Mwari*, refers to a God who is both male and female among the Shona, among whom the Lemba have lived in Zimbabwe over the past 200 years; the names Mwari and Mwali are used interchangeably by the Lemba as God's name.

Several of the Venda artists clearly portray the sacred feminine in their sculpture but the Lemba and Venda women, among others, seemed to find the concept of God as female a foreign one.

The works of Noria Mabasa (Mabasa, personal communications, 2001), Meshack Raphalalani (Raphalalani, personal communications, 2001) and Albert Munyai (Munyai, personal communications, 2001) in particular spoke volumes, in courageous ways that non-artists, especially groups who have lived under colonial domination, may find too dangerous to express.

Could it be that the act of discussion of God as Mother and Father would not take place in front of me, even though mythical symbols of both female and male deity are there? Haven't many other scholars had to make a leap of faith in this darkness?[16] (Journal entry, 2002). Still, having once read that there was a Venda word for Goddess, I was curious, and brought it up in my conversation with Lemba men in the town of Mmakaunhaye, including University of South Africa linguist Tom Sengani, when we were talking about the role of the senior aunt of the compound.

> DG: [Does she] have any special name, or title?
> TS: She doesn't have any other name except *makadzi*. You see, in our tradition, even with the Vendas, the senior aunt is an important person—like my aunt, with the spectacles on—she's the senior aunt here. So whatever thing you do, she has to be informed.
> DG: Does she have to approve it, or just be informed?
> TS: She must be informed, she can approve, but if she doesn't, do tell her. 'Cause she's sort of an intermediate between even family members, so that even if she disagrees with you, you must go and tell her.
> DG: You can still do it.
> TS: Yes.

I wondered, however, whether in practice many things would actually take place of which she did not approve.

I then told the group I had read the word *mudzimukadzi* in one Venda-English dictionary (Wentzel and Muloiwa, 1976)—and that it was translated to mean "goddess" [17].

Everyone was silent. Even Tom Sengani, who is in the business of words, seemed a bit puzzled by the question.

Uncle: (There's only) *makadzi*...
TS: *Makadzi*'s the senior aunt. *Mudzi*...
DG: is God?
TS: (simultaneously) is God.

As in so many other instances during this research, my interviews left me with more questions than answers. I relied on my senses, my eyes and ears; the art I saw spoke volumes, as can icon and even text when not layered with male-centered interpretations of humanity and deity. For me the Sacred Feminine was and remains clearly present—in between and behind the words, as meaning, as nuance, as Spirit.

Notes

1. Defined variously as the female in-dwelling presence of God, the feminine face of God and the Hebrew Goddess.

2. Organic inquiry is a methodology in which research is treated as sacred (see Clements et al, 1999).

3. Reaction to my suggestion of God as possessing female attributes brought reactions ranging from amusement to disbelief to extreme discomfort. One Sotho woman to whom I suggested this hastened to assure me that God is male in the bible. She had just given me a list of all the different types of African "churches" (religions); when I suggested that God may be portrayed as male simply because men likely wrote most of the bible, she quickly told me about another church—one she identified as satanic!

4. Patti Moskowitz, interview, 2001.

5. Further information on this can be found in the works of Carl Jung (Jung 1968), Betty De Shong Meador (Meador 2000), Judy Grahn (Grahn 1999) Margaret Grove (1999) and Vicki Noble (Noble 1991.)

6. A neighboring group living in the Northern Province. Ephraim Selamolela, a member of the Lemba Bhuba clan and successful entrepreneur with a number of different businesses, is married to a woman of Shangaan heritage.

7. A prayer taught to me by one of my teachers, author and activist Luisah Teish, a prolific storyteller and priestess of Oshun (Teish 2000).

8. Keren Friedman (Friedman 2001), a photographer, has provided stunning examples of this; she illustrates, for example, the use of henna by North African Jewish girls and women living in Djerba, Tunisia.

9. Anya's thesis was "Metamorphosis Of The Crone: Past, Present, And Future—How This Ancient Symbol Can Empower Older Women Today" (1999).

10. A private college in San Francisco that offers one of the country's two free-standing Women's Spirituality graduate programs. For further information, see http://www.newcollege.edu/womenspirituality/Default.htm.

11. My Israeli cousin and a librarian who helped me at an archeological library in Jerusalem insisted this meant either the wife or daughter of a kohen or priest, but the records from archeological digs at Beth Shea'rim in northern Israel translate kohenet as priestess. A stone had been found there with an inscription mentioning a kohenet (see Brooten, Women Leaders in the Ancient Synagogue, 1982).

12. Although these two have been shifted radically to encompass women as equal partners, thanks to the efforts of Jewish feminist women, scholars and theologians, and thanks to the work of such pro-feminist men as Zalman Schachter—Shalomi (Schachter-Shalomi 1997), David Cooper (Cooper 1998) and Gershon Winkler (Winkler 1998).

13. Intention, in Hebrew.

14. Plural for blessing (Hebrew).

15. There was a genuine willingness to consider the idea, or, among those espousing Goddess Judaism or feminist spirituality, a fervent belief in Her, among some of the liberal Jewish women I spoke with.

16. A number of colleagues have spoken to me of this same experience, including Margaret Grove (Grove 1999), Judy Grahn (Grahn 1999), Lucia Birnbaum (2001) and Dianne Jenett (1999).

17. No one verified this, however, or seemed ever to have heard the word. Either there is such a term and no one was willing to talk about it, or the authors were, perhaps, extrapolating. I find this unlikely, however, since it does not strike me likely that a missionary would go out of his/her way to include this term in a dictionary unless she or he had heard it from others.

The Black Stone

May Elawar, M.A.

I have always been perplexed by an ambiguity in Islam, a religion that vehemently opposes any form of 'idolatry,' yet reveres a black stone that is placed at the center of its tradition. In Mecca, the birthplace of the prophet Muhammad, a black stone with ancient and mysterious origins is part of the Kaa'ba, the direction towards which millions of Muslims worldwide turn to in prayer five times a day. It is also to Mecca to visit the black stone, with the hope of touching it or better yet kissing it, that two million pilgrims converge annually to perform the ritual known as the hajj.

My recent encounters with the Black Madonna and her African roots have brought the black stone of Mecca to the forefront of my mind. As I encounter scholarship on the dark mother's manifestation as the Shekinah in Jewish tradition, and the Black Madonna in the Christian tradition, I ponder the possibility of the presence of the dark mother within the Muslim tradition through the worship of the black stone in Mecca.

Growing up in a Muslim society in Kuwait that rigidly adhered to traditional Islamic doctrine, I find myself subconsciously drawn towards this area of research. Yet given the intensity of Islamic indoctrination that I experienced in school and society, it is not without trepidation that I relate the images, memories and values of the ancient dark mother goddess to the black stone in Mecca. In this endeavor I find myself bridging two distinct disciplines that I am immersed in contemporaneously: the discipline of women's spirituality and the Muslim discipline which has functioned as a backdrop in my life. With the black stone as the focus of my inquiry, I integrate contemporary women's spirituality research to retell the mythology of the stone from a perspective that is historically and geographically immensely broader than the

Muslim religion, a mythology that can be traced back to the African roots of the mother goddess.

Images of the Dark Mother and the Black Stone in Mecca

Approximately two million Muslims travel to Mecca in Saudi Arabia annually to fulfill one of the five pillars of Islam, the pilgrimage or hajj ritual. This holy city is the home of the Haram Mosque, a structure that surrounds an immense open courtyard with the granite cube of the Kaa'ba at the center. The Kaa'ba stands fifty feet high and is draped in a black silk cover called the *Kiswa*. Muslims claim that the Kaa'ba itself is not the object of prayer, and it contains no relief.[1] The only part of the building that has survived several renovations since antiquity is the black stone in the shrine's east corner at shoulder height.[2] Surrounded by a silver band, the part of the black stone that remains visible is remarkably similar in shape to a vulva. (see picture).

"The black stone now enshrined in the Kaa'ba at Mecca," writes Barbara Walker in the *Woman's Encyclopedia of Myths and Secrets*, "was the feminine symbol of the Goddess, marked by the sign of the yoni and covered by the ancient mother like a veil."[3] However, centuries of Muslim overlay have obscured the ancient meaning of the black stone as a center of worship and pilgrimage, and it becomes necessary for my inquiry to research the era prior to the emergence of Islam and its traditions.

My journey through pre-Islamic Arabia can begin 70,000 years ago by placing Mecca in the vicinity of the first phases of human migrations out of Africa. Mecca, which lies midway along the west coast of Arabia in an area named Hijaz, is fifty miles east of the Red Sea. Worship of the dark mother probably existed from this early date in the Hijaz given its proximity to the Sinai, which has been described as a natural bridge between Africa and the rest of the world by Lucia Chiavola Birnbaum in her book *Dark Mother, African Origins and Godmothers*.[4]

Greco-Egyptian geographer Ptolemy writing in the second century CE called the city Markoba, the temple.[5] Historians have attributed Mecca's long existence to the Zamzam well, the sole water source in a barren valley surrounded by treeless rugged peaks.[6] "Its usual climate has been described as a combination of suffocating heat, deadly winds and clouds of flies…No crops seem ever to have grown there. In its prehistoric period, this place without sown land was considered too sacred for regular habitation."[7] Perhaps in antiquity the sacredness of Mecca was also associated with the falling of a meteor in the area, the black stone which is venerated into the present time.

The Koran does not explain the remote origins of the holy place at Mecca,[8] it speaks only of an era of Abraham and his son Ishmael and their command from god to construct the sacred house (Koran verse 5: line 100). However, Islamic tradition did not rest on scriptural testimony alone and eventually created a mythology that traces the Kaa'ba and its sanctuary back to what they identify as the beginning of creation, to the time of Adam.[9]

Islamic myth relates how the Kaa'ba, originally built by Adam, was damaged by the flood sent to punish the people in the generation of Noah. The Kaa'ba was rebuilt by Abraham when he brought his concubine Hagar and his son by her Ishmael to Mecca, following trouble between them and his wife Sarah, and his other son Isaaq. Ishmael helped his father rebuild the Kaa'ba, and at that time, monotheism and the hajj rituals were instituted.

It is believed that members of Ishmael's tribe continued to be faithful to Abrahamic monotheism as manifested chiefly in the Kaa'ba and it rituals; however, they became so numerous that many had to spread out into other parts of Arabia. As they left they took stones from Mecca to remind them of the Kaa'ba and performed rituals imitating those at the Kaa'ba in the localities where they settled. To explain the subsequent emergence of idolatry and paganism, Islamic tradition describes how in the course of time the monotheism of Ishmael's tribe began to degenerate as people began to forget the Meccan origins of their stones. Eventually, small settled populations emerged at fixed shrines in the oasis, and the Bedouins, constantly in transit, carried their gods and goddesses with them. The objects they worshipped were principally trees, stones and heavenly bodies, or the deities that resided in them.[10] One aspect of worship was a widespread cult of stones that were totally shaped or unshaped into some form of rudimentary idol. Pilgrimages to the Kaa'ba at Mecca were also an integral part of worship.

Specifically addressing the black stone, Islamic tradition claims that it was sent down by god and entrusted to Abraham as a white stone. "A white sapphire from the garden" that turned black from the sins of the children of Adam and at the touch of menstruating women in pre-Islamic times.[11]

Expanding beyond traditional Islamic mythology, women's spirituality sources demonstrate that the worship of black stones has many precedents in antiquity. The vessel and the stone were the primary images of the Goddess, beginning as her epiphanies in the Neolithic era and ending with the mysterious images in Alchemy and Grail legends.[12] Black stones represented the Goddess in several cultures, write Baring and Cashford in their book *The Myth of the Goddess*. They associate the Goddess Cybele with the Kaa'ba describing her worship as a black stone in Anatolia and later in Rome. "The earliest form of the Goddess Cybele's name may have been Kubaba or Kumbaba, and one of the five ideograms of Kubaba's name was a lozenge or a cube which may represent the sacred black stone that was the testimony for her presence on earth..It is likely that her cult spread eastward towards the Euphrates or that it was indigenous throughout this vast area of land," write Baring and Cashford.[13]

Linking the black stone in Mecca to the Goddess Cybele, is akin to linking the Black Madonnas in Churches to pre-Christian Goddesses As a manifestation of the Goddess Cybele, the black stone can be traced even further back in time to Africa. Evidence provided by Lucia Birnbaum links the worship of Cybele with the worship of her predecessor Isis, whose origins were in Nubia.[14] The black stone as the epiphany of the Goddess is how I would begin my alternative version to the Islamic myth of Adam and Abraham as the original founders of the Kaa'ba.

"We can recover the lost myths of the Goddess through her images," write Baring and Cashford. "Wherever we find the cave, the moon, the stone, the serpent, bird and fish, the spiral, meander, labyrinth, the wild animals, lion, bull, bison, stag, goat and horse, rituals concerned with the fertility of the earth.."[15] we are in the presence of the images that once represented the Mother. In descriptions of historical Mecca, Muslim tradition is filled with these images of the Goddess. The sacred rock and a sacred spring (Zamzam) in Mecca are at the heart of the sanctuary in pre-Islamic Arabia, both of which remain an integral part of Muslim worship and ritual.

The serpent is prevalent in stories describing the pre-Islamic shrine in Mecca. When ninth century Muslim Historian al-Azraqi interviewed descendents of the prophet's tribe, the Quraysh, in Mecca, they told of a snake that was sent by god and sat in a pit inside the Kaa'ba to guard money and goods deposited by pilgrims at the sanctuary. They also described the horns of a ram that were hanging on the wall facing the entrance.[16]

The serpent reemerges in Islamic stories recounting a time when the prophet was thirty-five years old and his tribe, the Quraysh, decided to rebuild the Kaa'ba. However, they were afraid of incurring the guilt of sacrilege if they tore down the old structure, and "their hesitation was greatly increased by the appearance of a large snake which had taken to coming everyday out of the vault to sun itself against the walls of the Kaa'ba. If anyone approached it, it would rear its head and hiss with gaping jaws, and they were terrified of it. But one day, while it was sunning itself, God sent against it an eagle, which seized it and flew away with it. So the Quraysh said amongst themselves: Now we may indeed hope that God is pleased he hath rid us of the serpent."[17]

During the same incident of rebuilding the Kaa'ba, the serpent motif is also found in the foundational structure of the old building. According to historian al-Azraqi, when the walls were torn down to 'the foundation of Abraham', the builders came upon large green cobble stones placed side-by-side, like the humps of the camel.[18] These stones have also been described as linked necks of camels or intertwined fingers.[19] A man put a crow bar between two of these stones to lever one of them out, but at the first movement of the stone a quaking shudder ran through the whole of Mecca, and they took it as a sign that they must leave that foundation undisturbed.[20] When I draw out the humps of a camel placed side-by-side, a serpentine design emerges. I have not encountered any mention of these stones in contemporary descriptions of the Kaa'ba building, but given the precedent set forth by the Prophet's tribe by not removing them, I would predict that they are still there.

The main Muslim resource on pre-Islamic Mecca, *The Book of Idols*, describes oracular dreaming around the Kaa'ba and divination arrows that were used to forecast the future.[21] In addition, this text describes a myth that resembles ancient fertility rites between the goddess and her consort as taking place within the Kaa'ba structure. It is told that Isaf and Naila, two lovers who had sexual relations inside the building of the Kaa'ba were transformed into stone and subsequently worshipped by pilgrims to Mecca. Islamic tradition claims that they were petrified into stone and placed inside the Kaa'ba in order to warn people of their misdeed, but as their origin became remote, people began to worship them with their other idols. Eventually the two stones of Isaf and Naila were placed on the two hills outside the main mosque, and pilgrims to Mecca began the ritual of running between the two hills seven times.[22] This ritual is still practiced today as part of the Islamic hajj. The hills of Isaf and Naila have been renamed Safa and Marwa and a whole new mythology is attributed to them involving Hagar, Abraham's concubine, and her son Ishmael.[23]

Perhaps the most well-known feature of pre-Islamic Arabia among contemporary Goddess tradition scholars is the worship of the three Goddesses Manat, Allat and al-Uzza. Mentioned in what has come to be known as the Satanic verses of the Koran, these Goddesses constitute a major part of *The*

Book of Idols, which grants the Goddess al-Uzza the longest section in the whole book.

Manat is the most ancient of the three Goddesses, and her center of worship was along the coast of the Red Sea between Mecca and Medina. It is noteworthy to mention that as the oldest of the three Arabian Goddesses, Manat's worship was closest to Africa which lay just across the Red Sea. All the Arabs including Quraysh worshipped Manat, asserts al-Kalbi in *The Book of Idols*. They offered sacrifices to her and brought her offerings.[24] Her name has been linked to the Semitic word for hope and has also been explained as a version of the name Anath, the Canaanite Warrior Goddess mentioned in the Ugaritic texts.[25]

Among the treasures seized by the Muslims upon Manat's destruction by Ali, the Prophet's son-in-law, were two swords which had been presented to the Goddess by a devotee. These swords were given to, and used by, Ali in subsequent wars for the spread of Islam.[26] Manat is still present through her swords which have become a national symbol of Saudi Arabia. The swords are crossed in the shape of the letter 'x', and a date palm stands in the top center of the letter 'x', which, as will be described later, represents the Goddess al-Uzza.

The Goddess Allat stood in Taif and was represented by a cubic rock.[27] Herodotus referred to Allat as the primary Goddess of the Arabians, and Merlin Stone states that the name Allat is cognate with the title of Asherah as Elat in Canaan.[28] Her worship continued until the Prophet dispatched someone to burn her temple to the ground. The current mosque at Taif is built above her sacred site, and *The Book of Idols* describes the left minaret of the mosque as standing in the place of Allat.[29]

Al-Uzza was worshipped more recently than Allat and Manat. Her name means glory in Arabic. Merlin Stone states that her worship was most often associated with the planet Venus and at times described as the star Sirius, sacred star of the Egyptian Goddess Isis.[30] The name al-Uzza may also be linked to the name of the pre-dynastic Egyptian Cobra Goddess, Ua Zit, writes Stone, who was closely linked with the image of Isis.[31] Her idol was situated in the valley known as *Nakhlat al Shamiyah* (valley of the date palm). Al-Uzza's devotes built a house over her in which people used to receive oracular communications.[32]

The Book of Idols, describes al-Uzza as the greatest Goddess among the Quraysh,[33] and the prophet sent one of his finest warriors Khalid ibn al-Walid to destroy her. It is in the destruction of al-Uzza that I first encountered the motif of the angry black woman, an image that is repeatedly found in the

Islamic myths describing the destruction of places of Goddess worship. *The Book of Idols* describes this incident as follows: Al Uzza was a she devil and used to frequent three trees in the valley of Nakhlah. The Prophet sent al-Walid to cut down the three trees. When he cut down the third tree, he found an Abyssinian woman with disheveled hair and her hands on her shoulders gnashing and grating her teeth. Al-Walid dealt her a blow "which severed her head in twain and lo she crumbled into ashes."[34] Another translation of this incident refers to the woman as "the naked black old woman."[35]

The old black woman appears upon the destruction of the stones of Isaf and Naila. "There came out of these two stones a grey haired black woman who was tearing at her face with her nails, naked, pulling at her hair and crying out in her woe.[36] The 'old lady' was also the name given to the custodians of the Kaa'ba well into the Islamic era, they were the Banu Shayba, sons of the old Lady, an old Meccan family.[37]

The old lady, the serpent, the stones, the date trees are all ancient images of the Goddess and were prevalent throughout Arabia in the pre-Islamic era. These images continue to exist in Saudi Arabia and Mecca underneath the centuries of Islamic overlay. The black stone, the Saudi symbol of the swords with the date palm in the middle, the ritual of Marwa and Safa in the Hajj, were all co-opted by the Prophet and all contribute towards locating the ancient mother goddess in contemporary Islam.

Memory of the Dark Mother in the Rituals of the Black Stone

Further evidence that the ancient goddess is still present at the heart of Islam can be found through an exploration of contemporary hajj rituals which have remained the same for centuries. The pilgrimage to Mecca has been described as one of mankind's most enduring rites.[38] For almost fourteen hundred years since the emergence of Islam and back to antiquity, it has provided a spiritual destination to millions of men and women around the globe.

Three months before his death, the prophet Muhammad led ninety thousand followers on a pilgrimage to Mecca which has come to be known as the farewell hajj.[39] He co-opted the hajj as an expression of Islam and designated a pilgrim's route that integrated diverse pagan rites into a coherent ritual performance that pilgrims still execute today. In the hajj rituals, Muslims follow to the letter every step that the prophet took on his farewell hajj, thus the black stone became part of the Islamic ritual because the prophet Mohammad became extremely emotional in the presence of the black stone and kissed it with tears shooting from his eyes.[40] Omar, the second Caliph, is quoted as saying aloud, "I know you are nothing but a stone, and you have no power to do either good or evil, and if I had not seen the prophet greet you, I would not do so."[41] The gesture of greeting the stone may be accompanied only by the words "In the name of god; god is most great; god alone we praise, glory be to god."[42]

The hajj is considered to be the religious apex of a Muslim's life. "Simply to have the Kaa'ba physically before them brings tears to many pilgrims' eyes."[43] Similarly, Birnbaum describes the fervor that Black Madonna festivals and pilgrimages evoke in Europe associating this emotion with the memory of the dark mother which is closer to bodily resonance than cognitive remembrance.[44] Women pilgrims to Black Madonna sites speak of undergoing a rebirth or transformation. China Galland writes, "To say that one is longing for darkness is to say that one longs for transformation, for a darkness that brings balance, wholeness integration, wisdom, insight."[45]

Several accounts describing the experience of pilgrims to Mecca stress the intense emotional and transformational aspects of this journey. The hajj is continually described not just as a ritual act but as an experience to be felt. Malcolm X wrote that his experience of the hajj forced him to rearrange much of his previously held thought patterns, and to toss aside some of his previous conclusions.[46]

Pilgrims ritually circling the Kaa'ba start their circumambulation at the black stone and salute or try to touch or even kiss the stone in passing. This corner of the Kaa'ba building has been described by one pilgrim as the hallucinating whirlpool at the black stone corner.[47] "I am no longer the abstract believer that I was formerly, only a few instants ago," the pilgrim writes, "that believer who was so anxious to understand and to analyze….to find the right words to describe all this to explain it to intellectuals like himself, that philosopher that believer, I no longer know him, I no longer recognize myself in him. Now I am merely a man with tears running down his face."[48]

The Values of the Dark Mother and the Black Stone

In *Dark Mothers: African Origins and Godmothers* Lucia Chiavola Birnbaum writes that "knowledge of African origins may help dispel bigotries grounded on ignorance which may be our largest obstacle to social justice."[49] The necessity for tracing the history of the black stone in Mecca back to the African dark mother stems from a desire to bring back the knowledge and awareness of our common ancestry. My hope is that this information would help us transcend contemporary conflicts and wars grounded in a false perception of our inherent religious, ideological, ethnic and class incompatibilities.

Throughout her book *Dark Mothers*, Birnbaum describes communities of popular resistance to injustice and racism at sites where the Black Madonna is worshipped. Birnbaum identifies the values of the dark mother as justice with compassion, equality and transformation.[50] The early community around the Kaa'ba upheld standards reminiscent of the values attributed to the dark mother. Mecca was regarded as an asylum in the desert which welcomed the gods and goddesses of many tribes. "From the beginning people seem to have flocked there because the place was sacred. In a stark desert, made inhospitable by raiding and intertribal wars, the attraction of such an asylum, where safety is guaranteed and water is free, must have been great."[51] All were welcome as long as they followed the rules of the sanctuary, "all violence and fighting was forbidden."[52] In this environment of religious tolerance and spiritual enlightenment, the Arabic language flourished as poetry contests became part of the rites of the pilgrimage. "Poetry contests were held, fixing verses inscribed with animal skins to the Kaaba."[53] "The pre-Islamic rites at Mecca embodied an inexplicable element, something ancient and almost pre-cerebral, that matched the volcanic landscape all around it."[54]

The time when the city welcomed gods and goddesses from many tribes has long gone, and at the present only Muslims are allowed into Mecca. However, Muslim pilgrims are still expected to abide by certain rules while within the sacred precinct. Violence is prohibited during hajj, even down to disturbing the local wildlife. No anger or profanity is permitted as pilgrims continue to behave in ways conducive to peace and spiritual dedication.

Malcolm X, on pilgrimage to Mecca in 1964 wrote: "There were tens of thousands of pilgrims from all over the world. They were of all colors, from blue-eyed blonds to black-skinned Africans. But they were all participating in the same ritual, displaying a spirit of unity and brotherhood that my experiences in America had led me to believe never could exist between the whites and the non-whites."[55]

Perhaps, reawakening the ancient memory of the dark mother through her image as the black stone in Mecca would reawaken her values of non-violence and equality. Perhaps the memory that we are all her children would usher the world into a new era of peace, harmony and religious tolerance.

Notes

1 F. E. Peters, *The Hajj: The Muslim Pilgrimage to Mecca and the Holy Places* (Princeton University Press, 1994) p. 9.

2 Michael Wolfe, *One Thousand Roads to Mecca* (Grove Press: NY, 1997) p.xxi.

3 Barbara Walker, *The Women's Encyclopedia of Myths and Secrets* (Harper: San Francisco, 1993) p.51.

4 Lucia Chiavola Birnbaum, Ph.D. *Dark Mother: African Origins and Godmothers* (Authors' Choice Press: San Jose, 2001) p.45.

5 Wolfe Op cit., p.xv.

6 Ibid., p.xv.

7 Ibid., p.xv.

8 Peters Op cit., p.3.

9 The whole section describing the traditional Islamic myth regarding the origins of the Kaa'ba is taken from *The Book of Idols* as translated by Faris Amin Nabih (Princeton University press: Princeton, 1952)

10 Peters Op cit., p.20.

11 Ibid., p.6.

12 Anne Baring & Jules Cashford *The Myth of the Goddess: Evolution of an Image* (Arkana: London, 1993) p. 653.

13 Ibid., p.395.

14 Birnbaum, Ph.D. Op cit., p. 13.

15 Baring & Cashford Op cit., p. 40.

16 Peters Op cit., p.12.

17 Ibid., p.46.

18 Ibid., p.47.

19 Ibid., p.62.

20 Martin Lings *Muhammad: His Life based on the Earliest Sources* (Inner Traditions International: Vermont, 1983) p.42.

21 *The Book of Idols* Op cit., p.24.

22 Ibid., p.25.

23 Peters Op cit., p.33.

24 *The Book of Idols* Op cit., p. 12.

25 Merlin Stone *Ancient Mirrors of Womanhood* (Beacon Press: Boston, 1990) p.124.

26 *The Book of Idols* Op cit., p. 14.

27 Ibid., p. 14.

28 Stone Op cit., p.123.

29 *The Book of Idols* Op cit., p.15.

30 Stone Op cit., p.124.

31 Ibid., p.124.

32 *The Book of Idols* Op cit., p.16.

33 Ibid., pp.16–28.

34 Ibid., p. 28.

35 G. R. Hawting *The Idea of Idolatry and the Emergence of Islam: From Polemic to History* (Cambridge University press: Cambridge, 1999) p.139.

36 Ibid., p.69.

37 Peters Op cit., p.238–239.

38 Ibid., p.xiii.

39 Ezzedine Guellouz *Pilgrimage to Mecca* (Saudi Ministry of Information) p.22.

40 Ibid., p.24.

41 Ibid., p.104.

42 Ibid., p. 104.

43 Wolfe Op cit., p.xxi.

44 Birnbaum, Ph.D. Op cit., p.23.

45 China Galland *Longing for Darkness: Tara and the Black Madonna* (Penguin Books: NY, 1990) p.152.

46 Wolfe Op cit., p.499.

47 Guellouz Op cit., p.108.

48 Ibid., p. 100.

49 Birnbaum, Ph.D. Op cit., p. 27.

50 Ibid., p.xxvi.

51 Wolfe Op cit., p.xvi.

52 Ibid., p.62.

53 Ibid., p.xvi.

54 Ibid., p.xvi.

55 Ibid., p.449.

Bibliography

Al-Kalbi. *The Book of Idols*. Translated by Nabih Amin Faris (Princeton University Press: Princeton, 1952)

Baring, Anne & Cashford, Jules *The Myth of the Goddess: Evolution of an Image* (Arkana: London, 1993)

Birnbaum, Ph.D., Lucia Chiavola *Dark Mother: African Origins and Godmothers* (Authors Choice Press: San Jose, 2001)

Galland, China *Longing for Darkness: Tara and the Black Madonna* (Penguin Books: NY, 1990)

Hawting, G. R. *The Idea of Idolatry and the Emergence of Islam: From Polemic to History* (Cambridge University Press: Cambridge, 1999)

Lings, Martin *Muhammad: His Life Based on the Earliest Sources* (Inner Traditions International: Vermont, 1983)

Peters, F. E. The *Hajj: The Muslim Pilgrimage to Mecca and the Holy Places* (Princeton University Press: Princeton, 1994)

Stone, Merlin *Ancient Mirrors of Womanhood: A Treasury of Goddess and Heroine Lore from Around the World* (Beacon Press: Boston, 1990)

Walker, Barbara *The Woman's Encyclopedia of Myths and Secrets* (Harper: San Francisco, 1983)

Wolfe, Michael *One Thousand Roads to Mecca: Ten Centuries of Travelers Writing about the Muslim Pilgrimage* (Grove Press: NY, 1997)

Publication of the Saudi Ministry of Information *Pilgrimage to Mecca*

AKASHA MA*

Kalli Rose Halvorson, M.A.

Offered to Kali's blissful reality as the female consciousness outside, yet at the root, of space and time

* Akasha (Sanskrit): A free or open space, vacuity; the ether, sky, or atmosphere; the subtle and ethereal fluid that fills and pervades the universe as the vehicle of life and sound; located in the air, or out of sight.

> Kali, please join this meditation
> of honor and surrender
> to your startling space:
> the deep field of dark matter, dark *mater*, dark mother.
> Each burst of galactic light, a dazzling ovary;
> each ovary, a radiant milky purse of hundreds of billions of stars;
> each star, a glowing solar egg up to billions of light-years distant.
>
> I know, you've made it clear..galaxies, stars and such
> are simply images of your omnidynamic consciousness.
> Your female energy of awareness is the operating system
> that projects, sustains and dissolves
> the dimensions of time and space.
> Your virginal sentience the inimitable motherboard

that emanates, nourishes, destroys, dematerializes, and regenerates
the innumerable living beings, planets, planes and sphere of
  existence.

Ma, you are so silent.
Have I imprisoned you here in galaxies and stars, time and space,
consciousness, awareness, and sentience?
Perhaps you have no limits whatsoever..

Are you also timeless and formless, then, entirely removed
from birth, growth, stability, decay, death, dissolution, rebirth?
Do you repose non-physically
in the most primordial, powerful element—
the essential stillness and emptiness of the void?

YES

Then Goddess, spell your identity now!
If I whip up the spacious splendor
of your solar eggs spinning in time,
blend in the prime source code of your consciousness,
layer on the vast peace
of your absolute transcendence,
would the recipe be faithful
to your supreme Mother Reality?

"Nay, not so!" reply the Angels,
golden lightbeings now hovering low.
"You must cook your dish on Kali's stomping ground of
  cremation—
her landscape of nuclear fusion
between space and time,
and the void of emptiness.
Do you see how her unique black light mediates
between Mother Nature's space and time
and Father God's emptiness?

Kali's burning oven bakes away any tension between these two
   warring parties,
actively resolving their feud for the future.
She firmly guides you to embrace them both,
at peace with your vanishing past."

The lightworkers vanish,
having revealed the secret
of why black Kali emanates as such a passionate lover.
Since she consistently gives rise to oneness at every point,
in every direction and dimension,
her sovereign parthenogenetic essence bridges naturally
to the one from whom she is essentially indistinguishable:
Lord Shiva, her cosmic twin, entranced consort, and enchanted
   spouse!
Kali plays all the cosmological parts,
yet shares them all with her adoring and mystified Lord.

Moreover, since her maternal theology never divides,
and always unites,
she fights in victorious defense of every loving union.
A lioness enthusiastic for precisely this battle,
she teaches that the ecstatic wedding of every duality
is the state of perfect realization
in which our universe continually participates.

Kali, Kali, Kali, help me hold
the totality of your inconceivable Mother Reality
in some warm corner of my own lotus heart.
I would find it there forever, and become a great lover like you.
My deep space desire is to unite with you
every more directly and effortlessly,
the sight, the sound, the sense of you
implicit in all things.

The Goddess and the Sacred Art of Adornment

Laura Amazzone, M.A.

The sacred art of body adornment is a ubiquitous phenomenon that transcends time and space. At the heart of this sacred art is an understanding of the enormous spiritual value, power and protection inherent in the symbols and design of all forms of jewelry. The impulse to beautify and adorn the body is irresistible and reflects the wearers' place in the cosmos as well as their social status in their tribe, cultural or ethnic group. Peoples of past and present have bedecked their bodies with treasures from the bountiful body of Mother Earth—terracotta and other clay beads, flowers, gold and silver, white and other metals, grasses, feathers, elephant hair, horn, bone, palm leaves, shells, bird eggs, beetles, resins, barks, and seeds—thus imbuing their bodies with the essence of the Divine. One striking cross-cultural commonality is the expression of the richly ornamented and bejeweled human body as a microcosm of the greater macrocosmic whole. Jewelry expresses complex human relations with other realms, may articulate links to our ancestors, and serves to define and regulate the social interactions of the living.[1] Jewelry reminds us of the cyclical nature of our existence and is a celebration of our connection to Spirit.

Also apparent in the bodily display of ornamentation is the connection to and expression of sexuality. The shape of a necklace emulates the shape of a woman's yoni or vagina: the primordial gateway of life and death honored and recognized as such in pre-patriarchal and indigenous cultures around the world. If jewelry is expressive of a culture's worldview, then its relationship with women's mysteries, such as birth, menstruation, and death, enhance its significance. The relationship between the sacred art of adornment and female sexual and spiritual power is clearly expressed through the worship of the

Divine Mother. Remnants of the Goddess persistently resurface in folklore, lullabies, ritual, women's stories and expressions, food, weaving, embroidery, and other art forms.[2] We also find evidence of female centrality and autonomy through the language of jewelry and its symbols around the world.

The language of jewelry tells a rich story of past and present and demonstrates the cosmological understanding of the Female Divinity who governs all cycles of existence proving She is, indeed, everywhere! In looking at the roots of jewelry and its cultural expression around the world, there is an evident force behind the creative impulse that has been inspired by a worldview that holds the Divine as Mother.

Ancestral and Cross-Cultural Connections

Ever since I was a child, my love for jewelry and my love for traveling have gone hand in hand. I inherited my passion for jewelry and self-adornment from my beloved grandmother, Mammy. Always bedecked in jewels and ringing sweet musical notes whenever she moved, she was a sight to behold. My Mammy wore rings on every finger, tinkling bracelets cascaded down her slender arms, shiny necklaces and sparkling earrings enhanced her beautiful Danish and Welsh face. Emulating the brilliance of my Mammy's body ornamentation from as early as I can remember, I have covered my body with jewelry just as people in cultures around the globe have done for millennia. Every part of the body can be embellished with jewelry: headdresses, nose and earrings, mouth ornaments, necklaces and neck rings, fingers, belts of sumptuous chains, tinkling anklets, belts, and beaded body coverings. I have always felt mesmerized by pictures of heavily adorned tribal and native peoples in cultures around the world and spent many years living abroad in order to experience this magnificent creative inspiration expressed through the medium of jewelry first hand. My travels and explorations showed cross-cultural connections of styles, designs, material, and symbolism across the continents. One prominent commonality among the human race is the art of body adornment.

In contemporary American culture, wearing jewelry seems to serve no utilitarian purpose but is instead an expression of wealth and beauty. However, jewelry in its variety of forms has been worn for thousands of years as amulets and talismans and is believed to hold spiritual power. Jewelry can help heal and balance energies in people or even the environment. In the contemporary United States and other parts of the modern world, wearing and creating jewelry has too often become an unconscious spiritual practice, but looking deeper into the significance of jewelry and adornment, one finds a profound connection to the Goddess, Creator of Life and Death.

I am a feminist and devotee of Goddess in Her manifestation as Dark Mother. To me the Dark Goddess is Earth Mother and Mother of the Cosmos. She is the dynamic, creative force that manifests and permeates all existence. She is able to hold life's paradoxes and contradictions. She is the womb, the pregnant void; She is fierce and She is nurturing, wrathful and compassionate. I, like my ancestors, celebrate my female body and profound connection to Her by adorning myself with jewelry.

Sacred Language of Myth and Symbol

Myths and symbols enable us to comprehend the mysteries of the universe in a language that communes with our entire being, not just our rational minds. Jewelry is not merely for aesthetic pleasures and devoid of meaning. Jewelry symbolism functions as a metaphorical language communicated from wearer to viewer. The art of body ornamentation is an expression of one's values and ontological worldview. Symbolically, jewelry conveys the richness, complexity, and completeness inherent in nature. Perhaps the human impulse to adorn our bodies stems from a deep-rooted reverence for the natural cycles that govern our existence and the felt-sense of interconnectedness that living harmoniously with these cycles evokes. In all likelihood, people began wearing jewelry to symbolically mark significant life occasions such as birth, menarche, marriage, and death, and to ask for protection and blessings of the Divine.

The instinctive human need for play through creative expression could be another motivation behind creating beautiful ornaments for self-adornment. Spontaneous and delightful floods of creative ideas have inspired artists for millennia. Most often the chosen form of expression and symbolism reflects the world around the artist. Even the process of creating jewelry can be a reverent act. While this may no longer be the case in the commercial production of jewelry in many countries, the process of creating jewelry has most often been an invocation of the divine. In many cultures, before creating a piece, the artist will say prayers to a chosen deity asking for guidance and inspiration. The artist surrenders to the divine creative force and opens to receive the sacred transmissions that are then channeled through the language of symbols into the piece.

Symbols are a sacred narrative that can be found in ancient cave dwellings, on pottery, jewelry, goddess figurines, and other archaeological treasures dating back as early as the Paleolithic (33,000 B.C.E.). Archaeomythologist, Marija Gimbutas regards symbols such as the chevron, meander, spiral, net, animal motifs, and circles found on various archaeological artifacts as a pictorial "script," thus a language of goddess-centered cultures.[3] Symbolism found on amulets, beads, and other jewelry around the world depict earth-centered cultures, whose peoples most probably revered God as Female and expressed their cosmological understanding through their artwork. Gimbutas discovered in her numerous excavations; "systematic associations in the Near East, southeastern Europe, the Mediterranean area, and in central, western, and northern Europe indicate the extension of the same Goddess religion to all of these regions as a cohesive and persistent system."[4] Similar earth-based female-centered symbology is also found in Africa, Asia, Oceania, and the Americas. Not only do ancient relics reveal colorful, stylized, and complex patterns and designs that mimic the wonders of nature, but also present a rich heritage of our earliest ancestors that celebrates the sacrality of the earth and the female body.

History of Jewelry: Our Earliest Adornment, Beads

In considering the historical roots of jewelry, grave burials provide a great amount of information. Just as examining the burials of Old Europe demonstrates that our ancestors lived in egalitarian, matrifocal, peace-loving cultures,[5] grave goods also show us the importance of adornment throughout the ages. Beads are among the most common items found in graves[6] and date back to at least 38,000 B.C.E. in La Quina, France. Dubin, author of the comprehensive work, *History of Beads* explains why beads would be included in the burials. "The idea of an afterlife, that something human lives on, required symbols of permanence that would remain intact at the grave after the completion ritual."[7] The richness and abundance of beads in a grave reflects the status of the individual and their lineage.[8] "They mirror the culture of which they are a part and tell a great deal about the social, political, economic, and religious lives of the people who have made and worn them,"[9] and may be considered to be "symbolic repositories of sacred knowledge." [10] In a sense, what adornment represents and the properties it imbues to the wearer are as valuable to the dead, as they are to the living.

The first beads were made from materials found in the natural environment. The earliest found bead dates to 38,000 B.C.E., which predates the earliest known figurative art by about 5000 years. [11] Larger quantities of beads do not appear in Western Europe until around 31,000 B.C.E, [12] and around 28,000 B.C.E. strings of beads rather than single beads appear. From 26,000–20,000 B.C.E. in the Gravettian culture of central and Eastern Europe "beads of shell, tooth, and bone turn up with increasingly small holes. The smaller beads, moreover, begin to occur arranged in neat rows across the bones (sometimes the skulls) of the deceased." [13] In other parts of the world, such as India, Korea, and China, there is further evidence of beads dating to the Upper Paleolithic. [14]

If the ancients understood the earth as sacred, then all of its fur legged, winged, and finned inhabitants would be an intrinsic part of the mysterious whole as well. Early humans' relationship with these creatures whether through dependence on their flesh for survival or observance of these creatures' habits in order to invoke protection would account for the use of animal teeth, horns, fur, sinew, and bones in their amulets. An amulet is a charm or pendant that is charged with certain powers to protect or aid the wearer. By wearing parts of an animal's body, the wearer and creator of the beads maintained a measure of control over its spirit. [15] One of the earliest known groups of beads found is a cache of various animal teeth from 31,000 B.C.E. in Grotte du Renne, a cave at Arcy-sur-Cure in France. [16] Beads dating between 30,000–18,000 B.C.E. have been found in sites all over Old Europe suggesting that they were the material possessions of a culturally advanced people. Evidence has shown a "rich array of bone tools, as well as necklaces with beads of animal teeth, shells, and pebbles. Some of the beads were *carved in the shape of female breasts and torsos* and were probably associated with rituals of fertility[17] (italics added). The association between the fecundity of the earth and fertile life-giving power of the female body is evident in a wide variety of bodily accessories and depictions of the Goddess.

String skirts dating from as early as 20,000 B.C.E. on female figurines in present day France or depicted in drawings around the world often have beads and metals attached to the strings to "attract the eye precisely to the specifically female sexual areas, by framing them, presenting them, or playing peek a boo with them." [18] Of all the Paleolithic goddess figurines found, the breasts and pubic area are enhanced and sometimes ornamented. Neolithic goddesses around the globe are also richly decorated with symbolic jewelry, and female body parts are nearly always pronounced. Even later depictions of Goddesses almost always are ornamented; for example, the famous dancing yogini from the Mohenjo-daro civilization of the Indus (Saraswati) Valley 3500–1500 B.C.E. wears bangles up her arm and a pendant that expresses fertile abundance; the Sumerian Inanna wears lapis lazuli; and Egyptian Goddesses Nut, Hathor, and Isis all are depicted through various mediums adorned with beaded faience necklaces. In fact, in every culture throughout the ages, one can find representations of the Divine Feminine wearing beautiful jewelry. The proliferation of goddess images lavishly adorned in jewelry suggests a celebration of the creative and life-giving force as female that has been celebrated for millennia throughout the world.

Beading and Bleeding

Did one culture create the first beads, and then through trade and cultural diffusion pass the art on to others? The answer to this question is not clear. As Anne Richter, author of *Jewelry of Southeast Asia* suggests,

> Theories of cultural diffusion are fascinating, but they are mostly speculative. Many have not been supported by archaeological evidence. The idea that cultural changes are mainly introduced by waves of immigrants fails to account for spontaneous local developments. It is impossible without further and extensive archaeological research, to determine whether or not artistic similarities are merely coincidental, or sprang from a shared matrix of ancient ideas and habits of perception.[19]

Looking to other scholars' research on early cultures, we find another possibility that could account for the practice of beading and adornment around the world: menstruation.[20]

Many scholars contend that women invented timekeeping through charting their menstruation by notching bones.[21] Vicki Noble writes in *Shakti Woman*, "The earliest artifacts are menstrual calendar bones, notched with correct lunar cycles, tabulating pregnancy and menstruation."[22] As we have seen, beads are among the earliest artifacts of human civilization and were a likely method for keeping time. Researcher Alexander Marshack, author of the *Roots of Civilization* notes that the marks found on Paleolithic bones are "exact lunar tallies, and they fall within…a complex storied tradition involving at the center a female creatrix figure and all of her characteristic symbols."[23] The kinship between animals and humans at that time was expressed and honored, as we have already seen through the tooth and other animal part beads. It is likely that animal bones notched with lunar calendars and colored with ochre red[24] were used as beads in addition to being a method of keeping time. This may have also provided the basis for an elaborate system of mathematics and science that our ancient ancestors understood and developed over thousands of years.[25]

In her poetic and intriguing book, *Blood, Bread and Roses: How Menstruation Created the World*, scholar, poet, and activist Judy Grahn posits that consciousness was created by our pre-human ancestors recognition of the connection between women's bodies and menstrual cycles with the moon. The moon has long been a symbol of the ever-constant flow of life and creation from death to rebirth, to fruition, then disintegration into death. The waxing, full, waning, then dark of the moon is a living metaphor or, as Grahn would say, *metaform*, reflected in the menstrual cycles of women's bodies. The correlation between women's bodies and the moon could very well have provided the incentive for the first creation of jewelry, beading. Grahn believes the development of human consciousness and our ability to separate self from other derived from our ancestors' relationship with their menses. Shuttle and Redgrove also address this connection between menstruation and the moon, and continue to point out that "our words for 'mind' and 'civilization' came from words which mean 'moon experience.'"[26] Further evidence for the relationship of jewelry, women's bodies, and the creation of culture is found in the Latin word, *mens*, and *mensis*, meaning month, moon, and measurement. In German, the word for menses, *Regel*, also means measurement. Beads could have been created in order to measure the days between women's bleeding that correlates with the 28–29 day lunar cycle. Moreover, stringing beads obviously requires a sense of measurement. As one of the earliest expressions of abstract thinking, beads contained concepts of protection, prowess, beauty, prestige,[27] and most importantly emphasized human's understanding of their interrelationship with the natural world. The direct correlation of women's menstrual cycles with the lunar cycle perhaps incited ancient people to use beads as a form of family planning or birth control as they still are used today. In a village outside of Soroti, Uganda, local women line red, black, and white beads on a tray that indicate when they are bleeding and ovulating and correspond to the waxing and waning of the moon. The need to celebrate and express the mysterious parallel between women's bodies, reproductive capacities and the larger forces of the cosmos, particularly the moon, could be one explanation for the original creation of beads.

Another connection between menstruation and jewelry goes even deeper. As we will see, beading and the harvest were associated through ritual practice. Our menstrual blood is rich in minerals, as is the body of Mother Earth. In addition, menstrual blood can be used as a potent fertilizer, and there is little doubt that our agricultural ancestors knew this. Durdin-Robertson describes blood as "vibrationally potent and required by earth as a sacrifice that takes no life."[28] Feminists and supporters of Rudolph Steiner's agricultural biodynamic movement agree that the vibrational quality of menstruation has an enriching effect on our gardens and household plants.[29] Just as women's bodies attune with the moon cycle when exposed to the influences of natural light, planting and harvesting has always corresponded to the moon cycle. The similarities between fertile fields and the menstruating bodies of women of childbearing age are evident. Thus, it does not come as a surprise that ancient Asians strew beads around the temple grounds as an offering and request for a fruitful harvest.[30] The relationship between women's reproductive cycles, the lunar cycle, and harvest had a crucial impact on the development of ancient civilizations where women were creators of culture.

In Paleolithic and Neolithic cultures the earth was seen as bountiful Mother. Grahn suggests that our Paleolithic and Neolithic ancestors considered clay and dirt to be the flesh of Mother Earth, while rich deposits of rock, mineral, and stones were her menstrual blood.[31] Furthermore, Grahn notes that, "Metals and gems of ancient smiths and jewelers had religious significance connected to woman's blood and the earth's blood, even the blood of the sun. The Dogon consider the red metal copper to be an excretion of the sun, which is female."[32]

In Old Europe, the Copper Age Goddess was the "patroness of metallurgical crafts and mining."[33] From the late Neolithic (ca.5000–3000 B.C.E.), bronze, gold, and silver were used in Old Europe, the Balkans, the Aegean, and the Near and Middle East.[34] Anthropomorphic figurines and jewelry with stylized feminine designs, such as the double spiral, or pubic v rubbed with red ochre, have been found in graves along with beads reflecting a spiritual belief in the Divine as Feminine.[35]

Purposes of Adornment

It seems that beading, which led to other artistic jewelry forms, came out of women's menstrual experiences and served to mark women's powerful status as a menstruating woman in early societies. Adornment evolved into a way of

marking status and emphasized the unique natures of individuals as populations expanded and large scale communities developed.[36] Jewelry served as a
principle means by which cultures asserted their value system.[37] It also functioned as a repository of wealth. Jewelry is compact, easily portable, valuable in
trading, and can be easily hidden if necessary.[38] Its value can be redeemed during catastrophic life circumstances such as natural disasters or warfare. Beads,
and particularly cowry shells, have been used as money in Africa, Bengal, and
parts of Oceania. Resembling the shape of the vulva, cowries are also a quintessential symbol of female sexuality. The vulvic shaped cowries, used as
money, remind us of women being the originators of mathematics and science.[39]

As a status symbol, wealth is displayed at the joints: neck, ankle, fingers,
wrist, all places that enable us to move.[40] Mobility equals autonomy. Jewelry
draws attention and protection to these parts of our body. In considering the
profuse use of jewelry in tribal cultures, Borel notes, "how heavy, fragile, or
uncomfortable jewelry may be is of no immediate concern. But the opposite—the more profuse the piece, and the more difficult it is to wear, the
wealthier and more powerful the person is perceived to be."[41]

As a social indicator, jewelry chronicles the stages of life. All members of
certain tribes will each wear a certain symbol or type of jewelry, or members of
certain cultural groups will wear a similar piece expressing their affiliation with
each other and the ideology behind their group.[42] The complex of signals
embedded in jewelry is a visible language to community and expresses social
status, particularly personal and communal power:

> Rich jewelry, especially of the type that emphasizes the face, such as
> large ear ornaments, also demonstrated a heightened sense of majesty of
> the person, the importance of individual identity, and its power to persist
> and even flourish beyond death. The external beauty and preciousness of
> ornaments became attached symbolically to the inner essence of personal-
> ity. And it is in such mysterious transactions across the boundaries that
> divide the transient from the eternal and the public domain from what is
> intimate and personal that much of the meaning of jewelry still resides.[43]

All over the world today, certain symbols continue to be affiliated with particular beliefs signifying one's ideologies to the outside world, while also honoring the personal relationship between the wearer and their deities.

Protection and Ritual

Amulets, talismans, and other varieties of jewelry serve as a form of physical, psychological, and spiritual protection for the wearer. Tribal people around the globe pierce their ears, noses, and other parts of their bodies and adorn themselves with beads, metal, stones, and other natural materials for protection. In many cultures, it is believed that the soul can be seen and even manipulated through the eyes. Therefore, wearing large earrings, or an ostentatious necklace would divert a potential enemy's attention away from the eyes and to the piece itself. All around the world we find jewelry that protects the wearer as well as imparts some sort of power.

In addition to bringing protection, the more ornamented the body, the more it stands out both physically and symbolically. A heavily adorned body commands attention while it is dancing, during ceremonies and initiations. Jewelry has always held a crucial role in ceremonies and cultures all around the world integrate jewelry into their rituals. As representations of Divine forces, ornaments impart spiritual powers to the wearer. Special beads and pieces of jewelry are used as "prompters to insure the proper conduct of ritual and prayer."[44] As Borel points out, "ornament the body and it becomes theater; its wearers become performers in a show."[45]

When performing rituals, the decorated participants become vessels of the divine. Humans are transformed into deities when they are adorned in certain ornaments. In some cultures they are even worshipped as such. For example, in Nepal, the living Goddess Kumari always wears jewelry, but is even more lavishly and splendidly adorned when She assumes Her divine and royal roles within the culture's rituals, many of which center around the harvest.[46] "Personal adornment is an indispensable part of rituals; it intensifies their impact and expresses in visual terms a complex of symbols in ways that can be plainly understood by all the participants."[47]

Conclusion

As we have seen throughout the world and ages, beginning with the association between beading and menstruation, jewelry has functioned as an expression of human consciousness and abstract thinking, reflecting humans' ontological worldview. It has served to enhance certain powers of healing, empowerment, and/or protection while also being an art form, status symbol, manifestation of beauty, expression of feelings, token of membership in a particular group or belief system, representation of the divine, and/or an indication of commitment. The proliferation of jewelry throughout the centuries addresses deep spiritual, psychological, and physical concerns. Humans, honoring their interdependence on Mother Earth, have turned to Her bounty for inspiration and drawn freely from Her seeds, leaves, bones, feathers, teeth, tusks, seashells, hides, horns, eggs and many other natural materials. The creative incentive behind this craft and the modes of expression are infinite and boundless. No matter which culture one explores, whether ancient or contemporary, one will always find the sacred art of adornment. The symbolic language on jewelry is endless, yet a common thread of nature worship is woven throughout pieces from around the globe. If one looks closely enough, one will see that the Creatrix of Life and Death, the Great Goddess, Mother of the Universe, has been a predominant influence on the sacred art of adornment from earliest times.

Notes

1 Ann Richter, *Jewelry of Southeast Asia* (London: Thames and Hundson, 2000) 7.

2 Lucia Chiavola Birnbaum, Ph.D., *dark mother: african origins and godmothers* (San Jose: iUniverse, 2001).

3 Marija Gimbutas, *The Language of the Goddess* (New York: Harper Collins, 1989) xv.

4 Ibid.

5 Marija Gimbutas, *The Civilization of the Goddess: The World of Old Europe* (New York: Harper Collins, 1992).

6 See Gimbutas 1992. Also see Lois Scherr Dubin, *The History of Beads: From 30,000 BCE to the Present* (New York: Harry N. Abrahms, Inc., 1997); Ministry of Culture, Villa Blance Thessaloniki, *Greek Jewelry: 6000 Years of Tradition* (Athens: Archaeological Receipts Fund, 1997); Richter, 2000; Borel, 1994; and Barber, 1994.

7 Dubin, 26.

8 See Richter, 2000; Borel, 1994; and Dubin, 1987.

9 Dubin, 17.

10 Ibid.

11 Ibid., 21.

12 Ibid.; Ministry of Culture, 15.

13 Barber, 43.

14 Dubin, 25.

15 Ibid., 22.

16 Ibid.

17 Ibid.

18 Elizabeth Wayland Barber, *Women's Work: The First 20,000 Years* (New York: W.W. Norton & Company, 1994) 59.

19 Richter, 10.

20 To understand the influence of menstruation on the creation of art and culture see Vicki Noble, *Shakti Woman. Feeling our Fire, Healing our World, The New Female Shamanism* (San Francisco: Harper San Francisco, 1991; Judy Grahn, *Blood Bread and Roses: How Menstruation Created the World* (Boston: Beacon Press, 1993); Penelope Shuttle and Peter Redgrove, *The Wise Wound: The Myths, Realities and Meaning of Menstruation* (New York: Grove Press, 1988); and Monica Sjoo & Barbara Mor, *The Great Cosmic Mother: Rediscovering the Religion of the Earth* (New York: Harper & Row, 1987).

21 Noble, 1993; Grahn; Alexander Marshack, *The Roots of Civilization: Revised and Expanded* (New York: Moyer Bell Limited, 1991); Shuttle and Redgrove, Sjoo and Mor.

22 Noble, 1991, 17

23 Marshack in Noble, 1991, 17.

24 Marshack.

25 Marshack in Vicki Noble, *The Double Goddess: Women Sharing Power* (Vermont: Bear & Company, 2003) 24.

26 Shuttle and Redgrove, 128.

27 Dubin, 26.

28 Lawrence Durdin-Robinson, *The Cult of the Goddess* (Enniscorthy, Eire: Cesara Publications, 1974) in Noble, 1991, 15

29 Noble, 1991, 15

30 Dubin, 17.

31 Grahn, 240.

32 Ibid., 237.

33 Gimbutas, 1991, 118.

34 Ministry of Culture, 15.

35 Gimbutas, 1991; Ministry of Culture; Noble, 2003; Birnbaum, Ph.D.

36 Dubin, 7.

37 Borel, 23.

38 Ilay Cooper and John Gillow, *Arts and Crafts of India* (London: Thames and Hudson, 1996) 73.

39 Noble, 1991; Durdis-Robertson; Shuttle and Redgrove; Grahn.

40 Borel, 18.

41 Ibid.

42 In the Women's Spirituality movement the spiral and a variety of representations of the Goddess predominate, while Hindus and Buddhists can be seen wearing prayer beads and other jewelry with other Eastern symbolism. For many lesbians the double axe or rainbow bangles and pins are important indicators of their affinities. Teenagers may wear friendship charms, rings, beaded pins, and woven bracelets. Goths, hip hoppers, and punks don their own preferred symbols, while for others even choosing gold over silver, precious over semi-precious stones, or seed beads over plastic all carry a statement about one's status in society.

43 Richter, 11.

44 Dubin, 17.

45 Borel, 24.

46 Gabriel, 12.

47 Borel, 27.

References

Barber, Elizabeth Wayland. *Women's Work: The First 20,000 Years* (New York: W.W. Norton & Company, 1994).

Borel, France. *The Splendour of Ethnic Jewelry* (London: Thames and Hudson, 1994).

Birnbaum, Ph.D., Lucia Chiavola. *dark mother: african origins and godmothers* (San Jose: iUniverse, 2001).

Cooper, Ilay and John Gillow. *Arts and Crafts of India* (London: Thames and Hudson, 1996).

Dubin, Lois Scherr. *The History of Beads: From 30,000 BCE to the Present* (New York: Harry N. Abrams, Inc., 1987).

Durdin-Robinson, Lawrence. *The Cult of the Goddess* (Enniscorthy, Eire: Cesara Publications, 1974).

Gabriel, Hannelore. *Jewelry of Nepal* (London: Thames and Hudson, 1999).

Gimbutas, Marija. *The Civilization of the Goddess* (New York: Harper Collins, 1991).

_____. *The Language of the Goddess* (New York: Harper Collins, 1989).

Grahn, Judy. *Blood, Bread, and Roses: How Menstruation Created the World* (Boston:Beacon Press, 1993).

Marshack, Alexander. *The Roots of Civilization: Revised and Expanded* (New York: Moyer Bell Limited, 1991).

Ministry of Culture, Thessaloniki, Villa Blance. *Greek Jewelry: 6,000 years of Tradition* (Athens: Archaeological Receipts Fund, 1997).

Noble, Vicki. *The Double Goddess: Women Sharing Power* (Vermont: Bear & Company, 2003).

_____. *Shakti Woman. Feeling our Fire, Healing our World, The New Female Shamanism* (San Francisco: HarperSanFrancisco, 1993).

Richter, Anne. *Jewelry of Southeast Asia* (London: Thames and Hudson, 2000).

Shuttle, Penelope and Peter Redgrove. *The Wise Wound: The Myths, Realities, and Meanings of Menstruation* (New York: Grove Press, 1988).

Sjoo, Monica and Barbara Mor. *The Great Cosmic Mother: Rediscovering the Religion of the Earth* (New York: Harper & Row, 1987).

Guernica, Again

Janine Canan, M.D.

The sky is crying!
The war has begun.
Everyone on earth throws
their bundle of fear onto the fire.
And prayers, prayers
for the salvation of the innocents.
The sky bursts with tears.
The war is starting again.

*

One hour of war
is too long.
All this desire to kill
makes our world filthy.
The whole earth is shattered
by these bombs.
The land of our mothers
becomes a morgue of grieving.

*

The sun comes out.
White clouds swim the blue
and spring resumes her flowering.

Peace cannot be stopped.
Little mind stumbles into pure joy.
Friend calls out to friend.
Life is innocent and has no eyes for hate.
Let the war be over soon.

Iberian Pietá

Oh Lady of Montserrat,
the world is a child who sits on your lap
and leans against your pounding heart.
May our minds be wide and wise
as your all-loving heart.

*

The sorrow of creation is so heavy in Iberia,
the weight of masculine power—Rome, Carthage,
Germania, Arabia, Napoleon, Franco—wave upon wave
across her lands—invasion, torture, death.
Not until this oppression ends will she dry her tears.

*

Even through the iron bars of Spain—
immovable, intimate—
shines forth Our Mother.
In every cathedral, mosque, museum and temple.
In every human being, animal, plant, planet and star.

Crying for the World

Today I am crying.
Crying for the chimpanzee who lives in a cage.
Crying for the tree whose limbs are sawed off.
Crying for the woman blown-up by soldiers.
Crying for the baby starving in her mother's arms.
Hot tears roll down my cheeks onto the ground.
Oh, let everyone in the world be peaceful.
Let everyone be happy.

Lady of the Pillar

Holy Woman in your wide red skirt
upon your jasper pillar,
wood-carved Mary journeyed
all the way from Jerusalem, from crucifixion,
from the origin of the world, and before—
> *You are the core,*
> *You are the nub,*
> *You are the womb,*
> *You are the bud opening.*

Sweet Mother of Us All,
creatrix of the cosmos,
Goddess of the sun and stars,
You who are all light, Dark Lady
of Africa of the Soul—
> *You are the core,*
> *You are the nub,*
> *You are the womb,*
> *You are the bud opening.*

You we love, perfect
embodiment of the feminine force
that creates, informs and loves this world.
To You we turn, praying over and over,
be with us, dear Mother—
> *You are the core,*
> *You are the nub,*
> *You are the womb,*
> *You are the bud opening.*

The Spanish Goddess

Hera Hagstoz, M.A.

Whatever we call her by name, a dark female divinity has always been venerated in Spain. In modern times she has represented the subaltern, heretical
underbelly to a deeply Catholic and, until quite recently, fascist state. While
not always continuous, and certainly not without some difficulty and repression, the divine feminine has maintained Her hold in the subaltern cultures of
Spain. Recently, this phenomenon has taken the form of Black Madonna
worship. At first she would appear to be a Christian icon, but there are strong
Goddess overtones.

Over the millennia, there have been many different cultures occupying the
Iberian Peninsula. Its auspicious position between the greater European sub-
continent, the Mediterranean Sea, and Africa, played a large role in its multi-
cultural and, at times, tumultuous history. It functioned as a colossal land
bridge between Africa and Europe and we can still see the evidence to this day
in the differing cultures between the North and South of Spain. The peninsula
also acted as a sort of buffer zone between the Celtic/Iberian northern regions
and the northern tribal societies of Africa. The south of Spain, in particular,
has become a distinct blend of Iberian, African, and Mediterranean customs
and traditions; some going back much further than one might at first imagine.

This essay will focus mainly on the southern coastal areas of Spain because
I feel that this area was the keystone of the larger Iberian Peninsula, where the
migrations from Africa passed as well as having to bear the brunt of successive
colonization by eastern Mediterranean cultures. It is also an area that has
always been abundant in goddess iconography and symbolism; home to the
Millaran Eye-Goddess in the Neolithic, the Goddess Tanit/Astarte of the

Phoenicians during the Bronze Age, as well as the black madonnas of medieval and modern times.

Paleolithic Spain 30,000–10,000 BC

During the Paleolithic period of Spain, the Iberian Peninsula was a much different environment than it is today. Europe was experiencing a mini ice age and the creatures that walked the land would be considered exotic for today. There is ample evidence that there were giant cave bears, saber tooth lions, hippos, woolly mammoths, as well as the horse, deer, and bison. Human remains from this period are scarce, but there is evidence of stone tool technologies. It may be important at this point to emphasize the deep cultural connection that early humans in Spain shared with their African neighbors.

It is a well-known fact that art in and of itself is a distinctly human passion that originates somewhere between the desire to create reality on one's own terms and to express the inner nature of the human psyche through a concrete medium. In other words, art is and of itself a metaphor for the reality of human existence. Therefore, it is not without some respect and admiration that we should view the art left behind in caves and on stone as thoughtful meditations on life by the artists who drew and painted the magical pictures. Emmanuel Anati, an Italian archaeologist, also draws this same conclusion about the correlation between creating art and ideas of the divine. "The boundary between religion and art, for Anati, is not clear. His timeline of the path of creative art in the caves and cliffs of the world begins 40,000 years ago in central and south Africa, then into other parts of Africa; 35,000 years ago from Africa into Asia; 34,000 years ago from Africa into Europe...." (Birnbaum 2001, xxxv). "The matristic nature of this original world civilization is suggested in Anati's finding that the color red ochre was pervasive in African cave and cliff drawings 60,000–50,000 BCE when Africans carried this sign of the dark mother with them when they migrated to all continents" (Ibid, 7). Along with the importance of the color ochre red is the depiction of animals and humans involved in ritualistic scenes also a hallmark of ancient rock and cave art. "Figures dancing, singing, playing musical instruments, engaging in initiation rituals, with body decoration and masks, characterize the art of the entire heterogeneous African continent, according to archeologist Umberto Sansoni. African art of Africans south of the Sahara suggests that they venerated their ancestors, considered animals and all life sacred, and that they lived without violence" (ibid).

Like the African rock and cave art, the art from Spain also has these features in abundance. In particular one famous rock painting known as "Dancing Women" of Cogul has within it almost all the elements necessary to suggest that women were valued and sacred to the community. The figures are painted either in ochre red or black paint and the scene's main characters are larger than life women whose breasts seem to play a large symbolic role. They surround one lone male figure who is much smaller yet has a large phallus quite out of proportion with the rest of his body, much like the breasts on the women. There are also a quite a few animals included in the group; most notably a deer which has a transparent abdomen in which we can see two black spots and several cows or bulls. My interpretation of this scene is that it is one of high sacred fertility. The inclusion of animals perhaps means that human fertility was seen as integrally linked to the animal world. Whatever the true meaning of this picture may have been, it is quite clear that the women are the key figures and that it is a scene without violence. The dating of this scene is contested, but it is mainly held that it was created somewhere in the post-glacial period roughly 20,000–14,000 BC.

Neolithic Spain 5000–2000 BC

Worship of the female divinity continued from the Paleolithic down through the Mesolithic into the Neolithic cultures of Spain, represented as birth giver and priestess in cave art. This worship seemed to reach its zenith during the time of the Megalith builders of the Neolithic. These people were farmers who lived in fortified settlements and buried their dead communally in circular tombs. It has been suggested that this tradition stemmed from the eastern Mediterranean regions.

Along with the paintings, grave goods can tell us a good deal about the religious ideology of these people and from this we can see that divine female was conspicuous.

> At Barsella and Blanquizares were flat, undecorated plaques of bone shaped like the stone amulets of the Ghassul culture of southern Palestine and anthropomorphic 'double-anchor' pendants which seem to be derived ultimately from the conventional representation of a pregnant goddess, with raised arms and sprawling legs, familiar from painted frescos of c. 6000 BC at Çatal Hüyük in Anatolia. The Cueva de la Pastora yielded rarer types: a twin-lobed stone pendant of predynastic Egyptian affinity, a crutch-headed pin, no doubt derived ultimately, like the parallels cited

from the Danubian lands, from Anatolia, and a sherd which recalls the
incised symbolic eyes on the Neolithic pottery of Sicily (Stentinello) and
the painted eyes on the Chalcolithic pottery of Hassuna (Iraq) and Mersin
(Cilicia) (Savory 1968, 90).

It therefore appears that the influence of Neolithic Goddess iconography
from the greater Mediterranean area was beginning to make an appearance in
the indigenous cultures of Spain. The Eye Goddess that begins to appear in
Spain is representative of a whole range of matrifocal tendencies exhibited by
the Neolithic cultures of Spain. "The large eyes with which the Goddess is
portrayed strongly suggest the epithet "All-seeing" for her. However, the symbolism which surrounds the eyes speaks for an even more fundamental
attribute, namely that the eyes, like the Goddess's breasts or mouth, are a
Divine Source. The idea of divine moisture from the eyes is present in the
markings on artifacts of the Mesolithic and Pre-Pottery Neolithic periods
(Gimbutas 1991, 51).

A finale note on the Neolithic Goddess of Spain is the transition which
must have happened slowly from the nomadic cave dwelling gathering/hunt-
ing communities to the more sedentary farming communities. The tradition
of communal burial within caves slowly changed to burial within tombs which
becomes apparent with the tholos and rock-cut tombs of the Tagus culture.
These tombs seem to be an adaptation to the symbolic desire to return the
deceased to the womb/cave. Caves have always represented a birth/death
motif in the human psyche and have also always been utilized in their aspect as
earth tombs/wombs. The artificial creation of cave-like tombs on the part of
the Neolithic communities seems to be a sort of compromise to the reality of
living as farmers in fortified communities that lacked access to cave sites.

An important point to recognize is the strong matrifocal symbolism in the
tomb shapes themselves. "During the Neolithic, graves and temples assumed
the shape of the egg, vagina, and uterus of the Goddess or of her complete
body. The megalithic passage graves of Western Europe quite probably symbolized the vagina (passage) and pregnant belly (tholos, round chamber) of the
Goddess. The shape of a grave is an analogue of the natural hill with an
omphalos (stone symbolizing the navel) on top, a universal symbol of the
Earth Mother's pregnant belly with umbilical cord, as recorded in European
folk beliefs" (Gimbutas 1991, xxiii).

The Millaran Eye Goddess

The term, "eye goddess" comes from the Near East where apparently the cult originated[1]. Whether or not there was any direct influence is up to question, but it well known that the Millaran culture did have contact and therefore was influenced by the cultures along the North African coast. Much of what we know about the Millaran culture comes from their grave goods, however there are a few well-preserved settlements that have left us a somewhat sketchy picture of their life style. It appears that the Millarans were farmers and metal workers who lived in fortified towns around 2800–2000 BC. They lived in the south east of Spain and their influence extended far to the western coast of Spain, as can be seen in the construction of later tholos tombs of the Tagas culture (near the Tagus river in Spain and Portugal) as well as grave goods representing direct trade between the two cultures. It seems that Los Millares, the site the culture is named after, was an epicenter of cultural influence, and may represent an outside influence, possibly a colonization of the area by eastern Mediterranean peoples.

Distinctive of the Millaran culture is a magic symbolism represented in female figurines whose eyes are accentuated to the point that they became the defining feature of their divinity. Cylindrical idols where carved out of stone, ivory, and bone and placed within the tombs. "Its eyes are regarded as having sacred power because it seems to surpass all other creatures in visual acuity. This ambivalent image is a dim reflection, diffused through time, of the owl as an incarnate manifestation of the fearsome Goddess of Death. She was revered as a divinity and perhaps respected for her grim but necessary part in the cycle of existence" (Gimbutas 1991, 190).

In addition, I would like to suggest another possible connection between the original "Eye Goddess" Ishtar and the Millaran Eye Goddess. Ishtar, also known in the eastern Mediterranean as Isis or Astarte, was in some of her different aspects both a celestial Goddess and an underworld Goddess, her two halves symbolizing death and regeneration. As stated above in the footnote, Ishtar was characterized by the very same eye symbols, which we now understand to be associated with the owl. While being a bird of prey, it is also specifically a bird of the night. I would like to suggest a third connection that involves astronomy and stars in particular. If we are to see the eyes as a "radiating sun motif" (Ibid, 56), could we not also see them as a nocturnal sun sign; in other words as stars? It is well known that Isis was connected with star symbolism as portrayed by her starry mantle. Could the Millaran Eye Goddess be

Astarte/Isis/Ishtar? Even if there is no direct cultural connection, which there may be evidence for, it is interesting to note that many of the tombs along with their megalithic structures were laid out according to astronomical calculations. Also of note is that "[t]he west European Eye Goddess is known almost exclusively from sepulchral artifacts-either as large stone stela standing at the entrance to megalithic tombs, or as a figurine, bone phalange, stone cylinder, or schist plaque deposited within" (Ibid, 55). So, in a somewhat roundabout way, we can see here a symbolic connection between funerary astronomical concerns, the owl/Eye Goddess, and a new culture which brought with it this specific motif, associated in the Levant with Ishtar.

Regardless of whether or not there will ever be any physical proof of the Levantine roots of the Millaran culture, it seems that their new symbolism was not all that different or incompatible with the older, indigenous spirituality. For instance, in keeping with tradition, red ochre was used as a ritual element. Also of interest is the ambiguous sexuality of these pillars and stone idols, representing a Goddess, yet being phallic in shape. That these pillars stand just outside of the womb-shaped tomb seems to be an obvious reference to the regeneration aspect of death.

The Millaran culture was eventually overtaken by the aggressive incursion of horse riding nomads from north Eastern Europe, categorized as the Bell-Beaker civilization. Around 1900 BC, three hundred years after the collapse of Old Kingdom Egypt and Troy, the Millaran culture was overrun with a vastly different social/religious/political system which was patriarchal, violent, and although undoubtedly creative and artistic in its own right, highly stratified socially. That this change came about rather violently, as it did in other parts of Europe, is evidenced by the abrupt halt within the stratigraphy of Millaran culture after a certain date. "...at Vila Nova de São Pedro the occupation layers which formed on top of the ruins of the inner walls contained Bell-Beaker pottery instead of Millaran types, and at Los Millares and near Seville the communal tombs received secondary burials with Beaker pottery, weapons, and gold ornaments. All over the peninsula in the last quarter of the third millennium the Beaker nomads become culturally dominant, and soon afterwards spread rapidly to most parts of western and central Europe" (Savory 1968, 165). This marks the end of a relatively peaceful epoch. After this period evidence of the female divine exists, but in a diminished fashion.

The Spanish Tanit (Bronze Age 2500–500 BC)

The main trend of the Bronze Age in areas all over Europe was the increase in weapons used for human combat and the omnipresence of highly stratified, patriarchal societies. Also known in its later stages as the Orientalizing period, it is at this point that the Great Goddess becomes associated with subaltern cultures and it becomes harder to find examples that haven't been diluted by patriarchal ideological systems or recorded in history as merely sexual extensions of the new patriarchal gods. It was also during this time that we begin to see active colonization by eastern Mediterranean cultures, notably the Phoenicians, the Greeks, and finally the Romans. This does not mean, though, that the indigenous cultures ideologies were completely obliterated, or even lost when the takeovers happened. Some of the invading cultures merged with the indigenous cultures, for example the Phoenicians.

The cult of Tanit in Spain has not been well documented at the present moment. Much is known of the Carthaginian Tanit, whom it is said, demanded child sacrifice; although the libel of child sacrifice has now been repudiated by archaeologists.[2] The main differences of the Spanish Tanit is that there have been no topheths found and also no conclusive findings of human sacrifices to her. This may be due to the co-mingling of indigenous belief systems with the colonial mythologies as mentioned above. I believe that Tanit represented a Goddess of Death and Rebirth, specifically associated with the death of infants and children.

> In any case, Tanit definitely corresponds to Astarte of the East Phoenician pantheon. Rare in the inscriptions of Carthage, and yet contained in the theophorous names, Astarte evidently gave way to Tanit. The significant title of mother, accorded to the latter in certain inscriptions, indicates her nature, which is confirmed by the Greek identification with Hera and the Roman with Celestial Juno. The symbols which accompany her in the illustrations—dove, pomegranate, fish, palm tree—clearly suggest her functions as goddess of fertility (Moscati 1999, 139).

If Tanit was indeed Astarte, she was a Goddess of death and rebirth, governor of souls and perhaps through her connection with the North African Lamia or Neith, a guardian specifically of children. "Astarte ruled all the spirits of the dead who lived in heaven wearing bodies of light, visible from earth as stars. Hence, she was known as Astroarche, 'Queen of the Stars.' She was the mother of all souls in heaven, the Moon surrounded by her star-children to whom she gave their 'astral' (starry) bodies" (Walker 1983, 70). In respect to this aspect of Tanit, I would also link her to the Christian Mary. Like many goddesses of Death and Regeneration, the myth that accompanies them deal with the loss and subsequent rebirth of a son/daughter/lover/self; this holds true for Demeter, Astarte, Isis, Innana, and recently Mary. In her mythological connection to Astarte of the eastern Phoenician pantheon, Tanit also represents an early form of Mary. "Scholars who really understood the mystery of Astarte recognized in her one of the ancient prototypes of the virgin Mary. In Syria and Egypt her sacred dramas celebrated the rebirth of the solar god from the celestial Virgin each 25th of December. A newborn child was exhibited, while the cry went up that the Virgin had brought forth. Frazer says, "No doubt the Virgin who thus conceived and bore a son on the twenty-fifth of December was the great Oriental goddess whom the Semites called the Heavenly Virgin or simply the Heavenly Goddess; in Semitic lands she was a form of Astarte" (Ibid).

One of Tanit's main sanctuaries in Spain was found on the island of Ibiza in the Mediterranean Sea. "An extremely significant discovery, made on the Isla Plana at Ibiza, was a group of clay statuettes of the type familiar to us from Bythia. Here again the body consists of a vase to which the head, arms, and sexual organs have been attached. We sometimes note necklaces and ornaments round the neck. Like those of Bythia, the figurines were probably intended to commend the sick to the deities (hands indicating the part of the body concerned). Most of the statuettes of the Isla Plana have eyes superimposed, a characteristic which recurs in certain copies from other localities in Spain (Alcoy, Carmona, Cadiz)" (Moscati 1999, 237–238). The eye motif is an old tradition in Spain, and as I stated above in the section regarding the Millaran Eye Goddess, can be seen in this instance to have a direct connection to Astarte through Tanit.

Also of significance is that in the modern day town of Eivissa, once a main center of the Phoenicians called Dalt Vila or Upper Town, there is now a cathedral dedicated to the Virgin Mary. Also located in the same area is Puig de Molins, which is the largest and best preserved Phoenician necropolis containing over 3000 tombs within its multiple hypogeums. As I have stated before, the Church often built its sanctuaries near, if not directly over older indigenous sites of worship. This necropolis was no doubt a sanctuary of Tanit as well as other gods, and so it makes sense that a cathedral, which was started in the 15th century and completed two hundred years later, was dedicated to Mary.

The Cult of Mary/Mari

With regard to the fact that I am purposefully skipping a large chunk of time between the Phoenician influences in Spain and the medieval period of Spain, I would like to discuss the cult of Mary as the Christian Mother of God as well as witchcraft, who among other deities, worshiped a Mari. Keeping in mind the successive waves of influence from the Roman occupation to the Muslim occupation of Spain, I would like to examine the coincidences surrounding the repression of the feminine divine in the state religion of Christianity and the ironic connections between the Holy Virgin Mother of God and the demonized Mari figure.

During the years of the Inquisition in Spain, also routinely called the Age of Exploration and the Scientific Enlightenment, the feminine aspect of God was almost obliterated in the waves of mass hysteria and political intrigue surrounding the massacre of so called witches.[3] Jews, heretics, pagans, Muslims, and even Christians were routinely accused of witchcraft in some form or another and either tortured, burnt at the stake, or both to atone for their sins against the state and god. It was indeed a bleak time for the Goddess and those who followed her ancient traditions. However, it seems as though the Church left a loophole in its ideology, when all over Europe massive cathedrals were built in honor of the Virgin Mary. These immense structures, with architecture reminiscent of subterranean caves or grottos, took at times hundreds of years to build and required successive generations of craftspeople and excessive amounts of money to complete.

> Gothic cathedrals were dedicated not to God or Jesus but to *Notre Dame*; they were collectively called 'Our Ladies' or 'Palaces of the Queen of Heaven.' Many of them were built over pagan shrines of the Great Goddess. Rome's cathedral of Santa Maria Maggiore was built over the sacred cave of the Magna Mater. Santa Maria in Aracoeli on the Capitoline Hill was formerly a temple of Tanit. Mary's churches throughout Italy were founded on shrines of Juno, Isis, Minerva, Diana, Hecate. One church was even naively named Santa Maria sopra Minerva: Holy Mary over (the shrine of) Minerva. At Chartres, the heathen idol of the *virgo paritura* (Virgin Giving Birth) was preserved in the so-called Druid Grotto underneath the cathedral. It was said to be a black statue of Mary (Walker 1983, 609).

The Virgin today is still worshiped reverently by women and men throughout the Christian world and remains one of the most beloved figures, sometimes surpassing Jesus himself. It seems to me that much of the reverence for the Great Goddess was condensed within the Virgin Mary of Christianity and at the time of the Inquisition was an acceptable outlet for the otherwise repressed need to worship a female divinity.

> Above all, Christian authorities feared Mary might be the channel through which Goddess-worship could reestablish itself, for she inspired utterances similar to those the ancient Mother inspired, like Goethe's: 'Supreme and sovereign Mistress of the World!'...Oh Virgin, in the highest sense most pure, oh Mother, worthy of all our worship, our chosen Queen, equal with the gods.' The secret, ineradicable heresies of Marian worship received graphic form in the famous Vierge Ouvrante—Mary as a statue that opened to show God, Jesus, angels, and saints contained in her (Ibid, p. 610).

At the same time, there were secret cults concerned with the older deities such as Artemis, Diana, Astarte, Isis, and an interesting figure named Mari.

> Medieval Spain knew the Goddess Mari as a Lady or Mistress who lived in a magic cave and rode through the night sky as a ball of fire. This may have meant the red harvest moon, or possibly the moon in eclipse—always a dire omen. The Goddess Mari was said to give gifts of fairy gold and precious stones, which might later turn into worthless lumps of coal by the light of day. In later centuries, the same worthless gifts were given to 'bad' children by St. Nicholas at Christmas (Ibid, 585).

Mari may have been worshiped by the Basques, an area that was steeped in "witchcraft" during the Inquisition. "Much more significant, however, than these connections with old pagan places of worship (caves, springs, and dolmens) is the strong belief which exists in parts of Guipuzcoa and Vizcaya, that Mari, a mountain spirit believed to inhabit the highest peaks of mountains like Amboto, Aizkorri, and Muru, presided over the witches. This spirit is also called 'Lady' (Dama) and 'Mistress' (Senora), and can make storms. The legends which exist about her make us think of chthonic deities like Proserpina and others" (Baroja 2001, 237–238). This linking is also extremely significant in terms of the Death and Regeneration Goddess lineage of Spain. Mary is the Christianized version of this wild Goddess of Death and Rebirth. She too loses a child and sees him reborn. She too was a Goddess of Mourning and Hope.

Along with Mari, sometimes known as Black Mari, there is the phenomena of Black Madonnas.

> Black Madonnas may be considered a metaphor for a memory of the time when the earth was believed to be the body of a woman and all creatures were equal, a memory transmitted in vernacular traditions of earth-bonded cultures, historically expressed in cultural and political resistance, and glimpsed today in movements aiming for transformation. Differing from white madonnas, who may be said to embody church doctrine of obedience and patience, and differing in shades of dark, what all black madonnas have in common is location on or near archaeological evidence of the pre-Christian woman divinity, and the popular perception that they are black (Birnbaum 2000, 3).

Black Madonnas in Spain are still worshiped to this day as is the case at Montserrat near Barcelona in Spain. La Moreneta is the name given to this Black Madonna who attracts throngs of worshipers who wait in long lines to gain an audience. She is about three feet tall encased within a glass dome. There is a hole in the glass where her hand stretches forth a globe. People are allowed to touch this and quietly say a prayer or make a wish. Her small size is surprising, not only because she seems more monumental in theory, but also because she commands such deep respect from those worshipping her.

Within her mountain top sanctuary is a great deal of iconography associated with the Goddess. There are Medusas, Gorgons, snakes, fish, stars, birds, and even dragons. A striking element to the sanctuary is a second smaller chapel. In this darkened chapel one may sit and meditate after touching the Madonna. One views her from behind, although it is not very well lit and one must look high up to see her. There is a seemingly conspicuous placement of a statue of St. George defeating the Dragon. It is directly behind the Madonna and is quite gruesome in contrast to the serenity of the sanctuary. I imagine it to be a representation of the suppression of the dangerous feminine qualities of the dark mother. The Dragon in particular has a long history of being associated with the Goddess and most recently in Christianity as the Devil. Here again we have the powerful repression of an underworld feminine deity; Hell or Hel being an ancient Scandinavian Goddess of Death, the horned devil, a twisted version of the horned Hathor or Isis in her underworld aspect. It is an interesting placement for this statue, aligned strategically at the apex of the church's cross shape. The dragon gazes up in anguish at the back of La Moreneta who in turn gazes resolutely down onto the main body of the church as if to say "Gaze upon the virtuous Madonna, but pay no attention to the Dragon behind her veils." At the same time as the Church denies the presence of the dark goddess of prehistory, it makes a dramatic show of its patriarchal suppression, perhaps as a warning to those who would question. It did seem interesting to me that the quiet chapel behind the Madonna was also home to a Dragon and all those praying to the Madonna's back were at the same time turning their backs on the death of the Dragon.

Conclusions

The Great Goddess of prehistory, and by proxy the people of the land, has evolved and struggled and has had her rituals eclipsed by the modern cult of Christ, and yet still maintained a hold, albeit a subliminal one, on the people of Spain. People still honor the Goddess, perhaps unknowingly, when they pray to the Black Madonnas, or hold processions of Mary on certain occasions. They are still honoring a dark female divinity, even if they do not consciously realize it, when they admire the Gaudi's La Sagrada Familia, visit La Moreneta of Montserrat.

Even if not on the surface, there are still many subaltern elements within Spain that carry the elemental teachings and social behavior of an older matristic ancestry. Black Madonnas, social justice movements centered on non-violence, and the tradition of carnival all hold within them a seed of ancient wisdom left over from Spain's ancient past. These seeds have been kept alive precisely because they are hidden under layers of socially acceptable beliefs of the dominant culture, but they are easily spotted once uncovered.

It has been the aim of this article to illuminate the past in a way that emphasizes the female divine so that one day these dormant seeds may someday regenerate the peaceful and balanced practices of the ancient cultures they represent. As the Goddess teaches us again and again, there is never a death without a rebirth.

Notes

1 "…emphasis on the eyes as opposed to the particular sexual features, and to the exclusion of all else save hints at necklaces or facial tattooing, is a specialization which seems to appear in Syria about the end of the fourth millennium and to be related to a particular cult, identified with Ishtar, at the temple of Brak with its numerous clay idols" (Savory 1968, 160).

2 e.g. S. Moscati

3 For an excellent study of the witch trials read *Ecstasies—Deciphering the Witches Sabbath* by Carlo Ginzburg.

Bibliography

Baroja, Julio Caro. 2001. *The World of the Witches.* Trans. Nigel Glendinning. London: Phoenix Press.

Birnbaum, Ph.D., Lucia Chiavola. 2000. *Black Madonnas feminism, religion, & politics in Italy.* San Jose, CA: toExcel.

——. 2001. *dark mother african origins and godmothers.* San Jose, CA: Author's Choice Press.

Gimbutas, Marija. 1991. *The Language of the Goddess.* San Francisco: Harper San Francisco.

Moscati, Sabatino. 1999. *The World of the Phoenicians.* Trans. George Weidenfeld & Nicolson Ltd. London: Phoenix.

Savory, H. N. 1968. *Spain and Portugal The Prehistory of the Iberian Peninsula.* New York: Frederick A. Praeger, Inc. Publishers.

Walker, Barbara G. 1983. *The Woman's Encyclopedia of Myths and Secrets.* San Francisco: Harper & Row Publishers.

The other side breaks on through

Anne Bouie, Ph.D.

"We are not bodies and people with 'souls'" We are Souls temporarily identified with the body and times in which we have incarnated. I am not a body with a soul; I am a Soul with a body..."

This essay seeks to share and understand the experiences of three women, each from very different backgrounds with the Other Side. These women were all "minding their business"—or so they thought—when they were snatched from this presence and time back into another with force, certainty, and awe. This briefly shares their stories, the talks we shared, and our efforts to make meaning out of this work as it relates to the Dark Mother.

The Women

Wanda in Cachoeira, Bahia in Brazil

It goes without saying that Bahia is a magical place. It seems to be one of those places on the Earth where the veil between the worlds is much thinner, where one can sense the presence of the Earth, the Ancients, and the Other Side. I got that sense in Oaxaca, Mexico, in Big Sur in Monterey, California, in the Cmargue in the South of France, in Taos during the off-season, and in the Sea Islands in South Carolina. There are other places where the Veil is thinner, and it may be that these places do not speak to every Soul. They speak to me and I have experienced wonder, power, and healing at each of these places.

I had been anticipating the trip to Cachoeira, and had felt the presence of spirits and souls throughout our stay in Bahia. Joel, our guide and teacher, had told us that this was the site where the Africans who worked in the sugar cane fields first arrived. These were people from the Congo who were farmers, planters who knew and loved the Earth. I have studied slavery, and knew that sugar cane was the worst crop—hardest on the slaves. These plantations had the highest mortality rates of any crop grown in South or North America. It was not until I went to Cachoeira that it hit me with a knowing that these fields were not "plantations." They were death camps. They were places where Africans worked until they dropped dead. The life expectancy on the plantation was five to seven years; there were no great efforts by the Portuguese to save lives. They simply imported more Africans. Indeed, we were told that the Daughters of the Good Death were organized during the 1700s to stop the bodies from simply being thrown into the ocean. They organized to give the deceased a "good death."

I saw and experienced Wanda's encounter with the Other Side first hand. Wanda has an outgoing, cheerful and lighthearted presence t hat can veil her depth, determination, and intensity. She has an infectious sense of humor and daring; she said she intended to wear a thong on the beaches of Brazil, and she did—with sass and flair.

Our first stop in the area was at a restaurant that had formerly been a convent. The grounds and building were nicely tended. As we walked the grounds I noticed that Wanda was bent over and seemed not well. Suddenly a sound of terror, disbelief, horror, agony, and helplessness emerged through her that I have never in my life heard before—or since. She was doubled over in agony, sorrow and grief; pain was the least of the emotions being expressed. It was overpowering. Members of the group surrounded Wanda as she sobbed uncontrollably. It seemed as though the sound of horror and disbelief that "this could be happening" would never stop flowing from her. It finally ceased, Wanda recovered, ate lunch, and seemed as though nothing had happened.

I felt the pain and agony there, but not nearly to the extent Wanda did. I was disconcerted, and I saw many in the group keeping an eye on me as well. Later, as I wandered through the grounds, I came to an old, old tree in a courtyard toward the back of the convent. I made an offering to and for the Souls I felt around me. I acknowledged the pain, shame, degradation, death and sorrow that seemed to surround the place. As I made the offering, the wind came up as if to acknowledge and accept my prayers.

When I talked with Winnie, she was absolutely certain that the energy and feelings predated the Africans who served as slaves. I was certain that it was the Africans. She was adamant that it was not the Africans, but people who were there before them…the "indigenous" Indians who, like their kin in North America, were almost eliminated by the conquering Europeans. She was absolutely certain that she had been there, that she had been used as a channel by the Souls who lingered there. She said that torture and death had been there, that she had seen and experienced it herself.

Vera in Machu Pichu in Peru

Vera is a gracious, sophisticated woman who has traveled the world. She began traveling to exotic places twelve or so years ago to many of the world's most beautiful places—Istanbul, Africa, India, Spain, and Peru—which was the site of an experience that changed her life, opened her heart, and helped her commence journeys to realms unknown to her before. She had long been interested in Spirit and had been into shamanic journeying for some time—a marked departure from her conservative, traditional Catholic upbringing as a modest Latina. Her journey began in a new age, metaphysical church through a friend who introduced her to the Santeria tradition. She studied, practiced, but chose not to take the final steps to become ordained as a priestess of Oshun, the Yoruba entity of love, romance, and all things beautiful whose home and shrine are the River Niger in Ogugbo, Nigeria. From there she studied in the temples of Isis, the original face of Oshun.

She feels that each of the opportunities to learn, study and commune were "steps in the process; points on the journey" that she felt unfolding as she placed one foot in front of the other. It was a reading she had with a healer and mystic that impressed her with her connection to the Divine and her quest to experience personal healing and evolution.

Her journey with a shaman to Machu Pichu in Peru was the site of yet another more "up front and personal" encounter on the Other Side that made itself known, felt, and experienced as never before in Vera's life. She was in a Catholic school, on the way to Machu Pichu, where nuns lived, on the second story of the cloister looking down on a courtyard—so perfectly laid out and perfectly rectangular "it could have been a volleyball court."

As she was looking down at the court, she experienced an excruciating pain in her neck. Overcome with emotion and about to break down in sobs and weeping. She had the urge to escape, get out of there; "I have to hide so no one sees me, because I'm going to explode." She ran away from the courtyard and crouched down into as small a little ball as she could. The shaman leading the group rushed over to ask what was wrong.

She haltingly cried, "Something terrible happened to me back there!" She went back to the hotel room where she sat on the side of the bed and "cried, and cried, and cried" as if her heart had been torn asunder with grief, fear, shock, and pain. She could not move her head in any direction; the pain was relentless, she felt so "tragically sad." Her roommate "came and went" leaving her there, confused, in shock and in pain.

She says, "I finally collected myself and went down to the hotel bar to get a drink. As I sat down, the waitress looked at me, and saw the distress. Concerned, the waitress asked, 'What's wrong, can I get you anything? What's happened to you?'" Vera related the day's events to her. The woman exclaimed, don't you know where you were? Don't you know what happened there? You were looking down at what was the site of an altar in ancient times! They used to take young girls who had not begun their menses there to be sacrificed! They would kneel before the altar and their heads would be chopped off."

"As soon as she said that," Vera remembered, "the pain left my neck; I was no longer in a state of dread and panic. I could move my neck!"

Before Vera had had time to digest this experience, the Other Side confronted her once again. On the way to Machu Pichu, the shaman desired to perform a ritual. They were seated in a circle underneath a canopy of trees. Each member on the journey was called to the center of the circle to be sprinkled and blessed with holy water. As the ritual was progressing, her turn came, and she entered the circle, "I fell backwards; when I sat back up, I screamed, and started pulling up the grass, almost hysterical. The shaman leaned over me and sprinkled me with holy water, hitting each one of my chakras." Shortly, she recovered and went on with the journey.

Vera speaks of impressions and sensations of her experiences. She was obviously startled, taken aback. She did not anticipate the experiences, and, at some levels of consciousness, she felt unprepared for them. She did not have anyone with whom she could process the experience; her roommate had left her alone in tears in her room. She said that the shaman leading the trip did not say anything to her, nor did any of the other members of the party.

Eleanor in Toledo, Spain

Eleanor's first trip to Spain was with her brother and his family to celebrate a niece's graduation from college. They were having a wonderful time; Eleanor, the eldest, was enjoying time with her brother and the family. The trip was thrilling, but "uneventful" until they arrived in Toledo. Eleanor says that to understand and appreciate the depth of her experience there, it is necessary to "understand her brother," whom she described as a card-carrying member of "atheists of the world." Her brother was "not religious in the spiritual or cultural sense of the word. It seems as though he was almost disdainful of anything spiritual. Eleanor says that he scoffed at her experiences with the spiritual and metaphysical. Eventually she stopped sharing them with him.

At Toledo the remains of the synagogue are just that—a small shell of remains of what was obviously a lovely former place of prayer and worship. It is ironic that Toledo has a bust of Maimonides in the center of the city because today not one Jew actually lives there. While the town is exquisite, it also has a sense of mourning, loss, sorry, and shame…the killing and expulsions of the Jews seem to linger to this day.

Eleanor says they entered the synagogue, sat down, and felt "nothing." They sat, chatted, and ventured upstairs. There the experience began. She was overcome by terror, grief, pain, and panic. Even more startling—so was her brother. He was completely overwhelmed by fear, tears, and pain that he had never experienced, or expressed, before—in this lifetime. They looked at one another, hugged and cried together, completely overwhelmed, not quite understanding what was happening, or why. As the tears receded, Eleanor says that she and her brother, without a shadow of a doubt, realized and knew that they had been there, in that synagogue, before. Eleanor says she felt the terror and the fear, and the shame, at being unable to find, save, and help her younger brother. She witnessed the slaughter of Jews from the second floor, separated from her brother; she was killed there, and so was he. They relived that terror and sorrow all over again there, together. Her brother was stunned and nearly in shock. They collected themselves and left the synagogue. Eleanor says this experience marked a change in her relationship with the Other Side; when her brother made his transition, she got word from him that "she had been right all the time."

I was with Eleanor on this second journey to Toledo; I listened to her experience, saw her become tense and apprehensive as we approached Toledo. She now knew what was in store for her, but felt no more "ready" than she had been the first time. "I know I'm just going to lose it; I know I'm gong to cry. I know this," she kept saying. She says now that she knows she was there, and that she, as Soul, experienced this terrible time, five hundred years ago. As we approached the remains of the temple in Toledo, she did, indeed, begin to cry. She stood at the wall that reminded me of the Wailing Wall in Jerusalem. She was oblivious to people around her; some stared with amazement, with disdain, with empathy. She did not choose to linger, collected herself and went on with our tour of the city. Later, she shared her thoughts of this second experience. It confirmed and affirmed the first experience. She says she needs to return to Toledo alone to have time to "be" there, to actually be in the city and in the synagogue, as well as allow herself just to "be: while there. She says she know there is more for her to learn and experience, and mach to be shared when she returns.

What do they have in common with one another?

I listened to Eleanor's story in astonishment; it sounded so much like the stories of Wanda and Vera. The "coincidences" started to become phenomena with certain patterns, and, possibly, certain meanings. It seems that all three women were "chosen" to transmit memories and experiences of grief, destruction, death, and utter despair. In all three situations, the conquerors were simply decimated by the conquerors. There was no mercy, no kindness, and no quarter given. They did not seek the experiences—at least not consciously. I am sure that at a deep level of their Being, they did, indeed, seek the experiences, and, as a result, were guided and shepherded by their own ancestors, angels, guardians, and guides—those with love and concern for them, their evolution as Souls, and perhaps, most importantly, to help them become helpers and healers.

A long and winding road

Each of the women is very spiritual and has traveled a "long and winding road." Vera was raised in a conservative Catholic home as a "good girl" who went from her father's rule to her husband's home where she suffered emotional and physical abuse. A turning point came when she realized, beyond doubt, that her husband tried to kill her, and not only felt he had the "right" to do so, but would be supported by their families and surrounding community. She has done a great deal of work with Oshun and Isis, the Egyptian incarnation of the Dark Mother, and has been initiated as her priestess. She has a graduate degree and now works with battered women.

Eleanor was raised religiously and culturally as a Jew. Her roots are intact and precious to her. She is a university professor of multicultural studies where she works with new teachers. Interestingly enough, she teaches at a Catholic college. Wanda is a massage therapist, practicing Reiki, and works as a healer.

In short, each of the women work in areas to heal, restore, and affirm those who have been hurt and wounded—those who frequently had been given no quarter, had no place to turn, and no voice to speak on their behalf. All of them now work and speak and serve as advocates. Is this mere "coincidence?" I think not. Clearly, the values of the Dark Mother are manifest in their work, and in their experiences. All have experienced being the "dark other" in this incarnation. All have carried the projections and fears of others, and have paid "high dues" for doing so.

A conscious choice to align with the values of the Dark Mother

In this incarnation, none of these women have been given the option of being able to "choose" whether or not they will acknowledge being "the dark other." It is easy for any of us to pull out our "dark other" parts when we seek to gain credibility, access to a group, or membership in a certain circle. But when it is easier, and more "appropriate" to repress, deny, or ignore the "dark other" in our lives, heritage, or background, we do so, as the youngsters say, "with a quickness!" These women have chosen not to separate themselves from their awareness and honoring of the Dark Mother, and the values for which she stands: justice, compassion, Truth, and equality.

The need for healing in the world.

There are many Souls still with us. There are places where their presence is readily felt. The plantations throughout the American south; the fields of Cachoeria; the grounds of Dachau, the killing fields of Cambodia, Wounded Knee, the potato fields of Ireland, and the blood-soaked savannah of Ruwanda. All these places were the site of horrible things. Very bad things happened there. People were stripped of their dignity, their humiliation witnessed by those powerless to help and those who could authorize it to continue. The pain of witnessing can be as great as the pain of experiencing. What is there to say to someone whom you have seen divested of privacy, their boundaries violated, their very Soul assaulted?

These experiences were about the powerless being assaulted by the powerful…the dark people of the world being used as scapegoats by people unwilling or unable to seek harmony and accept the Truth that there is Enough for all of us—all of us.

These women are channels to let us know that until the suffering of the past is acknowledged, respected, honored, and addressed, it seems that there can be no peace for us on this side of the Veil. Vera experienced the pain of sacrificial victims, Eleanor the slaughter of innocents, and Wanda the decimation of a people. The Earth needs healing; the Souls are calling for it, and yet we have no means of responding. Or do we?

An openness to the past and our journeys as Souls

None of these women once mentioned the word "fear." None talked of trying to deny or break free of the experience with the other side. In the one case I witnessed, Wanda's, there was no way she could break out of it, she evidenced no fear and like Vera and Eleanor spoke of the experience in a very matter of fact manner. When I asked them what the experiences "meant" to them and what they intended to "do" with them, at first they answered, "What do you mean?" Vera, in her matter of fact way, said, "Well, I don't *do* anything with them; I just see them as points along the way on my journey." So, too, with Eleanor, and Wanda, though each said their experience was clarified and made more meaningful in our discussions. All these women seem to understand and accept the fact we can be guided, taught, and used as healers and helpers. They evidence a comfort level with the Unseen that is instructive and amazing at the same time. Vera says her father was the only guard who worked the night shift in the Old Place in San Juan, Puerto Rico because he was the only one who was not afraid of the spirits there.

Rejection of the Unknown and the Dark as evil

If we are to grow as Souls, an acceptance of the reality of the Other Side is essential. I believe the Dark Mother teaches us fearlessness. I believe her darkness is a reminder that the dark is not our enemy, nor a scary or bad place. The Other Side is the source of the Light…where all things germinate…where we retreat to find solace and wholeness. If I am afraid of the Dark, I cannot use the Light.

Acceptance of traditional and indigenous teachings...and humility

If the experiences of these three women teach us anything, they illuminate the validity of traditional and indigenous teachings. These teachings help people acknowledge and work with the Other Side as if it were a natural part of this life, which indeed it is. The acknowledgments of ancestors, guides, the ability to interpret dreams, and all the esoteric wisdom that has been hidden away, is needed if the experiences of these women is to be respected and understood. In traditional societies, elders and teachers help understand and make proper use of traditional teachings. In our society, all too often the "logical" dismiss the "illogical" the "educated" dismiss the "illiterates" and we all suffer. There is so much to be learned from those the Dark Mother nurtures and protects. If there were more elders and teachers with us, Vera, Wanda, and Eleanor would not, alone, have to "make meaning" or sense of these occurrences. There would be a context for the experiences. As it is, we must create a context.

Openness and the need for real communion

The conversations I shared with these women have helped me grow. It is amazing to find so much similarity across so many apparent "differences" in age, ethnicity, and culture. Hubris and a lack of openness can cause much harm. I know that many times I have caused myself and others harm because I thought "I knew." Only later did I learn that I did not know at all, or know enough. Only later did I realize that my blinders—society's or my own—kept me from seeing, or caused me to see through lenses that could not illuminate. I have learned that I do not know, and have to be open to teaching and help.

I have also learned not to twist the Teachings, the Truth, or the Way, for my own ends. I have learned that everyone of color is not more moral than those who are not of color. I have learned that there are men with more sensitivity and intuition than many women who would dismiss them out of hand. I have learned to discern, and not simply "see." In fact, I have learned that all too often, the unspoken, unacknowledged worldview that underlies my assumptions often contributes to the very problems I seek to solve, and that block me from the Truth I seek.

What do the experiences mean to me

The reality of these experiences has helped me lose my fear of the Dark, validated, beyond a doubt, the existence of the Other Side, and increased my desire to communicate with Spirit as embodied by the Dark Mother, the angels, guardians, guides, and all those with love and concern who seek to cross the veil.

I see my opportunity to travel as an opportunity to learn, gain illumination, and reinforce my commitment to healing—and accepting that I am a healer and a seer. Intimations are not to be dismissed, dreams have to be remembered and written down. I can talk with my father, even though he has made his transition; he is present whenever I wish and he intercedes for me. My ancestors have given me "a charge to keep" in this incarnation. I don't how it all fits together, but I do know that I am willing to show up. I am willing to acknowledge the travail of my ancestors and thank them for choosing to survive. I am willing to divest myself of teachings, ideas, and assumptions that get in the way. I am willing to be honest about what it is I do not know so that I can be taught—even—and perhaps especially—if the Teacher comes as a dark Woman. Ashe.

The Cone of Power: Visions and Manifestations of a Symbol in Western Culture

Vivian Deziak Hahn, M.A.

The terrain of the mysteries is the edge where power encounters power,
for mystery is the arising of powers that are uncharted and untamed,
that will not follow the logic of naked force,
and so act in unexpected ways.
Mystery is surprise.[*]

Introduction: the web of connection and becoming

The creation of the Goddess is a world in motion. Her body is the cone: the effulgent point from which all life flows. She is Shiva dancing, the moment when Mary and the angel Gabriel touch, the bird's song at dawn, the nipple and the baby's mouth sucking. Her vulva is the triangle and the seed—swollen as in preparation for birth. Her energy is movement and form. Inherent in the dazzling black dormancy of life, She moves out like birds flying in "V" formation. Her coiling and uncoiling spiral is the waxing and the waning of the moon, the blueprint in cells, the Crane Dance of Her priestesses. Her opposing and interlocking spirals appear on plaques, altar spaces, dishes, vases, and figurines, signifying the serpentine connection that unifies all life. At times of illness and death, when life's energy slackens, Her whirling and spinning cre-

116

ate a joyous sensation of the triumph of life; She is always becoming. She is the honeycomb, the tracks of deer, and daylight dying. She is the birth-giver, the death-wielder, and the exquisite power of lovemaking. She is the Mother of All. The image of her vulva appears on the walls of caves; human beings painted Her there over thirty thousand years ago, knowing her as Source.

Gradually, the world in which she is known and honored disappears. Her body is dismembered; Her places of worship are destroyed. Her people are vanquished. She who both destroys and regenerates becomes the witch of the night, cavorting with demons and sleeping with the devil. Her Cone, Her Pillar—the symbol of Her power as the life force—becomes the mask, the hood, and the tool of those who seek power over others. Her images are veiled, hidden, consigned to remote corners of the churches of the male god. The breath of god, the word of god, the hand of god, the image of god as judge, censor, conqueror, and divine king now reigns. Her web of connection and becoming breaks apart, leaving fractured minds and tattered souls. But She survives.

This essay explores the historical and religious significance of the cone as a symbol of power within western culture. Human power manifests within cultures in two basic forms—a power-over and a power-with. Power-over is linked with domination and control[1] and is at the heart of all violence, oppression, and war. Power-with is social power—the influence a human being can exert among equals.[2] Power-with is rooted in a power-from-within that appears in the human sense of mastery and the ability to know our needs. As this internal power moves outwards toward a connection with others, it sustains us and allows us not to command, but to influence and suggest and to listen.[3] Power-with was intrinsic to the worldview of the culture of the Great Goddess. The Goddess herself was (and is) a manifestation of the unity of all life.[2] Her power was present in water, stones, animals, trees, mountains, flowers, and humans, and therefore, sacredness—and[3] equality—were evident throughout the entire creation.

The original potency of the symbol of the cone as generative power has been co-opted. Reversing the cone's symbolism as life force and creative power, the agents of the European Inquisition used the cone (the pointed hood-mask) as a symbol of power-*over* in condemning to death thousands of women, Jews, lepers, and others labeled as heretics. Ku Klux Klansmen adopted the symbol of the pointed hood from the Inquisition and used it to commit racial murder. In contemporary times, feminist scholars and neo-pagan priestesses are in the process of reclaiming the ancient meaning of the symbol of the cone.

My relationship with the symbol of the cone began as I traveled to Spain in March 2003 as part of a study tour investigating the culture and images of the dark mother divinity of Africa.

I was particularly interested in seeing two of the most well known black madonnas of Spain—Montserrat and the Virgen del Pilar in Zaragoza—as well as the image of an Iberian priestess or goddess, La Dama de Elche. As I would learn, the image of the divine child sitting on the lap of the Montserrat virgin holds a pine-cone, a cone-related symbol of the generative and creative force of life.[4] The tiny body of the Virgen del Pilar is itself a cone of power; she is draped in a triangular-shaped robe and placed atop a pillar (also a symbol of the life force).

During the tour, I had a frightening yet transforming experience with the cone of power in the medieval Cantabrian town of Santillana del Mar that vividly demonstrated the violent effect of power-*over*. Six women from the tour and I encountered the living history of some of the women of Santillana del Mar. We discovered that many of the women and men of the town had been persecuted and murdered as witches by the Spanish Inquisition. One of the most potent and disturbing images I confronted during the experience was that of the chief inquisitor—a figure in cone-shaped hood—who sat in judgment of the people he condemned to death.

Mesopotamian Shadows: ancient roots of the cone symbol

The symbol of the cone has an ancient history. A 28,000 year-old mammoth ivory pendant-bead found at Dolni Vestonice in Czechoslvakia is carved in the shape of two breasts at the base of a conical neck.[5] An almost identical image painted in ochre red appears on the wall of the prehistoric cave of Le Portel in France (12,000 to 10,000 B.C.E.).[6] The Greek Aphrodite, imaged in her most elemental form, was a white marble cone. Coins from Cyprus, Aphrodite's legendary birthplace, bear images of her shrine at Paphos, showing the conical stone or *betyl*, which "housed" her divine essence.[7] Kings and priests of ancient Sumer and Egypt wore conical-shaped headdresses, which signified their divine status. The Great Goddess was often represented with winged arms and a conical hat and/or robe.[8] The conical or triangle-shaped robe is a distinguishing feature of many of the Black Madonna statues found throughout Europe.

A stunning image of Aphrodite riding on a goose, painted on a Attic cup dating from the 5th century B.C.E., depicts the goddess holding a spiral-shaped vine, out of which sprouts a cone that overlays an image of the crescent moon. Here the heavenly Aphrodite (her garment is studded with stars), as sister to Astarte and daughter of the Neolithic Bird Goddess, holds within her hands the ancient symbols of the divine female as life force; she balances them carefully between the thumb and forefinger of her right hand. Elmer G. Suhr notes that the thumb and forefinger of her left hand are "exactly in the position for drawing fibers of flax or wool" from a distaff,[9] while her right hand reaches upward "for a new supply of fibers."[10] She is "drawing her fibers" from the pregnant, creative energy of the source of life. As cosmic spinner, Aphrodite brings life forth from the whirling, spiraling cone of the moon.

The people of ancient Mesopotamia inserted clay cones into walls of buildings, believing that the cones would bring good fortune to their cities.[11] These fashioned cones were aniconic forms of the generative power of the divine. The moon was believed to possess divine energy in the form of the *pneuma*, and the spiraling rotating motion of the moon's cone-shaped shadow directed the vitalizing force of the *pneuma* toward the earth in the form of rain, dew and mist.[12] If the moon could transmit the essence of life through its cone-shaped shadow, perhaps the same energy could be recreated and reinforced with the shape of the cone.

While the city dweller during the 5th millennium B.C.E. continued to place cones in the walls of city buildings, with the hope of prosperity, the nature of life in the city began to change. The earliest settlements in Mesopotamia were similar to Catal Huyuk in Anatolia (Turkey)—peaceful, egalitarian and matrifocal.[13] The Great Goddess was the supreme deity.[14] With the appearance of urbanization came the formation of larger territorial and political units. The use of irrigation to develop more land for agriculture created both financial and power inequities.[15] Gender, for the first time, was correlated with power or powerlessness.[16] Women lost social status and male deities usurped the power of the female divine. A social system developed that honored power-over above power-from-within and power-with. War became common; the king, the warrior, and the hero appeared as new positions of power and status for men.

The Mesopotamian vision of the cone of the moon as the disseminator of the creative life force—a vision which included the image of the female divine—faded. The power of the god, the warrior, and the hero who seeks power-over others by disdaining the goddess, raping women and conquering and oppressing those who are less strong grew and gradually restructured the world. The cone in the wall—symbol of creativity and prosperity—was forgotten. The cone-shaped nail used to build the king's palace, the pointed sword used to take life, and the peaked hood that masked the identity of the one who condemned became the new shape of power.

In a world dismembered, the cone manifests as a symbol of power-over. The image of the cone appears as the hooded penitent—face hidden by sin—who carries a statue of the sorrowful Virgin Mother or an image of the torn and bloody body of her son. The cone is the grand inquisitor, in black hood and robe, who watches the woman's body burn. The symbol of cone materializes as the pointed hood of the Ku Klux Klansman who wields the power to terrorize and to commit murder.

Inquisitorial Minds: the cone and the witches of santillana del mar

We women sit in a circle. Most of us are tired. We're been traveling long hours on a bus and staying up late. Frictions and tensions have arisen among us. We are beginning to confront what cultivating spirituality among women really means. Some of us have gathered in this circle to process our feelings and to ground and focus our intentions. Earlier in the day, a few of us had walked into town, remarking on the charm of Santillana del Mar, buying earrings in shops and enjoying each other's company. We visited the local church and had discovered a sarcophagus containing the remains of a Christian saint, Juliana. The image on the sarcophagus depicted Juliana with bird's feet and with a chain tied around her waist, with the other end wrapped around the skull of demon. We were intrigued, wondering about Juliana and her story and the imagery associated with her.

The woman who leads the circle asks if we want to try to make contact with Juliana—to ask her about her life and her death. Some of the women are eager, replying quickly in the affirmative. Others remain silent; perhaps they are frightened or skeptical. My own skepticism arises, but I remain silent. Either I am too tired or I don't want to be perceived as a skeptic. Perhaps both. I have participated in this type of "encounter" before and have observed that what most frequently manifests is the overly active human imagination.

The circle leader guides us in a meditation designed to relax us and to bring our minds into an altered state. I sit on the floor next to her, feeling tense, tired, and the stiffness of the muscles in my back. The woman establishes the circle, grounds the energy, and draws the spirit of Juliana in, asking the women to speak about what they are seeing and feeling. Women speak of darkness, a sword, of pain and sadness. I am aware of a tightening sensation around my neck. I attempt to clear my throat several times and take several deep breaths. The feeling of tightness persists and gets stronger; a gurgling sound erupts from my throat. The circle leader is aware of my distress, and I hear her asking us again what we see. Suddenly my inner field of vision is flooded with the image of a huge flock of birds—geese, swans or ducks. They have been startled suddenly and are taking flight. I hear myself ask the women if they see them. The ground is suddenly covered with blood; it's on the straw, in the dirt, everywhere. Do the other women see it? I say again that I see blood everywhere. I am aware that some of the women are crying.

The circle leader touches my shoulder gently. She begins to ground the energy and slowly closes the circle. Afterwards, we speak in the circle about what has taken place. I speak about the choking sensation in my throat and the sense I have that Saint Juliana had been beheaded. Some of the women appear frightened. One traditionally Catholic woman quickly gets up to leave, her daughter following her. Later we hear that the woman had been so unnerved by what had happened that she had fallen on the stairs and cut her head. Another young woman shares that she is too scared to sleep in her room by herself. Feeling guilty for frightening her, I offer to sleep with her. She says she needs some fresh air and wants to go outside. I agree to go with her. Five others from the circle go out with us. We huddle together in front of the hotel, gaze at each other in silence, wondering what to do next. As we try to comfort the frightened young woman, I am trying to make sense of what happened. My rational and logical mind is reeling.

One of the women suggests that we walk up to the church. Perhaps being with Juliana will provide comfort and understanding. We walk the empty cobbled streets, passing the area where earlier we had laughed together and bought souvenirs. Approaching the church, we come to a portion of the street that has sunken down, a grated opening is placed there and water gushes up, flooding the street. There is a narrow street that turns to the right at this point and next to the street, a wall. The circle leader, who works as a psychic, is drawn to this wall and suggests that we all place our hands on it. Immediately we are filled with feelings of intense suffering and pain. I am forced to pull my hands away, the sensation is so strong. What was this place? Something horrible has happened here. One of the more calm and adventuresome of the women decides that she will climb the wall and look. We are frightened and warn her to be careful. She nods her head and disappears around the corner and into the darkness. The rest of us stand waiting, feeling apprehensive. The woman returns in a moment, saying it is far too dark to see anything. I feel a sense of relief. We continue walking up the hill to the church. Once in the courtyard, we discover that the door is closed and bolted shut. It seems that Saint Juliana will be offering us no comfort tonight.

Wiccan practitioner Starhawk perceives groups as entities—as "beings" in and of themselves, with minds, hearts, spirits, energy, and emotions. [17] She notes that when a task needs to be accomplished or work needs to be done each member of a group assumes a specific role. She identifies five major roles that manifest in nonhierarchical groups: the Crow, the Grace, the Dragon, the Snake, and the Spider. [18] Crows represent the direction of the East, the realm of mind and vision; they keep an overview of the group's tasks, they fly high, see far, and suggest new directions. [19] The Graces monitor the group's energy and work to direct and channel it. Representing the South and Fire, the Graces provide the raw energy that allows the group to expand. [20] Dragons represent the Earth and the North. They are nurturing and grounding; they establish and guard the group's boundaries. [21] Snakes see the under-view of the group. They detect feelings and emotions by burrowing into the ground and looking below the surface. They represent the West and the watery element in a group. Snakes shed their skins, and are continually reborn. [22] The spider spins a web that connects points across space, providing the group with a leader who acts as both its center and its spiritual heart. [23]

On this night in Santillana del Mar, the members of our group of "Inquisition Busters" (as I have come to half jokingly call us), functioning in a powerful nonhierarchical manner, assumed our necessary roles as we unwittingly (or not!) embarked on our journey. Psychic Spider served as our leader. She guided us through the process, using her psychic ability to take us into the deep realm of collective human pain. Drawing upon her considerable creative "wit," she was able to bring us home again. Crow-girl, the woman who scaled the wall and was courageous enough to initiate our walk into the darkness, stood often on the edge of the experience, maintaining a somewhat detached and calm perspective. Crow-mother, both a Priestess and a Mason, who also remained at the edges of our experience, reminded us as we approached the wall that it was midnight and Ash Wednesday. "It's the Witching Hour," she said. "And there are seven of us!"

Little Dragon, a woman who had previously identified strongly with the image of the dragon, filled the role of the protector of the group's boundaries. She even referred to herself afterwards as the "prowler," the one who stalked the periphery. Our group contained two Graces—Daughter Grace and Sister Grace. These two women held the energy we encountered and allowed me to embody it, while keeping hold of my "shirt strings." Daughter Grace reached in at the last moment to bring me back, otherwise, I might not be here to write our story. And I? Well, I am Snake—the underbelly of the group, the one who was to be charmed, the one to shed her skin-identity for a short time in order to touch the living soul of herself, or the soul of a woman like herself, who in the past had suffered greatly.

And so we stand in the courtyard of the church, in the darkness, and suddenly, we hear a door slam. A woman is walking toward the wall. She darts down the narrow street and just as quickly emerges again, looking our way; she beckons to us, and then moves rapidly down the street into the darkness. She is an exact replica of our leader, Psychic Spider. One of us says to her, "There's the other you!" We all laugh, but a bit nervously. Psychic Spider tells us that sometimes in her work, her "psychic-double" appears to offer her assistance and guidance.

As I hear Psychic Spider's words, I am drawn—no, pulled—in the direction of the wall and toward the narrow street. With my hands in my pockets and a sense of deep intention, I leave the courtyard. None of the women go with me. I pass the wall where we had felt the pain and I approach and enter the narrow street. One of the women calls my name. I walk onwards, not answering. The street is dark, empty, and silent. As I am halfway down, I hear the women's voices again. One of them is saying, "Where are you going?" I see an arch leading into a courtyard; I pass through it. Sister Grace shouts, "Vivian, you can't go in there. It's somebody's home." I shout back in anger, "This is nobody's home!" Standing at the doorway, I am looking into the darkest room I've ever seen. Crossing the threshold, I feel an incredible coldness and a deep sense of horror. On the ground, in the darkness, are two sacks—glowing and white. One sack, the smaller one, is thrown across the top of the other, sideways, haphazardly. The sacks form the shape of a cross. The pain I feel is indescribable; I am fearful that I will never come out of here alive. The women are calling me, begging me to come out. Sister Grace stands at the threshold, repeating my name. Someone grabs my arm, and I turn to see Daughter Grace with a look of absolute horror in her eyes; tears are streaming down her face. I begin crying now too, sensing her pain and her fear. We hold each other tightly and stumble back across the threshold.

Demon-spirits and suffering souls are everywhere; they fill the courtyard. The demon-spirits want me and the souls need me to hear and to understand their pain. And HE is there too, the inquisitor in his cone-shaped hood, his eyes staring; he is watching and waiting. "Don't you see him?" I shout to the women. Psychic Spider looks to the place where he sits and turns to me, with a quizzical look on her face. "Who's there?" She asks. I suddenly feel as if I am dying; Psychic Spider feels it too, and she shouts for the women to form a circle around me. The demons come closer. I squat on the ground and make grunting noises, birth pangs. Everything is dark and suddenly so very far away. I hear Daughter Grace crying; she is repeating over and over, "Those are my mother's eyes, those are my mother's eyes!" She is looking into mine.

It's totally dark now; I can't breathe. I no longer care. *Something* calls me; I open my eyes. Psychic Spider's face is very close to mine. She is reciting the Lord's Prayer: "Our Father, who art in heaven, hallowed be thy..." I hate her. I glare at her. I want her to stop saying those words. She knows it and keeps on reciting, "Thy kingdom come, thy will be..." I stand up now and Psychic Spider is telling me she wants me to come out of this place with her. I want to say yes, but the demons are close, the souls are grabbing and pulling me; their pain is so strong, searing. "Let's do a strip tease!" says Psychic Spider. "Come on, Vivian, dance with me!" She begins humming the traditional striptease tune, as she pulls her scarf from around her neck and wiggles her body. I begin to laugh and I join in the dance. Together we—the group of women—dance down the street, toward the wall, and back into our lives.

Later, as Psychic Spider and I talk about the experience, she asks me how I feel about having a child out of wedlock. I look at her, stunned. I tell her that thirty-four years earlier—the last time I had been in Spain—I had sat crying in the train station in Barcelona, alone and pregnant, abandoned by the man I had fallen in love with. Psychic Spider shares that what she "saw" during our experience in Santillana del Mar was that I had been a woman condemned by the Inquisition for my sexuality—I had given birth to a child out of wedlock, and that Daughter Grace was that child. In the cold, dark room, in the courtyard, near the wall, I had seen our bodies in the glowing white bags. Psychic Spider tells me that the Inquisition used a co-opted version of Jesus' Lord's Prayer to identify witches. "Heretics" would refuse to recite this prayer. Psychic Spider believed that I would hate her for reciting it, but she hoped that it would make me angry enough to draw me back. It did.

The morning after our experience, Crow-girl, Little Dragon and Daughter Grace returned to the wall and the courtyard. The wall surrounds a building that houses an Inquisition museum; instruments of torture are on display inside it. The dark, small, and cold room I had entered was in the light of day neither small nor dark. It was a large and empty hall, containing no glowing sacks or bodies. But rising above the wall, down the narrow street, by the courtyard where we women did our "sexy" dance back into the world, there is a recreation of the image of the inquisitor. He sits in silence, watching, hidden behind his pointed, cone-shaped hood.

Raising the Cone: reclaiming symbols and bodies

Spiritual teacher Eckhart Tolle believes in the existence of a collective human pain-body, which is the pain that has accumulated in the collective human psyche over thousands of years through disease, torture, war, murder, madness and other factors.[24] Certain races or countries in which extreme forms of strife and violence have occurred possess a heavier collective pain-body.[25] Everyone's personal pain-body is connected with and partakes of the collective pain-body.[26] Tolle also believes that all women are a part of the collective *female* pain-body, which has been created over the centuries by the subjugation of women and by the violence perpetrated against them through slavery, exploitation, rape, and the loss of children.[27]

I believe that the six other women and I, who came into contact with the suffering souls (witches and others persecuted by the Spanish Inquisition), had entered into the collective pain-body of the country of Spain. The husband of one of women of our group, when he was told the story, replied, "I believe that when people have been tortured and murdered in a particular area, their spirits remain there, still suffering and struggling to find peace." Spain's history of the persecution of others—heretics, Jews, lepers, the poor, and Muslims as well as witches—has been long lasting and violent. The Spanish Inquisition, as an instrument of persecution and torture, was not officially abolished until 1834.[28] The pain of those men and women killed by the Inquisition still hovers ominously over the land. Many women on our study tour had unpleasant and/or frightening experiences and feelings of negative energy and pain—in Zaragoza, in Toledo, and, particularly, our group in Santillana del Mar.

During the experience in Santillana del Mar, one of the most powerful moments for me was when Psychic Spider mobilized the other women to form a circle around me. I could feel their protective energy and the power the six mustered to guard me was amazing. The protective energetic cone of power that the women created "met" and warded off the destructive power-over of the Inquisitor, whom I knew wanted me to die, like the others.

One of the most devastating effects of the torture and murder of so many women during the times of the Inquisition was the loss of the ability of women to gather and work together collectively. During the height of the witch-hunts, often out of fear, women turned against each other; women doubted and distrusted other women. Children—often daughters and grand-daughters—accused and testified against their own mothers and grandmoth-ers. One of the Inquisition's greatest "successes" was the destruction of the power of women's communities.

I recall that after we women emerged into the main square after doing our "striptease" out of the narrow street, a car parked at the side of the road flashed its lights and I became frightened again, because I knew they were signaling us that they were still watching. We walked as a group back up to the courtyard of the church and stood there, stunned, still frightened, but feeling happy to be alive. Two men stood at the "wall of pain" talking, laughing, and glancing our way. I pointed to the men and told Psychic Spider that they were still after us. "That couple?" she asked. "That's not a couple." I replied. "It's two men—two inquisitors." Where Psychic Spider and the other women perceived a couple—a man and a woman—I saw two men dressed in clothes of the 16th century and wearing pointed beards similar to those seen on figures in royal portraits. "I have to let them know I'm not afraid anymore!" I told Psychic Spider. "I have to walk down there and look them in the eye." "Yes, okay." She replied. "But we other women will be watching you and protecting." I think that at that moment I smiled for the first time all evening. Walking toward the two men, I glared at them and then walked to the other side of the street and stood facing them. They were laughing at me and mocking me, letting me know that "things" weren't finished yet. But as the other women came walking down the street toward me, the "men" were suddenly gone—a young couple stood kissing by the wall, glancing at me as if I was quite strange.

The work I did to heal my own personal pain-body that night feels immense. I continue to process the impact of the inadvertent suffering I caused "my daughter of the 16th century," when she was killed with me as a "product" of my "sin." We women, either unconsciously or as Psychic Spider believes, by *non*-consciously agreeing to work together as a group of women, were able to generate power-from-within and power-with to reclaim an ancient symbol of the life force—the cone. Using the cone of women's power, we entered into the collective pain of human suffering and began to transform it. Psychic Spider tells me that our work has just begun.

Before leaving Madrid, I visited the Museo Arquelogico Nacional to see La Dama de Elche—the 5th century B.C.E. image of a female figure with a cone-shaped headdress. La Dama's "cone of power" has been traced through Spanish folk culture into contemporary times in the form of the *peineta* or large comb worn by 19th century C.E. Spanish women and by female flamenco dancers. Gimbutas believes that in the goddess culture of Old Europe the comb was also a symbol of the regenerative power of the divine. [29] European peasant women still wear combs for protection and healing. [30] The cone and its affiliated forms, currently *re*appearing in western culture, are symbols of the power-*with* inherent in the creation of the Goddess and remind us of Her capacity as genetrix to give life, to take it—and to renew it ever again.

Notes:

* Starhawk, *Truth or Dare: Encounters with Power, Authority, and Mystery*, (San Francisco: HarperSanFrancisco, A Division of HarperCollins*Publishers*, 1987), 4.

1 Starhawk, *Truth or Dare: Encounters with Power, Authority, and Mystery*, (New York: HarperCollins Publishers, 1990), 9.

2 Ibid.

3 Ibid, 10.

4 Marija Gimbutas, *The Language of the Goddess*, (New York: HarperCollins Publishers, 1991), 321.

5 J. C. Cooper, *An Illustrated Encyclopaedia of Traditional Symbols*, (London: Thames and Hudson, 1978), 42/

6 Buffie Johnson, *Lady of the Beasts: The Goddess and Her Sacred Animals*, (Rochester: Inner Traditions, 1994), 45.

7 Sigfried Giedion, *The Eternal Present: The Beginnings of Art*, (New York: Bollingen Foundation, 1962), 230.

8 Geoffrey Grigson, *The Goddess of Love: The Birth, triumph, death and return of Aphrodite*, (London: Constable and Company, 1976), 157.

9 Jean Markale, *The Great Goddess:Reverence of the Divine Feminine from the Paleolithic to the Present*, (Rochester: Inner Tradtions, 1999), 187.

10 Elmer G. Suhr, *The Spinning Aphrodite: The Evolution of the Goddess from Earliest pre-Hellenic Symbolism through Late Classical Times*, (New York: Helios Books, 1969), 99.

11 Ibid.

12 Ibid, 55.

13 Ibid, 54.

14 Starhawk, *Truth or Dare*, 37.

15 Ibid, 36.

16 Ibid, 38.

17 Ibid, 39.

18 Ibid, 276.

19 Ibid, 277.

20 Ibid, 278.

21 Ibid, 279.

22 Ibid, 277.

23 Ibid, 280.

24 Ibid, 282.

25 Eckhart Tolle, *The Power of Now: A Guide to Spiritual Enlightenment*, (Novato: New World Library, 1999), 138.

26 Ibid.

27 Ibid.

28 Ibid, 139.

29 Henry Kamen, *The Spanish Inquisition: An Historical Revision*, (London: Wedenfeld & Nicolson, 1997), 304.

30 Gimbutas, *Language of the Goddess*, 322.

31 Ibid, 300.

Picasso: The Man Behind Guernica and its Symbols

Karen N. Villanueva, M.A.

To go on a pilgrimage is to open oneself fully to the experience of the moment. This is my once in a lifetime because now is all that there ever is, the only guarantee. As a pilgrim, I was in Madrid at the Museo Nacional Centro de Arte Reina Sofía gazing upon the great work of Pablo Picasso called *Guernica* from every angle. I went back to see it twice. Much has been written regarding the symbolism in the images that Picasso employed: the bull, the horse, woman with dead child, etc. Yet, there has been little investigation into how Picasso saw himself and how this compelled him to respond to the attack upon Guernica. As a supplicant not schooled in the fine arts, I ask who was the man and what was his message.

On February 5, U.S. Secretary of State Colin L.Powell addressed the American people and members of the United Nations from the Security Council Chambers at the U.N. Headquarters in New York. The tapestry of *Guernica* from the estate of Nelson Rockefeller which had hung in the council chambers since 1985 was covered by the "baby-blue banner and the UN logo."[1] The work of art, depicting civilians as the victims of war, had too much in common with our planned assault against Iraq, a parallel that the Bush administration and U.N. officials clearly did not want the public or the media to make.[2] The plan of attack called "Shock and Awe" was aimed at destroying the Iraqi people "physically, emotionally and psychologically."[3] These were the same ideals behind the Nazi bombing of Guernica and the U.S. dropping of atomic bombs over Hiroshima and Nagasaki.[4] We with the power will wield it. We will bully because our might makes us right and we can. The

Bush Administration encourages us to believe that we are liberating the Iraqi people from a ruthless dictator. Death is the ultimate liberation.

Like Bagdad, Guernica (Gernika) is a town of cultural and religious significance to the Basque people with little military strategic value. [5] Basques have long struggled for recognition as an independent people. They speak their own language, Euskara, have long recognized female lines of inheritance in contrast to the rest of Spain, and live by their own legal code, fueros. [6] Guernica is home to the sacred oak, a tree where tradition dictates Basque leaders to pledge their allegiance. It was here on April 26, 1937 at 4:40 p.m., the height of rush hour, that Hitler tested his Condor Legion's "experimental Squadron" and decimated not only the population of this town but many of the recent refugees from the bombed town of Durango. It was Monday, market day, one of the busiest days of the week. [7] Approximately 1,654 people died, one third of the population, and 889 people were wounded. [8] When news of the massacre reached Paris, over one million people flooded the streets in protest. [9] How similar to their reaction over news of the U.S. plans to bomb the people of Iraq.

The targeting of Guernica was not just an attack against the Basque but symbolized the envy, jealousy and hatred of Spanish dictator Francisco Franco and then General Emilio Mola for the richer and more industrialized cities of the Basques and Catalans: Bilbao and Barcelona. [10] Throughout his long life, Franco hated the Basque and Catalan nationalists. [11] The Catalan, too, are a people with their own culture and language, Cataluña, similar to the Oc language, or langue d'Oc, of Provençal France. [12] The vernacular of Oc-speaking Catalan, Cataluña, was noted as barely distinguishable from that spoken north of the Pyrenees, the land where the Kabbalah was cultivated among Jews, Cathars and troubadours alike. [13] Ultimately, the world would soon discover that the Germans were only practicing in Spain for their plans to destroy and dominate Europe and the world.

In January of 1937, Picasso was asked by architect and Catalanista, Josep Lluis Sert, to create a large mural for the Spanish Republican pavilion for the Paris International Exhibition. [14] The Spanish ambassador in Paris desired that the artists of the pavilion demonstrate that the Republic, not Franco and the Nationalists, represent the Spanish people and their accomplishments. [15] Picasso was at first reluctant to accept the commission because of its intended use as a tool of political propaganda and daunting size, 11'6" H x 25'8" L. [16] Yet, he was so moved by the tragedy of Guernica that within six days he began work on the subject, a vision of the horror of that day in shades of gray. Colors that, in my opinion, express that little in this world is black and white; there are often truths behind truths that contradict truths.

From the amount of preliminary work that Picasso put forth, it is obvious that he thought a great deal about the message that he wanted to convey. He completed 45 preliminary studies; there are 7 photographs that document the progression and changes in the painting as he completed it. [17] Dismayed by the rumors that he was sympathetic to Franco and the insurgents, Picasso made the following public statement that clearly expresses the intent of *Guernica*: "How could anybody think for one moment that I could be in agreement with reaction and death?…In the panel on which I am working which I shall call *Guernica*, and in my recent works of art, I clearly express my abhorrence of the military caste which has sunk Spain in an ocean of pain and death…"[18]

Picasso was born Pablo Ruiz Picasso on October 25, 1881.[19] He spent his early years in Málaga, known as the capitol of the Costa del Sol. The port city was founded by the Phoenicians, also known as Canaanites, before siding briefly with Carthage, and before becoming a Roman municipium, a town governed by its own laws. [20] From 711 to 1487, Málaga served as a port city to the Kingdom of Granada, after which it fell to the Christians who laid a four-month siege. [21] The Dark Mother is well known to the people of Málaga. Located in the region of Spain called Andalusia, Málaga and its neighbors boast of high concentrations of the goddess Tanit figures of Carthage. [22] Canaanites, also, were known to have settled many of the areas that later welcomed Israelites, or Jews. [23]

Picasso's father was Don José Ruiz Blasco, an art instructor for most of his life, and museum conservator while they lived in Málaga. [24] His mother was Doña María Picasso y Lopez. She was said to have contributed to Picasso's short stature and dark coloring. [25]

Picasso dropped the traditional, paternal surname, Ruiz, in favor of his mother's maiden name, Picasso. Some have speculated that this was because the name Picasso was of Italian origin, and thus more distinguished than the common Spanish name of Ruiz. [26] Others have speculated that he favored the melodic sound of the alliteration, Pablo Picasso. However, the root of the name Picasso is "pica" meaning spear or lance and that may have had its own appeal to him that I will discuss later. Or perhaps with the name, Picasso, he chose to honor a hidden heritage with a name that pointed to his maternal birthright, Judaism. Jewish birthright is traditionally inherited through the maternal line. To be born a Jew is to be born of a Jewish mother. [27] There are scholars that claim that all the Jewish people left Spain, while others contend that those who were not killed converted, or pretended to convert to Catholicism. It is these, the pretenders, and their descendants with their complex adaptations and secret lives that make up the fabric of Spanish Christian society.

At the age of three Picasso was taken to his first bullfight by his father. [28] The corrida, or bullfight, has a tremendous history in Spain dating back to the Iberians. [29] The practice of the bullfight was reinforced by the Phoenicians, Canaanites, who had established trading posts that later developed into cities such as Malaca, present day Málaga. [30] They worshipped the great bull-god Baal, and brought their cult as well as their trade to Spain. [31] By the time of the invading Romans and their cult of Mithras, worship of the bull was well established in Spain. [32] The tradition of the corrida flourished with the Visigoths as well as the conquering Moors. "Accustomed to hunting the wild boar with javelins and from horseback, the Moors utilized the technique in the corrida as well." [33] The Catholic Church attempted to squelch the practice but found it impossible. So, in the time-honored tradition of the institution of the Catholic church, what could not be destroyed was incorporated. Notably, at the end of the reign of Isabella, Rodrigo Borgia became Pope Alexander VI of Spain. He not only had a love of the corrida but brought it with him to Rome. [34] In present day Spain, every festival of note and feast days of prominent saints are celebrated by the corrida.

Introduced by the Moors, horses are an integral part of the bullfight. After the bull is taunted by the Toreadors to determine his stamina and lassitude, the Picadors enter the arena on horseback. Although padded with protective covering, the horse is often gored to death. As demonstrated in much of his work in the 20's and 30's, the art of the bullfight was to influence Picasso greatly. This may be due in part to sharing the passion with his father. In addition, his love of the corrida may be due to the Phoenician (Canaanite), Jewish and Moorish ancestry he shared with the people of Andalusia.

As a young adult in Barcelona, Picasso was a member of a group of artists and philosophers called Valhalla, the Norse heaven for heroically slain warriors. [35] It is certain that during this time he attended the opera and saw the works of artists such as Wagner at Els Quatre Ghats. It may have been the influence of Wagner that inspired the name of the group. The activities of Valhalla are uncertain, however. It is suspected that they may have had strong interest in the mysteries of Wagner's themes. [36] One of the greatest of Wagner's operas, considered by some, is Parsifal.

Like Parsifal, Picasso may have envisioned himself as the "pure fool," one who lives perfectly in the present with no thought of the past or future. The fool is innocent and open to surprises. His destiny is unknown. [37] This may well explain why Picasso's personal life was fraught with passionate affairs. Also, it explains the childlike nature of his art. The fool of the Tarot corresponds to the number zero. In order to begin an adventure, you must begin at the beginning, and for the mathematician this is Absolute Zero. [38] It is the pure and noble fool, Parsifal, who begins Wagner's opera and finds his way to the castle of the grail, Montsalvat. He must save the King by recapturing the sacred spear (pica) before returning with the wisdom he has attained in the world.

Montserrat, the name so like the grail castle, Montsalvat, was noted as the place that inspired Wagner's Parsifal and the home of the Holy Grail. [39] Surrounded by rocky pinnacles called the "Guardians of the Holy Grail," Montserrat is a monastery outside of Barcelona that was founded after the discovery of "La Morenata", the little brown woman, in a cave in the mountains. She is the Black Madonna of Montserrat. Like many other madonnas found in trees and caves, she refused to be moved and thus, the monastery and church were forced to form around her. Caves are often associated with the Dark Mother. [40] La Morenata is the patron saint of the Catalans. In Medieval times, pilgrims from as far as Cathar country in Provençal France were known to have walked from their homes to see her. [41] She is so important to the people of Catalan that in 1936 she was substituted with a copy and hidden to protect her during the three years of the Spanish civil war. [42] Doubtless, Picasso felt at home with the Dark Mother of the Catalans, so reminiscent of the Canaanite Astarte and Carthaginian Tanit of his native home, Málaga.

Along the pilgrimage route to Santiago de Compostela, we also encounter centers of Kabbalistic learning such as Tudela and Gerona, north of Barcelona. At one point, Gerona boasted of the second largest community of Jews in Spain, second only to Barcelona.[43] The Hermetic and Kabbalistic traditions were absorbed by the mystery schools like the Freemasons, Rosicrucians and many others. [44] Even the cult of Mithras shared the mystery school tradition with exclusively male initiates and seven grades of initiation symbolized by a seven-rung ladder thought to lead to immortality. [45] Author W. Kirk Mac Nulty notes that, "There [was] a rich exchange of ideas among the students of Christian, Muslim and Jewish mysticism during the period of Muslim rule, and with the expulsion of the Jews in 1492 a large volume of Kabbalistic literature was diffused throughout North Africa and Europe." [46]

Kabbalah, also Qabalah and Cabala, is a Jewish mystery school that emerged from the oral wisdom tradition. Much of this wisdom survives as the book called the Zohar. Symbols and imagery are utilized in the Kabbalah to both understand the Divine and to harness this power for one's benefit and use, or the benefit of humankind. Kabbalistic practice is a request for miraculous intervention and the belief that if the proper language and symbol are used it will make it so. Rather than understanding the Divine as an aloof, non-interested being, it is an active force that may be understood by progressing through various stages of learning and meditation. This school of thought seems to have flourished in the 12th and 13th centuries in the Mediterranean areas of Spain, France and Italy, particularly in areas where we find Black Madonnas, Grail lore, Cathars, troubadours and Jews speaking a language known as Oc or Cataluña.

Picasso was probably familiar with Grail history and lore, and familiar with, if not knowledgeable, of esoteric teachings like the Kabbalah, not only because of his family heritage as a Jew and that he was raised in Barcelona, but because of the influence of his friends from Valhalla and his friendship with surrealist writers like Paul Eluard and Georges Bataille. He would have paused to wonder of the power that his name implies. It was known that the relics most sacred to the knights who guarded the grail were the chalice and the spear. [47] As told in John 19:34, one of the Roman soldiers pierced Jesus' side with a spear and from it came blood and water. [48] The grail story reports that this blood and water was captured in the chalice known as the grail. Thus the spear and the cup, or the chalice and blade, are forever linked. The Roman soldier became St. Longinus later in his life.

This spear has been called the "Spear of Longinus," "Spear of Destiny," "Holy Spear," and "Bleeding Lance." [49] Wisdom, it has been said, is the holy spear itself. It was lost to the Knights of the Grail but attainable through the "pure fool." [50] Spears from Tudela were highly prized. Perhaps this was because it was a City known for its Kabbalistic teaching. [51]

Possession of the sacred spear was said to endow a man with the power to rule the world. [52] Beginning with Herod the Great and throughout history, the spear has passed from leaders like Emperors Constantine and Theodosius to Charlemagne, Frederick II, and Kaiser Wilhelm before coming to its present resting place in the Hoffburg Museum in Vienna, Austria. [53]

Hitler was well versed in the esoteric knowledge of Judaism, the Kabbalah. For this reason, he sought the spear, and even the Ark of the Covenant. When his forces overtook Austria, he acquired the sacred spear and had it shipped to

Nuremberg. General Patton re-acquired it when the U.S. 7th Army liberated Austria and eventually returned it to the Hoffburg Museum.[54]

Central to the teachings of the Kabbalah is the Tree of Life. The tree consists of ten branches called sephirots. The sephirots are the ten divine structures that bring the world into being and compose the different levels of reality.[55] The great Hebrew and Jewish Mystical School scholar, Gershom Scholem, states that the word sephirot actually means sapphire and that there are ten jewels on the tree.[56] This is very much like the three jewels of Buddhism. Yet the more widely held definition is that sephirot means number.[57]

The painting, *Guernica*, may be divided into ten unique figures. These ten figures correspond to the ten sephirots in the following way:

<u>Bird</u>. The first of the symbols utilized by Picasso is a bird. The first of the ten sephirots, Kether, the source of all that is, a point that is just a beginning. If this bird is a dove, then it may represent the Holy Ghost, defined by Alexander Crowley as the phallus in its most sublimated form.[58] The dove is also an ancient pagan yonic emblem.[59] It is sacred to Astarte, Cybele, Isis, Venus, Juno, Mylitta and Aphrodite.[60] The dove represents wisdom, is a messenger of divine will, and signifies the activity of God.[61]

If the bird is a phoenix, then it may represent the resurrection of life, just as the phoenix arises from the flames of its dead parent.[62] Just as the soul is divine because it is neither male nor female but both, so is the phoenix divine.[63] If the bird is a vulture, then it may symbolize "the disintegrative processes which accomplish good while apparently destroying."[64] The bird may also resemble the swan shot by Parsival in the land of the Grail and is defined as ecstasy.[65] The Holy Grail, thought of as pure understanding, and the Holy Spear, wisdom, are said to be eliminated by perfect ecstasy.[66]

<u>Bull</u>. Early astronomers determined that it took 360 days for the Sun to circle the Earth. They hid this knowledge in their name for God, Mithras, the bull god, whose name adds up to 360 in Greek gematria.[67] The Sun is the father.[68] The second symbol utilized by Picasso, the bull, corresponds to the second sephirot, Chokmah, the father who is wisdom. The bull is a powerful phallic image of the paternal creative force.[69] In *Guernica*, the bull appears to encircle and protect the woman with the dead child in her arms.

<u>Woman with Dead Child</u>. There is no image that represents motherhood more clearly than the suffering of this woman holding her dead child. The third sephirot is Binah translated from the Bahir language as "mother of the world."[70] Mother is understanding and intelligence. She is intuition. She is the cup, the Holy Grail.

Horse. Picasso utilized the image of the horse to connote human suffering. The horse has long been used to symbolize the body of a human being carrying the weight of the spirit.[71] In contrast, the human spirit is burdened by the maintenance of the material personality.[72] The fourth sephirot, Chesed, means mercy, forgiveness and loving-kindness. This spirit of this sephirot was killed as if in the corrida by the destructive power of Hitler's forces. The horse, a mystical animal said to bring good fortune, is destroyed.[73]

Fleeing Woman. Picasso chose a fleeing woman to depict the fifth sephirot, Geburah, the first crisis. Geburah is the stage of severity and judgment.[74] The fleeing woman also represents the first of the three mothers: Mem, Shin and Aleph respectively water, fire and air.[75]

Warrior. The open eyes of the dead warrior foreshadow his intent to rise again.[76] He is the son. As the sixth sephirot, Tipareth, he represents truth, beauty and enlightenment.[77] Picasso has depicted him as dismembered and drawing a broken sword hilt. He reminds us that all that was good has ended in the destruction of Guernica but good will come again.

Light Bulb. The Ain Soph Aur is called the "Limitless Light." "If there is anything except nothing, it must exist within this 'Boundless Light.'"[78] The light is the blazing star, glory. It reveals the entire universe as it is in reality.[79] The seventh sephirot, Netzach, is drawn as a light bulb illuminating the scene of chaos.

Woman Fleeing Burning Building. The second of the three mothers is Shin, fire. Picasso draws her trying to escape a building engulfed in flames. She is the eighth sephirot, Hod. Her face expresses the horror of the comprehension that she is unlikely to survive.

Woman with Lamp. The third of the three mothers is Aleph, air. On her head, she wears the Mithraic cap, a symbol of freedom from materialism.[80] In her hand with outstretched arm, she bears the Lamp of Hermes to gain entrance to the secret house of wisdom.[81] Without the ever-burning lamp, the mysteries of the universe can never be solved.[82] The foundation of all things is three and the ninth sephirot, Yod, holds the power of three times three.[83] She looks upon the carnage with open-mouthed horror and the wisdom that no good can ever come from this devastation.

Flower. The tenth and final sephirot is manifestation, Malkuth. It is the daughter who brings the completion of creation to the next phase, beginning all over again. She is the Earth, the body and the hope of the next generation. She is barely visible in the painting and appears to bloom from the hand of the warrior, the son. It is the son who makes the world receptive for the daughter. The flower symbolizes beauty, resurrection and immortality. [84]

During a career that spanned almost ninety-two years, whenever Picasso was asked about the meaning or the significance of the drawings in *Guernica*, he was vague. Perhaps this was due in part to some vow that he took to some mystery school, perhaps Valhalla. Once when asked to explain his symbolism, Picasso remarked, "It isn't up to the painter to define the symbols. Otherwise it would be better if he wrote them out in so many words! The public who look at the picture must interpret the symbols as they understand them." [85]

It is my supposition that we as the general public were never the intended recipients of the message of the painting. If we derive pleasure or feel that we understand it, so much the better for us. The terror and horror are clearly there for all. However, Picasso was making a statement, sending a message that could be understood by someone. So, who was his audience? Who was meant to understand?

He knew that the symbolism was too sophisticated for Francisco Franco so he created *The Dream and the Lie of Franco*. This was a work that was more a caricature, or cartoon, than artistic work with a title and message that no one could doubt. *Guernica* was created to make a statement against a more sophisticated foe, Adolf Hitler, a bully and one of those who wielded power just because he could. I further believe that *Guernica* is a form of magical Kabbalah that I am not equipped to fully explain. Only Picasso could explain it and he chose not to. I also believe that in the end Picasso was satisfied that his message was received. After all, in the end, right won against might. Hitler was defeated. Are we as a nation comfortable with being the might as opposed to the right?

Notes:

1 The covering of the tapestry was so conspicuous as to merit note in the conservative newspaper, *The Washington Times*. Pisik, Betsy, "U.N. Report: The Picasso Cover-up," *The Washington Times*, February 3, 2003. http://washingtontimes.com/world/20030203–13680812.htm

2 Walsh, David, "U.N. conceals Picasso's 'Guernica' for Powell"s presentation," *World Socialist Web Site*, February 8, 2003, published by the International Committee of the Fourth International (ICFI). http://www.wsws.org/articles/2003/feb2003/guer-f08.shtml

3 The article quotes co-author Harlan K. Ullman from his Pentagon's National Defense University book on "Rapid Dominance" strategy. Smith, Gar, "Shock and Awe: Guernica Revisited," *AlterNet.org*, a project of the Independent Media Institute, January 27, 2003. http://www.alternet.org/story.html?StoryID=15027

4 Ibid. It is interesting to note that this article which clearly compares Guernica's bombing to the planned bombing of Iraq was written before the Colin Powell speech and the covering of the *Guernica* tapestry at U.N Headquarters.

5 Ibid.

6 Kurlansky, Mark, The Basque History of the World. New York: Penguin Books, 1999. p. 36.

7 Beevor, Antony, The Spanish Civil War. New York: Penguin Books, 1982. p. 166.

8 Ibid.

9 Walsh.

10 Kurlansky, p. 197.

11 Ibid. p.194.

12 Partington, Helen (project editor) et al, Spain. London: Insight Guides, 2002. p. 399.

13 Menocal, María Rosa, *The Ornament of the World: How Muslims, Jews and Christians created a culture of tolerance in Medieval Spain.* Boston: Little, Brown and Company, 2002. p. 221.

14 Mallen, Enrique, *The On-Line Picasso Project*, Department of Spanish Studies, Texas A&M University and the Picasso Museum, Málaga, Spain. http://www.tamu.edu/mocl/picasso, "January, 1937."

15 Ibid.

16 Ibid.

17 Hart, David, "Study Guides on War Art: Pablo Picasso (1881–1973): From the Spanish Civil War to Vietnam," *Responses to War Web Site*, August 26, 1999. http://www.arts.adelaide.edu. au/personal/Dhart/ResponsesToWar/Art/StudyGuides/Picasso.html

18 Blunt, Anthony, Picasso's Guernica. London: Oxford University Press, 1969. p. 9.

19 Walsh.

20 Partington, p. 226.

21 Ibid.

22 Birnbaum, Ph.D., Lucia Chiavola, *Dark Mother: African origins and godmothers.* Lincoln: Authors Choice Press, 2001. p. 130.

23 Ibid. p. 215.

24 Mallen, "October 25, 1881."

25 Ibid.

26 Ibid.

27 Unterman, Alan, *Dictionary of Jewish Lore & Legend.* London: Thames and Hudson, 1991. p. 104.

28 The Public Broadcasting Service, Barry Stoner, exec. Prod, Suzanne Duroux, writer, "Treasures of the World: Stories Behind Masterworks of Art & Nature," "Guernica: Testimony of War," "Questions of Meaning." http://www.pbs.org/treasuresoftheworld/a_nav/guernica_nav/gnav_level_1/5meaning_guerfrm.html

29 Conrad, Jack Randolph, *The Horn and the Sword: The history of the Bull as symbol of power and fertility.* New York: EP Dutton and Company Inc, 1957. p. 161.

30 Ibid. p. 162.

31 Ibid.

32 Ibid. p. 164.

33 Ibid. p. 167.

34 Ibid. p. 174.

35 Harris, Mark, "Wagner and Picasso," *The Picasso Conspiracy web site*, 1996. http://web.org.uk/picasso

36 Ibid.

37 Godino, Jessica and Lauren O'Leary, The World Spirit Tarot. St. Paul: Llewellyn Publications, 2001. p. 2.

38 Crowley, Aleister, (The Master Therion), *The Book of Thoth: A short essay on the Tarot of the Egyptians (Being the Equinox Volume III No. V)*. York Beach: Weiser Books, 2000 (originally published in 1944). P. 12.

39 Ellis, Havelock, *The Soul of Spain (with illustrations)*. Boston: Houghton Mifflin Company, 1931. p. 369.

40 Birnbaum, Ph.D., p. 93.

41 Ibid. p. 228.

42 Albareda, Anselm M. (nueva edicion, revisada y ampliada por Josep Massot I Muntaner), Historia de Montserrat. Montserrat: Publicaciones de L'Abadia de Montserrat, 1974. p. 129.

43 Scholem, Gershom (edited by R.J. Zwi Werlowsky, translated from the German by Allan Arkush), *Origins of the Kabbalah*. New Jersey: The Jewish Publication Society, Princeton University Press, 1987 (originally published in 1962). P. 365.

44 MacNulty, W. Kirk, *Freemasonry: A journey through ritual and symbol*. London: Thames and Hudson, 1991. p. 11.

45 Harris, Mark, "The Mithraic Cult," *The Picasso Conspiracy web site*, 1996. http://web.org.uk/picasso

46 MacNulty, p. 12.

47 Winkler, Franz E. (narrative reductions of the operas by M.G.H. Gilliam), *For Freedom Destined: Mysteries of man's evolution in the mythology of Wagner's Ring operas and Parsifal*. Garden City: Waldorf Press, 1974. p. 75.

48 *New American Standard Bible*. Nashville: Thomas Nelson Publishers, 1977.

49 Tucker, Suzetta, "Spear or Lance: Flow of Blood & Water," *Suzetta's Christian Legends & Symbols site*, 1998. http://ww2.netnitco.net/users/legend01/spear.htm and Loeffler, Ron, "The Spear of Longinus," *Lazy Boy's Rest Stop site*, 1998. http://sxws.com/charis/relics8.htm

50 Jones, Charles Robert Stansfield (a companion of the Holy Grail sometimes called Frater Achad), *The Chalice of Ecstacy: being a magical and qabalistic interpretation of the drama of Parzival*. Chicago: Yogi Publication Society, 1923. p. 16.

51 Kahane, Henry and Renée Kahane in collaboration with Angelina Pietrangeli, *The Krater and the Grail: Hermetic Sources of the Parzival*. Urbana: University of Illinois Press, 1965. p. 125.

52 Loeffler, Ron, "The Spear of Longinus," *Lazy Boy's Rest Stop site*, 1998. http://sxws.com/charis/relics8.htm

53 Ibid.

54 Ibid.

55 Unterman, p. 175.

56 Scholem argues that, "The word is not derived from safar, to count, but from sappir, sapphire. They are thus sapphire reflections of the divinity, and Psalm 19:2: 'The heavens declare the glory of God,' is interpreted by the

author in accordance with this etymology: 'the heavens shine in the sapphirine splendor of the glory of God,'" p. 81.

57 Crowley, p.16.

58 Ibid. p. 56.

59 Hall, Manley P. *The Secret Teachings of All Ages* (The Diamond Jubilee Edition.) Los Angeles: The Philosophical Research Society, 2000. p. LXXXIX.

60 Ibid.

61 Ibid.

62 Kahane, p. 108.

63 Kahane, p. 109.

64 Hall, p. LXXXIX.

65 Jones, p. 5.

66 Ibid. p. 36.

67 Crowley, p. 27.

68 Ibid. p. 29.

69 Hall, p. XCI.

70 Scholem, p. 75.

71 Hall, p. XCII.

72 Ibid.

73 Gomariz, p. 75.

74 Crowley, p. 18.

75 Ibid.

76 Gomariz, p. 285–6.

77 Taken from notes from a lecture delivered by Pamela Eakins, M.A., author of *Tarot of the Spirit*, on April 28, 2003 at the California Institute of Integral Studies.

78 Crowley, p. 13.

79 MacNulty, p. 18.

80 Harris, "The Mithraic Cult," and Hall, p. CXXI.

81 Hall, p. CXXI.

82 Ibid.

83 Eakins, M.A. lecture.

84 Gomariz, p. 181.

85 The Public Broadcasting Service.

Bibliography

Albareda, Anselm M. (nueva edicion, revisada y ampliada por Josep Massot I Muntaner), *Historia de Montserrat*. Montserrat: Publicaciones de L'Abadia de Montserrat, 1974.

Beevor, Antony, *The Spanish Civil War*. New York: Penguin Books, 1982.

Birnbaum, Ph.D., Lucia Chiavola, *Dark Mother: African origins and godmothers*. Lincoln: Authors Choice Press, 2001.

Blunt, Anthony, *Picasso's Guernica*. London: Oxford University Press, 1969.

Celdrán, Pancracio, *Creencias Populares (Costumbres, Manías y Rarezas: con su explicaci n, historia y origen)*. Madrid: EDIMAT Libros, 2000.

Conrad, Jack Randolph, *The Horn and the Sword: The history of the Bull as symbol of power and fertility*. New York: EP Dutton and Company Inc, 1957.

Crowley, Aleister, (The Master Therion), *The Book of Thoth: A short essay on the Tarot of the Egyptians (Being the Equinox Volume III No. V)*. York Beach: Weiser Books, 2000 (originally published in 1944).

Daix, Pierre, *Picasso*. London: Thames and Hudson, 1965.

Ellis, Havelock, *The Soul of Spain (with illustrations)*. Boston: Houghton Mifflin Company, 1931.

Godino, Jessica and Lauren O'Leary, *The World Spirit Tarot*. St. Paul: Llewellyn Publications, 2001.

Hall, Manley P. *The Secret Teachings of All Ages* (The Diamond Jubilee Edition.) Los Angeles: The Philosophical Research Society, 2000.

Harris, Mark, "Hitler & the Spear," *The Picasso Conspiracy web site*, 1996. http://web.org.uk/picasso

_____, "The Mithraic Cult," *The Picasso Conspiracy web site*, 1996. http://web.org.uk/picasso

_____, "Wagner and Picasso," *The Picasso Conspiracy web site*, 1996. http://web.org.uk/picasso

Jones, Charles Robert Stansfield (a companion of the Holy Grail sometimes called Frater Achad), *The Chalice of Ecstacy: being a magical and qabalistic interpretation of the drama of Parzival*. Chicago: Yogi Publication Society, 1923.

Kahane, Henry and Renée Kahane in collaboration with Angelina Pietrangeli, *The Krater and the Grail: Hermetic Sources of the Parzival*. Urbana: University of Illinois Press, 1965.

Kurlansky, Mark, *The Basque History of the World*. New York: Penguin Books, 1999.

Leal, Paloma Esteban, *Guernica*. Madrid: ALDEASA, 2001.

Loeffler, Ron, "The Spear of Longinus," *Lazy Boy's Rest Stop site*, 1998. http://sxws.com/charis/relics8.htm

MacNulty, W. Kirk, *Freemasonry: A journey through ritual and symbol*. London: Thames and Hudson, 1991.

Mallen, Enrique, *The On-Line Picasso Project*, Department of Spanish Studies, Texas A&M University and the Picasso Museum, Malaga, Spain. http://www.tamu.edu/mocl/picasso

Menocal, María Rosa, *The Ornament of the World: How Muslims, Jews and Christians created a culture of tolerance in Medieval Spain*. Boston: Little, Brown and Company, 2002.

Partington, Helen (project editor) et al, *Spain*. London: Insight Guides, 2002.

Pisik, Betsy, "U.N. Report: The Picasso Cover-up," *The Washington Times*, February 3, 2003. http://washingtontimes.com/world/20030203–13680812.htm

The Public Broadcasting Service, Barry Stoner, exec. Prod, Suzanne Duroux, writer, "Treasures of the World: Stories Behind Masterworks of Art & Nature," "Guernica: Testimony of War," "Questions of Meaning." http://www.pbs.org/treasuresoftheworld/a_nav/guernica_nav/gnav_level_1/5meaning_guerfrm.html

Scholem, Gershom (edited by R.J. Zwi Werlowsky, translated from the German by Allan Arkush), *Origins of the Kabbalah*. New Jersey: The Jewish Publication Society, Princeton University Press, 1987 (originally published in 1962).

Sinclair, Andrew, *The Discovery of the Grail*. London: Century, 1998.

Smith, Gar, "Shock and Awe: Guernica Revisited," *AlterNet.org*, a project of the Independent Media Institute, January 27, 2003. http://www.alternet.org/story.html?StoryID=15027

Tucker, Suzetta, "Spear or Lance: Flow of Blood & Water," *Suzetta's Christian Legends & Symbols site*, 1998. http://ww2.netnitco.net/users/legend01/spear.htm

Unterman, Alan, *Dictionary of Jewish Lore & Legend*. London: Thames and Hudson, 1991.

Von Eschenbach, Wolfram (translated by A.T. Hatto), *Parzival*. New York: Penguin Books, 1980.

Wagner, Richard (opera guide series editor: Nicholas John), *Parsifal*. New York: Riverrun Press, 1986.

Walsh, David, "U.N. conceals Picasso's 'Guernica' for Powell's presentation," *World Socialist Web Site*, February 8, 2003, published by the International Committee of the Fourth International (ICFI). http://www.wsws.org/articles/2003/feb2003/guer-f08.shtml

Winkler, Franz E.(narrative reductions of the operas by M.G.H. Gilliam), *For Freedom Destined: Mysteries of man's evolution in the mythology of Wagner's Ring operas and Parsifal*. Garden City: Waldorf Press, 1974.

New American Standard Bible. Nashville: Thomas Nelson Publishers, 1977.

Sardinia: Land of Dea Madre

Leslene della Madre

I have been back from my study trip to Sardinia and Italy for over a month now. As I re-settle into my familiar life, I feel different. Traveling to lands and sacred sites where evidence of the Goddess is irrefutable gives me a new spark and added hope. Since these times in which we live are indeed perilous, as the global wanton dis-ease of the hatred of women spreads, going unnamed and unnoticed, while simultaneously claiming victory as the number-one most inhumane, degrading, violent, deadly, destructive, disastrous and unspeakably painful force on our planet, I felt nurtured by the living presence of the Great Mother, Dea Madre, in Sardinia.

When one has an opportunity (and I am fully aware that this opportunity is not afforded most people in the world, therefore, I am deeply and profoundly grateful for it in my life) to stand on and touch the Motherland where her children lived in complete and total respect for her presence and abundant bounty, one can experience a profound change at a cellular level. While I believe this same consciousness existed here in the soil of my birth (USA), there is something tangible still existing in Sardinia, an island off the coast of Italy, thought by some to be Atlantis, whose rugged and serene shores are graced by the turquoise-sapphire waters of the Mediterranean. Sardinia her-self *is* the Great Mother. Her immense beauty and great diversity—oak cork groves, stunning grottos sheltering millions of years-old stalagmites, mysteri-ously shaped granite rocks carved by the mistral winds of time, millennia-old olive trees, brilliant red poppies dancing among ancient ruins, stunning ances-tral triangle wells of the Goddess, Neolithic sacred sites, beehive shaped rock-hewn structures, uterine shaped giant tombs, and ancient Goddess figu-rines—have given her the name "Dea Madre", or Goddess Mother.

Because Westerners, white ones in particular, have generally not been raised with the lineages and legacies of our ancient ancestors, many of us are bereft of a true deep connection to the wisdom of the mother—as if we are cast adrift floating on a turbulent sea waiting for rescue, not knowing our own plight. In Sardinia "Dea Madre" lives in the hearts of the people—she is a primal living legacy. Here in the USA, Goddess reality is usually marginalized into some sort of "esoteric feminism", suggesting that feminism itself is a nonviable world-view. Nothing could be more viable. In Sardinia, everyone seems to know Dea Madre. Even though Christianity made its arrogant presence known in Sardinia, it did not entirely usurp the pagan/goddess reality it encountered. To this day, in some parts of the interior, people practice earth-worship and paganism, maintain a form of matriarchal family structure, hold land in common and pass on healing ways through the oral lineages of women.

I asked our guide about the rich Italian *strega* (witch) tradition. He replied that *strega* has a reputation like witch does in our culture—something bad and scary, quite similar to the demonizing of women healers in patriarchy, as in the inquisition. I was saddened to encounter this reality. It shows the presence of the ubiquitous layer of patriarchal domination that we must eradicate. Even though I was sad about yet another way in yet another place of the normalized disrespect of women, I was nonetheless happy to hear what he had to say about the Sardinian women living deep in the interior. He spoke of female healers in a very respectful way. He told us the Sardinian women healers, known as *majarzas,* keep paganism alive and do not accept money for their services. He was proud to report this—proud to be Sardinian where paganism/earth spirituality is still a way of life for some, and very clear about communicating that Christianity had not taken the earth out of his people.

Tracking the African roots of the Goddess was the focus of our study trip, organized by feminist cultural historian, Lucia Chiavola Birnbaum, whose theory about African migrations and return Semitic migrations found validation as we uncovered crucial evidence she identifies as central to her theory. For instance, we visited ancient Neolithic burial sites, like the necropolis of *Montessu*, circa 3500 BCE—graves cut into the hillside with spirals and pubic V's etched in stone, flushed with red ochre and the Dea Madre carved into rock (excitedly pointed out to us by a tour guide who was just leaving the site who wanted to make sure we saw her. His words about her came off his lips as easily and as naturally as a simple greeting. Not only was I stunned by her carved image in the rock, I was also stunned by his "of course, there is Dea

Madre, you must see her" passionate manner. A man, no less—a man not threatened nor in competition with the Goddess Mother. That, in and of itself, was also a remarkable experience). Lucia's "theory" (I personally don't view this as a theory at all, but rather irrefutable fact), explicitly explained in her book, *dark mother, african origins and godmothers*, posits that African migrants traversed every continent of the globe, taking with them the values of a dark woman deity—equality, nurturance and justice with compassion—some 50,000 years BCE. We visited other sacred sites confirming this—the likes of which I did not know before going to Sardinia. Some of the iconic Goddess Mother imagery bears a likeness to the *Cycladic* Goddess imagery, and some of it I had never seen before, though the corpulent round shape of her was very familiar to me from my travels to other sacred places in Europe, and through the work of the late eminent arecheomythologist, Marija Gimbutas, as well as through other feminist researchers and scholars like Monica Sjoo and Barbara Mor.

Structures, said to be constructed circa 1500 BCE by the mysterious *Nuragic* civilization (a Bronze age culture from 1500–500 BCE are large stone bee-hive like structures. There are several thousand of these structures throughout Sardinia, and this culture is the subject of much debate.), a sacred well renamed by Christians as St. Cristina's, took our breath away. There in the countryside was this magnificent sacred 3500 year-old ritual well, its triangular/yonic opening carved into the earth with steps leading down to the sacred waters of the goddess. To us, it was unmistakably a well constructed in the shape of Tanit, the North African goddess of Carthage, widely known throughout the ancient Mediterranean. The stairs descend to a small pool of water, held by a large rounded stone-hewn structure resembling a uterus deep within the earth. Looking up through the uterus-shape one could see spirals of light winding to the top where a perfectly round opening emerges above ground. At the equinox, the sun's rays penetrate the triangle, touching each step as the light meets the sacred mirror waters within the body of the mother, reflecting directly up through the womb-opening at the top at ground level. Every 18 ½ years the moon, at the solstice, on her path of descent, is mirrored in the circular opening, her light bouncing off the sacred water within, traveling up the stairs, emerging from the yonic gateway at ground level. This sacred place is indeed an amazing feat of astronomical architecture. This year, 2004, the moon will work her magic at this most holy well at the time of the winter solstice. I could feel the presence of Dea Madre as I sat at the edge of the stairs, witnessing the dripping water from the uterine wall of stone, scooping the precious water in my hand and anointing myself with it. I could feel the deep veneration and peace of her wisdom and the very ancient, global, yoni-versal (meaning the "song of the yoni"—from my perspective, a truly wonderful way to perceive the "universe") presence of her being.

After such an experience, I was shocked to hear a male tourist view the well and exclaim "phallic" something. Though I don't know exactly what he was saying, as he was speaking Italian, I could feel his lack of understanding at what he was viewing. I felt deeply protective, and felt a call to educate. I went to the small information sign posted to the side of the well, and spoke to the woman who had been with him (the man had apparently gone off somewhere else) and told her that it was not a phallic site at all, that it was a sacred site of Dea Madre, whose likeness was shown on the sign. She listened to my English as best she could, and I felt that we had an understanding that women are sometimes able to share regardless of cultural and linguistic differences. It is common to find a strong male bias in archeological explanations, both in scholastic writing, in museums and at sacred sites, so why wouldn't the man have thought this to be another "god/he" place? However, I remain impressed by the general acknowledgment of Dea Madre in Sardinia. A recent publication about this sacred well, *Il tempio a pozzo di Santa Cristina*, by Franco Laner, which I bought at the small on-site gift shop, speaks to the goddess mother symbolism of Tanit. Thank Goddess.

As we wound our way through the pristine beauty of the countryside of Sardinia, we stopped at archeological sites and museums that further validated the evidence of Dea Madre as well as the presence of African influence. For me, this tour was more than an academic interest. It was a deepening of my connection to the understanding of ancestral origins, sacred earth spirituality, reclaiming the true religion of our planet, restoring feminine power to its rightful place as well as uncovering the layers of truth smothered by the patriarchal lies of his-story. Entering a church in the capital of Sardinia, Cagliari, I was completely taken aback by the deep ebony statue of a nude African tribal woman resting in the corner to the left of the front entrance. Her presence was totally astonishing. The explanation was that St. Augustine, to whom the church is dedicated, was African, and I might add, a terrible misogynist. And yet, here in the house of "god" was this African woman divinity. I felt the church was really hers. There were also many symbols of female divinity and paganism, such as a carved snake coiled around the base of a pedestal, spiral and yonic motifs on altar boxes and remarkable black madonnas.

Black madonnas are plentiful in Sardinia. Lucia's observation is that black madonnas appear along African migration routes. Patriarchal explanations say they are black because they are reflecting the fact that they were carved from wood, or that they are covered with smoke from a fire. However, when I stand in the presence of a black Madonna, I can feel her ancient origins wearing the garb of Christian co-option. I have felt this before in a church in Malta. In one church we came across a Dutch artist whose particular area of interest was Ethopia. He had a display of his art depicting the black Madonna amidst her people—it was so inspiring to me that I bought one of his vibrant and brightly colored paintings: the black Madonna at Pentecost surrounded by shining, adoring African faces. To me, his rendition of the Madonna holds within it the memory of the very ancient dark mother of all (see my article *Luminous Dark Mother* at www.awakenedwoman.com under my old name, Leslie McIntyre). The adoration in the eyes of the people he painted glows with the same deep love one can witness between mother and child.

Many places in Sardinia abound with tales of miracles of the Madonna. Even though my interest usually circles around more ancient cultures, I found myself completely amazed at the religious focus on Dea Madre in her contemporary form as Mother Mary within the more christianized places of Sardinia. The focus was not on Jesus—it was on the feminine—the mother, Dea Madre. In one small sanctuary we visited, we found a rosary in the gift shop in the shape of the biological symbol of the female! It was reminiscent of Tanit, as the ancient memory of the Goddess appeared before us in this form. We were all stunned, astonished, moved. And needless to say, many of us purchased the rosary. The picture on the little card tucked in the pocket of the carrying case is a black Madonna.

In many churches of the Black Madonna, and no doubt, churches in general, there are traces of early paganism, Goddess spirituality and earth-worship. We saw amazing black stone spiral pillars surrounding black Madonnas, yonic symbols, spiral motifs, snakes, rosettes, statues of nurturing women, and folk art. In Rome, I was deeply struck by a magnificent large stained-glass window of three honeybees, well known to be sacred to the Goddess, particularly in pre-patriarchal Crete and the Mediterranean. Honeybees are a cooperative matristic society, something we could all stand to learn from and remember from our ancestors. There they were, in great colored-glass beauty, emanating the radiance of the goddess as the light of the sun held them in her warm embrace. This church, as are so many, was built on a holy goddess site of the ancient Near-Eastern Goddess, Cybele.

In one church I visited, I had a very unusual experience. Some churches have a place where one can purchase religious art—postcards, iconography, posters, and rosaries. When I went to pay for some postcards, the elderly man behind the counter came around and spoke to me in excited Italian, which I didn't understand. He beckoned me to sit down, and kissed me on both cheeks. He gifted me a large poster of Mary and a card with a picture of St. Monica, the African-born mother of St. Augustine, with a poem titled "Prayer for Mothers." I couldn't help but feel that he knew on some level I was a Goddess Mother devotee, a mother myself, and that Dea Madre, Mary, St. Monica and myself were all the same Mother. I also felt he had a deep reverence for mothers in general, which is rare, and had absolutely no shame in expressing his true and deep veneration of the Goddess to me. Though he probably did not use the word "Goddess", his sharing about her was unmistakable.

Visiting the Villa Giulia Etruscan Museum in Rome was a very interesting experience. After having seen the ancient tomb of the "Giants", *Coddu Vecchu*, a *Nuragic* megalithic monument in Sardinia resembling a large uterus with a yonic entrance carved in stone in the front, I was deeply impressed by the people who built such a structure. I was then amazed to see hand-fashioned terra cotta uteri resting on the shelves of artifacts from the Etruscan culture in the museum in Rome. The mysterious Etruscans, inhabiting northern Italy somewhere between 900–800 BCE, were a pre-Indo European culture favoring egalitarianism far more than the Greek and Roman world. I felt I was seeing once again another thread of the ancient Mother Goddess as she wove her way through the chthonic, psycho-spiritual, biological flowing memory-field of her many children, first from Africa to the rest of the world.

The actual building of yonic/womb/tomb structures and the handcrafting of clay wombs by peoples from these two different cultures spanning hundreds of years reveal a definite message for anyone willing to see. Upon viewing the clay uteri, I remembered that my friend had previously pointed out to me a famous and unusual swaddled baby Jesus figure in a church we had visited. It struck me that the swaddling looked very much like the clay uteri I had viewed in the museum. Perhaps the swaddling was symbolic of the mother's womb. Viewing the clay forms also gave me pause for reflection on the great stone beehive type structures of the *Nuragi*. My mind swirled with pictures of honeybees, beehives, and the bee-body shape of the clay uteri. I could feel a kind of ancient intuitive connectedness with the ancestors across time.

Because I was on a spiritual pilgrimage paying homage to the Goddess Mother, which is my passion, I was deeply impacted by the patriarchal split I experienced as well. This split is everywhere—including deep within our own psyches. It is a split reflecting the usurpation of the ancient values of woman-centered life and female divinity by androcentrism and narcissistic, phallocentric, "religious" domination. At the same time I saw the black Madonna in the extravagant churches I saw the black Madonna begging on the steps of the church, outside the heavy doors. The dark-skinned women, old and young alike, sitting at church entrances, begging for money to eat, to feed their children, or for medicine, posed a stark contrast to the veneration of the black Madonna icons gracing the very ornate inner sanctuaries of these gilded structures, considered to be places of worship. My heart ached for the obvious and arrogant inequality, as the men inside the churches (priests, etc.) didn't seem to see their Madonna sitting on the steps outside, begging for mercy.

When I gave them money, their faces lit up with a kind of eternal/maternal love that held no anger or malice. I was particularly moved by one woman. She was very old, it seemed, bent over like a tree that had been constantly blown by a forceful shaping wind. She walked the sidewalk in front of a church, humbly holding her small cup in front of her. I could not see her face, as she was so bent over, though I could feel her timelessness. I stuck a bill under her fingers so that she had a grip on it. I said *"Buon giorno"* to her, and she replied, *"Buon giorno"* in a sweet, quiet voice. I felt she was Dea Madre, bowed by the pain of women's oppression, walking, walking, waiting to be seen. The gift of her sweet presence will be with me for the rest of my life. I feel to be that sweet in the midst of such burden is something that only an old woman can know.

Then there was the dark-skinned gypsy mother with her two children sitting on the sidewalk—Dea Madre of the streets. Her darkness wasn't because she was carved from wood or covered by smoke. Her two children fearlessly approached me, holding out their small hands, eager to receive anything my white privilege would give them. I gave them some loose coins, which felt like a pittance. I walked along on my way, the image of their mother staying with me, her presence asking me to open my heart. I went back to her and gave her some money and took some bag lunches we had been given that were packed with an abundance of food and gave them to her. I looked into her face, and saw myself. I experienced her open heart brimming with love and gratitude welling up in her deep brown eyes. There she was once more, the begging Dea Madre. These women meant more to me than I can say. I know that when the women and children are cared for the same way the stone churches are, Dea

Madre will truly bless us with her grace. Until that time, we are destined to suffer in confusion, because if she who gives birth, and has done so since the dawn of time, beginning with the first dark mother of Africa, is not venerated, then so goes all life.

I have brought home with me the sights, sounds, smells and tastes of a little-known place that will live in me for a very long time, particularly the many faces and mysterious presence of Dea Madre. I am thrilled the archeological evidence in Sardinia provides Lucia with further affirmation of her passionate discourse on our African heritage and human beginnings, for the values of the dark woman deity must be restored in order that peace be remembered and sustained. It is equally important we remember the dark mother as the mother of all, for she is the living truth. Our ancestors knew what we must remember. This truth is finding its way into the scientific community as in astrophysics, for instance, in which the "Mother Universe" theory explaining what happened before the so-called big bang (which I call the big she-bang) posits our genesis from "a timeless dimension that has always existed and always will, bearing daughter universes down an endless corridor of time." (*U.S. News and World Report, Mysteries of Outer Space*, p.14.) A theory, I might add, not unlike the very way the honeybee recreates itself.

To Dea Madre

I feel you sighing through the starry mists of ancient mistral time
Your great granite breasts nurture Earth and Sky
My daughter-self, fruit of your great sacred womb
Breathes your sweet essence.
Liquid turquoise and sapphire gently lick your sandy softness,
Red, blue, purple, yellow and pink
Ecstasy
Flowers across your expansive earth body.
Red magenta blood cork trees glisten in your
Musty forests.
Great, great grandmother olive tree,
Roots alive held deep in your dark body,
Branches catch the whisper of your voice on the wind...
Dea Madre

My heart weeps for you and for me and for us all
You, begging on the sidewalk, dark eyes shining
You, walking the cement sidewalk, pacing, waiting
You, dark mother, your children with hands open
Searching my face for coins
My heart opens
I can think of nothing else
I see you and my spirit cries
"What has happened?"

The Dowry

Lorraine Macchello

La riconoscenza è la memoria del cuore
(Gratitude is the memory of the heart)

I never met my grandparents. Never felt their touch or heard their voices. I have photographs of three of them, but none of my maternal grandmother, for none exists. She is ever-changing in my imagination, without features or shape, yet always a woman in her late fifties, her age when she died. She bequeathed nothing to me, for I had yet to be born. But here in San Francisco, worlds away, my hands have held the dowry she made for my mother; I have slept in the sheets, eaten on the tablecloths, dried my face on the towels.

"See this blanket, Lorraine," my mother would say to me. "Your grandmother spun the yarn for it from our own sheep." And she would tell me about this woman I never knew, stories which usually came to her when we made beds together, folded laundry, or when I watched her roll out a lump of egg-and-flour dough into a perfect circle of pasta. The memories would tumble forth, and my grandmother became almost mythical as I listened throughout my life.

Filomena Cardellini lived and died in the comune, or county, of Pesaro, on the Adriatic coast of central Italy. She spent her married life in Montecchio, one of the many towns in the rolling hills leading to the sea, never traveling beyond the distance one could walk from village to village.

She was born in 1862, before Italy was yet unified as a nation. In her late teens she went into servitude as a kitchen maid for a family of seven. Her employer was the overseer of eight parcels of land, farmed by sharecroppers for the landowner, the marchesa. Filomena lived in the main house for ten years, and was the servant chosen to make delicate egg noodles—the very special dish of their region—when the marchesa visited her country estates. When she married my grandfather, Giovanni Barbieri, she sacrificed the abundance of the marchesa's lands and resumed the meager life she had known before. Her daughters never heard her utter a reproach or a complaint, but understood, when they were older, their father's pain that he could not provide a better life for them. When on special days, their table proffered meat or eggs, Giovanni would feign a lack of appetite and take only a small portion. The girls, when they were small, believed him; but certainly Filomena knew.

She gave birth to three daughters. One died in infancy; the youngest was my mother, Maria. Filomena, according to my mother, was "una donna chiusa"—"a closed woman"—reserved and stoical. She was dignified and proper. She laughed very little, and when she cried she shed silent tears. If ever she had feelings of joy, she did not express them. She and Giovanni did not shout at each other in anger, nor did they sing and dance, nor were they openly affectionate. Theirs was a life of restraint, dedicated to each other and their daughters. They lived in a house which Giovanni had inherited from his father, peasants without land to sustain them. "We were well off compared to some others; we always had plenty to eat," my mother used to tell me. But it is common for children to not recollect hard times, when they are insulated by their youth and the adult world that protects them. For their parents it was a struggle to survive, to overcome the harshness of time, place, and class.

The little family always had good bread. They were the proprietors of a large brick oven, and my grandfather provided the wood, twigs, roots—whatever fuel he could find in the surrounding countryside—to heat the oven for their neighbors' use. For every batch of bread baked, a loaf was left as payment. They chose for their table bread made of the whitest flour, from what they knew to be the cleanest kitchens; the less choice loaves they fed to the few chickens and the pig they kept in the stable adjoining the house. They also had two sheep, which provided them with pecorino cheese and wool for Filomena's spinning wheel.

Giovanni would be gone for days and weeks at a time when he could get work on road construction crews. He worked for the nearby farmers during planting and harvesting but received no money. For this labor he was paid in wheat to make flour, grapes to make wine, olives to make oil. After the harvest, the farmers permitted the townspeople to glean what was left. The women and girls in their long skirts, their hair protected with bandanas from the sun and dust, would comb the fields for the lost stalks of grain, using their aprons as sacks.

And the young people supplemented family meals by stealing from the farmers. My mother would recount that "it was always Irma who was brave enough; I was too timid." Her sister Irma would sneak into a field for a few ripe peaches or bunches of grapes to be eaten with their bread, running home with her loot to be shared with the family. It was an accepted way of life: the farmers grew the produce and the villagers pilfered some of it.

Most of the economy was based on a barter system. What little money Giovanni could earn went for shoes, clothing, food staples to augment their small supplies. On rare occasions when he had business in Pesaro, he would walk the seven or eight kilometers, spending a few cents at the docks for a fresh fish.

When Irma and Maria were still little girls, some of the scarce cash was allotted for cloth and thread for their dowries. They would marry one day and, when they did, the groom's family would provide the roof over their heads, and the bride's family enough linens to last their lifetimes. A bride was more marriageable if she came from a family who had planned well for her future. Giovanni sheared their two sheep; Filomena combed and washed the wool clean, spun it into coarse yellowish yarn, then wove this into thick blankets. One of these, heavy and lumpy like a Berber rug, was my bed cover all the years I lived in my parents' home in San Francisco.

There was variety in my mother's dowry—the everyday things one needed to run a household and the personal items of clothing for the bride. The finer things, made from precious store-bought cloth from Pesaro, were entrusted to a woman in the neighboring village of Farneto, whose skillful embroidery created the most beautiful pieces. These were brought out during Easter week on the day the priest came to bless a family's home; on a couple's wedding night; or when in death a body lay on its own bed, watched over by praying relatives and neighbors.

On the small patch of dirt behind their house Giovanni grew hemp. After it was harvested, there followed a long process of soaking it in the nearby river, separating and combing the stalks into thinner and thinner fibers, until it was pliable enough and fine enough for Filomena's spinning wheel. On long winter days, my grandmother spun the endless spools of thread that she would later weave into strips of cloth, long enough to be made into sheets. On hot summer days she and her daughters carried the cloth to the river, dipped it in the limpid running water, and spread the long pieces on bushes to bleach and dry in the sun. Dip and dry, dip and dry, until the cloth was white enough for a mother's gift to her daughter-bride. Many years later, in my bed, my skin rubbed against these sheets—a bit rough, but always slightly warm in winter and cool in summer. They still smelled of the earth and the river and the sun.

From the time they could hold a needle, Filomena gradually taught her daughters how to make the cloth into towels, tablecloths, napkins—some with tiny initials of the bride-to-be embroidered inconspicuously in a corner. Some they embellished richly with deep crocheted borders and raised embroidery. The needlework on pillowcases conveyed messages: "Happy Dreams" and "Love Eternal." The towels were decorated with four-inch-high initials—M.B.—in beautiful flowing script. Everything was white.

The dowry did not come to America when my mother came in 1921 to marry my father, crossing the ocean in steerage. "Don't bring your linens, Maria," my father Carlo wrote her. If all goes well, we will return to Italy in a year or two." She brought only a few sheets and towels and her bridal undergarments.

They did not make their fortune so easily or so quickly, and events gradually assimilated them into their new homeland. Six years later, in 1927, when a friend was going back to "the old country," he was asked to bring as much as he could of my mother's dowry. By then her father had died, and her inheritance was in the hands of her in-laws, my father's family. They packed an ancient trunk with only part of her belongings, fortunately all of the prettiest things, and tied the dilapidated box with ropes for shipment.

The remainder of it, rolls and rolls of cloth tied with thread, stayed stored in the house of my uncles for another twenty years, my mother never relinquishing her claim to it. In 1949, my father returned to Italy and learned that some of it had been damaged by shrapnel in the bombings of World War II, but much of it was intact. He brought it all home to San Francisco.

When my eldest daughter Ronda was about to be married in 1975, my mother gift-wrapped a box for the bride with several almost-new things from her dowry. Then she set aside two similar packages for my other daughters, Carla and Paula. The most beautiful things, three or four of them, still new, rest in the cedar chest in my room. Sometimes I rummage through them with one or the other of my daughters. We unfold and admire the handiwork and talk of my mother and of my mother's mother.

These treasured pieces of the dowry are all the physical evidence that remains of my grandmother and the life lived around her hearth. They are the central themes of all the stories my mother ever told me about her. I never saw a photograph of her or heard her voice, yet I feel I know her well.

Stregoneria: Italy's "Old Religion" from Historical to Modern Times

Marguerite Rigoglioso, M.A.

For this inquiry I set out to investigate the following questions: What is Italian witchcraft? Has it ever been a bona fide religious system, or merely an incoherent amalgam of magico-religious practices handed down from an earlier era? What are its origins and how has it manifested throughout history? Is it practiced today? If so, in what form? Has Italian witchcraft been carried by Italian immigrants to the shores of America? If so, how does American stregoneria compare with Italian stregoneria?[1] This article represents my preliminary historical and ethnographic research on the topic.

Evidence for the Existence of Italian Witchcraft

In *Ecstasies: Deciphering the Witches' Sabbath*, Carlo Ginzberg examines testimonies in the European witch trials from the 14th through 17th centuries and teases out a deep substratum of popular beliefs and practices that amount to a hidden shamanic culture operating in Italy during that period. Ginzberg determines from trial records that an ecstatic cult existed at the time, one centered on the veneration of a female deity or female spirits variously named Diana, Herodiana, Herodias, Abundia, Richella, Madonna Oriente, la Matrona, the "Good Mistress," the "Teacher," the "Greek Mistress," the "Wise Sibilla," the "Queen of the Fairies," and so forth. She is a deity at times "surrounded by animals, intent on teaching her followers 'the virtues of the earth.'"[2] Testimonies indicate that men and women, but above all, women, would ritually meet with her in shamanic trance, usually at night. One group, the benandanti of Friuli, fought during such episodes against malevolent "witches" who threatened the fertility of the fields. Sometimes shapeshifting into animals or insects, other times riding on animals' backs, they would end their journey by joining an otherworldly "procession of the dead."[3] Various references to "toads" and ointments in the trial records, suggests Ginzburg, indicate that practitioners may have induced such trances by ingesting or topically applying hallucinogenic substances derived from toads' skin or psychoactive mushrooms.

We now move to the late 1800s. Self-styled folklorist Charles Leland, in poking around the Romagna region of Tuscany (between Forli and Ravenna), stumbled upon what people there called "la Vecchia Religione," the Old Religion. This tradition, he claimed, "is really not a mere chance survival of superstitions here and there...but a complete system."[4] Its practitioners venerated the goddess Diana "and her daughter, Aradia (Herodias) the female Messiah."[5] In several remarkable volumes, Leland compiled as much as he could of the mythology, folklore, and spells still being utilized by the streghe in the last decades of the nineteenth century. He traces the origins of stregoneria back to the Etruscan period, showing how the spirit entities still being addressed by the latter-day streghe preserved names and attributes of the old Etruscan gods. Leland's books are a remarkable compendium of lore, ceremonies, and incantations to effect cures, attract love, remove evil influences, bring certain things to pass, evoke spirits, insure good crops or a traveler's safe return, divine events, cast harm upon enemies, and so forth. The practices, he notes, remained in the hands of "mystic families, in which the occult art is preserved from generation to generation, under jealous fear of priests, cultured people, and all powers that be."[6] A tradition that was predominantly the province of women, the rites and secrets were passed on in families to younger female members by female elders.

A century later, we find Italian American Leo Louis Martello in his 1991 book *Witchcraft: The Old Religion*, confirming the notion that the Old Religion has been passed all the way down through family lines to the present day. He writes, "The strege [sic] (Witches) in our family go back for centuries. My grandmother used to read the old Tarochi deck of cards, from which we get the modern Tarot. She was the village strega and both envied and hated by priests."[7] In 1951, when Martello himself was 18, his extended Sicilian family in New York initiated him into the tradition as well. Italian stregoneria—and Sicilian stregoneria in particular—Martello says, survived throughout the centuries by becoming an underground phenomenon during and after the Inquisition. That his relatives observed him from afar for years before initiating him to make sure that he would do justice to the tradition and could be trusted to maintain craft secrets, he notes, is characteristic of strega families.[8] It is because of the secrecy enshrouding the tradition, he maintains, that stregoneria is not more widely known than it is today.

Enter Raven Grimassi. An Italian American who also claims to come from a strega family, Grimassi has taken Italian stregoneria out of the broom closet, making certain aspects of it available to the wider public. In his several volumes, including the 1995 *Ways of the Strega. Italian Witchcraft: Its Lore, Magick and Spells*, Grimassi presents a remarkably systematized religion, a reported blending of several northern and central Italian stregoneria practices, which, he says, is "an attempt to restore the original Tradition."[9] As such, the stregoneria he describes has a coherent cosmology, mythology, and set of specific practices. While some hereditary streghe complain that aspects of Grimassi's stregoneria are inauthentic, "borrow" too heavily from Leland's work, ignore the many regional varieties of stregoneria, and wrongly incorporate aspects of American New Age philosophy, many agree that at least some of the folklore and rituals he offers are indeed grounded in strega traditions.[10] A growing number of Americans interested in paganism are turning to stregoneria à la Grimissi to guide them in their work in covens or as individual practitioners. Grimassi himself heads a coven in California.

And what of Italy today? Has the strega tradition survived in that country and are there those who claim to still be practicing la Vecchia Religione? My preliminary research indicates yes. Fabrisia, a hereditary Italian-American strega I interviewed who now lives in Tennessee, says that several male witches from the Bologna area have corresponded with her via the Internet since discovering her Web site on Italian witchcraft (www.Fabrisia.com). "They are hereditary witches and tell me that what they practice has been passed down to them through their families and hasn't changed since the 1500s," she says.[11]

Farther south, in Sicily, we find that popular magic is still widely used. "A very large number of people from all classes believe in magic in Sicily," ethnologist Elsa Guggino says.[12] However, she notes that practitioners of magic there are generally not called "streghe" because that term is understood to signify the diabolical "witch" image that is now widely considered to have been creation of the Catholic church. Rather, they are known by a plethora of names, including "maga, mago (the masculine version), magara, ma'ara," and so forth. They are generally hired by others to perform a variety of rituals that will assist in the physical and psychic healing or protecting of the clients themselves or their loved ones, as well as to cast and cure the "malocchio," or evil eye, a spell intended to cause harm to another person. Sicilian magic is highly syncretic, with many elements of Catholicism (prayers, names of saints) entering into the spells and rituals (something that was hardly present in the stregoneria of northern Italy during Leland's time). While the maghi that Guggino describes are not of the "New Age" variety (the latter exist but do not fall under the scope of her research), they have not stated to Guggino that they are practicing the Vecchia Religione, either. Interestingly, Guggino has not found evidence for the latter. Given that Leo Martello and other streghe of Siclian origin provide compelling anecdotal evidence that the Old Religion was still operating in Sicily at least as recently as 35 years ago, however, it may well be that Guggino has not been privy to the phenomenon because the strega families have maintained their iron curtain of secrecy. Clearly this remains an interesting avenue for further research.

Roots of Stregoneria

What are the antecedents of stregoneria? Perhaps the most dramatic document providing clues in this regard is the so-called "Gospel of the Witches," a poetic piece possibly based on oral traditions that Leland claims to have obtained from a Romagnolo strega he referred to as "Maddalena." While its authenticity is disputed by some scholars, many contemporary hereditary streghe embrace it, asserting that it contains lore and rituals that they were taught by their families.

The document tells how Diana has a daughter by her brother, Lucifer, god of the sun and the moon, and named her Aradia. Diana sends Aradia down to earth, where Christians are oppressing the believers of the old ways, to teach them "witchcraft." Thereafter, Aradia leaves and tells her followers to call upon her once a month at the full moon out in nature, to adore their Queen, Diana.[13]

Aradia, says Leland, is Herodias, who was regarded very early on in stregoneria folklore as being associated with Diana as chief of the witches. And, in fact, the carefully researched scholarly work of Ginzburg, mentioned earlier, confirms both the association between these two figures as well as their connection with Italian witchcraft, at least as far back as the 14th century. Leland further notes that Herodias is a name that comes from West Asia, where it denoted an early form of Lilith. Both figures, he says, had Isis as their precursor.[14] The link between Diana and Isis is further underscored by the fact that they shared many sacred attributes, including the crescent moon (also a symbol for "horns") and the lotus.[15] Thus, from this chain of associations alone we can possibly trace the origins of stregoneria to the religion of ancient Egypt, which venerated Isis. Isis was also venerated in Europe during the Roman Empire.

Stregoneria also obviously descended from other, earlier mystery religions of the Mediterranean. Leland traces stregoneria in the Romagna region to the magico-religious practices of the Etruscans, a non-Indo-European people whose existence in Italy has been dated to somewhere around 1000 B.C.E. Many of these practices, including occult remedies for disorders, were carried into the early Roman period. Authors such as Cicero, Tacitus, Livy, and Virgil explicitly state that their divination and religious practices were drawn from Etruscan sources. In fact, Etruscan books of magic were popular in Roman times, and the information contained therein was not just reserved for the elite but shared by the common people.[16]

It is significant to note that one of the attributes of Diana, as with her Greek precursor, Artemis, was as protector of women in childbirth.[17] Streghe, her priestesses, thus also had an important role as midwives, dispensing herbs to help usher along the birth process and ease the pain of labor. The two main herbs cited as being sacred to Diana are rue and vervain. An important symbol for Italian witches is the "cima di ruta," a sprig of rue in whose branches are objects such as a key, the moon, and so forth. Rue was used as an abortive agent.[18] Is the "sprig" of rue a symbol of women's power to take away life? If so, the wearing of it by streghe as a sign of loyalty to their craft and to Diana could thus have been as a defiant, subversive statement indeed about women's power (particularly during the time of the Inquisition)—and one that I suspect remains largely buried in the collective unconscious, even in the minds of most streghe today, many of whom proudly wear it as their emblem. The sprig of rue may thus well be a signifier for the chthonic (or underworld/death) mysteries, pointing to stregoneria as a practice ultimately chthonic in nature, itself.

Further evidence for this notion can be found in the fact that the lore and iconography surrounding Diana in the classical Roman era is also connected to that of the Greek goddesses Demeter (herself considered a form of Isis[19]), Persephone, and Hecate, whose chthonic-based religion was widely practiced in southern Italy and Sicily.[20] Diana was closely associated with Hecate as queen of the witches, and in this aspect was considered a deity whose realms were nocturnal (hence her association with the moon) and underworldly.[21] We can also see echoes of the mother-daughter/descent myth of Demeter and

Persephone in the story of Diana and her daughter Aradia, who "descends" to earth to help humankind.

Sicilian Witchcraft

Sicilian Witchcraft seems to have had its own particular flavor. Leo Martello claims that witchcraft in Sicily descended from the religion of the early inhabitants of the island, and traces it to at least as far back as the Sikelian peoples, 1500 BCE (who may have been related to the Etruscans, or Etruscans themselves). He discusses the origins as being associated with goddesses who eventually were syncretized with Demeter and Persphone under the later Greek occupation of the island beginning in the 8th century B.C.E.

Historical evidence linking stregoneria in Sicily to the Demeter and Persephone religion (or its Sikelian antecedent) is not unequivocal but still suggestive. In "'The Ladies from Outside': An Archaic Pattern of the Witches Sabbath," Gustav Henningsen examines approximately 70 case records of trials of Sicilian witches held from 1547 to 1701 by the tribunal of the Spanish Inquisition in Palermo. The trials involved "donne di fuori" (women from the outside), as they were called, a title that was alternately applied both to witches themselves and to supernatural, fairy-like entities who accompanied them on their nocturnal sojourns.

Henningsen determines from the trial records that a "Sicilian fairy cult" was thriving on the island at least during the time of the Inquisition, if not even earlier. It was led mainly by women who served as "charismatic healers" and cured ills caused by the fairies. Several nights a week, they would "rush out in spirit…and take part in the meetings and nocturnal journeyings."[22] Interestingly, many of the names used to address the fairies were identical to those that northern Italian witches used for their deities (as cited earlier in Ginzberg), although Henningsen does not directly mention Diana or Herodias among them. The striking similarities point to the strong ties that must have existed between Sicilian and northern Italian witchcraft, strengthening the notion that the practices in both places originally derived from a common source (the Etruscans?). And the fact that two of the names used in both places are "The Greek Lady" and "the Wise Sybil" becomes particularly significant in the case of Sicily. I strongly suspect that "the Greek Lady" was a reference to the ancient goddesses Demeter and/or Persephone. I also suspect that the mention of the "Wise Sybil" reflected an archaic memory of the sybils who functioned in an oracular fashion on the Italian peninsula in Roman times.

Martello claims that his Sicilian grandmother conducted rituals at Lake Pergusa, which, as I have demonstrated elsewhere,[23] was sacred to Persphone at least as far back as Roman times. If Martello's claim is accurate, this demonstrates an unbroken chain of ancient beliefs and practices that existed in Sicily into the modern era.

It is interesting to note that the Sicilian-American streghe themselves whom I have met seem to have what could be considered a certain "underworldy" quality about them. By that, I mean they have a no-nonsense intensity and an air of mystery and secretiveness about them, and they maintain a concern with combating negative spirit forces operating in their environment and in society. The fierceness of Sicilian streghe has also been noted by Martello and others. "Unlike most other Witchcraft traditions," he writes,

> the Sicilian and some Italian branches do not hesitate to threaten the deities...This Sicilian quality is not one of disrespect of blasphemy. It is one of positive self-assertion, a recognition of our own inner divinity, and a sense of personal power in our own lives that neither man nor God nor Goddess can undermine.[24]

Contemporary Italian-American Witchcraft

Contemporary Italian-American streghe I have interviewed echo Martello's claim that in Sicily, Italy, and among Italian Americans in the United States, the old religionists have survived to this day by raising their children publicly as Catholics, while privately and deliberately teaching them the old beliefs and practices. One of the most prominent Sicilian-American witches is sixty-something Lori Bruno, who counts among her ancestors Giordano Bruno, the Italian heretic who considered Diana an important deity, held that witches were the midwives of social reform, and maintained that the Egyptian religion as transmitted in the Hermetic literature was superior to Christianity. For his views, he was burned alive. Thus, along with stregoneria, the fear of authorities was handed all the way down to Bruno's own generation. "In our studies, we don't write anything down," she says. "I was taught that you don't leave paper lying around or the 'Inquisition' will get you."[25]

Bruno, who grew up in Brooklyn, says that her family's practices involved regularly calling on the old gods, including Diana, Apollo, Hecate, Demeter, Persephone, "and the ancient Siculian [Sikelian] goddess," on occasions such as the full moon and other holidays. Other rites included burying red eggs in the east at sunrise on Easter morning, and burying silver coins with honey in the ground, she says, "to honor the Earth Mother."

Minnesota resident Bellezza Squillace observes that in her family the teachings of the Old Religion were frequently enfolded in women's activities such as cooking or sewing.[26] Rolling a ball of yarn for knitting, for example, was an activity that allowed one to problem-solve on a right-brained, intuitive level. "One person had the skein of yarn on either hand, the other person was making the ball," she explains. "A rhythm was created, like the swaying of the ocean, as the arms went up and down and the hands spiraled. This was the 'entering of the maze,' a time in which the two of you would talk about the issues at hand. By the time you finished, you had new insights into your life."

Squillace recalls how her relatives also told her stories about figures such as Medusa, the Sirens, Hecate, Demeter, and Persephone, as well as the Italian witch Befana and Saint Lucia. These stories served as "another method of instruction in problem resolution," she notes. The fierce female entities known as the Furies, she learned, could be called upon for assistance, a practice she herself has used in extreme situations. "They are called in to right an injustice perpetrated by someone in a position of authority or to avenge the matriarchy," she explains. "I've invoked them in two different rituals. Once I did it to help catch a man who was raping and killing women, and burning their bodies in a park. The next day the man was arrested."

While Squillace's family considered these activities as natural as breathing, they did teach their young charge that their members were "different," somehow set apart from the mainstream, and that their differences should not be advertised to anyone. "They told me, 'We believe differently, but you still go to church. You go along,'" she recalls.

Fabrisia, who grew up in a large Italian-American community in Massachusetts, also recalls that "in church the old Italian ladies said 'Ave Diana' instead of 'Ave Maria.'"[27] Fabrisia remembers her grandmother turning the statue of Mary away from what she was doing when she was out in her herb garden harvesting plants for remedies and spells. Her paternal grandmother, great-grandmother, and aunt, all of whom were born in northern Italy, identified themselves as "streghe" and told Fabrisia they were practicing their own "religion." They began teaching her from a young age the family traditions, particularly the knowledge about herbs. Not surprisingly, one of their favorite plants was rue.

Fabrisia remembers that it was typical for her female relatives to hang wind chimes all over the yard. "My aunt believed that when the chimes rang they announced the presence of a fairy," Fabrisia recalls. She also remembers her elders regularly leaving food out in the garden as an offering to the deities. One ritual they taught her, which Fabrisia uses regularly, invokes protection from a bad storm. "You go to each door of the house, lay pennyroyal down as an offering, and recite: 'Winds of the East, winds of the West, I beg you give us rest. Winds of the North, winds of the South, I ask you please blow around me,'" she says. "I did that ritual one day when a tornado swept through our town in Massachusetts. I saw my gas grill go up and down without tipping over, and we could feel the wind going around our house while on the house across the street the shutters and shingles came ripping off. We hardly had any damage at all. Now any time there's a storm my kids say, 'Ma, quick! Get the pennyroyal!'"

This article has given just a brief overview of the roots and history, as well as some of the contemporary manifestations, of Italian, Sicilian, and Italian-American stregoneria. Clearly much more study remains to be done, particularly in Italy itself, where tantalizing stories of the existence of a strega "underground" are continually reported but have proven elusive to investigate. Hopefully new information will keep coming to light as streghe on both continents share their knowledge more publicly, and as scholars continue to follow the ancient threads that connect such knowledge back to their historical sources. The revelation of such a rich body of information will no doubt serve as an ever greater source of empowerment and nourishment for Italians, Italian-Americans, and anyone seeking an authentic connection with spirit.

Notes

1 I should note here that the word for witchcraft in the modern Italian language is "stregoneria." However, various writers, including Charles Leland and Raven Grimassi, refer to it as "stregheria" (or even the misspelled "stregeria,"), claming that this is the term historically used by its practitioners. As at this point in my research I have not yet confirmed whether witches in Italy have in fact ever called their craft "stregheria," I will use the term "stregoneria." In addition, ethnologist Elsa Guggino (personal conversation) maintains that in Sicily the word "strega" is used disparagingly to describe someone who practices malevolent magic; other words such as "maga" are used instead to denote practitioners of the healing and magical arts. Sabina Magliocco also notes this and disputes both the idea that there was ever a "unified organization of Italian Witches" in Italy, as well as the idea that Italian-American witchcraft constitutes a bona fide survival of this earlier religion. See Sabina Magliocco, "Spells, Saints, and Streghe: Witchcraft, Folk Magic, and Healing in Italy," The Pomegranate 13 (summer 2000): 4–22. My article serves as an interesting counterpoint to hers. While Magliocco makes many excellent points that I agree with, I choose to take more at face value than she does the reports of researchers such as

Charles Leland and the claims of streghe such as Raven Grimassi, Leo Martello, Lori Bruno, and others that a secret "underground" religion based on the old ways has been operating for hundreds of years on the Italic peninsula and Sicily, and that this religion has been carried by Italian immigrants to the United States. I therefore come to somewhat different conclusions about the nature and possible origins of Italian and Italian-American stregoneria than she does. I contend that there is still a great deal more research to be done before any conclusions can firmly be drawn about the validity of the historical claims made by contemporary streghe. For simplicity's sake I tend use the word "strega" (and its plural, "streghe") throughout this paper to mean "witch" in all senses of the word. Also for simplicity's sake, I use the feminine form of the word in Italian for both men and women.

2 Carlo Ginzburg, Ecstasies: Deciphering the Witches' Sabbath (New York: Random House, 1991), 131.

3 Ibid., 155.

4 Charles G. Leland, Etruscan Roman Remains (Blaine, Wash.: Phoenix Publishing, Inc., n.d.), 9.

5 Charles G. Leland, Aradia: Or the Gospel of the Witches (New York: Samuel Weiser, Inc., 1974), viii.

6 Leland, Etruscan Roman Remains, 4.

7 Leo Louis Martello, Witchcraft: The Old Religion (New York: Citadel Press, 1991), 33.

8 Martello, "What It Means to Be a Witch," Occult (January 1974): 4, and interview with Martello, April 14, 2000. This was, as it turns out, to be Martello's last interview before he died in June 2000.

9 Raven Grimassi, Ways of the Strega. Italian Witchcraft: Its Lore, Magick and Spells (Saint Paul: Llewellyn Publications, 1995), xviii.

10 Information relayed during interviews with my informants, April 2000.

11 Interview with Fabrisia, April 2000.

12 Interview with Elsa Gugguno, April 14, 2000.

13 Leland, *Aradia*, 1–6.

14 Ibid, 103.

15 Frederick Elworthy, The Evil Eye: The Origins and Practices of Superstition (London: Collier Books, 1958), 355.

16 Leland, Etruscan Roman Remains, 11.

17 Elworthy, 350.

18 Gatto Trocchi, Magia e medicina popolare in Italia (Rome: Newton Compton, 1982), 86, 106.

19 Diodorus Siculus, Library of History: Books IV.59-VIII, translated by C.H. Oldfather (Cambridge, Mass.: Harvard University Press, 2000) 283 (69.1).

20 See Peter Kingsley Ancient Philosophy, Mystery and Magic (New York: Oxford University Press, 1995) and In the Dark Places of Wisdom (Inverness, Calif.: The Golden Sufi Center, 1999).

21 Leland, Etruscan Roman Remains, 151.

22 Gustav Henningsen, "'The Ladies from the Outside': An Archaic Pattern of the Witches' Sabbath," in Early Modern European Witchcraft: Centres & Peripheries (Oxford: Clarendon Press, 1990), 195.

23 See Marguerite Rigoglioso, M.A., Mysticism, Mother Worship, and Misogyny in the Navel of Sicily: A Spiritual History of Enna, Lake Pergusa, Demeter, and Persephone (Ann Arbor, Mich.: UMI Dissertation Services, 2001), UMI #1403470.

24 Martello, Witchcraft, 145.

25 Interview with Lori Bruno, April 6, 2000.

26 Interview with Bellezza Squillace, April 9, 2000.

27 Interview with Fabrisia.

Bibliography

Elworthy, Frederick. The Evil Eye: The Origins and Practices of Superstition. London: Collier Books, 1958.

Ginzburg, Carlo. Ecstasies: Deciphering the Witches' Sabbath. New York: Random House, 1991.

Grimassi, Raven. Ways of the Strega. Italian Witchcraft: Its Lore, Magick and Spells. Saint Paul: Llewellyn Publications, 1995.

Henningsen, Gustav. "'The Ladies from the Outside': An Archaic Pattern of the Witches' Sabbath." In Early Modern European Witchcraft: Centres & Peripheries. Oxford: Clarendon Press, 1990.

Kingsley, Peter. In the Dark Places of Wisdom. Inverness, CA: The Golden Sufi Center, 1999.

_____. Ancient Philosophy, Mystery, and Magic. New York: Oxford University Press, 1995.

Leland, Charles G. Etruscan Roman Remains. Blaine, WA: Phoenix Publishing, Inc., No date given.

_____. Aradia: Or the Gospel of the Witches. New York: Samuel Weiser, Inc., 1974.

Magliocco, Sabina. "Spells, Saints, and Streghe: Witchcraft, Folk Magic, and Healing in Italy," The Pomegranate 13 (summer 2000): 4–22.

Martello, Leo Louis. Witchcraft: The Old Religion. New York: Citadel Press, 1991.

_____. "What It Means to Be a Witch," Occult (January 1974): 1–9.

Rigoglioso, M.A., Marguerite. Mysticism, Mother Worship, and Misogyny in the Navel of Sicily: A Spiritual History of Enna, Lake Pergusa, Demeter, and Persephone. Ann Arbor, Mich.: UMI Dissertation Services, 2001. UMI #1403470.

Siculus, Diodorus. Library of History: Books IV.59-VIII. Translated by C.H. Oldfather. Cambridge, Mass.: Harvard University Press, 2000.

Trocchi, Gatto. Magia e medicina popolare in Italia. Rome: Newton Compton, 1982.

una piazza: SicilianSummer evening

Gian Banchero

1

the twilight now has waned into night

2

a large star and the Crescent moon being suspended in blackness are
illuminating a one time Arab-now-Christian campanile

3

evening birds are sing-songing to each other

4

From under the tolling little bell
Burnt day workers in various corners have laid themselves down
to a sleep;

5

a few well dressed men have now eaten old-time frugal suppers
circle around and around and around this piazza
conversing in hushed tones.

Sweetly,
somewhere from behind a closed shutter
wet thick china-ware is heard settling against each other
as a woman washer of dishes
sings
in
minor
key
to a baby who already sleeps well

The Speech I Never Spoke

Chickie Farella

Sam'n Nella Farella's 50th Anniversary
(from anthology *Dialogues Of My Mother's Guilty, Superstitious and Subservient Ways*)
(April 30, 1949–1999)

Seven years ago I fled Chicago to the southern California desert and my folks snowbird home for a three week hiatus to write and to heal. They say the desert is a healer. That 3 week stay transformed into nearly permanent residency because I know it's *not* my last stop, just a separation that led to a divorce from a nearly 20 year marriage which I know **is** my last stop.

Recently, I went back to Chicago for my folks' 50th anniversary party. I had a little story prepared, however, to my surprise, so did my sister. Usually I am the long winded pain in the butt at the family gatherings cause my brothers really dislike speech making. It's something they just don't do. Nor do the men like the women making speeches. They call us the "big mouths" of the family. So I decided to leave the job for my sister so I could eliminate the moaning and "Madonning!" when I would take the podium. But I have decided to share what would have been my speech with you today.

I have a Califorinia friend by the name of Patty Gammino. A very talented, educated woman, also transplanted from the east, who possesses an uncanny romantic idea of relationships that I left behind a long time ago. My mom and pop just love her, and she them. My mother especially likes her cause she's "back east" down to earth as opposed to much of the uppity country club "land of the nips and tucks" desert mentality. Last April, the day before they were to return back to their home in Chicago, we had Patty over for dinner. At the end of the evening, they exchanged their hugs goodbye and she and I went to the corner watering hole for a cocktail. After a half a glass of wine, she turns to me and says, "Your folks are sooooo in love!" I said, "What?"

"Their sooo in love...they're lovebirds!" I put my drink down and asked, "Patty, were you at the same dinner table with me? Lovebirds? get real, Gammino!

"Yes I was at the same dinner table with you. They're DARLING together. You and I should only be as lucky to have a relationship like theirs!"

Now here's a gal that retired early in the marketing end of the publishing business, executes her own stock trading and owns investment property..not too shabby, right? So I said, "Patty I'm not quite as drunk as I'd like to be yet, so let's take a stroll down memory lane here this evening. I believe that one minute after you walked in the door, dad got up from his "sofa-throne" and wanted his salad before you even sat down to have a welcomed glass of wine, when mom yelled at him about his rudeness and he said, 'Oh Nell, it's just Patty'. Not to mention that she and I both fought with him BEFORE you arrived cause he refused to put on a nice dinner shirt and insisted on wearing his tee shirt with a couple of marinara spots picked up from lunch." Patty just giggles. Then, if my memory serves me well, he left the dinner table before we completed our meal cause Wheel of Fricking Fortune just tuned in and I believe the shrill of mom's voice turned my pop's one syllable name into two: 'Saaaaaaaaaa-aaammm, don't you dare leave us at this table! We haven't finished our meal!!!!'

'Oh Jeez, Nell...It's just Patty...she knows how I am don't you Patty'?

'Sam you would do this if Patty were the Pope! You do this every time we have company! It's embarrassing!" Patty giggles again. "There so in love."

"Awe Come on Patty...whadya blind? They just put up with each other. They saved two other people by marrying each other, for Christsake!"

"Chickie, you just don't see it because you NEVER pay attention! You have to pay attention." So I shrugged my shoulders, ordered a Sambuca and said, "Ya know Gammino, you may be a smart cookie, but emotionallly YOU'RE wacky and you and I will NEVER agree on the subject of relationships, ever!

Next day

That morning I went into the kitchen. Dad's head is buried in the newspaper and mom's in the kitchen in her robe half asleep performing her daily ritual of making HIS cream of wheat. She had another insomnia night. Now this cream of wheat thing he's got going drives me nuts cause he refuses to let ME make it for him when my mother has a bad night. It doesn't matter that I have catering experience, because he thinks she is the only one who can make it without the lumps. So sometimes I will dare say, "Well then…Daaad…how about some toast instead cause ma's not feeling very good?" His answer…"I don't tell you how to do your business, don't tell me how to do mine. End of story. Case is closed. Anyway, as she's stirring the cream of wheat, "Guess what, Ma? Patty Gammino thinks that you two are the hottest couple in the desert." Mom's eyes began to open, she wrinkled her little forehead, and banged the wooden spoon on the pan to shake off that extra stupid cereal he eats and says, "What? Jeez, I love Patty, but she must be a little on the goofy side, huh? How did she come up with that, babe?"

"WELL, She's always felt that you and your little Mr Wonderful here, are the perfect couple. I believe the term she used was LOVEBIRDS!" which I pronounced in my sarcastic falsetto. At that point Dad lowers the newspaper and lifts his eyes above his readers to look at me with that very dry "Jack Benny/BillCosby" look. "I said it before, I'll say it again. Deez people in the desert are a little on the wavy side. I think it's the sun."

We finished breakfast, took our showers, got dressed and headed for the airport. As we piled ourselves and the luggage out of the car, I gave HIM a big hug, (ya know he drives me crazy but I miss him so much when he leaves, dont ask me why…I think it's cause he really is so cute to me when I think of him so far away…I dunno) "I told him to behave and help mom unpack when they get to Chicago in…which…pfff…I knew that was a waste of MY breath. You see my father is not well, God love him, worked very hard to make us a living for many years; however my mother spoiled him very early on so he has always chosen to remain as a nonparticipant of any and most all "3d"s: dual domestic duties. Before I hugged HER, I reminded her to make sure that Chicago O'Hare has a wheel chair for him cause his diabetic legs would not make it through the airport. She says…"Yeah, yeah, yeah. You just drive home safely, MISSY, and don't forget there's lots of nice meat in the freezer! You better eat good while I'm gone!" I looked down at my "gotta lose 10 pounds body" then at the luggage attendant and asked him, "Sir, do I look like I missed any meals lately?" He politely said, "Maam, I'm not goin' there; I dont' go there when my wife wants me to go there, I'm sorry."

THAT EVENING she made the usual call informing me of their safe and sound arrival. Here's how it went.

"Hi Babe"

"Hi Ma, how was the flight?"

"Well your father topped himself."

"Really? Ya sound like you're outta gas, Ma. Are you ok?

"If I've told him once, I've told him a thousand times, "Wear your suspenders on the plane."

"Yeah, Ma, and I'm sure he said, "Don't f———bother me!" right?"

"Right. He doesn't like that the security alarms go off when he walks through, but it's not a big deal cause they know it's from the suspenders."

"So he got his way as usual, right ma?"

"Well…you know your father."

"Too well. So what happened?"

"So we get on the plane, and as he reaches up to put his briefcase into the overhead storage area, his pants fall down to the floor for all the passengers and attendants to see him in his jockey shorts, belly and skinny legs."

"Well that must have been a REAL turn on! Did any female flight attendants attempt to "hit" on him?"

"Oh God forbid! I was so embarrassed! I wanted to die right there!"

"Ma, there are worse things that can happen. Take it easy! Now what about the wheelchair. Did you order a chair to be at O'Hare when you arrive like I told you?"

"Well that's another story."

"Really? I never would have guessed. Let's see. Did Mr. Wonderful, "It Has to be MY idea first and should NEVER make any F———common sense," refuse the chair Ma, Hah?"

"Well…you know your father."

"Too well. What happened?"

"Well, you know how BIG O'Hare is…It's as big as the city, for Chrisakes!"

"Yeah, Ma, I know, and…

"Well, when we arrived he had to stop every 4 or 5 steps cause his legs were hurting him so bad, and I was carrying everything and my back was killing me" *(At this point I should tell you that my mother is about 4'10")* and then he had to go to the bathroom! Well, I had to search for a John for him cause he just couldn't make the walk and then when I found one, I couldn't find HIM, and I had all this stuff, and my back was killing me so I had to yell in the middle of the airport for everyone to hear: *"SAAAAAAA—AAAAAAAAM! WHERE ARE YOU? I FOUND A TOILET!"*

"Gee, Ma, I'm really sorry I missed that."

"I was so embarrassed!"

"By the way, Who picked you up from the airport?"

"Well, that's another story."

"Really? I bet."

"When we got home, Jim…

(Jim is their neighbor and best friend to them. He's a generous kind man and performs the "ddd's" "dual domestic duties"at their home that leaves mom guilt ridden because he won't accept a cent. Yet dad, better known as Mr. BYG = "Born Without Guilt" happy as a clam and will always say, "Just cook for him, Nell. Jim don't care.")

"Jim and I carried *all* the luggage in, and you know Jim was yelling at me for lifting the bags, but I had to help…I couldn't let him do it alone, could I?"

"So where was dad when all this was taking place? He didn't help with the luggage, Ma? and don't tell me about his legs, Ma. I *know* what he can do…Ma, and I know what he can't do. I swear to God, Ma, you're gonna go first and if you do I *will* strangle him with my bear hands. THIS HAS TO STOP. NOW! Here it comes again! Where was he when all this was taking place?

"STOP, CHICKIE! Listen! I'm sick and tired of you and your sister yelling at me when I talk about your father. You know sometimes I need a friend to talk to just like you. God knows I've licked up hundreds of your and your sister's wounds, without yelling or judging you. If you continue to talk to me with that tone I'll just hang up!"

"Sorry, Mom, I'm really sorry." I lowered my tone and realized how alone in this she is and asked, "So where was he when all this was taking place?"

"*Well…*"

"Maaaaa?'

"Well…I heard him calling me while I was outside and I went in and found him at the top of the stairs in the family room, and at this point I had really had it, babe, I really had it with him!"

"What did he want?"

"*Well you know your father.*"

"Maaaaaa, talk to me!"

"He said, 'Nell ya get up here. There's something wrong with the remote control and I'm missing the Bulls game!'"

Now to most of you this should be the end of this story. It's not. I was very very angry. All laughs aside, my little 73 year old mommy is the only sib out of four who hasn't had a heart attack and THAT is NOT funny to me. The only way to sublimate this anger was to take a deep breath, hold it, let all out…and sit at my trusty computer and let my fingers do the talking. I then went into my fax program and said, "I'll fix Patty Gammino with this little gem!"

She called me immediately after reading the dialogue.

> "They're so in LOVE!" she says with even more conviction.
> "Awe, come on Pat, you can't BELIEVE that!"
> "Oh yes I do. You just don't see it! It's because you've never pay attention! You have to *pay attention!*" I was too frustrated to give her an inch...so I filed that thought. I filed it away and refused to respond to it!

A year has past. This past February I was in my room working for about four hours. I took a big stretch and decided to break and go into the living room to check what was for dinner and if mom needed me to go to the store. As I walked in, I stopped abruptly. The soaps were on, the sound was down and mom was sitting in her little corner of the sofa in her little peach moo moo house dress, resting her short curvy legs, her knees uniformly together, sound asleep with her little lips perched outward, and as she exhaled her breaths, I noticed my father was staring at her. I pulled back around the corner quietly to watch something I had never witnessed in my entire life, ever!

There I was, for five minutes, watching my father watching my mother while she sleeps.

I PAID ATTENTION!

Wisdom Scroll

Max Dashu

Maat by Max Dashu

Her name means true, right, real. She wears the ostrich feather, symbol of natural Law. In the first act of creation, a great Egg formed out of the primeval waters of darkness. From it emerged the boundless spirit of the sun, causing movement and life, forming all beings according to Maat. It was Maat who laid out the course of the sun at creation.

"Your right eye is Maat and your left eye is Maat, your flesh and your limbs are Maat...you are because Maat is."

The heart is weighed against her feather of truth.

Spider Grandmother by Max Dashu

Creation stories of Arizona and New Mexico praise Spider Grandmother or Spider Woman. The Keres peoples call her Tse-itsi'nako, Thought Woman. She brought everything into being through the power of her mind. The Hopi remember her as Kokyangwuhti, who chanted the creation song over the Earth's twin poles, setting stability and circulation in prder. She created all living beings from earth and her own saliva, then spun shining webs of creative wisdom over them and inspirited them with her chant.

In some traditions, old Spider Woman causes the Corn Mother—or her daughters—to emerge from the underworld, and instructs them to enliven all beings by singing over their images.

Khokhmah by Max Dashu

"Wisdom," the power guiding creation, is praised as "intelligent, holy, unique, manifold, subtle; mobile, clear, unpolluted, distinct, invulnerable, loving the good, keen, irresistible…"

In the Book of Proverbs, "She is a Tree of Life to all who lay hold of her."(3:18) She sings, "The one who finds me, finds Life.: (8:35) Khokhmah builds a house of seven pillars.

In Ben Sirach (24:4) she declares, "My throne was in the pillar of cloud."

In late antiquity she was venerated as the all-wise creatrix and genetrix Sophia.

Xi Wang Mu by Max Dashu
(Queen Mother of the West)

Xi Wang Mu is called "the Original Breath of the Great Yin" and "Mother of All Creatures," whose life spans she dteremines. She gives life, causes and cures diseases, and imparts mystic wisdom. Energies of new growth surround her like a cloud. In her garden, hidden in the clouds of the Kun Lun mountains, the peaches of immortality grow on a colossal Tree. It is a ladder between Heaven and Earth, along which spirits and shamans travel. Xi Wang Mu is attended by a host of faeries and immortals. A three-legged raven is one of her magical emissaries. The Taoist classic Zhuang Ze says of Xi Wang Mu, "Nobody knows her beginning, nobody knows her end."

Kali Mahavidya by Max Dashu

Kali is the first of the ten Great Wisdoms. Seated in the cave of the heart, she brings about spiritual and material transformation, burning away impurities and cutting through illusion. "resuming after dissolution Your own nature dark and formless, You alone as One, ineffable and inconceivable. You are the beginning of all, creator, protector and destroyer that You are...Taking the form of the Void, in the robes of darkness wrapped, who art Thou, Mother, seated alone in the shrine of Samadhi? From the lotus of Thy fear-scattering feet flash the lightnings of love. Thy spirit-face shines forth with laughter wild and loud."

Sapient Sibillia by Max Dashu
("Wise Sibyl")

Memory of the prophetic sibyls of Cumae turned, in medieval Italian tradition, into a pagan mountain goddess. Wise Sibillia lived in a subterranean paradise in the high Appenines. Seekers entered it through a grotto with a magical spring-fed lake. Within were caverns full of marvels and treasures, where the immortal Sibillia and her faery women regularly assumed serpent form. They taught the arts of magic. Sibbilia blessed those who visited her mountain, and when they returned to the world they passed the rest of their days in joy. It was said that whoever stayed longer than a year could no longer leave, but remained deathless and ageless, feasting in abundance, revelry, and amorous delights.

Ahame: Medea Under the Stars by Patti Davis

Eye Idol I (ca. 2500–2000 BCE)
Museo Arqueologico de Sevilla, España
Jodi MacMillan 2003

Eye Idol II (ca. 2500–2000 BCE)
Museo Arqueologico de Sevilla, España
Jodi MacMillan 2003

Flamenco. Cuevas de Tarantos, Granada, España
Jodi MacMillan 2003

Your hair becomes the sky
Aikya Param

Monica Sjoo

Sehkmet temple in Nevada desert

Monica Sjoo 2000

Monica Sjoo

Paper Dolls © 2000
Tricia Grame
70" x 45" acrylic

Vessel Series, I © 2001
Tricia Grame
48" x 36" mixed media

Spirits and Sprites

Jean Rosenthal Harris

If you know of what you sing, death is but the center of a long life.

—Old Druidic saying

One:

I'm at Stillwater cove on the rugged Sonoma Coast, perched on a favorite rock observing the action. Pelicans are swooping around me and two pelicans share a rock to my right. Then one flies away. The remaining pelican turns his head sideways and his eye is giving me the once over. Then I notice his strange looking beak moving up and down and it seems he's speaking. It's hard to hear because of the sounds of the wind and the waves but I'm sure now the pelican is talking to me.

"Hello over there, on the rock. "You Jean! yes you! I've been waiting for you," he's yelling in what is clearly a Yiddish accent. "My name is Mendel, I'm sure you heard them talk about me. I have a lot to tell you and there's not much time. You don't have to look around like that! Who else do you think I'm talking to? Don't be fooled by this pelican business. It's temporary. But I know who you are and you know who I am as you'll soon find out. Listen, it's like this: I'm what they call here a sprite; What's a sprite, you're going to ask? Well I'll tell you. A sprite is a spirit, only backwards. You understand? When the spirit finds a body, any kind of a body, it becomes a sprite. Like me in this pelican outfit. *Farshsteist?*

"It happens after you die. Your body they make into fertilizer but the *nishome* or spirit that lives inside of you, it's always around, like electricity, they can switch us on and off. You get me?

"You see, the truth is…nobody knows how it works. Not anymore than you did when you were running around in a suit and a tie. All I know is I

189

was dead one minute, and the next I was floating around in space till a bird caught me and flew me here, inside of it, like Jonah in the whale.

"It changes…all the time it changes, we spin around like smoke. I'm spirit today, a sprite tomorrow. Like now I'm in this pelican outfit. Tomorrow I could be in the body of a cat. Or a doorman. It's crazy, and sometimes you forget who's who.

"That's how some of us get to help out with our loved ones…to do now what we couldn't do then. We can only help out for three generations, then they move us some place else.

The pelican is speaking rapidly, in profile, out of the side of his long beak and with one large eye looking directly at me. The eye appears to be pulsating in that queer pelican face. The fog is coming in now and I pull my hood around me. This is going to be one long and bewildering day. I sit there staring at this pelican and listening closely to every word.

"This is going to be a long story sweetheart, so you better get comfortable, the pelican says," reading my thoughts.

"How I got here, it's like this…I come from a long line of Lithuanian Jews. We lived in a small town *Kovna*, what the Lithuanians called Kaunas. For centuries we lived peacefully with the *goyem*.

"In my body life I was your grandmother Leah's father Mendl, a tanner by trade. That's right! Don't act so surprised! It's true. Leah, your grandmother, the one you never got to meet! She was the oldest of my five daughters. Do you know the story? They must of told you how I arranged a marriage for her with Aaron, a respected Torah scribe. I thought it was the right thing to do. What did I know?

"But as soon as I died, I saw everything in a different light including the troubles coming thirty years down the road. For my family and for all our *landsleit*.

"I decided the best thing to do was get them out of Europe, one way or the other. First, I worked on Aaron the Torah scribe, (my daughter's husband) and I tell you I kept up a constant *tumult* in his head until he couldn't stand it no more. "*Gevalt!*" he yelled, covering his ears. "I have to go to America!" he told Leah "and I want you and the children to come with me!

"But I couldn't get his wife, my own beloved daughter Leah, who also happens to be your grandmother, to go along with him. Talk about stubborn! Just like her mother, you couldn't get her to listen. I tried everything in my power, but she wouldn't leave…refused to budge. *Eingeshpart!* Just like my wife! I hope you're not like that!

I have no time to reply. This pelican is talking a mile a minute.

"So in 1905, Aaron went alone to America and Leah, left behind, went straight to the Rebbe and got a divorce. Just like that! If I had fingers, I'd snap them. Your mother Helen was only nine...her brother Arky was four. Aaron went alone. The *mishoogener*, they called him, but I knew he couldn't help it...he had to go.

"In a few years time, I went to work on your mother Helen and she was easy. I saw to it she found certain books to read, certain pamphlets which stirred up her dreams. She was smart for her age. Had a head on her shoulders. Of course she wanted to go to America! And I put it into her head she might even find her father. Can you imagine this, Helen, at age thirteen, Helen asks her mother to let her go on a summer vacation to the States but already she knows in her heart she's never going back? Some Helen! Smart as they come. I did a good job with her. You're lucky you had such a mother! She's one of my success stories.

"Well, to make a long story short, your mother Helen finds herself in New York City, age 13, the year is now nineteen hundred and nine and she's all alone, strange language, you can imagine, but she doesn't complain. She uses her *kop* and finds a room, a job, night school, learns English, supports herself, what they call *chutzpah*.

"So like I'm telling you, in a few years time, your mother Helen is made a buyer of ostrich feathers (would you believe the first woman to hold such a position?) and soon she 's making enough money to move to her own apartment, buy the latest fashions and dress to kill, even when she's s riding in the subway.

"Having a good time until World War One started. The American President said it was supposed to be the war to end wars. What did they know? Who could imagine World War Two and the Holocaust, still to come? Even I, personally, couldn't see that far ahead. I wasn't yet what they call a full-fledged sprite.

"In human bodies, we can see only what's in front of our noses. But when we're rid of the bodies, we get to see more....we can look back three generations and we can see ahead three generations.

"where was I? Well, it was up to Helen to bring our family seeds to America. As it turned out, I figured right. Helen was the only survivor of her family because she was here.

"I already know what you're thinking so let me save you the trouble...even when we can see ahead what's going to happen, we can't help. We're not in charge....that's all they tell us, so if you think you 're going to die and then you'll know everything, forget it, it's not like that! I'm telling you, they don't tell you much more than you knew before. If there's floods, fires, plagues, wars, we can't stop the destruction or what looks to us like destruction. It's happening out of our reach. We can't even stop the pain to the people we're watching. All we know there is something else going on higher up. So be it! who am I to argue? What we CAN do and we're encouraged to do, is bring in a little light after the darkness, open up the heart it shouldn't get too tight, help them forget, and sweeten the taste of life with hope. That's all! And that's plenty!

"There wasn't a thing I could do about that *shandedicke* time still to come for those left in Europe. The best thing was to help your mother Helen here in America. And I'll tell you how I did it. Just listen to this: this is where the story gets interesting. I'm hanging around New York City one day keeping an eye on Helen, and I whoosh into an old friend from the Old Country. We went to *Cheder* together and when we were kids we used to hang around the bakery his father owned, just to keep warm and eat *kichel*. When I knew him all those years ago, he was apprenticing to become a maker of spinning wheels. Now he's a spirit!. just like me. Tells me he died age 95 from a bump on the head he got in his barn. He was a tall guy.

"Mendl!" he exclaims "What are you doing here?" And I tell him the *gantze geshichte*.

"Then he tells me he's also running all over the place keeping an eye on his grandson, a certain Sgt. Abraham Rosenthal who's here in New York on a 3 day pass. Don't ask where the two of them have been! Camp Cody, New Mexico, Brownsville Texas, Sioux City, Iowa, the *gantze veldt*. How do you like that?

"And where do we meet like this, my old friend Yankl and me? We're flies in the subway….the IRT to be exact, flying around together, watching our two grandchildren go down the steps and into the train marked Bronx, and in the meantime Yankl and me, we're trying to exchange a few words and catch up. It's rush hour, the trains are packed, and it happens to be *erev Rosh Hoshanna*.

"Suddenly the handsome soldier Abraham, (Yankl's grandson) is tugging on another man's sleeve. "Excuse me sir," he asks. "Is this the train for Caldwell Avenue?" The man shrugs. My friend Yankl looks at me, and you won't believe this but we get the same idea at the same time.

"Both of us, we concentrate our thoughts on our grandchildren to stand near each other, to hold on to the same pole. Abe is carrying an address in his hand. I have Helen give him the once over. Oh is he good looking! kind eyes, she likes what she sees, and his accent reminds her of home, even if he is in the uniform of the United States Army.

"Excuse me Sgt, did you just ask directions to Caldwell Avenue?"she says, looking directly at him. He turns to see where the voice is coming from, and when he sees her, his eyes almost pop out of his head. She looks just like Theda Bara!

"Yankl and me are in our fly-suits, and trying to figure out how to wink. 'Follow me,' Helen tells Abe and they get off together at the next station so she can point out his train. Now we have to work quick…get to their instinct button. Yankl and me, we both know how it should go….this is a love match if we ever saw one and in this place you get extra credit for those. We make Helen follow her feelings, give Abe her address and for Abe to show up the next day with a heart-shaped box of chocolates.

"So while Helen is showing Abe the sights of New York, Yankl and me, we're dressed up as two pigeons, and we follow them everywhere. Up and down Broadway! There are so many pigeons in the streets, nobody pays any attention. It's a perfect disguise. Yankl and me, we're eating breadcrumbs and shmoozing and bragging about our families. We're sitting under a bench in Central Park and the puttee wrapped legs of his grandson Abe and the gray suede boots of my granddaughter Helen are dangling in front of us. They don't even know we're here. It was a love match if I ever saw one."

Out of nowhere there's a great whoosh of wings and Mendl, my talking pelican is shoved off the rock and displaced by another pelican. Mendl flies a circle and returns to the same rock, lands, and faces the other way now, making room for the new pelican. Now I 'm looking into his other eye, and he doesn't take it off me.

"Okay as they say," says this other pelican." Enough telling my story when I'm not here. I'm Yankl, in case you're wondering, Yankl. And if you don't mind, Mendl. I'll tell my own story. Then our Shindl sitting here listening to all this, can put it together for herself."

When he calls me Shindl, I cry. My mother called me Shindl, because she said when I was born and she first saw me, my eyes were shining. How could a pelican named Yankl know this?

The pelican that's Mendl and the pelican that's Yankl turn their heads to face each other, cross their beaks over one another a few times, and then settle down.

Yankl takes over the story. "First, you have to know your father Abraham, or Avreml as we called him, was my only living grandson but even I have to admit he was a difficult case. He no sooner got settled someplace, he wanted to see someplace else.

"First he wanted to visit his aunts in Leeds, England, so I went along as a pebble in his pocket. Then he took me on a long boat ride to Palestine to see his father and sister, and before a year is over we're on our way to Galveston, Texas in America. I hide out in a camel, a donkey, a goat. Don't ask! *Shlep shlep shlep*...But did he stay in Galveston? No! This Abe was impulsive and I had my work cut out for me. Still he was worth it, what a sweet guy, liked to laugh, make others laugh, very kind. But who am I telling this to? You know that better than anybody, *Shindl*. He was your father.

"The only *tzooris* with Abe was he craved adventure. He wanted to see the world. Just like his poppa did, traveling to South Africa all those times and then going to Palestine to buy land from the Arabs and the Turks.

"Abe was no better. He's here in America only a few months, and already he enlists in the New Mexico State Guard to go capture the bandit Pancho Villa and teach him a lesson. What kind of a lesson, he wasn't sure himself.

"Oy, was it hot in the desert! Let me tell you, but did Abe mind? No! it reminded him of Palestine. He was the only Jew in the regiment. When they found out how good he cooked and baked, they put him in charge of the Quartermaster corps. He was baking *teiglach* and *kichel* and *rugelach* for those cowboy-soldiers...and did they love it! Don't ask! Abe even cooked them *cholent* for *Shabbas*, but they thought they it was stew. Stew on Saturday.

"There's a war going on in Europe, and in 1917, Captain Pershing begins to disband his special forces so he can go run things over there. Now listen to this! Abe's Captain Murphy who happened to be a Doctor, was from Sioux City, Iowa. Abe followed his Captain back to Sioux City and had it in his mind to enlist in the Infantry. The infantry! I almost *plotzed* when I heard that. Everybody knew the Infantry was the first ones gassed and it would of been goodbye Abe. I had to work fast.

"I called in an old friend, and if it hadn't been for this buddy's help, we'd of been in big trouble. Abe's Captain Murphy, when he was a young man, he had a good spirit working for him. MacGuiness, his name was, Irish, but we got along, we understood each other. Regular buddies. We liked working together, and I'll tell you something.... just the way MacGuiness was watching Dr. Murphy, Dr. Murphy in real life was keeping an eye on your poppa Abraham. That was our arrangement. So instead, Capt. Murphy got Abe to enlist in the Sioux City Ambulance company and that saved his life."

The pelican that is Mendl says. "In this place we work together. We like to help each other out. It's a regular kibbutz! Everybody co-operates."

"Now this is the interesting part," Yankl continues, ignoring Mendl.

"Look what I dreamed up! I gotta give myself credit here! When your poppa was on that ship coming from Alexandria, Egypt to Galveston, Texas, he met a family of Jews from Argentina. All the men had a circle of gray hair in the middle of their foreheads. 'It runs in the family', they told him and as far as they were concerned, that's it, but the truth is I'm the one who made up the whole idea. Good, no?

"Five years later, didn't I arrange for a Corporal with the same gray circle of hair on his forehead to meet Abe in the Jewish Welfare Board in Ft. Dix, New Jersey? What about that! Of course the Corporal was related to the people from Argentina! Naturally they got to talking and that's why Abe went to the Bronx on his 3 day pass instead of Philadelphia."

The pelican that is Mendl tilts his head to the side, then shudders slightly, at the same time repositioning himself on the rock. His head is erect and it's clear he wants the floor again.

"Back to Helen and Abe, your parents," Mendl takes over again, "so that's how they met! I know they told you the story many times but even they didn't guess it was because of Yankl and me in the IRT. And think about this for a minute...Momma came originally from Lithuania, and Poppa was born in Poland just across the border from her home town. When they spoke Momme Loshen it was sweet for both of them. All that way he had to come, from Poland to England to Palestine, then to Galveston, Texas; Camp Cody, New Mexico; and Sioux City, Iowa before they could meet in the New York Subway.

"You see what I mean? How it weaves together! A cloth doesn't make itself. We have to do our part. And so it goes for three generations.

"One year later, when the war ended, and Abe came back from France with my friend Yankl boasting to me how hard he had to work to keep his grandson alive, Helen and Abe married and moved to Sioux City, Iowa, where Abe's Captain Murphy became their family doctor and delivered their two children, first your brother Norman and six years later, you, Jean.

two:

Following day. Sun illuminates the scene. A school of small herring is trapped in Stillwater Cove and the seals are having a picnic. Sushi to go. The sea is a swirl of activity and the skies above are throbbing with life. Pelicans dive into the water to feast near the seals, and the gulls and egrets fill the air with activity. I return to my rock, and there are dozens of pelicans, swarming about. Exchanging places from rock to rock. There are so many pelicans, I can't tell them apart.Soon I realize one of them is staring at me intently.

"Mendel?" I ask,. "Is that you?"

"Of course it's me, he says," Who else? Where was I with my story? So you get the picture now?. You see how it all weaves together? It's too bad we only get to be around here for three generations before we go someplace else. But in our sprite-time, we can do a lot of good. Do you ever stop to think about why, sometimes after someone you love dies, then good things start to happen to you? Who do you think makes that happen? The spirit of the one who just died! He's going to work for you.

"Take for an example when your brother Norman was shot down in an airplane during World War Two, who do you think it was jumped into the parachute with him and saved his life? Who went through the year and a half in Prisoner of War camp with Norman, and the long death march, and finally saw him home safely to marry your best friend Janice and to father Leslie and Stephanie and to grandfather the two sets of twins? Well, it was Aaron, your *Zaidy*! Helen's father, that's who saved him! I'm not saying he did it all alone. He had help. In a crisis, you get to call in all the help you can, spirits working other places, if it's not so important, they come to help you.

"This was the spirit that used to walk around in a body called Aaron, who left his wife and children and traveled to America, and which put into Helen the dream to come to America also…Just believe me when I tell you it was Aaron, making up for all the pain he caused a long time ago when he was in the body of a man. Yes, it was Aaron who jumped into the parachute with Helen and Abraham's son Norman. Believe me!"

Up to this point the other pelican has said nothing, but somehow I feel it's Yankl, the more reticent of the pair. He says politely: "we also helped out."

"Sure sure," Mendel says, "everybody helped. Listen, I got to go now. The fishing is good and who knows how long it'll last? See you tomorrow!"

three:

The next day the seals have left the cove, the fog is rolling in and we're down to a handful of pelicans and the usual gulls. I look over the assortment of pelicans. I can hear Mendl's voice calling me from a tree. I look up and it's a blue-jay. The bird is talking:

"The pelicans had to follow the herring, but I still have more to tell you, so I changed outfits till I'm finished. I look good in blue, don't you think? Yankl is here also, in the other tree and he's coming over soon. First, he has to finish dressing. I got to admit, it's his story as good as mine.

"Mendl talks so much it's hard to get a word in, move over Mendl, I want to say something, too."

Another blue jay is rocking on a branch below Mendl. At first I think it's Yankl but his accent is different.

"First, permit me to introduce myself, Madam, I'm called Ziggy, my full name is Sol Zygmunt but everybody calls me Ziggy. I also come from the old country. From Warsaw, to be exact. I was grandfather to Maurice and Israel Maimoni. Two brothers.

"It was like this: the Miamonis were assimilated middle class Jews. The family lived in Warsaw for generations. The brothers went to University, graduated as Doctors, and even Maurice's wife was a University graduate, a teacher. They were not interested in following the traditional path, and they knew they needed a more promising future than they could have in Poland.

"At the University, the brothers read the writings of Theodore Herzl and the rationale for a Jewish homeland in Palestine. It seemed the only solution. The pogroms in Poland were getting worse every day and it didn't take a genius to figure things out.

"Their parents encouraged them to pioneer. They were getting old and couldn't leave the family business, but the brothers the Doctors should go.

"Now I was given Maurice to keep an eye on. Israel had his own guardian, an uncle I believe. Anyway, this was my first experience as a sprite and I wanted to make good. I liked this Maurice. He was intelligent, spoke five or six languages, was interested in new ideas, thought things over for himself, and he was what we call a *mentch*.

"It was decided the brothers would go to Palestine alone, and if they liked it, they would send for their wives. First the brothers went to the old city of Jaffa, but soon found their way to Petah Tiqvah, the first Jewish settlement funded by Baron Rothschild.

"There, they planted orange trees, fixed up an old house studied Dr. Ben Yehuda's conversational Hebrew, worked with other *chalutzim* to drain the swamps, both suffered a bout with malaria, but within a year the brothers managed to open a small medical clinic, the first in Petah Tiqvah, providing care for Arabs and Jews alike. Then, they wrote for their wives to join them.

Mendl pushes Ziggy aside here.

"I hate to interrupt," he calls out, "but I have to explain something and without that, the story doesn't make sense."

"Go on," Ziggy says gently. "I know you won't rest in peace until I let you interrupt my story.

"No offense, please," Mendl says, "but the story doesn't make sense if you don't tell her that my people were also in Petah Tiqvah AT THE SAME TIME. That's the whole point! Listen Jean, your parents were married six or seven years, they had a nice life in Sioux City, they had your brother Norman. But your grandfather Moshe wrote to them to come to

Palestine, to help in the family business which was prospering. Rosenthal's was the first Jewish bakery in the whole country! Everybody wanted their challah!

"Your mother wasn't so crazy about the idea, but I already told you what a hothead Abe was, so he talked her into going. With your five year old brother Norman. They sold what little they had, said goodbye to their friends, and left Sioux City for Petah Tiqvah. The year 1925.

"You still think all is just coincidence? Are you beginning to get the picture? You see how things happen? That's all I wanted to say. Go on Ziggy! It's your turn!"

Ziggy, a gentle spirit as he had been a gentle man, says"Thank you Mendl." He pauses a moment.

Yankl, who had been quiet all this time, blurts out:

"It *is* amazing, when you think about it, how you and Arturo, the children of these two families will meet in California more than 70 years later."

"Not only that," Mendl interrupts again. "Your mother was a patient at their clinic. It was Arturo's father, Doctor Maurice who told her finally to leave, Palestine was not for her, her health depended on it, she should go back to wherever she came from. He also told her she was pregnant."

"In the meantime, Maurice's own wife Anna became pregnant. She begged Maurice to leave Palestine, the life was not for her, they should try to go to the United States. He did what he could but their visa was turned down. America wasn't taking any more Jews.

"Finally, in the Fall of 1926, with Anna, seven months pregnant, they book passage for a ship to South America. Now here is where I get really busy. I have to do a lot of finagling to make things come about. Maurice and Anna were of the opinion they were going to Panama but I knew Panama was dirt poor, people struggling, no future, so I arranged for an old friend of mine, another spirit without an assignment, to take the body of a passenger on the ship. Maurice was an engaging man and soon made friends with this passenger. I had him sit at their table so they could get to talk. I even gave him a ring of the Freemasons because Maurice belonged to the brotherhood. My man urged them to change their mind about disembarking in Panama. "You will have a better chance in Colombia," he advised them. They never saw him again.

It took six weeks for Anna and Maurice to get to Bogota, but finally they arrived in the clean city, high altitude, good air, and there in January of 1927, in the Bogota Maternity Clinic, Arturo was born to Anna and Mauricio Maimoni."

"And my family," Mendl interrupts again, "My family went back to Sioux City, Iowa. Abe got his old job at the Iowa bakery, Norman started Public School, and Helen gave birth to you, Jean, at the Sioux City Maternity Hospital in January 1927.

Yankl, who has been quiet all this time, finally whistles out: Magic. There's no other word. Magic."

"That's our story," Mendl says. That's what we all wanted you to know."

It was quiet for a moment while I tried to absorb all I had heard.

Mendl again: "People talk about timing but they don't know how it works. Yankl, Ziggy and me could show them a thing or two. Don't forget we all knew each other in Petah Tiqvah back in 1925…when the two sets of parents first met each other. You Shindl, had to come all the way from Sioux City, Iowa and Brooklyn, New York to the Bay Area of California some fifty years ago, and Arturo, how do you think he got here all the way from Bogota, Colombia? Who do you think gave him the idea to go to Cal Tech in Pasadena and Berkeley for graduate school? Go on! Tell me! Don't you think it's funny that you both lived here for so many years, living other lives, it's true, and now, in your Seventies, you meet for the first time! You're going to tell me that's a coincidence!

"I think we should explain," Yankl says, "that sometimes we make ourselves known just for the fun of it. we like to make pictures drop on the floor or books to fall off the shelves, things like that, to bring attention. Take for example the first night Arturo spent at your house Shindl. You went to sleep outside on the deck, it was a warm night. Sometimes during the night Eddie's self portrait fell off the wall in the bedroom where it had been hanging over thirty years. Fell to the floor, just like that! Now don't tell me you thought it was an accident! You knew. You knew it was Eddie's spirit saying something, or trying to say something and it got through, it was okay, you realized this was Eddie's last gift to you, he was moving on down, off the wall, making room for another to come into your life. Nine years of grieving is enough already. He wants to see you happy. What else? So he goes to work and calls us in and he gets in touch with Arturo's parents to bring the two of you together. It would be perfect! And it is! Don't you agree?

"Can you imagine all the commotion going on around here? All of us who've worked with Arturo and all of us keeping an eye on you Jean, all these years, all the parents and grandparents, every one of these *nishomes* is going crazy congratulating themselves and clouding around, what a great idea it is…Arturo and Jean should find each other…now, at this time. It's brilliant! Then we sort of shift places and plot another twist. And you think you have free will?"

Glossary of Yiddish terms:

chalutzim—early Zionist pioneers
cheder—Hebrew school

cholent—slow simmering stew
chutzpah—nerve
eingeshpart—stubborn
farshteist?—do you understand?
gantze geshichte—the whole story
gantze veldt—the whole world
gevalt—a cry for help
kichel—egg cookie
kop—head
landsleit—hometown people
mishoogener—crazy man
momme loshen—mother tongue
nishome—soul
plotzed—fainted
rugelach—rolled cookies
shabbas—Sabbath
shandedicke—shameful
shlep—drag
teiglach—honey cookies
tumult—loud noise
tzooris—trouble
zaidy—grandfather

Goddesses Around the World

Mara Lynn Keller, Ph.D.

Goddess spirituality is one of the fastest growing spiritual movements in the world today. Like a creative fountain, Goddess spirituality overflows into contemporary music, dance, visual arts, film, fiction, scholarly works and ritual celebrations. It is a primary spiritual path that can lead to personal, social and ecological relationships of balance, compassion, justice, ecstasy and love—and it one of the best aspects of living in the Greater San Francisco Bay Area, where every day, women and men, supported by our thriving local Goddess community, recover their sense of wholeness and their Divine connection as they awaken to the Goddess within.

Why is the Goddess so important? There is no panacea for all our modern ailments, yet to many, the Goddess symbolizes our best hope for a viable, sustainable future. This is because she represents an antidote to the imbalances that so grievously plague the world: imbalances between the sexes, humans and other species, the rich and poor, different races, cultures and religions, war and peace. Given the appalling spoiling of the environment, the difficulty of inter-personal relationships, racial and class conflict, escalating violence between the sexes, the lack of conflict-resolution skills, the massive extinction of species and the lack of respect for future generations, many have turned to the Goddess and her wisdom traditions out of frustration with the limitations of the religious as well as secular choices offered by the dominant cultures of the world, which might be characterized as patriarchal fundamentalisms.

If flaws in modern culture result largely from over-masculinization, over-population, over-exploitation of labor and natural resources, over-militarization, etc., then the Goddess is a powerful symbol and catalyst for what is most needed. She represents the sacredness of the feminine, keeping population in balance with the natural environment, honoring each person's innate talents and creativity, seeing that all people are well-nurtured, resolving conflicts peaceably, recycling and protecting resources for future generations, and successfully building multi-cultural societies with harmony among different races and cultures.

Many people assume that violence and warfare have always been primary modes of self-defense and wealth-acquisition, that survival and progress depend on these above all else; and that there are no other choices. But if we look at non-traditional history, for example, if we look at the herstory of women's spirituality around the world, we find there are other possibilities that recommend themselves to us. We learn of cultures where humans live in balance with the rest of nature, where men and women live harmoniously together, where there is a strong sense of community and a shared development of social well-being. This is why a deeper look at Goddess cultures, past and present, is relevant to us today.

African Cosmological Goddesses of Creation and Abundance

The work of Dr. Lucia Chiavola Birnbaum, in concert with others, documents the migration of peoples with their religion of the "dark mother" out of Africa to all continents of the world during the Old Stone Age, beginning c. 50,000 BCE. Thus humans share not only a common biological inheritance but also a common spiritual heritage. If we could acknowledge and affirm this common ground, it might have the power to heal our divisions and guide us to a better future.

Black Goddesses, sacred ancestors and holy queens have peopled Africa from Egypt in the north to Zimbabwe in the south. Powerful examples of the African Goddess are found everywhere. A running or dancing Goddess with a field of grain between the horns of her headdress from which falls a shower of seeds or rain, has been called the Horned Goddess, but might as easily been named the Goddess of Abundance. Pre-dynastic Egypt offers another marvelous image: a bird-headed, human breasted Goddess who stands with arms outstretched as if about to take flight. Might the ancient belief that a bird symbolized the human soul, help us now safeguard the declining flocks of birds and their migratory routes?

Neith, like Nut, is an Egyptian Sky Goddess, Queen of Heaven, whose body births the sun and moon each day, and from whose breasts falls the rain that nurtures all life. The Great Mother Goddess Isis, with her male counterpart Osiris, is the "Giver of Life." When Osiris was killed by his brother Seth, Isis searched everywhere for her beloved and, gathering the scattered fragments of his dismembered body, restored him to life; she then bore their son Horus. Isis is the original Black Madonna. Her loving partnership with Osiris annually restored fertility to the Nile Valley so all people would find abundance.

In many African nations it was the power of the Goddess that supported the emergence of historic queens, just as early Pharaohs of Egypt drew their legitimacy and their power to rule from the Great Mother. Makeda, Queen of Sheba, is an example of the wisdom and magic embodied in the historic and mythological queens of the African continent. Her poetry invoked Holy Lady Wisdom as, *"sweeter than honey, more joyful than wine, more illuminating than the sun—causing the heart to understand."* How do we find the wisdom of an understanding heart, not only in our daily lives but in social and international affairs as well? Why don't we demand that today's heads of nations pursue the same purposes as the great African queens and Goddesses: to feed the people, raise the children with love, celebrate the sexual union of partners, and foster the creative talents and arts of each individual! Might the growing presence of the Goddess today support the emergence of more politically empowered women and men committed to these same values?

Middle Eastern Goddesses of Sacred Marriage and Freedom

The Sacred Marriage of the Goddess Inanna and her beloved Damuzi was central to the religion of ancient Mesopotamia, where (as in Egypt) divine lovemaking caused the fertility of the land and the people to be renewed each year. To this myth of celebration was added, during the rise of patriarchy in Sumer, the story of the Descent of Inanna.

Descending to the Underworld ruled by her sister Eriskigal, herself dragged down as the "spoils" of a warrior, Inanna loses all earthly attributes and powers, dies, and hangs on a hook as rotting flesh; until rescued by her faithful woman attendant. Since Damuzi had been unwilling to offer his life to save Inanna, he is consigned to stay in the Underworld for half of each year.

Sacred stories invite multiple interpretations. The myth seems to say that if one woman is abducted and raped, no woman is free to live her life unscathed, but must somehow reunite with her underworld sister in order to restore personal and social wholeness. And, if a man pursues his own power with disregard for the Goddess, he will be able enjoy those powers only half of the time, but spend the other half with the shadowy dead.

The historical spread of patriarchy is further seen in the myth where the young God Marduk destroys his mother, the primal Goddess Tiamat of the Deep, recreates the cosmos out of her body, then makes humans into his slaves. It is not surprising, then, that the Sumerian word for 'freedom', '*amargi*', means 'return to the Mother'.

For over a thousand years, from the 18th to 7th century, the Goddess Ishtar was praised with a beautiful salutation: "*Ishtar, Queen, Goddess of All, Lady of Heaven and Earth, Queen of Heaven, Goddess of the Universe, who walked in Terrible Chaos and brought life by the law of Love. Out of Chaos bring us Harmony, and from Chaos lead us by the hand.*" We might want to pray this prayer also, to clarify our intentions so that a social order of love rather than of fear and greed will prevail.

Near Eastern Goddesses of Cosmic Order and Culture

In ancient Anatolia, now Turkey, there was an abundance of Goddess reverence for at least 7 millennia, from the Agrarian Age until the Christian era. She was called Anna, Mother, and Hannah, Grandmother; Arrinna, Sun Goddess; Cybele, Aphrodite, Artemis. Her priestesses were called *Melissai*, honey-bees, producers of sweetness. At Ephesus, people built a magnificent temple for Cybele-Artemis, where hundreds of inscriptions refer to her as "founder, saviour, commander, guide, advisor, legislator, queen, spreader of light, controller of fate, great, magnificent..." (Ergener Anatolia: 49). What it would be like if we had such a role model who was consulted in everyday matters and celebrated in community festivals!

The great temple of Cybele-Artemis was finally destroyed during the Christian era, but Ephesus was declared the birthplace of Mary, Mother of Christ, and a church was built nearby. The Mother of Mary and Grand Mother of Jesus was Saint Anne, Anna. It is important that religions honor mothers, grandmothers and daughters, as well as fathers and sons and grand-fathers!

Cyprus and Crete: Goddesses of Partnership, Peace and Artistry

The 5th century BCE philosopher Empedocles wrote of the pre-patriarchal peoples of Cyprus: *"No war-god Ares was worshiped, nor the battle-cry; Nor was Zeus their king nor Kronos nor Poseidon; but Cypris [Goddess of Love] was Queen."* They brought their artistry as offerings to the Goddess, not animal sacrifices; nor was it their custom to eat animal meat.

Crete, during its Goddess epoch from c. 6000 BCE to 1450 BCE, was a highly artistic multi-racial society settled by peoples from Anatolia, the Middle East, North Africa and Old Europe. The people's love of nature and devotion to the Goddess were expressed in their open sensuality and pleasure in adornment, lively, beautiful art and writing. The internal harmony of this multi-cultural civilization was evidenced by the lack of defensive fortifications of the temple cultural centers and the absence of any images of war or military rulers. An Archaic hymn asserts that peace and justice were attributes of Nature herself, and that *"all wild living things were held about by wealth-loving peace."*

This graceful civilization of the Goddess was dominated by warriors from mainland Greece, beginning c.1450 BCE. After 1100 BCE, the culture not only in Crete but also Greece collapsed into a Dark Age that lasted some 300 years. Then, after another millennium, warfare again overran populations and ecosystems to such an extent that Europe descended into another Dark Age, this time lasting a thousand years. Now, only a few centuries since modern cultures began expanding, chronic warfare and the decimation of peoples and environments threaten us with another massive regression. When will humans become collectively wise enough to interrupt these cycles of violence? Perhaps memories of the ancient Goddess cultures can inspire us to create new alternatives.

Far Eastern Goddesses, Gentle and Fierce

In the Far East, as in most other cultures, we find both gentle and fierce Goddesses. Tibetans revere the Buddhist Boddhisattva Green Tara, Goddess of

Com-passion, as well as the wrathful Red Tara, who acts out the rage that results from karmic pain. In Tibet, returning to the womb of the Mother Goddess is a meditation for union of the human spirit with the divine; as is the tantric spiritual-sexual union of woman and man.

In India, the Goddess has ten thousand names, at least. Prakriti is Mother Nature. Lakshmi is Goddess of Abundance, Great Mother who feeds all. Shakti is the Goddess of activating energy who stimulates her male partner Shiva to contemplate the divine unity of all that is. Durga is Earth Mother, and Kali her fierce warrior daughter, who like Durga, feels compelled to protect her people against evil forces. Goddess devotees today often call upon Durga or Kali to find the courage, strength and fierce compassion needed to work against rape, child incest, the sexual traffic in women, destruction of forests and clean rivers, and other desecrations that plague us. Devotions to the Goddesses continue today, and their sacred festivals are enthusiastically attended by millions of men and women, where priestesses dance to embody the Sacred Feminine.

In China, the descendant of the Goddess of Nature is Kuan Yin, Goddess of mercy and compassion. Her redemptive powers use the skillful means of wisdom and compassion to purge all karmic woes. In Japan, the Buddhist Goddess of Compassion becomes known as Kwannon.

In Japan's Shinto religion, Kami spirits—the awesome powers of nature and all auspicious beings and events—are revered. Since the 7th century CE, Amateras——u, the Sun Goddess, has been chief Kami, and until the last century, Japanese Emperors claimed divinity by tracing their lineage directly to her. A few years ago, during inauguration ceremonies, the Japanese Emperor is said to have participated in a secret ritual of sexual union (symbolic or otherwise) with the Sun Goddess—as the means to become empowered to rule.

European Goddesses of the Mysteries of Birth, Sexualty, Death and Rebirth

In Greece, the Great Goddess held all within the cycles of birth, death and regeneration, and she was worshiped as Creator of the Universe, Earth Mother, Mother of the Gods, Goddess of the Hearth, Love, Social Justice, Arts, Crafts, Plants and Animals, Moon, and more. By the time of classical Greece, the earlier Goddess cultures were firmly subordinated to Olympian Zeus, who was worshiped for bringing success in battle to his followers, and who also established rape as the standard for sexual relations.

The Goddess religion continued to share its Mysteries of Love through the rites of Aphrodite, Goddess of Love, Beauty and the Arts; and of the Earth Mother Demeter and her Daughter Kore-Persephone, who birthed, raised and fed the people, and gave the laws of a peaceful and civilized way of life. Although their sacred story became overshadowed by the Daughter's abduction and rape and the Mother's grief, the primary transmission of the Goddesses' rites was to bring humans to the major gateways of life—birth, sexuality, death and rebirth—with love. Demeter, Goddess of Abundance, *"mingled in love-making and sleep"* with a mortal man of Crete, then gave birth to Plutos, Plenty. Plenty was depicted in Greek art cradled in the arms of Irene, Goddess of Peace—expressing the profound belief that peace, not war, brings the fruits of prosperity.

The Goddess' Mysteries were also celebrated in Italy. The primary Goddess of the pre-patriarchal Etruscans was Turin, Goddess of Love. Later in Rome, she was Magna Mater, Ceres, Juno, Diana, Venus. Sicily serves as a living museum of the many treasures and layers of the European cultural history of the Holy Mother. Its folklore and popular icons of the Black Madonna carry the memory of the Dark Mother from Africa into the present.

In the British Isles, the Goddess was Brigid, Lady of the Lake, Rhiannon, Morrigan, and Mab, Queen of Fairies. In Scandanavia She was Freya, Goddess of Love; Ilmatar, divine Creatress; and Mielikki, Goddess of the Forest. Especially in France, the Holy Mother was worshiped in great medieval cathedrals built in honor of Our Lady. Even after the effort was made to deny all divinity to the feminine, as witnessed by the burning of witches, devotion to the Goddess persisted (albeit disguised) in reverence for the Shekinah, the Indwelling Presence of God; Hochma and Sophia, Holy Wisdom; and Mary, Queen of Heaven, Mother of God.

The Americas' Grandmothers and Other Goddesses

In our own homeland, America, we see many faces of the Goddess and come to realize they are all ultimately One. In Native American cultures, while different male and female deities may be worshiped, it is understood they are part of the Great Mystery. Spirit grandmothers and grandfathers, Goddesses and

Gods, are here to help us see we are all held within the unspeakable beauty and infinite intelligence of the Great Mysterious.

In Mexico, the Goddess was Chicomecaatl, Heart of the Earth; Tlazolteotle, Birth-Giver; and Tonantsin, whose indigenous roots blended with the Virgin Mary of the Spanish invaders to become the Virgin of Guadalupe, probably the most powerful spiritual influence in all Mexico. Today, those suffering persecution in Latin America pray to the Black Madonna as the Mother of the Disappeared.

In North America, for the Eskimos, the Goddess is Sedna, ruler of the Sea and all its creatures. To the Algonquin, she is Nokomis, Grandmother, who feeds all. To the Hopi she is Spider Grandmother, Creator of the Universe, Earth Mother and Corn Mother. The Hopi, whose name means "peaceful people," are a matrilineal and egalitarian farming community. Their cooperative and mutually supportive way of life is explained by the understanding that, *"Any time, anyone may need help. So we all help one another."* Hopi are taught not to be aggressive and not to kill, except when necessary for food, and then, nothing is to be wasted. The indigenous belief that humans are relatives to all that live, is powerful medicine for our survival.

Coming again to our home region of the Greater San Francisco Bay Area, we find that many of the leading practitioners, ritualists, artists and authors of the contemporary Goddess spirituality movement live right here! These include Jennifer Berezan, Lucia Chiavola Birnbaum, Jean Shinoda Bolen, Sandy Boucher, Z Budapest, Pamela Eakins, Ph.D., Riane Eisler, Rose Wognam Frances, Elinor Gadon, China Galland, Judy Grahn, Miri Hunter Huruach, Hallie Iglehart, Diane Jenett, Mary Mackey, Alexis Masters, Vicki Noble, Mayumi Oda, Arisika Razak, Charlene Spretnak, Starhawk, Luisah Teish, Alice Walker, and Patrice Wynne. A new generation of voices is emerging from the wonderful students of our sister graduate programs in Women's Spirituality in San Francisco at the California Institute of Integral Studies and New College.

We believe the world's Goddesses have a great deal to offer of truth and wisdom, pleasure and joy. While an understanding of Goddess spirituality around the world gives us deeper insights into human cultural evolution, the contemporary practices of women and men in circles honoring the Goddess and God are creating a new spiritual and social ethos that intends to transform the present, with its increasingly threatening military and economic woes, to a more peaceful and enlightened global culture, where humans and other species can thrive.

Athena and the Mirror

Susan Carter, Ph.D.

Helmeted, in full armor and wielding her shield, the goddess Athena is ready for imminent battle. This image of Athena is the role assigned to her by the patriarchal Greeks. Perhaps, for political reasons, other parts of Athena's characteristics—the earthier, more peaceful and reflective aspects—have been veiled or fragmented.

A careful reinterpretation of Athena's myths reveals her to be a complex deity: She is not only a fierce and determined deity, but also one concerned with more life sustaining and enhancing activities. Also, in comparing Athena to goddesses from earlier civilizations, many of their powers have been reduced to symbols on the clothing Athena wears in her portrayals. The myth of the slaying of Medusa, and Athena's part in it, dramatically illustrates how these goddesses' aspects have been fragmented and demonized. Recreating Athena's wholeness is not only important for understanding her real complexity, but also has implications for contemporary women.

The best-known myth concerning Athena is the account of her birth. Metis[1], Zeus' first wife and Athena's mother, is a goddess of exceptional wisdom. She has the ability to change shapes and thus evades Zeus' advances towards her. Nonetheless, Zeus eventually overtakes Metis, and she becomes pregnant with a girl child, who is to be Athena. Zeus also becomes aware that in the future Metis shall have a second child by him, a boy. This boy child is prophesied to become more powerful than Zeus, and to rule over him. As in other familiar tales of father-son rivalry, Zeus wants to make certain that this cannot happen. So before Athena is born, Zeus charms Metis, tricks her, and swallows her whole. This act destroys Metis, but not her unborn daughter,

Athena. Like Persephone who was abducted by Hades, Athena is violently and prematurely taken from her mother.

Athena is subsequently born from Zeus's head. In some versions, beginning with Pindar, it is said that Hephaistos assisted at the birth, splitting Zeus' head open with a double-edged ax or hammer. [2] In other versions, Athena is born from a "peak," which may be interpreted to mean the top of a mountain, rather than Zeus's head. [3] Yet Homer, in both the *Iliad* and the *Odyssey*, makes no mention of Metis, saying that Athena is simply Zeus' daughter. Athena is generated by Zeus alone and bursts forth from his head fully formed and radiant in her shining armor, a wonder to behold. Seemingly born without the benefit of a mother, she is, in fact, denied a mother. Moreover, she is born already a fully developed woman, capable of bearing and protecting children herself.

Several details in the accounts of Athena's myths reflect what happened in Classical Greek society. One is the account of Metis being ultimately unable to avoid Zeus' advances, despite her shape shifting. This makes a strong point—if the goddess of wisdom (and cleverness) could be overcome, then surely a mortal woman would not stand a chance in denying a man. In fact, Athenian lawgivers, (e.g., Solon, in the sixth century BCE), contributed little, if anything, to protect women from unwanted advances or rape by men. The violator in the case of rape was often merely reprimanded and went unpunished. In the case of seduction outside of marriage, however, where courting and actual love may have been involved, severe punishment was justified, including the death penalty. [4] The message was clear: men's ownership of women and their offspring, and their homes and attentions, were not to be challenged. Women's bodies, however, could be violated with little or no consequence to the man. Love was not a consideration in marriage. Indeed, in the Bronze Age marriage by capture was a variant to an arranged marriage, [5] and by the Classical period in Athens this practice had been ritualized. [6] Although there is no mention of rape by Zeus of Athena, it is through the association of her mother (and her fetus) being overcome by a powerful male, in this case Zeus, that Athena becomes a fully-grown woman.

The mythical precedent of Athena's birth from Zeus' head is used in early Greek society to argue that the father alone can beget a child. Father-right is formally introduced, defended, and validated through this version of Athena's birth. It is a story told and retold in Greek arts and drama. In Aeschylus' *Eumenides*, Apollo argues that the man is the source of life, and refers to Athena as a product of father-right when he states:

The mother so-called is not the child's begetter, but only nurse of the new-sown embryo; the one who mounts, the male, engenders, whereas *she*, unrelated, merely preserves the shoot for one unrelated to her...I shall show you a proof of this assertion: a father could give birth without a mother; near to hand there is one to bear witness—the daughter of Olympian Zeus, who was not nurtured in a womb's darkness but is the kind of shoot that no goddess could give birth to.[7]

Later, in the same play, Athena herself declares, "There is no mother who gave birth to me and I approve the male principle in all things and with all my heart—except in the matter of marriage, and am very much my father's child." [8] Athena is thus portrayed as a father's daughter: heady, intellectual, and almost always depicted with her armor, symbolic of defensiveness. She is thus identified with the male upper world.

Although Athena aligns herself with the emerging patriarchal order, she also brings to her duties some of the aspects of Metis. She is reflective, full of mercy and wisdom. She offers the quality of restraint and lucid intelligence. [9] She often interrupts mortals at times of rash action. In the *Iliad*, she stops Achilles as he is about to slay Agamemnon because he wants to claim Achilles' concubine as his own. As Stassinopoulos explains, "The goddess intervenes: 'Cease,' she whispers. Athena is standing beside Achilles, personifying his own inner wisdom, whispering, yet clearly heard over the tumult of wilder passions. She represents both the 'nearness of the divine at the moment of severest trial' and the embodiment of the wise counsellor we all carry in us." [10] The portrayal of Athena in mourning (from the Acropolis, c. 480–450 BCE) may depict her reaction to being unable to stop all rash actions and warring in her land. Helmeted and leaning on a staff, her head is bent, her gaze downward.

Athena is above all a goddess of culture—she is a patron of cultural forms, a culture-bearer. She not only protects the cities, but also ensures that its citizens are productive. She is the teacher and patron of weaving, wool working, carpentry, and handicrafts—crafts that require the ability to formulate and hold in mind an image of an end state. [11] In various myths Athena is asked by other gods and goddesses to weave dresses and robes in order that they may achieve certain ends as well. In order to seduce mankind, Zeus asks that she create a dress for the first woman, Pandora. Hera requests a special robe to lure her husband away from the action on the battlefield. Athena creates items of great beauty and utility. Despite increasing male domination in both public and private spheres, "respect for the female as life-giving and nurturing crept back into human consciousness via the manufacture of textiles. Denied biological parenthood, Athena and other mythological women regained a claim to maternity through the imagery of wool working." [12] Further, in the *Statesman*, "Plato uses Athena's weaving as a metaphor for the political process, and provides the bridge between Athena's nurturing of the arts that sustain the life of the community and her patronage of the art that binds the community together." [13]

All these references to Athena hint at her original identity, before she became an Olympian deity. Athena was once a great mother goddess and a household goddess, both a protective divinity and guardian of the house. She, along with Demeter, is perhaps the closest link to the old Great Goddess of Crete. She was both a tree goddess and a snake goddess, [14] and thus not strictly of the upper world. Presiding at least 1,000 years before the Classical Greek goddesses, Athena is also a direct descendant of the early Minoan palace goddess, who became the Minoan shield goddess of the Mycenaean era. [15] Parts of Athena's story relate to both aspects of the Minoan goddess.

A connection to the tree goddess is apparent in the tale of the contest between Athena and Poseidon to determine who would rule Attica. As her gift to the people, Athena planted an olive tree and caused it to grow in rocky soil. For this she was judged victorious over Poseidon, who caused a salt spring to flow from a rock struck by his trident. The Acropolis was later erected on this same rock, but it was Athena who ruled, second to Zeus, over the city that was named after her.

A second link to the Minoan goddess is Athena's association with the snake. Artwork of the times often shows Athena in the company of snakes. The statue of Athena, c. 520 BCE, from the Archaic temple on the Acropolis, depicts a reflective Athena, gazing downward, with one arm slightly raised. Around her head is a wreath of snakes, and from the edge of her robe, a row of intertwined snakes creates a decorative and impressive border. The hand, which emerges from the robe, holds a snake's head. Other artwork shows a winged Athena with the same sort of snake border. [16] As R. W. Hutchinson concludes:

> The classical deity who embodied most of the spirit of the Minoan Snake Goddess was certainly Athena, not the fierce warrior goddess of Olympus as Homer represented her, but rather the maiden goddess as Pheidias saw her, the calm, benignant patron of the city, still faithful to her

bird (the owl), her snake, and her pillar, all familiar elements in the cult of the Household Goddess, the Snake Goddess of Crete, by one tradition the birthplace of Athena. [17]

Her association with the snake also appears on her shield with the depiction of the Medusa/Gorgon's head, replete with writhing snakes in place of hair. [18] The myth of the Gorgons [19] sheds additional light on the association of Athena with snakes.

The Gorgons were three sisters who lived in the direction of Night. They were named Sthenos, Euryale, and Medousa. Sthenos meant strength, Euryale pertained to the wide sea, and Medousa was also thought to have pertained to the sea. Medousa also means "ruleress." [20] Interestingly, she is the one sister of the three said to be the mortal one. It is Medousa, or Medusa, who is of the most interest in relation to Athena. If Athena did, indeed, come from Crete, she would have been a Greek goddess who came over the sea. Further, as the protector of the city-state of Athens, she was a ruler. These shared attributes suggest that Athena and Medusa derive from the same ancient figure.

Athena and Medusa's stories dramatically intersect through the adventures of Perseus. Perseus was the Greek hero whom Athena assisted in slaying the Gorgon. "This hero was named by his mother Eurymedon, as if he were a 'ruler of the sea' and Medousa's husband, not merely her slayer." [21] According to the myth, the look of the Gorgon could instantly turn men into stone. Athena's part in the story was to protect and guide Perseus in his task of winning the Gorgon's head. [22] She instructed him to not look directly at the Gorgon, but to use only the bright shield's reflection to see instead. In this way Perseus was able to sever the Gorgon's head without coming face-to-face with it, and avoided being turned to stone. Other versions of this myth tell of Athena handing a mirror to Perseus to assist him.

In short, the myth centers on an all too familiar theme: the Greek hero, aided by a goddess, uses violence to undermine female power, and is once again victorious through his violent measures. The myth of Medusa condones and validates male aggression through divine intervention and sanction. This may also reflect political changes in Greece, and "Zeus, as the embodiment of the new order, is also validated politically through the myth of Athena's birth through his head, since it is on her shield that the severed head of the gorgon finally comes to rest." [23]

Yet given the similarities and common associations between Athena and Medusa, a non-patriarchal interpretation is also possible. The Medusa/Gorgon's head is found at the shrines of both Artemis and Demeter, as well as in connection with Athena. The Gorgon could have once represented "the nature of a *function* for all the goddesses, and was only later identified exclusively with Athena."[24] Why would Athena assist Perseus in order to destroy that which may be recognized as a part of the goddesses and of her as well? Given Athena's attributes of reflection and sense of purpose, might she have had something else entirely in mind as she assisted Perseus in his quest?

Athena did give the mirrored shield, or a mirroring device, to Perseus—but perhaps not to help in the way that seems most obvious. Feminist scholars have speculated that the once positive attributes of the Medusa/Gorgon had been demonized in Greek society. Medusa appears to have been split off from more inclusive and complex goddesses, perhaps even an earlier version of Athena. Her stony gaze was a reflection of what was inherently wrong in the warring society. The unspeakable rage and hatred that must have arisen in the warriors of a city-state so often at war were projected onto her. Medusa stopped action and reflection, while Athena assisted it. They became opposites, but part of a whole. Perhaps *this* is the meaning of the Gorgon Medusa's head on Athena's shield.

While the snakes emerging from the Medusa's head writhe exaggeratedly, her gaze is still, cold, frozen. Athena, too, through her small and large actions—weaving, cultivation, and counsel in combat—displays a still, meditative quality. To be done well, her arts require stillness *and* action, reflection *and metis.*

In this case, the mirror Athena gave to Perseus may have been intended to reflect *his* image, as well as Medusa's. In it he might see his own hatred and rage. As May Sarton so aptly expressed: "I turned your face around! It is my face./That frozen rage is what I must explore—/Oh secret, self-enclosed and ravaged place!/That is the gift I thank Medusa for."[25] Athena could have also offered Perseus this gift—asking him to take a deep look at himself, and to reflect on the consequences of his past actions, as well as his intention to kill the Medusa/Gorgon. It is "perhaps the quality of self-disciplined awareness in Athena that [could] transform the terrifying face of instinct into a protective shield."[26] Such reflection might shock Perseus to his senses, and the Medusa (representing all women) would be spared from his sword, from having her head severed from her body!

Nonetheless, in the interpretation of the myth that prevailed, Perseus slew the Medusa/Gorgon, and her head came to rest as a symbol on Athena's shield. In this way the Medusa/Gorgon and Athena are integrated once more.

The powerful image of Athena holding her shield displaying the Medusa/ Gorgon's head is not necessarily a portrayal of the glorious victory of good over evil, or even of Athena's appropriation by patriarchal powers. Rather, it can serve as a reminder, a warning of what can happen when we are unable to look within and see ourselves fully—unable to see both the shadow and the light—either as individuals or as a society. When we become split, part of us dies. It may be a part that is necessary to live well and fully. Perhaps Athena displays this symbol in hopes that this kind of history does not repeat itself. She may be suggesting that we move fluidly between our many and varied aspects, to and fro like the weaver's shuttle between threads, to form conscious patterns in our lives and community. Or perhaps she is asking us to turn the shield around, back to our bodies without armor, back to the place of receptivity and creation, a place of reflection, back to the darkness, back to the womb, back to the mother, back to Metis. Is she trying to make us see that the only bloodshed we need is menstrual—that which gives life and does not rashly take it away? In this return, perhaps she asks us to reflect deeply, and choose wisely. By polishing our own mirrors and seeing ourselves fully we, too, may recover a more embodied whole.

Athene

I, Athene,
a father's daughter,
burst from the head of a male god.
I will not return there—
do not claim it as my own.

But look instead
to the womb of my mother,
who was swallowed
before giving birth.

Boldly now I turn
the father's shield around.
And in the turning,
re-turning,
conceive

the way back to
Metis' womb.

Reclaiming
the mother,
proudly reclaiming,
at last
I give birth
to myself.

—Susan Carter, Ph.D.

Notes

1 Metis has been variously translated by numerous scholars as "cleverness," "counsel," "prudent counsel," "intelligence", "cunning," and, most commonly, "wisdom." Metis has also been described as "divine personification of thought or counsel in Greek mythology" (see http://www.loggia.com/myth/metis.html from "Mythology—Greek Mythology").

2 Timothy Gantz. *Early Greek Myth, A Guide to Literary and Artistic Sources.* (Baltimore: The Johns Hopkins University Press, 1993, 1996), 1:51.

3 Carl Kerenyi. *Eleusis* (Princeton, New Jersey: Princeton University Press, 1967), 120. It is also interesting to note that this would connect Athena back to Earth rather than connecting her only to Zeus, the preeminent sky god of the Olympian pantheon.

4 Mary R. Lefkowitz and Maureen B. Fant., eds. *Women's Life in Greece and Rome: A Source Book of Translation* (Baltimore, Maryland: John Hopkins University Press, 1992), 45.

5 Sarah B. Pomeroy. *Goddesses, Whores, Wives, and Slaves* (New York: Schocken Books, 1975), 19.

6 Elaine Fantham, et al., *Women in the Classical World* (New York: Oxford University Press, 1994), 98.

7 Aeschuylus. *Eumenides* 657–667. Trans. A. J. Podlecki. (Warminster, England: Aris & Phillips Ltd., 1989).

8 Ibid 736–738.

9 For further discussion see Anne Baring and Jules Cashford. *The Myth of the Goddess* (London: Penguin Group, 1993), 338–340.

10 Arianna Stassinopoulos. *The Gods of Greece* (London: Weidenfeld & Nicolson, 1983), 141.

11 Anne Baring and Jules Cashford. *The Myth of the Goddess*, 338.

12 Eva C. Keuls. *The Reign of the Phallus* (Berkeley: University of California Press, 1985), 310. See also Figures 229, 230, and 231 in this book.

13 Arianna Stassinopoulos. *The Gods of Greece*, 140. For Plato's discussion about weaving and politics in its entirety see: *Plato's Statesman* 279a—283b. Trans. J.B. Skemp. (London: Routledge & Kegan Paul, 1952).

14 Both the tree and snake are associated with women, creation, and menstruation in world mythology. For further discussion see Judy Grahn. *Blood, Bread, and Roses: How Menstruation Created the World*. (Boston: Beacon Press, 1993), 57–68.

15 For further discussion see Anne Baring and Jules Cashford. *The Myth of the Goddess*, 337; Marija Gimbutas. *Goddesses and Gods of Old Europe* (Berkeley: University of California Press, 1974, 1982), 149; and Arianna Stassinopoulos. *The Gods of Greece*, 142.

16 See Figures 17 and 18a in Anne Baring and Jules Cashford. *The Myth of the Goddess*, 333, 334.

17 R.W. Hutchinson. *Prehistoric Crete*. (Baltimore, Maryland: Penguin Books, 1962), 209.

18 Numerous depictions of Athena with the Medusa/Gorgon's head appear in various Greek art mediums such as pottery (painted vases) and sculpture in art museums throughout the world. Several good examples are displayed in the Ny Carlsberg Glyptotek, Copenhagen, Denmark. For a published example see Figure 19 in Anne Baring and Jules Cashford. *The Myth of the Goddess*, 334.

19 For an archaeomythological investigation of the Gorgon see: Joan Marler. "An Archaeomythological Investigation of the Gorgon," *Revision* 25 (no.1, Summer 2002): 15–23.

20 Carl Kerenyi. *The Gods of the Greeks*. (New York: Thames and Hudson, 1951), 48–49.

21 Ibid. p. 50.

22 It is not to be forgotten however, that it was not Athena alone who assisted Perseus—the god Hermes also assisted in this task, since he knew where to find the Gorgon.

23 Anne Baring and Jules Cashford. *The Myth of the Goddess*, 341, 343; and Joan Marler. *Revision*, 22. Baring and Cashford contend that, "Perseus as a historical figure may have been the founder of a new dynasty around 1290 BC, in which case the myth may also be the recording of a decisive change in religious and political organization" 343. Joan Marler cites Diodorius Siculus (Sicilian historian from the first century BCE) who "wrote about Perseus battling a nation of 'valiant and bold' women warriors in Libya called 'Gorgones' (*Liber Quartus* 3.52.2)." She goes on to state that "some scholars argue that the beheading of Medusa by Perseus reflects an Argive conquest of Libya by the first wave of Achaeans, the suppression there of a matriarchal system, and the violation of the mysteries of the Libyan snake-goddess Lamia (Neith). Medusa, the Libyan queen who ruled the people of Late Tritonis, was killed by Perseus (the 'cutter' or 'destroyer') after she led her troops into battle against him." *Revision*, 21.

24 Anne Baring and Jules Cashford. *The Myth of the Goddess*, 341.

25 Mary Sarton. "The Muse as Medusa." *Selected Poems of May Sarton*. (New York: W.W. Norton & Company, Inc., 1978), 160.

26 Anne Baring and Jules Cashford. *The Myth of the Goddess*, 341.

Bibliography

Aeschuylus. *Eumenides*. Trans. A. J. Podlecki. Warminster, England: Aris & Phillips Ltd., 1989.

Baring, Anne and Jules Cashford. *The Myth of the Goddess*. London: Penguin Group, 1993.

Fantham, Elaine, et al. *Women in the Classical World*. New York: Oxford University Press, 1994.

Gantz, Timothy. *Early Greek Myth, A Guide to Literary and Artistic Sources*. 2 vols. Baltimore: The Johns Hopkins University Press, 1993, 1996.

Gimbutas, Marija. *Goddesses and Gods of Old Europe*. Berkeley: University of California Press, 1974, 1982.

Grahn, Judy. *Blood, Bread, and Roses: how menstruation created the world*. Boston: Beacon Press, 1993.

Hutchinson, R.W. *Prehistoric Crete*. Baltimore, Maryland: Penguin Books, 1962.

Kerenyi, Carl. *Eleusis*. Princeton, New Jersey: Princeton University Press, 1967.

———. *The Gods of the Greeks*. New York: Thames and Hudson, 1951.

Keuls, Eva C. *The Reign of the Phallus*. Berkeley: University of California Press, 1985.

Lefkowitz, Mary R., and Maureen B. Fant, eds. *Women's Life in Greece and Rome: A Source Book of Translation*. Baltimore, Maryland: John Hopkins University Press, 1992.

Marler, Joan. "An Archaeomythological Investigation of the Gorgon." *Revision* 25 (No. 1, Summer 2002): 15–23.

Plato. *Plato's Statesman*. Trans. J.B. Skemp. London: Routledge & Kegan Paul, 1952.

Sarton, May. "The Muse as Medusa." *Selected Poems of May Sarton*. New York: W.W. Norton & Company, Inc., 1978.

Arianna Stassinopoulos. *The Gods of Greece*. London: Weidenfeld & Nicolson, 1983.

Isis

Latonia Dixon

I existed before consciousness and
there was justice and balance.
I was there at your conception,
in the ecstasy of your Mother's glory.
You felt me in the fluid of your mother's womb.
I brought you feelings of trust, beauty,
intelligence, certainty, worthiness, and uniqueness.
I am the Dark Mother.

I was with you before you could speak,
before you were misunderstood.
I am the voice that whispered words of praise as
I held your hand when you were learning to walk.
I am the eternal peace that flowed through you
without any mental effort.
I protected you and never exposed you,
when you felt vulnerable and inadequate.
Instead I taught you boundaries.
I am the Dark Mother

I watched you as you were magical.
I caressed your soul.
I illuminated you with my love.

I told you that you are essential, indispensable, and important,
and that there is nothing wrong with you.
I accepted you unconditionally,
and loved you deeply.
I am the Dark Mother.

My grace is so relevant that you must pass me on to others
with confidence, admiration,
by being understanding, and non-judgmental,
through acceptance, innocence, and empowerment.
You feel my love, as it runs deep,
and you respond by relaxing and just being.
I have convinced you that I am never gone,
that I do exist.
You've experienced my gentle presence,
through the calmness of a spring breeze.
I am the Dark Mother.

I am the core of independence
I am spiritual wholeness
I am the logic of wisdom
I am truth, unification, and the erotic.
I am the insatiable expansion,
that fuels all innovations.
I am self-control and aspirations.
I am the Precious Reflection you see in the mirror everyday.
I guided you into your true authentic self,
who you are, into what you do, and have.
I breathe life into your soul.
You've known me for generations.
I am the Dark Mother.

She is Everywhere!

Velia Kroupa, M.A.

Prayer to Mary, the Black Madonna

Mother of dark soil,
Morning Star
and vast ocean—
Mother who births plants
winged creatures,
fish of the sea
and four-footed beasts—
Mother who nurses stars,
the planets,
the black universe—
Mother who suckles the children of the earth—
Mother who holds creation in her strong arms,
rocking it through the ages,
with the lullaby of life—
Show us your face, O Divine Mother,
Show us your face.

This prayer honoring Mary, the Mother of Jesus, is from *Resources for Peacemaking*, a section in the monthly publication *The Monastic Way*, created by Sister Joan Chittisier of the Benedictine order. The prayer reflects my personal devotion to Mary for whom I have a great love. My Baptismal name is

221

Maria Velia, which helps to explain why I always considered myself a "child of Mary."

This year I graduated from New College with a Masters degree in Women's Spirituality. My thesis has in its title the Rosary as a symbol of my healing process. The Rosary is a special devotional prayer to Mary that I dearly love. Because my heritage consists of Mexican maternal origins, I am strongly connected to the Virgin of Guadalupe, the Mexican patroness.

When I learned that Professor Lucia Chiavola Birnbaum from the California Institute of Integral Studies was leading a group to Spain to study and explore the Black Madonna, I quickly signed up to go. It was my first trip to Spain and as Spanish is my language of origin, I was excited to have the opportunity to speak it in Spain. And I hoped Mary would show her face.

Images of the Divine Feminine, in many forms, are found throughout Spain. She is Everywhwere. In the center of Madrid is the huge glorious Fountain of Cibeles (Cybele) represented in all the glory of her goddess nature. Two regal lions drive her chariot and angels are her porters behind the vehicle, ready to serve her. Along the Gran Via, a great avenue in the center of Madrid is a grand building, the Edificio Metropolis, that supports the beautiful statue of Winged Victory on its roof. This is a city that honors the feminine in mythology and religion. Although I found devotion to Mary, the mother of Jesus, everywhere in Spain, I will only mention the ones that I found especially meaningful to me.

Our Lady of Guadalupe

A statue of Our Lady of Guadalupe in the cathedral of Seville moved me and interested me because I knew nothing of her, so that my pilgrimage to Spain to find the Black Madonna resulted in just that. I found her. There is a town in Spain named Guadalupe. The story of this statue is part of the Spanish cult of Mary that attributes victories against invaders to the protection of Mary. When Don Rodrigo, the leader of the Visigoths, was defeated by Saracens in 711 and his people fled to the mountains, some of the knights on their way to Asturia took with them a statue of the Blessed Virgin. They placed her statue in an iron casket to keep it safe and buried it somewhere in a cave in the province of Estremadura in the northern part of Spain. The precious statue had been given to Bishop Leander of Seville by Pope Gregory the Great and was held in high regard by churchmen and secular people alike. The rule of the Saracens lasted for over four hundred years in Spain.

After the liberation, the country did not forget the promises made by its leaders to the Blessed Virgin for her intercession in their victory. Pilgrimages to sanctuaries in Covadonga, Saragossa, and other locations resulted in a strong cult of Mary that has withstood the test of time.

The Guadalupe shrine came into existence in 1326 when a cowherd named Gil found the casket buried in the earth. Pertinent documents verified its authenticity and though it had been buried for more than six hundred years, it was perfectly preserved. The Franciscan fathers were entrusted with her and the Shrine of Our Lady of Guadalupe became one of the most important pilgrim places in Spain. The Franciscan fathers who accompanied Columbus and later the conquistadors carried her statue with them. This inspired the Franciscans, and among them the first Bishop of Mexico, Zumaraga, to name the new shrine after the apparitions on the hill of Tepeyac in honor of the Virgin of Guadalupe in Spain. The new Guadalupe in Mexico was to outgrow, in importance, its prototype.

The original image of Our Lady of Guadalupe has distinctive Moorish and Spanish characteristics. Guadalupe, where the casket with the image had been buried, is also a mixed Spanish-Arab word meaning River of the Wolf. Estremadura was infested with wolves for centuries during the Middle Ages.

Our Lady of Montserrat

Montserrat is a magnificent mountain group, four thousand feet high, above twenty miles from Barcelona. The name, Montserrat, of Latin origin, means saw-edged mountain. It is formed by huge boulders that raise their immense bulk perpendicularly to that four thousand foot summit. It is similar to the inaccessible monasteries of Mount Athos in Greece.

The legend tells of shepherds who thought they saw light and heard music on the mountain. Guided by the shepherds, the bishop of Manresa found, in the cavern, a wooden figure of Our Lady and the Holy Child. He ordered that the statue be carried into the cathedral immediately. However, the procession with the statue never reached the cathedral because, after much marching, the small wooden figure became too heavy so that the Bishop decided to accept it as a sign and left it in a chapel of nearby hermitage. The statue remained there until a church was built on the top of the rocks near where it was discovered.

This statue is then most celebrated, the most important in Spain. It is thirty-eight inches in height and is known as "La Morenata" meaning The Little Black Madonna. The wood is now black with age; one of its most striking features is the dignified expression of Our Lady. In her right hand she holds a majestic orb.

All the kings of Spain have worshipped at this shrine, as well as shrines of most of the saints of the Catholic Church in Spain. Spain carried the Gospel to the western hemispheres. Spaniards were the missionaries who first taught their religion on the American continent. Most of the enthusiasm for this, I believe they derived from their devotion to the Blessed Virgin.

Today the monastery at Montserrat is occupied by the Benedictines. Their performance of the divine services if famous as is their choir school, the Escalonia, composed of forty boys. Its heavenly harmony persists.

Montserrat was my favorite Black Madonna in Spain. She moved me to tears. I love her.

El Pilar de Zaragoza

On the banks of the river Ebro, in Zaragoza, rises the Basilica of Our Lady of el Pilar, the jewel of the Baroque art in Aragon. The temple is visited by thousands of believers and pilgrims. It keeps the image of the Virgin of the Pilar at the center of an ancient veneration that dates back to apostolic times.

The legend is that the Blessed Virgin Mary began making appearances to believers even before she died. She appeared to the apostle James in Saragossa in 40 A.D. She appeared to the despondent missionary while he was in deep prayer and presented him with a column of jasper and a small wooden statue of herself. She instructed him to build a church there, the first ever dedicated to the Virgin Mary. She is said to have spoken: "This place is to be my house, and this image and column shall be the title and altar that you shall build.' And so the Basilica of Our Lady of Pilar was built.

James later returned to Jerusalem, where he was executed by Herod Agrippa in 44 A.D., thus becoming the first apostle to be martyred. The wooden statue and the jasper column still reside at Saragossa and are displayed on special occasions in the Compostella.

These Black Madonnas are dear to me because I discovered them late in my life. Though there were other Madonnas that I met in Spain that were new to me, such as the beautiful blonde and smiling White Virgin, the only Mary that looks into her baby Jesus' eyes and seems happy, the ones that I loved best were the Black Madonnas because their strength was palpable. La Macarena in Seville surprised me because I had never heard of her and because she seemed so richly dressed in gold.

Many other images of Mary throughout Spain reinforced the belief that she is everywhere. Indeed, she showed me her face over and over. I am grateful.

Mujer Azul

Dorotea Reyna, M.A.

i.

Where did I learn
This knowledge?
Restored like a cup
Of rainwater from
The pail?

Where did I know
To step where no one
Else ventured,
All alone?

How did I find
The cool of the river
By the blazing sun?

How did I trust
Woman's mystery
When all around me
I saw women in
Submission?

What reservoir
Now heals me even
As we pull away?

What alignment of
Blue planets?
Green galaxies?

How is it that I
Trust the one inch
Of me that has
Not been trodden
Or broken down?

Why trust
That inch?

ii.

There is a lady
Who is part
Portent and part
Holder of catastrophe

She is as old as
The ruinous galaxies

Surrounded by blue rings
She is as patient as Saturn
Comprehensive as the sea

She divides and redivides
Inside us; blessing the
Niña that forms,
Spirit's child

This lady questions
By her very existence

She is further away
Than a pearl, scarier than
Jesus.

iii.

Inside the Mexicana
She is never far away
Guadalupe,
Guadalquivir

She is the blue
Mantilla
In the sunniest smile
The comfort you never
Expected and now
Cannot live without

Agave-mujer
Blue sympathies from your
Thorniest roots

One taste of your elixir
And the conquistador's soul-rush
Is stilled

Inexhaustible mujer
They call you witch
Who heal by the touch
Who navigate surely the heart

No map-maker you are the
River quenching every damned
And blessed thing
You touch

iv.

Inside this blue kiss
You are agave
Delicate desert wine
Warmed by the bluest of
Midnight skies

Mexicana, your lips
Are surprisingly cool
I had imagined the fire
Of gitanas, but some new god
Has entered your kiss

V.

Tengo un libro
Éste libro
Sus palabras suenan
Dulces como las
Estrellas

Tengo un vientre
Capaz y sonrisa contenta

Acércate tú
Que ya me conoces
Para que yo te bendiga
Mientras te susurro

V.

(English translation)
"I have a book
This book
Its words sound
Sweet like the
Stars

I have a capable
Womb and a happy smile

Come closer
You already know me
So that I can bless you
While I whisper"

Guadalupe in the Heart of California

Jennifer Colby, Ph.D.

She is everywhere, but is there room for her, room in our society, room in our hearts?

Each December the metaphor of the Christian story of Mary's search for a place to give birth to her child is acted out in my tiny coastal California town by members of the Mexican community. For nine nights of *Posadas* the Virgin Mary in the form of a statue carried by children comes to the doors of the community and finds no room. She is ready to give birth and there is no place for her to spend the night. After singing at several houses, one door brings a different response. Finally this door is flung open with the recognition that she is the queen of heaven. A huge party begins with pozole, tostadas, tamales, children running underfoot, and piñatas bursting. I am *Maestra* (teacher) in this farming community south of San Jose, invited to join the hours of rosaries mixed with Spanish and English versions of Silent Night and children anticipating their bags of treats. The parents hope to give their children more than candy, an experience of their precious Mexico in their new land. They have brought images of the Virgin from their hometowns. In California prayers under the oak canopy declare she is here.

Far from the urban centers, I live in a rural area of California. I have made my own micro-geography the subject of my investigation of women's spirituality. This area from south of Hollister stretching to Watsonville is cut by the San Andreas Fault, and by four county lines. It is an area underserved by each county, forgotten by health care and transportation systems. What ties the region together is the social needs of migrant farm workers, the impact of growth as the Silicon Valley commuters arrive, and the geography of oak cov-

232

ered hills and rich farmland. It is the Pajaro River Watershed, whose tributary, the San Benito River, brings water from the Pinnacles and Indian Canyon through the Chittenden gap to the Monterey Bay. The Pajaro is a river neglected by most, altered by mining and levees, cursed during floods. School children plant trees by her banks where tourists once swam, and mourn her destruction down stream, where deforestation has destroyed the habitat of her namesake. Bird in Spanish, the mouth of the Pajaro was once home to thousands of species. I live in this watershed, on the San Andreas Fault, close enough to the Pacific for her breezes.

In my micro-geography, she is everywhere: in a sweat lodge in Indian Canyon, or in the Guadalupe chapel in San Juan Bautista, in a field of blue corn in Aromas protected with corn dollies, or in the Rodriguez Street Laundry in Watsonville where her altar is serenaded by the swoosh of turning dryers. She is celebrated by the local population as Guadalupe, the Virgin Mary, the goddess Tonantzin. In a 150-year-old adobe on the main street of San Juan Bautista, Galeria Tonantzin has offered a room, so to speak, for the Virgin by gathering together images by women artists from across the United States and beyond. For eleven years the exhibition "Images of the Virgin" has displayed art works in many media that have expanded our understanding of this icon. Artists and scholars have also gathered in San Juan Bautista each December for a yearly conference to explore why this image is so important to women today. The image of the Virgin has become a touchstone for women from various traditions. She is a symbol of the sacred female.

On December 12th you can rise with the San Juan Bautista roosters and celebrate holy mass at the Mission in honor of Our Lady of Guadalupe's feast day, followed by El Teatro Campesino's *La Virgen de Tepeyac* play every other year. You can also gather outside on the same morning under an oak tree in Watsonville where Guadalupe appeared. From Hollister to Watsonville, in my micro-geography, devotees of Mexico's Virgin Mary rise early to offer a home in their hearts to the Virgin, *La Morenita*, the little brown one. The basilica in Mexico City may be too far away for a pilgrimage, but the Virgin has sacred places here. Her story of appearing to the indio Juan Diego is enacted in the Mission, and the sacred image she left behind, the original being in the basilica in Mexico City, is reproduced and hung in special places. The earliest adobe walls of the San Juan Bautista Mission surround her image in the Guadalupe Chapel and a wall at Felipe's Mexican restaurant has been transformed by dozens of Virgin paintings. There you can eat a good chile relleno while contemplating her glory.

To celebrate her presence here I have invited women to San Juan Bautista for our yearly "Virgin Image" conference. They come from across the country in a kind of spiritual/intellectual/artistic pilgrimage to explore this phenomenon. College professors, young Chicana poets, grandmothers turned artists, therapists and business leaders gather to contemplate images of the sacred female, to walk the streets of San Juan, enjoy *El Teatro* and enchiladas at *Jardines*, and consider the *Virgen de Guadalupe* who has found a home here. The iconographic history of the Virgin image is explored as well as contemporary transformations of her image in women's art.

The amazing thing about an image is its ability to have multiple meanings and to transform to fill the needs of people. Can women re-image the traditional Virgin, make her less passive, and endow her with characteristics of powerful, everyday women? Many artists have. Black Madonnas are icons revered in special places across Europe, often where the church was built over an earlier sacred site, a healing well, a place where the goddess was worshiped. Is Guadalupe the Black Madonna of Latin America, her church built on the mount of Tepeyac where the goddesses were honored? The core of what the participants at the yearly gathering in San Juan Bautista have found out over ten years is that when women connect with images of the empowered sacred female they connect with their own power and sacredness. The images become a counter to the media exploitation of women as objects. Women become subjects, agents of their own lives, as they explore the images of the Virgin and she who is behind her.

Mother of God, or goddess herself, she brings a sacred story into a sacred landscape. Scholars with roots in Mexico, Poland, Italy, India, and Brazil have traced for us the threads of images of the sacred female in cultures that honor the goddess and honor the earth, and they have shown us how that memory has been kept alive in the image of the Virgin. We have also listened to local Coastanoan Anne Marie Sayers recall the Native American history in San Juan Bautista, giving us a local example of honoring the earth and honoring the balance between male and female and all living beings. Her values are brought to this particular place, my community, through both the indigenous people of the land and the icon of the Mexican culture, celebrated by women artists.

It is this rootedness in place, in the history of San Juan Bautista and the contemporary local community of artists, poets and actors, adults and children, farmers and business owners, Anglos, Native Americans, Chicanos and Mexican Americans, that makes Galería Tonantzin a home for these images of the Virgin. Artists have asked "what's under your skirts Guadalupe?" and found a powerful earth based, compassionate mother who calls her people to work for justice. Guadalupe has been the "estandarte" the banner leading the Mexican revolution and the farm workers' struggle for rights. She is celebrated in our town by the *Teatro Campesino*, the theatre troupe born in the long marches to Sacramento that created the farm workers union. Here in our part of *Aztland*, the sacred homeland of the Mexica/Aztec, she calls us to offer room in our hearts for compassion, care for the earth and justice.

At Galería Tonantzin Virgin images range from paintings of the traditional icon by Marina de Silva to complex collages by Lynn Aisawa that challenge the Virgin image as a prescription for female submission. Byzantine iconography is placed next to images of Black Madonnas of Europe, Africa and Latin America and images of Kali from Asia. This multicultural view of the Virgin Mary is centered on images of Guadalupe, the Mexican variety, so important to the local community. Chicana artists who transformed the image of Guadalupe were critiqued for raising her skirts, putting high heels on her, for suggesting a sexuality of the image. Chicana artists have explored Guadalupe's indigenous roots and her syncretic relationship to Tonantzin and Coatlique. Carmen Leon depicts Tonantzin as the mother of all embracing the Virgin—mother and child of the corn. Anglo artists also depict Guadalupe, embracing her cross culturally. During the 2000 conference the "Guadalupe Dialogue" explored the issues surrounding women from different cultural backgrounds embracing Guadalupe in their art. Chicana activists asked "What do you think you are doing when you use Guadalupe in your work?" Anglo artists responded that they couldn't deny that Guadalupe is speaking to their soul. Seen as the local manifestation of the dark mother, Guadalupe is embraced outside of the national and ethnic boundaries in which she appeared, but not without questions surrounding her appropriation.

In this dialog I spoke to the issues of living in California as our demographics change and communities become more Latino. In this context Mexican culture is influencing the dominant Anglo culture. How do we honor each other's experience and create art that is not a commercial appropriation similar to other ways global capitalism swallows up minority cultures? When members of the dominant culture embrace the image of Guadalupe do they embrace the values of justice she represents, embracing the marginalized peoples she appeared to? Guadalupe is still identified with the other, the altar in the back of the church that women pray to, not the Christ in the center. She represents the subaltern, feminine perspective that is not honored in our competitive, commercial society. Despite her marginalization by the powerful, she is everywhere.

One year during the *Posada* in Aromas the Virgin was carried in procession past the Protestant and Anglo American Christmas carolers in the park. I was struck with being in the procession with the marginalized of our little community, "asking for *Posada*", looking for a room for the night, while the triumphant carols declared the light of Euro-American male centered culture. The Virgins of many immigrant groups have carried the feminine principle of the dark mothers to our continent where they have encountered the stronghold of Protestant Patriarchy alongside displaced Native cultures. At Tepeyac in Mexico Cortez's Guadalupe of Extremadura encountered the multiple goddesses of the Mexica culture and the story of Guadalupe/Tonantzin was born.

In San Juan Bautista Franciscan missionaries encountered the Mutsun/ Ohlone/Coastanoan peoples of Popalucian, a site sacred to twenty-two surrounding villages. As the native peoples escaped the restrictions of the Mission they went to Indian Canyon, where today ceremony is continued on the only federally recognized Indian land on 350 miles of coastal California from Santa Rosa to Santa Barbara. Many believe that California Indians are extinct today, however the Coastanoan people who have survived are reclaiming their land and sacred practices. At the end of the nineteenth century it was safer for native Californians to claim Mexican heritage. Many women continued their ceremonies in secret, while on the surface being good Catholics. The gold rush brought a bounty on native California lives. Going underground this culture survived, reemerging today.

This carrying of the feminine principle in women's ceremony and devotion to Guadalupe has erupted in contemporary popular devotion and in women's art. Carol Whitehill's hand colored photographs of the Guadalupe shrine at Pinto Lake celebrate Guadalupe's local apparition in 1992 to a Mexican woman, a laid off cannery worker. After the apparition the familiar silhouette of Guadalupe was left emblazoned on an oak tree. This tree has become the pilgrimage destination for thousands who leave candles, flowers, and photos at this outdoor shrine. Guadalupe, moved out of the Watsonville church destroyed by the 1989 earthquake, finds a home in the natural world. Visiting last December 12th I witnessed early morning rituals with sage and tobacco, recalling the layers of indigenous belief that under gird devotion to Guadalupe. Amidst Mexican teens and grandmothers I said my own prayers and walked out to the water behind the tree to watch an egret soar. She was there, guarding the water and she led me to see that the next step on my activist path is to work to protect the Pajaro River Watershed. And so I have, through art, which is the best way I know how to, embarked on a project to tell the stories of the river.

The river brings me back to my micro-geography, to the sacred waterfalls of Indian Canyon, and the Gabilan mountain range. She is here without her Catholic layers of the Virgin Image, mother earth in a more pure form. She is also here at my home. Each oak tree has an opening, a vaginal form that could be the Virgin's silhouette, an echo of the opening of caves marked with red ochre, an aperture for the sacred female. I see her in the mountains across the valley, shaped like a woman's body. I hear her in the winds through the pines, in the voices of my beautiful daughters growing into women, in my husband's embrace. In my life connected to land, to the natural world and the political world of saving rivers, serving low income children, teaching social justice and racial and gender equity, and connecting women to their creativity. She is here. In my home I have made room for her and for her values of justice and compassion.

Where is there no room for her? The metaphor of the *Posadas* connects the story of the Virgin to the life of immigrants, wanderers through the ages who bring their sacred story into new lands, but are marginalized or forgotten. The meeting of cultures in the landscape is a theatre where power is acted out. We need to understand this history. Do we honor the Mutsen/Ohlone/Coastanoan of this watershed and our roots as part of the South West, the mythical homeland Aztland of the Chicanos, the South West that was part of the Mexican nation until 1848? These cultures honor this land as sacred. How do we recognize the Spanish land grants and the Mexican period, forgotten aspects of our California history not always taught when fourth grade children celebrate the gold rush and the railroad that brought Levi and Stanford while isolating the Chinese immigrants? Where is the story of the Virgins brought by Italian immigrants to Monterey, or the stories of courage by local Japanese farmers interned at Manzanar? How do we recognize Mexican farm workers for both immigrating and returning to their homeland, a land without borders? As the West was won by dominant Protestant capitalist values these stories were submerged. As Silicon Valley capitalists invade our farming community today they again bring dominant values into our midst. To counter that, artists and activists are engaged in re-membering our history and calling forth a future.

This spring in San Juan Bautista the gallery is filled with women's art, not the Virgin images, but collages of hope for peace in a time of war. Lavender and rose perfume fills the gallery with the scents of the goddess, and someone buys a necklace of amber beads. While talking about the future of exhibiting women's art and teaching classes here my hand forms a cup. I feel I have created a vessel, a space for women's art and a room for her. Galeria Tonantzin and Studio San Juan provide a gathering place for women to explore their creativity and spirituality and to connect to the sacredness of the land and to our multicultural history. As we sort out our commitments and connections as Californians living in a more and more diverse society we are challenged by the image and story of Guadalupe, by the Virgin of the *Posada* seeking a home, and by the respect of indigenous peoples for the feminine energies of Earth and Spirit. She is everywhere, especially in my micro-geography in the heart of central California and in women's art that calls us to remember the sacred female and her values of love and justice.

La Virgen Maria: Queen of Guatemala

Elizabeth Webster Shillington, Ph.D.

Studies of Mary in Mexico and Central America carried out by people in the English-speaking world tend to focus almost entirely on Our Lady of Guadalupe in Mexico, to the exclusion of many of the other rich forms of Marian devotion that exist in Central America.[1] Although little has been written about it, Guatemala is an example of a country where Mary's presence can be seen and felt everywhere. Indeed, *la Virgen María* is the Queen, Mother, Patroness, and Co-Founder of the nation. Through her the Guatemalan people have links to their own past, comfort in their present situation, and hope for the future.

The Conquest

The Virgin Mary arrived in Guatemala with the Spanish conquistadors, who, led by Don Pedro de Alvarado, conquered Guatemala in 1524. Both Spanish and K'iche' texts attest to her presence in the battles between the conquistadors and the native Maya. According to the Spanish chronicler Francisco Vasquez, Mary appeared on the battlefield as a beautiful white girl who defended the Spaniards and, together with her angels, blinded the Indians, rendering them ineffective in battle.[2] A similar story is told in a K'iche' version dating from the sixteenth century, which noted that the K'iche' could not defeat Alvarado because he was defended by a very white girl surrounded by "birds without feet" (the iconographic representation of angels).[3] In this version the K'iche' wanted to kill the girl, but the "birds without feet" protected her.

The Spanish lost little time in imposing their Catholic faith on the New World. The Maya were forced to live in newly laid out villages, each with a central square, an administrative building and a church that contained at least an image of the cross and of the Virgin Mary. Native religious shrines were converted to Christian use and the miracles and legends of the saints taught to the Maya.[4] Spain had thus far resisted the influence of Protestantism, so many of the traditions that were dying out in Europe were given particular emphasis in the newly colonized lands, especially those involving the sacraments and the cult of the saints.[5] *Cofradías* (brotherhoods) were established to care for the images of the saints, which were often housed in people's homes due to lack of space inside the churches. This practice gave members of the *cofradías* more privacy to carry out their rituals in a more traditional form than was officially sanctioned by the Church.[6]

The Maya of Guatemala resisted the new religion because it was being forced upon them, but they found many elements of Catholicism compatible with their own religion, including the altars, baptism, confession, incense, fasting, celibacy, pilgrimages, and the drinking of wine in a ritual context.[7] The cross was already an important symbol of the four directions. New names were given to old practices and deities, giving the outward appearance of compliance with the new religion. Even the *cofradías* were similar to the *chinamit* of pre-conquest times.[8] However, the old ways were not forgotten. Aspects of Maya religion that were repugnant to the Spaniards continued to exist, but in a more hidden form. Human sacrifice, for example, was still carried out, but in secret and sometimes with the added Christian element of crucifixion.[9] Members of the pantheon of deities were given the names of Catholic saints, but the associations with the original deities remained very strong.

Mary was introduced to the Maya primarily in her forms of *la Immaculada* (the Immaculate Conception) and *la Asunción* (the Assumption). The Spanish artist Pacheco, who was a member of the Inquisition, made it mandatory that the Immaculate Conception and the Assumption be depicted with the Virgin standing on a crescent moon and surrounded by stars.[10] Thus the Maya associated her with their Moon Goddess, who was depicted in their own art with a crescent moon.[11] The Moon Goddess was also the goddess of childbirth, weaving, water, medicine, agriculture, and maize.[12] Soon Mary became associated with those domains too. She was often invoked in prayers to the *Chacs* (rain gods).[13] In Chenalhó, people make an offering to the lunar Mary by throwing their clothes into the lake.[14] The Maya of the Yucatan refer to her as

"Beautiful lady, guardian (or embracer) of the maize."[15] The Tzotzil weavers in Magdalenas pray to Mary for help with their weaving.[16]

Mary is also sometimes referred to as the wife of Christ (*la mujer de Cristo*).[17] The Sun is often associated with Jesus and in Maya myth the Sun is married to the Moon Goddess.[18] Thus the ancient concept of the sacred marriage seems to exist quite naturally in Maya Catholicism.

There are a couple of significant differences between Mary and the Moon Goddess, however. The Moon Goddess was not faithful to her husband, the Sun, and she is often portrayed in myth and art as a bad-tempered old woman.[19] In contrast, Mary is the perpetual Virgin, sweet-tempered, beautiful, and young. The Moon Goddess is older than the Sun and is said to have once been as bright as he, but he blinded her in one eye at the request of the people so that they could sleep better at night with the dimmer light.[20] This myth certainly suggests to me the possibility of an earlier time when the feminine was more honored in Guatemala than it later came to be. This decrease in the power of the Goddess has, of course, its parallels in many (if not all!) ancient cultures.

Images of the saints, as well as that of the cross, are believed by the Maya to contain divine power and are thus worshipped as deities, rather than as representations of saints. Many statues of Jesus and Mary are considered to be miraculous and have large cult followings. The most important of these in present-day Guatemala is the Black Christ in Esquipulas. However, there are also some of the Virgin Mary that have had particular historical and religious significance.

Nuestra Señora del Socorro

The statue of *Nuestra Señora del Socorro* (Our Lady of Succor) is considered to be the oldest statue of Mary in Guatemala. It is believed to have arrived with the conquistadors who accompanied Don Pedro de Alvarado in the early sixteenth century. Due to this association, she is also known as *La Conquistadora*. Her very first title was *La Piedad* (Piety or Mercy), but this title was changed to *Nuestra Señora del Socorro* in 1527.[21] The first church built in the original capital of Guatemala was dedicated to Santiago, but it had an altar to *Nuestra Señora del Socorro*, where people came with their vows and prayers. In the early days few people attended masses held on Sundays or even on Christmas or Easter, but it was considered a sacrilege to overlook the mass of Our Lady on Saturdays. In fact, when the governors wanted to make a new decree or law and put it quickly before the people, they did so at the end of the Saturday mass for *Nuestra Señora* in the recently founded city.[22]

A number of images of the Virgin Mary in Guatemala have the title of *La Conquistadora*, which they have held since the time of the conquest. One of them is *Nuestra Señora de la Merced* (Our Lady of Mercy), who is also said to have appeared in the battles and revolts of the conquest of Guatemala and Mexico.[23] Another is *Nuestra Señora de los Remedios* (Our Lady of the Cures), a small statue that is reputed to have been brought from Spain by one of the conquistadors devoted to Mary. A disposition of Jorge de Alvarado on November 22, 1527 at the establishment of the City of Santiago of Guatemala ordered a chapel built for her, which is also recorded in a city document dated July 28, 1532.[24] The image of *Nuestra Señora del Socorro*, however, is the "official" *conquistadora*. She is considered by some to be the Mother and Co-Founder of Guatemala because she was the first woman to come with Don Pedro de Alvarado to Guatemala and is much more known and loved than he was.[25]

The statue of *Nuestra Señora del Socorro* is sixty-five centimeters high and is made of wood from an orange tree, giving her skin an olive color. It dates from the end of the fifteenth century, before the Council of Trent. The original figure, clad in a bright blue mantle, held the baby Jesus in her left arm and with her right arm offered him her left breast. In his left hand he held a little bird. Her oval face had a serene expression and her head of long, golden hair was covered with a mantilla. Not only was this statue a beloved image of Mary, but it was also considered an excellent example of Renaissance art with some Gothic characteristics.[26]

This image of *Nuestra Señora del Socorro* disappeared for a number of years after the decisions of the Council of Trent reached Guatemala in 1565. When she reappeared several years later in a less conspicuous place near the main altar of the church, she was no longer nursing the Christ child. She was elegantly reclothed, had a new head of hair, and in her right hand she held a silver bouquet instead of her breast.[27]

Nuestra Señora del Socorro played her most important role as the one to whom people came with petitions for rain and safety from earthquakes and volcanic eruptions. She became known as *la abogada del agua* (advocate for water).[28] In a series of liturgical processions imploring divine mercy, the primary images petitioned included those of *Nuestra Señora del Socorro*, *la Virgen del Coro* (the Virgin of the Crown), *la Virgen del Rosario* (the Virgin of the Rosary), *la Virgen de la Merced* (the Virgin of Mercy), and *la Virgen de los*

Pobres (the Virgin of the Poor).[29] These processions usually involved carrying the statue out into the streets or countryside where the Virgin could view the parched or ruined land. When, for example, a major volcanic eruption occurred in 1705, people prayed to *Nuestra Señora del Socorro*. As soon as they began their supplications the air began to clear and when the procession went out from the church the dark cloud that had remained over the volcano dissipated. She was also petitioned during many subsequent earthquakes and volcanic eruptions, especially the devastating earthquake of 1717.[30]

La Virgen de Candelaria

The most famous Marian pilgrimage site in Guatemala is that of *la Virgen de Candelaria*. She is a life-size statue of Mary that was also brought to Guatemala from Spain by the conquistadors.[31] Her shrine is in a church in the town of Chiantla in the highland area of Huehuetenango. Although the church itself has no particular architectural merit, the shrine is one of the most ornate in Guatemala.[32] The Virgin is covered with silver, stands on a silver pedestal, and wears a gold crown with diamonds and other precious jewels in it.[33] This image of *la Virgen de Candelaria* is thought to be miraculous. Pilgrims for centuries have visited the shrine from Mexico and all over Central America with their offerings and petitions.[34]

The legend surrounding this Virgin is similar to the one about Guadalupe in Mexico. According to popular tradition, an old Indian man was walking near Chiantla one day when he saw a beautiful lady floating down the valley on a maguey until she came to a stop at a particular rose tree. On subsequent days he continued to see the same vision until he understood that the rose tree was where she wanted a church built for her. The church was then erected on that spot and the town grew around it.[35]

In early colonial times, Don Pedro de Almengor, owner of the silver mine near Chiantla that still bears his name, in gratitude for many bounties, offered the Virgin a silver robe. As he wished the workmanship to be of the finest, he brought an artisan from Spain to fashion it. Still not content, he promised to make her niche of silver also...

Time went on. The mine gave forth of its treasures. But Don Pedro, oblivious of his pledge to the Virgin, thought only of amassing greater riches and neglected to make the silver niche for the Virgin...

Our Lady of Chiantla, grown weary of waiting, punished him for his failure to keep his promise. She caused the mountain-side to slide down upon the mine, sealing the entrance.

Thus, Don Pedro was entombed with all his miners and the silver mine of Almengor was never worked again.

Often at dusk, on the trail to Almengor, a bent over figure is seen on a mule: it is Don Pedro himself who passes by striving to carry the promised silver to the Virgin. He bears the great burden of his unfulfilled pledge and his spirit can find no rest.[36]

The *santos* (syncretized saints) of the Maya are not always beneficent. They can be vengeful when they are neglected or promises are not kept.[37]

La Virgen del Rosario

La Virgen del Rosario (the Virgin of the Rosary), also known as *Nuestra Señora de la Antigua* or *la Domina*, was commissioned by Dominican priest Friar Lope de Montoya in 1592. She was fashioned out of pure silver by three silversmiths in Antigua, Guatemala a few years later. According to popular legend, *La Virgen del Rosario* was travelling through America with the Christ child. When they reached Guatemala, he fell asleep, so she decided to stay there.[38]

In the early seventeenth century *la Virgen del Rosario* was reputed to be the best and most beautiful statue of its kind in the Americas.[39] It depicts a gracious and maternal Mary holding in her arms a sleeping child with a small dove between his fingers. At her feet is a crescent moon of silver. She and her son both hold a rosary. She is richly dressed and surrounded by a halo of seventy-seven stars. Her face is said to turn pale at times of national calamity or imminent disaster.[40]

In 1650 an Extraordinary Jubilee was declared for the Rosary, which was celebrated in Guatemala on February 12 of the following year. In a magnificent procession, the image of *la Virgen del Rosario* was carried from the Santo Domingo Church in Antigua to the Cathedral. A week later, on February 19, she was to be carried solemnly to her chapel, but on February 18 a large earthquake shook the city. A perpetual guard was set up around the statue, praying the rosary so that she would intercede for the people.[41] These earthquakes instigated a tradition of praying the rosary every day in the Church of Santo Domingo. Due to the protection received in the earthquakes of 1651, she was named "Patroness of the City against the Earthquakes." Her fiesta was then celebrated on the Sunday closest to February 18 every year.[42] Thereafter, whenever a volcanic eruption or an earthquake occurred, people prostrated themselves at the feet of the Virgin.

Early in the last century the bishops of Guatemala sent a petition to Rome with 35,000 signatures requesting that *la Virgen del Rosario* be named Mother, Queen, and Patroness of the Nation. Pope Pius XI agreed to a Pontifical Coronation *of la Virgen del Rosario*, naming her Patroness of Guatemala. Monseñor Luis Durou, Archbishop of Guatemala, as the Pontifical Representative, solemnly crowned the image of *la Virgen del Rosario* on January 28, 1934 in the atrium of the Metropolitan Cathedral before a huge throng of people, all calling her Queen and Patroness of Guatemala. In 1969 Pope Paul VI, in a papal bull, elevated the church of Santo Domingo to the status of the Pontifical Basilica of Our Lady of the Rosary. The Basilica was consecrated in 1970.

The *Fiesta de la Rosa* is celebrated on the first Sunday in May. On this day roses are solemnly blessed and distributed to the faithful. The blessing of Christ is invoked so that the roses transmit spiritual and bodily health. Miracles are reputed to have occurred for sick people who drink the water of these roses with faith, invoking with devotion *la Virgen del Rosario*.[43]

Semana Santa

The city of Antigua in Guatemala has hosted celebrations of *Semana Santa* (Holy Week) since the sixteenth century that are now second in the world only to those in Seville, Spain. One of the first of these took place when Antigua first became the capital in 1543.[44] Processions and *velaciones* (holy vigils) take place throughout Lent, culminating in Holy Week processions that draw visitors from around the world. The processions take place every Sunday in Lent until Holy Week, when several magnificent ones take place each day of Maundy Thursday, Good Friday, and Holy Saturday. In each procession a massive float of Jesus is carried throughout the streets of the city for twelve hours, borne on the shoulders of male volunteers dressed in purple robes, who switch with fresh volunteers at every block. Behind the float is a brass band playing a funerary march. A second (somewhat smaller) float of Mary follows and at the tail end of the procession are small pedestals bearing Mary Magdalene and Saint John. The people of Antigua prepare lavish *alfombras* (intricately patterned carpets) of flower petals and colored sawdust in the streets for the processions to walk over.

Mary appears in the processions of Lent and Holy Week as *La Dolorosa* (Our Lady of Sorrows) or *La Soledad* (Our Lady of Solitude). Although she is present in the processions in Spain, she is carried by men there.[45] In Guatemala, the women bear Mary on their shoulders as an act of penitence and devotion. Most of the sculptures used date from the seventeenth century. They are made from wood cut on the south coast during the waning quarter of the moon (but not on Friday since that would bring back luck).[46]

La Dolorosa appears in processions on the first Friday in Lent, each Sunday, the Friday before Palm Sunday, Maundy Thursday, and Good Friday. Holy vigils are held for her in two churches in Antigua on the Tuesday and Wednesday before Holy Week. In Guatemalan sculptural tradition, she is the most important figure of the passion after Jesus. She is typically depicted with her hands reaching out and her face looking heavenward, as if beseeching God to spare her son. She has the sword plunged into her breast that was prophesied by Simeon in the Gospel of Luke. Most of the churches in Antigua have a sculpture of *La Dolorosa*, which appears in the Lenten processions. These processional sculptures are usually much lighter than other sculptures. Their robes are of velvet with gold embroidery and they often have real hair pieces.[47] A couple of the more famous *Dolorosas* include *La Dolorosa* from La Merced Church in Antigua, sculpted by Pedro de Mendoza in the seventeenth century and a more recent one created by Guatemalan sculptor Santiago Rojas in 1963 in the church of San Bartolomé Becerra.[48]

La Soledad depicts Mary after the crucifixion. She is usually portrayed with an expression of deep sorrow, looking straight ahead of her with tears running down her cheeks.[49] In her hands she holds the three nails that pierced the hands and feet of Jesus and his crown of thorns. One of the most famous statues of *La Soledad* has been on display in La Escuela de Cristo Church in Antigua since 1664. Sculpted by Pedro de Mendoza, it depicts Mary with dark skin and black hair.[50] On the afternoon of Good Friday, *La Soledad* appears in a few processions following a statue of Jesus (*Señor Sepultado*) lying inert in a glass coffin. On Holy Saturday all the processions are only for *La Soledad*, carried by women dressed in black. It is a day that is focused entirely on the sorrow of Mary and only women are involved in those processions.

Other *Marías*

In addition to the images of Mary already mentioned, there are many others. She has over twenty-four titles in Guatemala, among which the following are most important:

Nuestra Señora de la Asunción	(Our Lady of the Assumption)
Nuestra Señora de Guadalupe	(Our Lady of Guadalupe)
Nuestra Señora de Belen	(Our Lady of Bethlehem)
Nuestra Señora de Loreto	(Our Lady of Loreto)
Nuestra Señora de las Mercedes	(Our Lady of Mercies)
Nuestra Señora de Morenos	(Our Lady of the Indigenous People)
Nuestra Señora de los Pobres	(Our Lady of the Poor)
Nuestra Señora de los Remedios	(Our Lady of the Cures)
Nuestra Señora de las Rosas	(Our Lady of the Roses)[51]

Our Lady of the Assumption gave her name to the present day capital of Guatemala, *Guatemala de la Asunción*, known in English as Guatemala City. She is celebrated every year in Guatemala from August 14–18, the main day being on August 15, which is celebrated as the feast day of the Assumption in all Catholic countries.[52]

Our Lady of Guadalupe has a significant presence in Guatemala, although not as great as in Mexico. On her feast day on December 12, *ladino* children in Guatemala dress up in *traje*, the traditional Maya clothing. The little boys sport fake moustaches in imitation of Juan Diego. In Antigua, a children's procession carrying a small statue of Guadalupe parades through the streets.

Conclusion

In the years since the conquest, the Maya of Guatemala have continued to endure horrific violence under the rule of the governing elite. They have suffered rape, torture, and innumerable massacres. Perhaps that is why the Holy Week processions remain such huge events in Guatemala. In other parts of the world, the Resurrection of Christ celebrated on Easter Sunday is the culminating point of the Lenten season. In Guatemala, however, the final day of Lent is Holy Saturday, when the sorrowful *Soledad* is paraded through the streets. Once she is returned to her place in the churches, everyone goes home to sleep and recover from the outpouring of energy and emotion. Easter passes practically unnoticed. The reality of the Guatemalan people since the conquest has been characterized far more by suffering, pain, and death than by hope and resurrection. Huge amounts of money, time, energy, and resources are poured into the Lenten processions depicting the passion and death of

Christ. When Easter finally arrives, the streets are deserted. Only the remnants of trampled *alfombras* and trash discarded by pilgrims from all over the world mark the fact that the suffering of Christ and his mother, Mary, have ceased…at least for a moment.

The conquistadors ushered in centuries of great suffering for the Maya, but ironically they also brought with them a means of providing some measure of solace in the aftermath of the destruction. Mary, the grieving mother, is an appropriate Queen for a country that has been so devastated by death and anguish. She knows what it means to suffer, to see a son murdered, to be helpless in preventing her loss. For Guatemalans of faith, she, perhaps more than the risen Christ, offers hope and consolation. With her pain they can identify; with Christ's dominion over death they can not—yet.

> *¡Ten piedad de nosotros, Señora!*
> *Nuestro canto va unido al fervor…*
> *Guatemala, de hinijos te implora:*
> *¡No la apartes jamás de tu amor!*[3]

> (Have mercy on us, Lady!
> Our song goes united in fervor…
> Guatemala, on her knees implores you:
> Never separate her from your love!)

Notes

Muchas gracias to Elizabeth Bell, Charlene Spretnak, Elizabeth McCullough, Ginger Hooven, John C. B. Webster, and Laura Amazzone, M.A. for their pearls of wisdom!

1 The paucity of material available outside Guatemala on Mary *in* Guatemala is typical of the way Central America tends to get overlooked in scholarly studies (except by anthropologists and linguists). Despite its proximity to the United States and Mexico, its invisibility may be partly due to the fact that the United States has contributed a great deal to its violent history.

2 Miguel Alvarez Arevalo, *Nuestra Señora del Socorro: presente en los 500 años de evangelización de America* (Guatemala: Serviprensa Centroamericana, 1989) 15.

3 Ibid.

4 Donald E. Thompson, *Maya Paganism and Christianity: A History of the Fusion of Two Religions.* Middle American Research Institute (New Orleans: Tulane University, 1954) 12.

5 Manuel M. Marzel, "Transplanted Spanish Catholicism," in *South and Meso-American Native Spirituality*, ed. Gary H. Gossen. (New York: Crossroad, 1993) 154–155.

6 Sandra Orellana, *The Tzutujil Mayas: Continuity and Change, 1250–1630* (Oklahoma: University of Oklahoma Press, 1984) 215.

7 Ibid., 208.

8 Ibid.

9 Thompson, 14.

10 Ibid.

11 Susan Milbrath, *Star Gods of the Maya* (Austin: University of Texas Press, 1999) 119, 150.

12 Sylvanus Griswold Morley, *The Ancient Maya* (California: Stanford University Press, 1947) 230; Nathan L. Whetten, *Guatemala: The Land and the People* (New Haven: Yale University Press, 1961) 291; Thompson, 28.

13 Thompson, 28.

14 Milbrath, 33.

15 Thompson, 28; Robert Redfield and Alfonso Villa Rojas, *Chan Kom: A Maya Village* (Chicago: The University of Chicago Press, 1962) 116.

16 Milbrath, 33.

17 Whetten, 291.

18 Milbrath, 23, 31.

19 Morley, 230.

20 Thompson, 7.

21 Alvarez Arevalo, 11.

22 Ibid., 14.

23 Ibid., 17.

24 Ibid., 18.

25 Ibid., 60.

26 Ibid., 33–34.

27 Ibid., 35. I assume this change was due to the section in the Twenty-Fifth Session of the Council of Trent that prohibits the adornment of a statue "with a beauty exciting to lust."

28 Ibid., 39.

29 Ibid., 37.

30 Ibid., 37–38.

31 Edith Hoyt, *The Silver Madonna: Legends of Shrines, Mexico-Guatemala* (Mexico: Editorial Letras, 1963) 23.

32 Adrian Recinos, *Monografia del Departamento de Huehuetenango* (Guatemala: Editorial del Ministerio de Educacion Publica, 1954) 302.

33 Recinos, 303; Hoyt, 23.

34 Recinos, 301; Hoyt, 23.

35 Hoyt, 23–24.

36 Ibid., 24.

37 Thompson, 26.

38 "Guatemala: Our Lady of the Rosary," The Mary Page. http://udayton.edu/mary/resources/engfour.html

39 *Reina Consagrada* (Guatemala: Delgado Impresos, 1995) 5.

40 "Guatemala: Our Lady of the Rosary."

41 *Reina Consagrada*, 7.

42 Ibid.

43 Ibid., 8.

44 Elizabeth Bell, *Lent and Easter Week in Antigua* (Guatemala: Impresos Industriales, 1995) 3.

45 Ibid., 4.

46 Ibid., 44.

47 Ibid., 47

48 Ibid., 59, 64.

49 These tears are often made of crystal. Ibid., 37.

50 Ibid., 75.

51 Arturo Dibar, *El culto a nuestra señora en la epoca del descubrimiento y de la conquista en Nueva España y tierra firme* (Guatemala de La Asuncion, 1971) 90.

52 R.P. Luis Diez de Arriba,. *Historia de la Iglesia de Guatemala. Tomo I: Periodo Colonial* (Guatemala City, 1988) 305.

53 "Himno de la Coronación," *Reina Consagrada,* 58

Bibliography

Alvarez Arevalo, Miguel. *Nuestra Señora del Socorro: presente en los 500 años de evangeliczacion de America*. Guatemala: Serviprensa Centroamericana, 1989.

Bell, Elizabeth. *Lent and Easter Week in Antigua*. Guatemala: Impresos Industriales, 1995

Dibar, Arturo. *El culto a nuestra señora en la epoca del descubrimiento y de la conquista en Nueva España y tierra firme*. Guatemala de La Asunción, 1971.

Diez de Arriba, R.P. Luis. *Historia de la Iglesia de Guatemala. Tomo I: PeriodoColonial*. Guatemala City, 1988.

Guiteras-Holmes, C. *Perils of the Soul: The World View of a Tzotzil Indian*. New York: The Free Press of Glencoe, Inc., 1961

"Guatemala: Our Lady of the Rosary." The Mary Page. http://udayton.edu/mary/resources/engfour.html

Hoyt, Edith. *The Silver Madonna: Legends of Shrines, Mexico-Guatemala*. Mexico: Editorial Letras, 1963.

Marzal, Manuel M. "Transplanted Spanish Catholicism." In *South and Meso-American Native Spirituality*. Edited by Gary H. Gossen. New York: Crossroad, 1993.

Milbrath, Susan. *Star Gods of the Maya*. Austin: University of Texas Press, 1999.

Morley, Sylvanus Griswold. *The Ancient Maya*. California: Stanford University Press, 1947.

Orellana, Sandra L. *The Tzutujil Mayas: Continuity and Change, 1250–1630*. Oklahoma: University of Oklahoma Press, 1984.

Recinos, Adrian. *Monografía del Departamento de Huehuetenango*. Guatemala: Editorial del Ministerio de Educacion Publica, 1954.

Redfield, Robert and Alfonso Villa Rojas. *Chan Kom: A Maya Village*. Chicago: University of Chicago Press, 1962.

Reina Consagrada. Guatemala: Delgado Impresos, 1995.

Thompson, Donald E. *Maya Paganism and Christianity: A History of the Fusion of Two Religions*. Middle American Research Institute. New Orleans: Tulane University, 1954.

Whetten, Nathan L. *Guatemala: The Land and the People*. New Haven: Yale University Press, 1961.

The Black Madonna: Primordial Ancestress

Deborah Rose, M.A.

When I embarked on a pilgrimage to France in search of the goddess, the last thing I expected was to re-enter Catholicism, the religion of my childhood. My conscious intention for the trip was to see the very earliest female imagery dating back to the Ice Age. And I did. I explored some wonderful museums and archaeological sites…but some other force was at work.

I kept bumping into black and brown madonnas in the crypts and altars of very old churches. Inevitably, there were many lit candles in front of the dark skinned statues, more than around the white Mary or Jesus. I noted this phenomenon first at Chartres. While the tourists were wandering around admiring the beauty of the stained glass windows, I saw a steady stream of pilgrims coming to pray to a very black mother and child statue that was perched on a ten-foot pillar. As I watched, dozens of people lit candles and kissed the pillar, leaving behind handwritten notes at its base. The spiritual pulse of the whole great cathedral seemed to be focused on a statue of a black mother.

French friends that I talked to had no idea why she was black and accepted it nonchalantly as one does with customs that have been around for a long time. This was my third trip to Chartres over a twenty-five year period and the first time I had noticed her. In the past I'm sure I simply ignored her and her worship because I was embarrassed by devotional Catholic practices as one is embarrassed by the things of childhood that were once very precious and then had to be thrown aside at the gates of young adulthood. Now as a grown woman searching for traditions that were older than the androcentric ones surrounding me, I almost couldn't believe what I was seeing: the devotions of the Catholic faithful were keeping alive a reverence for the mother energy that I suspected was older than that to the Christian Mary.

From a book called *The Cult of the Black Virgin*, I learned there are more than two hundred active shrines to the black madonna in France. Most of them date to the 11th and 12th century, some even earlier. They are all housed within Catholic churches and according to the author Ean Begg, the Church denies the significance of their darkness saying it is due to the soot of candle smoke over many years. His research, corroborated by a number of other books I have since read, reveals earlier pre-Christian goddess worship at almost all of the sites where black madonnas now exist.

For Example

In the great cathedral of Chartres, the black madonna statue I described above dates to the thirteenth century. A second madonna statue exists in the under-ground crypt next to an ancient and sacred well. The story is told that the Christian missionaries first coming to the area of Chartres found the indige-nous peoples worshipping a statue of a woman giving birth. The missionaries concluded this was a "pre-figuration" of the Virgin Mary and that the people were already Christians—they just didn't know it. A sanctuary was built around the original mother statue. She continued as the centerpiece of each succeeding church including the present cathedral built in the 1100's. During the French revolution the statue was deliberately destroyed and in 1856 a dark wooden sculpture was created to replace it.

Further south in the medieval town of Le Puy there is a high and holy hill that served as a pre-Christian sacred site. The worship of the Virgin Mary occurred here at a very early date and it is said to be descended from a cult devoted to the Celtic Mother Goddess Cerridwen. A cathedral was built upon the holy hill and on the main altar there is a very black madonna and child statue. In the Middle Ages five popes and fifteen kings came to see her as did Joan of Arc's mother, walking all the way from the west of France to pray for her daughter's victory.

The original statue was burned by the French revolutionaries. In the place where the statue was destroyed, a local farmer found an oval red stone inscribed with hieroglyphs and an image of a woman standing in a boat wear-ing a headdress of a crescent moon. This is an ancient symbol of Isis and curi-ously, before the Christian era the worship of Isis was the most widespread religion in the Roman Empire extending from Spain to Asia Minor, from

North Africa to Germany. Originally from Egypt, Isis was associated with the fertility of the black soil irrigated by the flooding of the river Nile. Her priests wore black and burned incense (as do Roman Catholic priests) and the most sacred of her images were made from black basalt.

Cybele was another great Mother Goddess whose cult was spread throughout the Roman Empire. From Asia Minor she was brought to Rome in the form of a black stone. By the third century BC, she had become the main deity of the area now known as Lyons. In the nearby city of Clermont-Fermont there is a holy well that was once associated with Cybele and is now part of the church of Notre Dame du Port. Next to the well is…a very black madonna sitting resplendent on a marble throne.

There are many goddesses connected to the black madonna shrines but Isis, Cybele and another dark skinned divinity called Artemis of Ephesus are the most prevalently referenced ones. This last one, Artemis of Ephesus, is different from the huntress Artemis so popular in Greek mythology. In her native Ephesus (Turkey), her statue was considered one of the seven wonders of the ancient world. And many of the black madonna statues in Europe are to be found along the tin trading routes of her followers.

But why? Why was—and still is—the image of a black mother so important in a white culture?

WHO IS THE BLACK MADONNA?

I returned to France a second and third time to search out the shrines to the black madonnas. I read through many books including the two French sources Ean Begg used to write *The Cult of the Black Madonna*. After thinking and thinking, the answer came through feeling, and the feeling was very deep and quite simple.

Each of us originated in the darkness of our mother's womb. And, as a species, we all came out of Africa. My twenty-five years of work in holistic healthcare makes me a firm believer in body memories and cellular consciousness. On an individual and collective level the body *remembers* the darkness as the source and the beginning. As a felt kinesthetic experience, the dark mother is the original mother.

This simple understanding has to be posited against the evolving institution of Christianity and the distortions that occurred to the image of Mary. To begin with, the historic Mary was probably not white. Some of the first paintings of her are attributed to St Luke and they are all brown skinned. In all likelihood Mary was ethnically dark or browned by exposure to the sun, or both. Her "whitening" has to be seen in the context of male antipathy toward the body, particularly the female body. The early Church Fathers considered women to be unclean, contaminated and evil.

In order to justify Mary's relationship to the son of God, she was split off from her female flesh. By decree of Church dogma, Mary's own conception was immaculate, that is, untainted by sexual intercourse and she in turn conceived her son through a shaft of light sent by God. In another dogma, her body was taken up into Heaven at death so her flesh always remained pure.

The Church Fathers may have tried to split off spirit from matter but the need of the human psyche is to have wholeness and the dark mothers, who have existed since the beginning, arose as the holders of the life force that is female—and embodied—in a period of white European history that devalued women and nature. If the "foreign" dark skinned goddesses had never been introduced to Europe I suspect the black madonnas would still have appeared to balance the whitened up Mary.

On my first trip to France, in the context of a goddess pilgrimage, I was "lead" out of the museums and into a dynamic and living worship of the black mother. It was as if I was being guided to see a stream of consciousness that had been obscured for centuries at a time and was only now becoming visible as a clear and continuous flow. I would name that stream as mother wisdom and the truth that it has to tell is that the mother is the first principle in human consciousness. This is not to say that male is insignificant or inferior but simply what we know first is the mother. Sperm meets egg within the body of the mother. She grows us inside her until we are ready to be launched out into the world and still, for many years, we need her for sustenance and support. This basic reality of human existence has been denied and demeaned for the last few thousand years by all the major Western world religions.

The Roman Catholic Church has been a major perpetrator of this denial and oddly or perhaps quite appropriately, it contains within itself hundreds of black madonna statues which embody the oldest truth on the planet, that is, that the miraculous and mysterious gift of life comes through the body of a woman and in the beginning that body was a black body.

These musings of mine were confirmed at the end of my last goddess pilgrimage to France. I had taken a "wrong" turn out of the mountains near the Spanish border and I found myself once again in the town of Limoux where Notre Dame de Marceille resided in a very old church on the top of a hill. She was an unusually young and beautiful dark skinned madonna statue. When I saw her for the first time I knew in my gut that she was an important yet unknown piece in the puzzle I was assembling and for these reasons, I was not surprised to find myself again in the vicinity of her presence. When I entered the church an elderly woman was already kneeling in front of the statue. She left and I lit a candle, offering my deep heartfelt thanks for all the blessings I had received on the trip.

Just as I was about to drive away, a middle-aged man who had been with the elderly woman beckoned me down a path. He was waving an empty plastic bottle. I followed his lead and we came to a small fountain where he introduced me to the woman who was his mother.

"*L'eau miraculous*" they both said to me pointing at the fountain. It was miracle water, not for drinking but to bless oneself. He took my hand, dipped it into the water and had me touch my third eye and then both my eyes. The woman told me she had a bad sickness in the stomach and she was praying for a healing. It was possible, she said, because this black madonna was very powerful.

I grabbed my chance: "*Pourqoui est la vierge noir?*" (Why is the Madonna black?)

The words came in a torrent.

He said: "*La vierge noir, elle est la terre, c'est tout!*" (The black madonna is the earth, that is the simple truth.)

She said that there were many many black madonnas and that they were "*primordiale, pre-historique, avant le Christ.*" She kept repeating the word "primordiale" in that wonderful French accent.

I asked if she thought the black madonnas represented the ancient goddess. Perhaps Isis, she said, perhaps something to do with the Greeks, but more significant was the universality of the mother: "La Mama" in her words. With great emphasis she told me that everyone everywhere worshipped the mother, especially where there was beauty or special and unusual features in the land. The mother, she went on to explain, existed before anything else.

I asked if she had studied these things. Oh no, she replied, she simply had a great passion for the black madonnas and through that passion, she understood them deeply.

I smiled broadly, trusting implicitly in the wisdom of this mother.

My search was clearly over.

*   *   *

The Gypsy Festival to Sara-la-kali

Every year on May 24th and 25th, the Romany—or Gypsy people as we know them—travel from all over Europe to the South of France, to an area called the Camargue, to celebrate themselves as a people and to honor their patron saint, Sara-la-Kali. I had heard about this colorful festival for many years and one year, finally, as part of a research project exploring the black madonnas of France, I went.

As I drove into the tiny tourist town of Les Saintes-Maries-de-la-Mer I had a fever. Through the haze of my altered state I saw a landscape that was utterly surreal: it was flat and swampy, swarming with mosquitoes and in the distance, wherever I looked, there were clusters of white horses and black bulls and an occasional pink flamingo. I felt completely dislocated and burning up besides. What the hell was I doing with my life—was I sick in my body or my head? Here I was driving around by myself in the South of France hoping the Gypsy festival I was about to attend would give me some kind of instant insight into the ubiquitous black Madonna so prevalent throughout all of France. But I didn't know when the festival was to begin and or even where it would be held.

The spirits, the angels, someone other than myself was clearly guiding my journey as I arrived in the small town filled that day with 7000 gypsies and 30,000 pilgrims disguised as tourists. Parking appeared easily and I walked into the main plaza around the church. I could hear the priest inside intoning louder and louder and the voices of the congregation beginning to sing passionately. I was startled to discover the Catholic child in me responding with equal emotion and tears flowed out of my eyes like rivers.

Then she appeared, the statue of Sara-la-Kali, held high by several men, wrapped in layer after layer of sequined robes. She was a glittering young woman, very dark-skinned and her gaze was piercing and direct. Local legend has it that this Sara came to France as the Egyptian "servant" of Mary Magdalene who was fleeing prosecution by both Jews and Romans seven years after the crucifixion.

Yes, Mary Magdalene in France. The legend dates to the Middle Ages. Her sanctuaries can be found in Sainte-Baume, Rennes-le-Chateau and at Vezeley and her name appears everywhere, particularly in the South, associated with cookies and towns and even an era of prehistory (the Magdalenian). The latest twist on the legend of Mary Magdalene comes from an American named Margaret Starbird, author of *Woman with the Alabaster Jar*. A devout and charismatic Catholic, Margaret pondered why an Egyptian "servant" became so highly venerated. Through research and revelation she decided that the young Sara was the child of Mary Magdalene and Jesus Christ! Perhaps that is why the Roma from all over Europe come annually to fete her as their queen. I am told that to the Romany people, Sara represents the Mother, the woman, the sister, the *Phuri Dai*, the source of all their blood.

I first heard about Sara reading China Galland's book *Longing for Darkness*. In China's visit to the church in the town of Les Saintes-Maries-de-la-Mer, she describes a family of Roma reverently approaching the statue of the black Sara. The women lit tall taper candles and the elder male of the group reached his hand through the many layers of Sara's dress to fondle the nakedness underneath. China finished the chapter with the sentence "I was breathless."

I will go on to tell you that in the fourteenth century the Roma people migrated from India where the gesture of touching the yoni was and still is a sacred act, totally foreign to contemporary Western religious traditions. Perhaps because the Roma are still a matrilineal people, this action is intended to honor, not abuse, as those of us raised under patriarchal rule would automatically assume. The Roma came, saw Sara, and named her Kali. Though I have never heard that the Roma are conscious of the connection to the Indian mother deity Kali, the synchronicity cannot be accidental. Both the Hindu and Romani languages translate the word Kali as "the black woman."

Sara-la-Kali is a young woman, not a mother, and so she cannot be formally classified as a black "madonna" yet she is part of the underground phenomenon of black females still actively being honored in the white culture of France. The festivity, though wildly popular and organized by the local priests, is in jeopardy of being banned by the Catholic authorities "at the top."

Today however was the day of returning her to the sea from whence she came. She was accompanied by *les Gardians*, men on white horses holding three pronged spears like the trident of Neptune; and Provencal ladies with dark hair swept back into buns arranged tidily with a piece of lace; and Romany men, swarthy and mustached, stroking their violins slowly; and Romany women, whose dresses were tight and colorful, and whose feet were the feet of the earth, naked in open-backed high heels, calloused and darkened with dirt. All of us walked together to the sea singing "Ave Ave A—ve Ma—ri—a."

The procession snaked through the streets of the town and along with Sara, I, too, faced into the waves, drenching my dress with delight and abandon. Only once a year does Sara see the sunlight and the sea. The rest of the days she lives under the earth in the basement of an ancient church, a place that should be cool and moist but instead is always hot with the burning of candles in her honor.

The heat of her crypt is matched by the passion of the Romany people. As soon as the official ceremony was over, as soon as the tourists left in their buses, the real festival began. Small groups of people gathered in the cafes and the plaza. Typically, the music would start with a man's high-pitched singing. Quick syncopated clapping would come out of the crowd, more men's voices, perhaps a guitar. Then the women began to dance, one or two at a time, feet stamping on the earth, hands fluttering around the head, hips moving in a way only a women's body can move, unselfconsciously and gloriously sensual.

I was filled with the particularly un-Catholic feeling of being deliriously alive in my body. Whatever symptoms I had arrived with had disappeared. I don't remember ever feeling so well.

The Black Madonnas in my Life

Necia Harkless, Ph.D.

Perhaps, what I write about in this essay would make more sense if I shared with you who I am. After eighty plus years as an African American woman I am still on my spiritual journey and also related to every human being Who is in quest of connectedness or wholeness. As I look back the journey seems so circular and like Thomas Merton, former Monk of the Abbey of Gethsemani ."..I have no idea where I am going. I do not see the road ahead..." I was born at a point in history when the world was closing its chapter on the French Revolution and Enlightenment and the dawn of the age of Industrialism with its twin companion Colonialism which was heavily invested in the riches of Africa and the labor that would increase the power of the New World.

It was in the 12th century BC that the Trojans were forced *to* fight with the Greeks over land, treasures and eminent domain, in what bas come to be known as the first trade war in history. It is now in the 21st century that America and England are engaged in what might be called another Trojan war in the same regions for basically the same reasons. The irony of the first Trojan war lies in the fact that Memnon, the King of the Ethiopians had *to* come *to* the aid of the King of Troy but gave up his life in mortal combat with Achilles, the immemorial Greek.

I was born in Detroit, two years after the end of World War I. My parents were products of the exodus from the south. Mother was born in Houston, Texas in 1894.She graduated from Prairie View Normal Industrial College in 1913. My father was born in Alabama in 1890. He graduated from Tuskegee in the class of 1914. My sister and brother kept the dream of my parents alive by becoming an art professor and arbitrator, of the highest rank, respectively. I have followed my passion through the world of Social Work, Education, Art,

Religion, and Ethnography, and am presently enjoying myself as a Donovan scholar at the University of Kentucky.

It was in my father's library that I read the Odyssey and Iliad of Homer and Aneid of Virgil and the strengths of African culture before it was denigrated by the missionaries and the other marauders. My first book was "The Poppy Seed Cakes" because I went to Majeske school and lived next to a Polish Immigrant community called Hammtramck, which no longer exists as I knew it. I also live in a polyglot American community of African Americans from the South and Canada along with the immigrants from Eastern Europe who took Americanization classes on the sun roof of the school, Majeske. Not being an immigrant caused me a great deal of grief, but my fears were allayed by my father because he said that I was already an American and we also owned our own home.

Our second home was in a Jewish neighborhood north of General Motors office Building and the Fisher Theater. I lived next door to a family that was a member part of the Purple Gang, across the street from George Shirley who later became one of the first African American stars at the Met. Two blocks down the street lived my father's classmate who reluctantly became the father-in-law of Malcolm X. There were some remarkable people in our neighborhood which became known as the "Gold Coast."

Our church was the First African American Baptist Church in Michigan known as the Second Baptist Church. The original members disassociated themselves by from the First Baptist Church, which was white, so that they could have a greater autonomy community. The church is still located in Greek Town on Monroe street in downtown Detroit. It was an Underground Railway Station for the slaves and freedmen making their flight to Canada. Speaking of coexistence, next door to church was a Greek candy store where we bought pomegranates and pistachios with a portion of our Sunday School money. My Church School superintendent was a West Indian who had been a missionary in Liberia. Next door to the store was a Greek restaurant where the turbaned men in their Greek costumes smoked the water pipe and dined. There I saw my first Black Jew and other mysterious figures from the Orient.

On the same Monroe street was the Roman Catholic Church with which we exchanged palms on Palm Sunday and around the corner was the traditional Greek Orthodox Church with the icons of the Holy Mother of God. This little world of mine in Detroit went sour during the racial upheavals of the sixties and seventies in Detroit. At the present time, it is trying to fight its way back.

Mother was the faithful and devoted Baptist and dad was the stoic Episco-palian that taught me the importance of cause and effect. When I was in col-lege, the rallying cry was "not what a world, but change the world, you have nothing to lose but your chains." Also the symbols of the French Revolution: Liberty, Equality and Fraternity were ultimately subsumed under the Black Fist during the long hot summers of civil unrest, the hegemony of the police and the bliss of Flower Children. After recently reading *God and Physics*, I began to understand that we are again at the brink of a new age which will be defined by new concepts in science, religion and the reclamation of the values of the Dark Mother (justice with compassion, equality, and transformation).

The Black Madonna has always been a part of my life, as she was intro-duced to my mother by a postcard from my father from Chambery, France while he was on leave from the army during World War I. Since Paris was off limits for all African American soldiers, my father had to find a place to wor-ship south of Paris. Dad worshiped in the Great Marian Sanctuary of Notre-Dame De Myans. On the back of the postcard my father wrote "My Love, This is the Black Madonna as she stands on the altar of the old church today. Every thing is pure gold only her face is black." I myself made a pilgrimage to Myans in 1994. The message over the entrance read: "Then saith He to the disciple: Behold Thy Mother."[1]

The Holy Mother had a great impact on my life as I was born two years after my father returned from France. When I was able to understand the importance of the postcard, I thought my mother was a Black Madonna and I would grow up to be one. I even thought I was a godlet because of the impli-cations of the scripture which said that my body was a Holy temple and the spirit of God lived within Me. I, of course, was asked out of Sunday School for such blasphemy.

I treasure a wall-hanging in my living room given to me by my mentor, Dr. William Y. Adams. It was painted by a Nubian artist at the time of the 1961 excavations of the frescoes in the great Cathedral at Faras in the Northern Sudan. The painting was a reproduction of one of the frescoes representing the Mother of God (Theotokos) and the Holy Infant blessing a Nubian prin-cess. The frescoes which offer a magnificent view and understanding of Nubian Christianity are on permanent display in the National Museum at Warsaw and the National Museum of Khatoum. I viewed them during my research in 1988.

"We now know that up top 535 AD, the Christian authorities had allowed the pagan peoples of Nubia to fetch away annually from the temple on the island of Philae the statue of the goddess Isis and to carry it into Nubia for the blessing of the crops. However it now seems that along side of the pagan creeds the new faith of Christianity was beginning."[2] According to Priese, the Metoitic kings of Kush maintained close cultural exchanges with Egypt between 204 and 185 BC when they managed to gain possession of the Island of Philae, the center of the Isis cult at the first cataract which was integral to the religious life of both the Egyptians and the Meroites.[3]

The internalization of the Cult of Isis by the Romans and the Greeks 300 years before Christ spread throughout the Mediterranean countries of Italy, Spain, Greece, France and as far as the land of the Celts and Britain. Isis is said to be the prototype for the mother and child cult of Christian faith that ultimately absorbed, displaced and transcended the fertility cult that exemplified the power of women. The groves and grottoes that were once sacred places of worship of Isis are now cathedrals adorned with Black Virgins or Madonnas reflecting the various styles of the Medieval and Renaissance period.

Sudanese Habits and Traditions of Christian Origin[4]

"The house of the new born child is swept. The dirt, the afterbirth and the midwife razor are all put together on a small raft made of wheat straw. An oil lamp and a big cake of wheat flower are also placed on it. The first or second day after the birth the baby is taken to the river by the midwife, accompanied by village women and children. They also carry with them, beside the little raft, a brass basin containing the kohl [eye-shadow] pencil, the kohl pot, some durra and dates. The midwife scatters the handful of durra on her way, right and left saying: 'This is the portion of the Mariya. Oh Angels '(This is reminiscent of the Marian processions of today in the villages of Europe.)

The women folk who accompany her chant and pray "By the Mariya! By the Angels and by his face, grant us, O God our desires." At the river, the small raft carrying the lighted oil lamp, the house dirt, the razor, etc. is left floating on the river. Before it is carried down the stream, a woman stealthily recovers the cake. The brass basin is filled with Nile water and carried to the baby's house, where it is jealously kept for some days, then the remaining water is thrown away with this water, the mother's breast are washed then the midwife carries to the mother the baby to nurse.[5]

The Sign of the Cross and the Child and Other Ceremonies

"In some villages...a little child of a good character—or a girl, according to the sex of the newborn baby—is taken to the mother's bed. The child is offered seven dates to bite and invited to lap with his (her) lips still wet to the mouth of the baby. It is believed that the good character of the boy (or girl) will so pass on [to] the newly born baby. If no good child is available an adult having good reputation, is invited to perform the action. If none of those present have the requisite condition (good conduct) the ceremony is postponed until the seventh day."[6]

"A sign of the cross is made by the midwife on the forehead of the newborn child with kohl immediately after birth. Other crosses are painted on the walls of the house with the blood of the sheep slaughtered for the occasion. Attention is paid not to break any bone of the sheep when it is butchered. The bones are collected and kept for one year, after which they are thrown away during the rain season."

"In some villages the mother stamps her fingerprints with the delivery blood on the wall near her bed. If the children of a women die in infant age, at the next birth she will make a sign of the cross on the wall with the first excretion of the baby. This will not be effaced (whitewashed) for at least 25 years."[7]

An Illumination and Worship at Jasna Gora

In August of 1988, my niece, Sharon Pitts, and I escaped the banks of the Nile that had risen over fifty feet high leaving villages submerged and bodies floating on the Nile to arrive safely in Warsaw. There we were met by an archaeologist at the University of Warsaw to view the frescoes of Faras. Since our research at Khartoum was disrupted by flood, we could not celebrate mother's birthday at the Royal Pyramids at Jebel Barkal. What was lost at Khartoum, was gained beyond my wildest dreams.

Upon returning home, I was able to share my experience in person with my mother about the Holy Mother in Poland as she had shared with her husband vicariously through the mail from France. As we knelt before Our Lady of Czestochowa and the Patron Saint in the Monastery of Jasna Gora to receive the Eucharist, I felt a great sense of the Mother of God and the Godhead in her presence. We were not alone among the sea of worshippers from all over

Europe and perhaps the States. I felt the surge of love in that great crowd who had made the pilgrimage to receive her blessings. My mother must have felt in her heart that I was privileged to have a similar experience to that of my father, seventy years ago in France. "She is indeed everywhere." It was three months after I had shared this experience with my mother, and three days before she died that she expressed to me over the telephone from Detroit, her love of life, her love of church, her children and her friends. Her last words to me were "God is Love."

The power of the Dark Mother has not been lost on the nation of Poland as Pope Paul makes his annual visit to Jasna Gora to kneel before her shrine. As a young factory worker, during the Second World War, Pope Paul had the feeling that he should distance himself from the Marian devotion of his childhood in order to focus more on Christ which became a painful inner struggle. The readings of Saint Louis of Montfort, who was influenced by the Spanish mystics, Teresa of Avila and John the Cross ended the struggle for His Holiness. As Pope, his motto became "Totu Tuus(I am Completely yours, O Mary").[8] Lech Walesa wore a replica of the Holy mother as a lapel pin both as a Solidarity leader and President and dedicated his Nobel peace prize to her.

The Shrine of the Black Madonna in Detroit, Michigan

The Shrine of the Black Madonna is another political and spiritual testimony to resistance and liberation. This time it is found in the African American community which had witnessed the unionization of the Ford Motor empire by the Reuther brothers in 1939 and two race riots in 1942 and 1963. The Shrine of the Black Madonna, originally known as the Central Congregational Church on Linwood Avenue in Detroit was, founded in 1956 by Rev. Albert C. Cleague, Jr. He became radicalized by the climate in Detroit because of inadequate housing for the poor, "ethnic succession"< "white flight", loss of jobs to non-union shops and cheap labor overseas. The church became the Pan African Orthodox Christian Church with Shrines and Bookstores in Detroit, Atlanta, Houston. Cleage shepherded his flock under his new name, Reverend Jaramogi Abebe Agyeman, until his death on February 20, 2000. Black Theology was the hallmark and Black Liberation his vision, as he preached self determination for black people.

I happened to wander in to watch an artist painting the Black Madonna for the church. It was during a conversation, the artist noticed my hands and became impressed with them. He asked if he could substitute my hands for the model's hands because my hands exhibited more strength. The Black Power Movement used the clenched fist as its symbol and message. In the eyes of the black artist, he wished to portray the strength of the African American mother and her hands should convey that message.

As you have noted, my personal experience with the Dark Mother has encompassed the ancient Isis, Our Lady of Myans, representative of the Roman Catholic in France, Our Lady of Czestochowa, representative of the Orthodox Church, and the Black Madonna of the Pan African Orthodox Christian in America. The first emergence of the Isis Cult was far back in antiquity, Our Lady of Czestochowa was first known about in 1100 AD and the Shrine of the Black Madonna in 1970.

Each reflects the unconscious power and spiritual response to the subliminal psychological and spiritual needs of humanity through the ages, based on the cultural expectations and modifications of the values of the dark mother: justice with compassion, equality and transformation.

Signs, Gestures and the Secret of Mary

In our world signs, signals and symbols are idealized reference points for how to feel and act in an ordered world. Yet we do not always act and respond rationally as we are captives of our subliminal longings. Our internal, subliminal world responds to these reference points both individually and collectively and their meanings are shared legacies of our past which extends back to primordial times. It is the Dark Mother that "carries the missing dark pole of the feminine archetype in our times."[9] Signs and symbols can be cult objects, artifacts, myths, legends and literature defining the culture for interior and ulterior purposes. The earliest known gestures are the upraised arms in reverence or celebration. The upraised open or clenched fist or the raised second and third finger as in victory. The handshake as a legal sign of agreement, the closed palms as prayer.

The painting by El Greco called "El caballero de la mano pecho"—The gentleman with his hand on his chest, is used as a springboard for questions in my own mind about the residuals from the fertility cults found in Christian symbols, images and ideas. I had seen this painting in the Prado when I was doing my Nubian Research. It was not so compelling to me until my focus was on the Dark Mother.

Thomas Peter Kunesh wrote a Master's thesis in Religious Studies to determine the meaning of the gesture used in the painting of El Greco that seemed singularly different in the portrayal of the right hand: fingers splayed except for the third and fourth fingers which are tight together. His perceptions may have been shaped by his ethnicity as a Native American.

The following abstract will give you the scope of his study:

"The hand gesture in El Greco's painting, here called the "pseudo-zygodactylous" gesture, is traced, through comparing similar gestures and iconographical scenes, to breastfeeding images of goddesses, e.g., the Virgin Mary, Hera, and Isis, nursing male infants. As theology and artistic stylization develop in Christianity in the medieval and Renaissance periods, the gesture is noted in paintings of the Virgin Mary in a nursing attitude but without a child, in a position of maternal care for mortals seeking heavenly salvation. The gesture later appears in art without a nursing context, used by saintly characters and, ultimately, secular figures such as El Greco's "Caballero." The gesture's symbolic meaning is extrapolated from these religious contexts, both artistic and literary: maternal (goddess) power and influence over the fate of human beings (mortals) in the afterworld, and men's desire to secure immortality through symbolic control of female deities, which ensures continued access to salvation (immortality)."[10]

The stunning conclusion of the Kunesh's study is "both historically and symbolically the pseudo-zygodactylous gesture links Mankind to God via Woman, the female element of intercession in conflict." This is particularly revealing with regard to the study of the Dark Mother. In his examination of art, history and the religions of the past, he felt that gesture itself perhaps has lost its original meaning. However, Kunesh found every example using the gesture was not created by a woman which led to his statement that "The salvific power of the divine mother is not abnegated or denied, but translated and appropriated by men."[11]

Kunesh arrives at his conclusion through a detailed iconographical analysis of six paintings in the Prado that display the p/z gesture painting has only the gesture in common with the other paintings, which are religious scenes with depiction of the breast. Also there is no action, no woman, no breast, no milk.

The following were paintings examined: (titles suggest content).

1. Mary nursing Jesus in "Rest on the Escape to Egypt" by Gerard David (1450–1523);

2. Mary squirting mil to the souls in purgatory in "LaVirgen dando su leche a las almas del purgatorio" by Pedro Machuca (1517);

3. Unknown Spanish gentleman, "El Caballero de la mano al pecho" by El Greco (1578);

4. Juno holding her breast for Hercules in "The Birth of the Milky way" by Peter Rubens (1577–1640);

5. Mary with her hand to her breast before Jesus in Mar'a, intercession ante el Hijo" by Matero Carezo (1666)

6. Bernard receiving milk from the Virgin Mary in "la Vision de San Bernardo" by Battolome Murillo (1665–75)

The earliest source maternal gesture was cradling the child while it nurses at the mother's beast. The female figurines from Neolithic and pre-Indo European times are examples of this basic gesture in the fertility cults. Isis suckling Horus is the proto-type for the Christian images of the Virgin Mary and her child Jesus through the millennia. The Kanesh study points out that in the ancient Near east the image evolved from nursing babies to nursing boys and grown men to the "sacral metaphysical nourishment of princes and kings/"

In the Kushite Twenty-fifth Dynasty (750 BC—350 AD), a silver plaque was found which portrayed a queen suckling the goddess, Mut. A study by J. Leclant shows that the king was suckled by a goddess on three occasions: at birth into the world, and after his death, and when he was reborn into the afterlife. It was through the persistence of the longing for nurturance, protection, and justice that the worship of the pagan deity or Dark Mother entered the Christian Church.

In 431 AD the Council of Ephesus determined that Mary was the Mother of God which became the orthodox teaching. It has remained centered in the eastern Mediterranean serving to reinforce the growing cult of Mary and her overwhelming adulation (called Mariology).

According to the study of Kanesh, the inclusion of the emotions in the paintings and the codification of the iconography took place with the portrayal of abstract qualities of the female goddesses such as Grace (Benignita), Charity (carita), and Sustenance (Sostanza), which are anthropomorphized as women and shown in some relationship to lactation. Could this be a precursor to the values of the Dark Mother, justice with compassion, equality and compassion?

The first appearance of the Virgin as mediatrix and the appearance of the gesture p/z is seen in a mosaic in the great west wall picture of the Venetian Tarcello Church in the 12th century. Her hands are raised with palms outward looking directly at the viewer fully clad. The p/z gesture becomes an abstract symbol as it is removed from the source, the Holy Mother or Mother Goddess. The gesture is taken up not only by Jesus to display his wound but it is shown with other mortals such as saints, apostles who adopted the gesture as they gained immortality through the right path for living, and they in turn could confer immortality on others through Mary. Kunesh suggests "as the gesture moves to human beings who gained immortality through correct living and correct worship, it is arguable that the gesture they were given was not borrowed from Jesus but from the original source, Mary"[12]

The gesture in reference to Mary has many meanings in modern literature. The sign signifies sustenance and salvation of humanity when the hand is placed on her breast or when it is bared. The evolution is seen as a basic gesture of nurturance and giving life to a more complex manifestation: immortality and salvation. The literature examined by Kunesh indicates that from the 12th century to the 15th century the concept of "Jesus as Mother" was imminent, "translating the concept of nursing to the preeminent Christian authority figure, Jesus Himself. Possibly the power of the Mary had been transferred to Jesus by inference and in the case of mortals by appropriation.

The Secret of Mary

The 21st century is pregnant with many possibilities for the values of the Dark Mother and the transformation of the universal church and those on our planet who are longing for wholeness and inclusion. Merlin Stone wrote *When God Was A Woman* was one of the early feminist writers to explain the worship of the prehistoric Mother Goddess. From a non-Christian perspective, she analyzed the creation story of Genesis which she describes as an allegory to Yahweh, the Hebrew God supplanting the Mother Goddess which was represented by the tree of life and the serpent of the Hebrew religion supplanting the worship of the Goddess. This notion derives ultimately from Sumerian mythology which is the oldest known mythology.

The Old Testament glorifies the Patriarchs and assigns a role of silence and subservience to the Matriarchs. In modern examination of the New Testament, Jesus was much more sympathetic to women. He was devoted to his mother for sixteen years and absorbed all of her wisdom. In the New 'Order of The Family of the Incarnate Word', commissioned by Rome in 1997, Pope Paul specifically recommends that the modern day Catholics should become familiar with the mystical theology of St.Louis DeMonfort as he did when he began to doubt the church of his youth. DeMonfort's *Devotion of Mary or The Secret of Mary*, is the invitation to reevaluate the role of Mary and the virtues of the Dark Mother. DeMonfort reinforces, for one, the conclusion of Kanesh's study that links mankind's salvation via women. St. Louis assures one that "following the order established by his divine wisdom, God ordinarily imparts his graces to men through Mary....God chose her to be the treasure, the administrator and the dispenser so of all if his graces and gifts pass through her hands. Such is the power that she received through him."[13].

The challenge of the Third Millennium is to embrace a more explicit universality that moves beyond the exclusivity of Christianity into a "total Incarnation of faith....to become truly "catholic" enough to include the myths of the dark-skinned peoples....who would see in religion [i.e. Christianity] only oppression and bitterness and pride."[14]

Notes

1 Harkless, Ph.D., Necia.D. *Poems and Images.* Lexington, Kentucky : Heart to Heart and Associates, 1995

2 Plumley, M.J. "New Evidence on Christian Nubia in Light of Recent Excavations"*nubia Chritiana.* Warzawa:Acadamie De Theologie Catholique,1982 pp.17–19

3. Priese, K.H. The Gold of Meroe, New York :Metropolitan Museum of Art, *p.11.*

4. Vantini, G."Christian Relics in Sudanese Traditions" in *Nubia Christiana,pp. 25–39*

5 ibid

6 ibid

7 ibid

8 Messori, V.,Ed. *Crossing the Threshold of Hope by His Holiness Pope Paul II,*New York: Alfred Knopf, 1994, pp.213–215

9. Gustafson, F.*The Black Madonnas,* Boston: Sigo Press, p. *xii*

10 Kanesh, http://www.darkfiber.com/pzabpreface.html

11 Kanesh, http://www.darkfiber.com/pz/middle.html

12 Kanesh, http://www.darkfiber.com/pz/middle.htlm

13 The Secret of Mary, http://www.romancatholicism.org/mary/secret.html

14 Weill, S.*Waiting for God,* New York: Van Rees Press, 1951,p.8

The Piggly Wiggly and the Black Madonna

Mary Saracino

"The sun spun in the sky," my father told me. "It twirled in place for a second or two. Then it stopped."

He had witnessed this miraculous phenomenon outside the Piggly Wiggly supermarket a few blocks from his house in Seneca Falls, New York.

"Herbie saw it, too," Dad added, as if mentioning his stepson-in-law would dispel any doubts I might have had about his sanity.

I sat across his kitchen table as he matter-of-factly related his tale. Calmly, with eyes as clear as sunlight, he sipped his afternoon coffee and nibbled a Stella Dora wafer cookie. I was visiting from Minneapolis, returning to my hometown for a short stay. I was not unaccustomed to my father's supernatural stories. He often talked of the numinous powers of saints and angels. He had even sworn that, as a teenager, his Guardian Angel had mysteriously dislodged a murderous chunk of crusty bread from his clenched throat. But never before had he spoken of errant suns.

It didn't spin wildly, my father insisted. The sun didn't cartwheel over the astonished horizon or bound over billowy puffs of clouds. It wiggled quietly, the way the tail of the grocery store's giant icon, a butcher-hat-wearing-pig, might wag in a soft breeze.

"I stared right at it and my eyes weren't injured at all," my father attested.

Until that astonishing moment it had been an afternoon like countless others. My dad and Herbie had routinely exited through the Piggly Wiggly's automatic sliding glass doors into the hot sunshine, arms full of grocery bags, heading home to their respective wives. "Phew, it's a scorcher," my father might have casually remarked as he glanced up at the sweltering orb, but on

272

this day, that rascal sun was not content to merely beat down upon their sweating heads. It danced before their dumbfounded eyes.

Heat stroke, one might be tempted to scoff. Every rational adult knows that the sun can't spin in the sky. Laws of nature not withstanding, Herbie corroborated my dad's story after the two men rushed home to reveal the miracle to everybody who would listen. Those chosen for the initial telling were members of the family who lived in and around the small town my father had claimed as his home for nearly sixty years. His confessors included my stepmother, Rose, Herbie's wife MaryAnn, my brothers and my father's brothers and sisters. Eventually the news spread to an assortment of neighbors and the priest at St. Patrick's Catholic Church. Some believed him. Some didn't. My father had a reputation by then of being a self-styled, modern-day mystic. Several times he had traveled to Medugorje, in what was once Yugoslavia, to visit the holy site where the Blessed Virgin Mother is said to appear. The sun spins in the sky there, too, when She is present, and people are able to stare directly into it, without harming their eyes, without the aid of sunglasses or pinhole viewing devices. The Blessed Mother's divine powers shield and protect the retinas of staunch believers.

When my father arrived home after his first trip to Medugorje he sadly confessed to me on the phone that he was not among the fortunate who had witnessed the Holy Mother's appearance. He had not seen the sun accomplish anything during his pilgrimage, other than to shine, shyly, in the sky. Other seekers on that rocky hillside in Yugoslavia had been more generously blessed. They had witnessed the Virgin Mother and Her miraculous spinning sun. My father's faith was strong and he believed their accounts. To commemorate the miracle, he collected small rocks from that holy hillside and brought them back to America, doling them out, like amulets, to his children, his mother, his siblings, his friends. When I flew out to visit him, he tucked a shard of Medugorje stone into the center of my hand, as well.

"Carry it with you," he urged. "The rocks heal people. Pray to the Blessed Mother. She will help you."

There were other wondrous claims. My father swore that the metal links on his rosary had changed to gold since he had encountered the essence of the Divine in Medugorje. Whenever the opportunity presented itself, he would pull the coil of beads from his pants pocket and proudly display them. "See," he would say with awe. "These weren't gold before. But look. Look at them now!"

When he unfurled his palm and held the transformed rosary before my eyes, I stared at the swirl of black beads and blinked hard. Although not the gleaming gold of a wedding band, the links appeared to be gold-like. I couldn't recall if they had ever been silver before Dad's pilgrimage. I nodded compliantly. "Yes, I see, Dad. They do look golden."

I could have suggested that my father bring his rosary to my brother Steve, a jewelry designer. No doubt Steve would have been able to verify whether or not the gold was authentic or merely tarnished pall. As inane as it seems, it never crossed my mind to scrutinize the authenticity of my father's statement. It simply didn't matter. Like a medieval alchemist, my father fervently believed that the silver had transmuted to gold. That was reason enough for me to let it be.

Other daughters might have tried to censor all such claims. They might have even urged their fathers to seek psychiatric help or petitioned to have them committed to a mental health unit. Still others might have called the *National Enquirer* causing an avalanche of Marion-crazed believers to descend upon my father's small town. The faithful would arrive in droves, kneeling and wailing in the asphalt parking lot in front of the Piggly Wiggly, their wide eyes staring, unflinchingly, into the stupefying sun, surrounded by a passel of jaded entrepreneurs hawking

T-shirts and statues of Our Lady of the Piggly Wiggly.

I did none of that.

The folks to whom my father had imparted the story of his spinning miracle simply took the entire incident in stride. So did I. *That's just Frankie* we agreed. Our attention soon returned to the mundane routines of daily life.

My father's talk of the sun moving, of golden rosary links, of healing rocks was as commonplace a topic for him as a chat about last week's Yankee game. Ever since I was a child, the Blessed Mother and the saints have suited up for Dad's starting line up—right beside Mickey Mantle and Joe DiMaggio. For him, the Piggly Wiggly spinning sun was just as thrilling, but no more extraordinary, than a no-hitter or a grand slam homer at the World Series. Things of the spirit world, visions beyond the veil, images of halo-headed holy men and women populated my father's everyday world. His devotion to the Virgin Mary was sacrosanct. Steeped in the religion of his southern Italian youth, this blend of canonical Catholicism and pre-Christian mysticism was the cornerstone of his faith. It comforted him through his joys and his sorrows.

It was not difficult for me to accept my father's faith-filled assertions as possibility instead of fact. He and I both believe in the power of the soul to experience things that the rational mind cannot comprehend. The traditions of my father's southern Italian Catholicism took root among a people that, in pre-Christian times, were followers of a more ancient longing. The blood of my father's faith mingled with that of ancient Greeks, Moors, and countless others who, over the course of thousands of years, had invaded my ancestors' homelands. Each conqueror brought their own distinct spiritual fervor, imposing it upon the conquered, until the result was an amalgam of creeds and practices. Sometimes God was even a woman. And dark-skinned.

My father's religion is rich in metaphor. It is a spiritual poetry that embraces the essence of mystery. It differed in texture and content from the strict Catholic doctrine taught to me by the Irish-American nuns in the All-American parochial school I attended as a child. My father's Catholicism was far more intoxicating than the stories and commandments pontificated by priests from the pulpit at Sunday Mass. The kind-hearted Irish-American pastor, Father O'Byrne, never mentioned the sun's ability to defy the laws of physics. His oration never included stories about saints with stigmatas, or martyrs plucking out their eyes, as Santa Lucia had done. The good Father stuck to safer material—New Testament stories about Jesus turning water into wine or walking on tempestuous seas.

I learned the juicier tales from my father's *Lives of the Saints* books, the majority of the reading material to be found on the shelves of the knotty pine built-in bookcase in our front parlor. I dreamed of renaming myself Agnes in honor of the saintly, fourth century Roman who declared herself a Christian and was martyred for her devotion. This girl, of perhaps twelve or thirteen, refused to renounce her Christianity and so endured torture and threats to her life. Stripped and paraded through town, as an example to all those who would wantonly display their faith, she sought only to cover her unclothed body with her long tresses and accept her impending death. She is depicted with a lamb, the symbol of her virginal innocence. I knew I was capable of such steadfast allegiance, although I secretly prayed that I would never be so fiercely tested.

Italian Catholic saints were brave and generous. Whether surrendering their worldly inheritance, like St. Francis of Assisi, or zealously championing the plight of children confined to the gallows, like St. John Bosco of Turin, these men and women embodied virtues and values that transcended the gritty, lurid details I devoured in the pages of their biographies. Who could not be persuaded to a life of compassion by St. Joseph, who had raised Jesus as if he were his own son? His selfless generosity enabled him to set a place at the table for a boy-child that he had not fathered, engendering a custom enacted to this day in Italian American communities across the country. On St. Joseph's feast day, March 19, Italians open their pantries and feed those less fortunate.

By the time I was ten years old, Pope John XXIII had pried open the clenched doors of tradition and heralded the way for a more pedestrian, ecumenical Catholicism. The *Lives of the Saints* were banished to the sidelines, a curious footnote in the annals of Catholic history. Priests donned less ornate vestments and faced their congregations in an attempt to suggest that they were merely members of the flock now, no longer overseers of the herds. They celebrated Mass, not in Latin, as they had for centuries, but in English or the vernacular language of their congregation. Anyone who still believed in Purgatory became suspect. Limbo disappeared. Indulgences fell out of favor. No longer could you merely say a few select prayers and earn a suspended sentence in Purgatory. Indulgences were once seen as an essential way to plea bargain with God, get Him to ease the duration of sin-induced punishment in return for good works on Earth (sort of like time off for good behavior). Now they were suddenly relegated to the status of off-color jokes; everyone had a favorite one but no one was allowed to mention it in polite company. The juicy, transcendental stories—the legends, upon which my father's faith thrived—were also silenced, shooed to the attic like crazy relatives.

Many positive changes emerged as a result of Vatican Council II, not the least of which was a lessening of the absolute power that the Catholic clergy held over the spiritual lives of parishioners. Somehow, in the transition, my father never succeeded in leaving behind his Old World way of seeing the Catholic cosmos. Whether consciously or not, he clung to the mystical traditions that gave his faith its richness, its deeper, psychological meanings. Why be a Catholic if you couldn't believe in the power of novenas to save souls? One might as well be a Unitarian. To my father's way of thinking, Heaven and all its saintly royalty, had not forsaken the true believer, no matter what kind of revolution Pope John XXIII had set in motion.

My journey away from Catholicism has been long and serpentine. My questioning started when I was six and my mother began an extramarital affair with the assistant pastor of our local Catholic Church. By the time I was thirteen, she had run off with him, taking my two sisters (one of whom was secretly the priest's daughter) and me with her, leaving behind my four brothers and, of course, my father. I learned, at a very early age, that the canonical rules were flexible. Priests weren't untouchable demi-gods; the Pope wasn't infallible. They were merely mortals trying to do their best to interpret the ways of God, just like anybody else.

Throughout my junior high and high school years I went to Mass every Sunday, alongside my two sisters, my mother, and my stepfather, who was by then de-frocked. Both my mother and her new husband had been excommunicated when they had run off together—he for turning his back on his priestly vows and his diocesan duties, she for leaving her marriage. Although they were legally married in a civil ceremony, their union was not blessed by the Church, which had damned them to the fires of hell. I thought it odd that non-Catholics were allowed to divorce and remarry while Catholics were sentenced to a life devoid of God's benevolent grace. What kind of God was that?

To further stoke the fires of my Catholic ambivalence, ten years after my mother left him, my father petitioned the Archbishop to annul their twenty-three year marriage. He had fallen in love with a widow named Rose and wanted their marriage blessed by the Church, an act that would have been forbidden to him as a divorced man. With enough witnesses and enough cash, my father was able to reverse the effects of the Holy Sacrament of Marriage, into which he had entered with my mother, and erase the Church's long-term memory. In the process, he relegated to illegitimacy, the souls of the six children he had sired with my mother. In the eyes of Mother Church, my brothers and sister and I became bastard-children. In a strange twist of canonical logic, the daughter of my mother and her priest boyfriend had become the only legitimate offspring in my family. Perhaps this is one of the reasons why my father has felt compelled to say Novenas for his sons and daughters, as if his nine-day devotions in our honor will placate his Catholic God, seduce Him into forgiving us our dubious birthright and accept us into the Kingdom of Heaven.

By the time I had entered my twenties my trust in the absolute authority of Catholicism had been severely diminished. I set aside the mandates of dogma and freed the pagan baby in my own soul. I began to explore what lay outside the fiefdom of the Holy Vatican See. At the all-women's Catholic college I attended, I was taught by nuns who wore street clothes instead of religious habits, and who were as comfortable quoting D.H. Lawrence as Deuteronomy. Having come out as a lesbian in high school, I no longer wished to affiliate with a Church that refused to accept the holiness of my sexual identity. Along the way, I was introduced to feminism and opened the door to a decidedly different spiritual sensibility. In graduate school, I was drawn to coursework on comparative religion and women's studies, unearthing the long-buried consciousness of the Divine Mother and redefining my sense of Spirit. God did not require a masculine face. Indeed, for centuries before the advent of Judaism, Christianity, and Islam, God was undoubtedly a woman.

For most of my adult life I have identified as a "recovering Catholic." This tongue-in-cheek assertion reveals more about my search to uncover my own spiritual beliefs than it does about my need to distance myself from my Papal past. In sifting through the rubble of my Catholic faith, I was able to cull authentic articles of faith from the glittering remains and safeguard them, discarding the gilded imposters that I had accepted without question. Along the way I created a richer doctrine, not one based on the rules and regulations of an organized religion, but instead one that encourages intellectual curiosity, invites doubt, and accepts the transformation of grace. I am no longer a Catholic, but I am very much a believer.

Many years ago my father sent me a shiny silver medal of Our Lady of Mount Carmel. Included in the package were two brown scapulars—one for myself and one for my partner, Jane. Dad was never without his scapular—a pair of small cloth squares, imprinted with the image of a saint or of the Virgin, joined by a ribbon of cloth, worn around the neck by some Catholics as a symbol of their devotion. He proudly donned this sacramental item, wearing it beneath his shirt every day. A pamphlet tucked inside an envelope explained the power of the small swatches he had sent me.

Your brown scapular of Our Lady of Mount Carmel is a gift to you from your Heavenly Mother. It is an assurance of salvation. "Whosoever dies clothed in this (scapular) shall not suffer eternal fire." This is the Blessed Virgin Mary's PROMISE, made July 16, 1251, to St. Simon Stock.

The text went on to assure that Pope Benedict XV granted an indulgence of 500 days *each time* the scapular was kissed.

"This is amazing," I exclaimed as I read the text. "It's like medieval Catholic voodoo. Where does my father find this stuff? Wasn't it banned after 1963?"

My mind careened down the narrow aisles of St. Patrick's Guild, a local Catholic gift shop, dodging racks of holy cards, cases of sacred medals, piles of scapulars sealed in cellophane packages. I was astonished that such archaic contraband, with its Blessed Mother's *promise* of salvation from eternal damnation, still existed after the pronouncements of Vatican Council II. I flipped the tiny sheet of paper and read the supplier's name: Holy Wounds Apostolate, Inc., P.O. Box 937, Wisconsin Rapids, WI 54495. I imagined fervent

Catholic guerrillas, working far into the night, in a scapular factory, nestled among barns and pasturelands in rural Wisconsin. Some of the workers cranked out brown, cloth scapulars as others folded the tiny paper pamphlets and diligently hid them inside cases of white plastic, glow-in-the-dark statues, before sending them off. They expertly packed each shipment, skillfully disguising its illicit, precious cargo.

My father could have been one of those tireless workers, staving off the impending darkness that threatened to immerse the modern Catholic Church in a sea of amnesia. Their mission was to insure that the Vatican would never forget that the faithful were yet in dire need of such iconography.

I set aside the pamphlet and added the new medal to the chain I wore around my neck. Its tinny edges clicked against the silver oval of a different Blessed Virgin Mother that my father had given me after returning from one of his trips to Medugorje. I feel a special kinship with Holy Mother Mary, partially because I was named in Her honor, and partially because She is the appropriated, and lesser rendition, of a more ancient spiritual memory: the Dea Madre, the Mother God. She, who had once been revered as Godhead, was now cast as God's human mother. These medals of silver are sacred objects. They are my graven images, worn as an act of rebellion against my Catholic childhood and against a religion that had systematically relegated the Divine Mother to the lower echelons of spiritual consciousness. Like the statue of the Black Madonna of Tindari, or the statue of Tara, the Tibetan Buddhist Goddess of compassion, that rest upon the altar in my home, these talismans invoke spiritual mindfulness; they are parcels of spirit that transcend my father's Catholicism, uniting his faith to mine.

My spirituality is a hybrid of my father's southern Italian Catholicism and my encounters with psychic healing, Tibetan Buddhism, and the Dea Madre. As incongruent as it may at first appear, my father's faith and mine are more similar than dissimilar. We both trust that the etheric eye has powers of second sight. While my father's visions are peopled with the saints of my childhood and with Jesus, the Blessed Virgin, and Joseph, mine are filled with spirit guides, psychic entities, and priestesses of the ancient, original God-figure of humankind, the Dark Mother. Dad relies on the power of holy cards and rosary beads. I read Tarot cards for insight and carry small rocks in my pockets to keep me grounded. Whatever outward manifestations our separate spiritual practices may take, in the end, we both believe that faith in things unseen has the power to heal, even if it defies the laws of science to do so.

My father's pilgrimages to Medugorje strengthened his faith in the unseen and in the supra-natural powers of the Divine to set the sun spinning in the sky.

In May 2001, I made my own pilgrimage. I traveled to Sicily to tour several Black Madonna sites. In that ancient land, the spirit of the Mother God thrives. By then I had long been drawn to the feminine face of divinity and had taken many Women's Spirituality courses during my graduate school days at the University of Minnesota in Minneapolis. I had read such classics as Merlin Stone's *When God Was a Woman* and Robert Grave's *The White Goddess*. Much later, as I was doing research for a novel on southern Italian immigration to American, I would come upon Lucia Chiavola Birnbaum's *Black Madonnas*. To my surprise, in her work I discovered an unexpected connection between my yearning for the dark female divinity and my desire to learn more about the reasons why my grandparents had been forced to leave Italy. My pre-Christian ancestors had most likely worshipped a female God; my Catholic forebears had undoubtedly knelt before a candle-clad altar and prayed to a Black Madonna.

Lucia Chiavola Birnbaum, I was soon to discover, was an eminent historian and professor of women's spirituality at the California Institute of Integral Studies in San Francisco. As a Sicilian American and an expert on the Black Madonna, she seemed the perfect guide for my very personal quest. When I learned that Chiavola Birnbaum was leading a Black Madonna study tour of Sicily in the spring of 2001, I signed up. Under her tutelage, my traveling companions and I visited ancient temple ruins, sites that had once been sacred to the Dea Madre, and upon which now stand Catholic churches, most of which are dedicated to the Virgin Mother.

On Sicily, the Great Mother's presence is as vibrant as the spinning sun. I encountered a pre-historic rendering of Her majesty on Levanzo, a small island off the coast of Trapani on the western (African) side of the island. On a clear and shining morning my traveling companions and I embarked across waters as deep as memory. A speeding ferryboat carried us to Natale Castiglione, the man who was to guide us to the Cava di San Genovese, the site of Upper Paleolithic and Neolithic cave drawings. Natale and his family had been the keepers of the Cava since the ancient drawings had been "discovered" by a woman from Florence, vacationing on the island in 1949. Natale's father had been the cave's first guardian, a duty he performed with serious tenderness. When he grew too old to act as the cave's gatekeeper and safeguard its precious images, he passed on the privilege and the obligation to his son.

My companions and I paid our guide fees and then piled into Natale's jeep. We bumped along as he drove us up a rocky hillside past abandoned buildings and barren fields. When at last we had arrived at the summit of the hill, Natale parked his vehicle and led us in our descent along a serpentine footpath down a steep incline toward a sea so beautifully blue it brought tears to my eyes. The wind blew steadily as we slowly made our way across the gray rocks and among the red wildflowers. At the base of the hillside, the waves swelled and rolled toward a rocky beach. There, in the crook of the shoreline, the ancient cave waited. Natale ushered us inside its dark womb. With lantern in hand, he shined light on the cave's undulant walls, permitting us to witness ancient images of tuna, porpoises, bison, deer, women, men, and spears. In a separate section, secluded in Her divine Holiness, we beheld a drawing, stained in sacred ochre red that had withstood the ravages of time and the ages. The simplicity of this etching belied its magnificence. Inside the dark chamber we could not have known if the sun was spinning in the cloudless blue Sicilian sky. It didn't matter, for my heart leapt at the image I was privileged to encounter, the icon of the Dea Madre left by a Paleolithic painter for my 21st century eyes to behold. There was mystery there and wonder enough to twirl ten thousand suns.

Throughout Sicily I witnessed subaltern sacredness. In the main sanctuary, at the Santuario Maria di Custonaci, I knelt before a painting of a dark-skinned Madonna nursing the Christ-child. The altar contained no crucifix, no images of Jesus, save for the tiny babe feeding at His mother's exposed breast. To the right of this Black Mother stood a statue of the Goddess Demeter, holding a cornucopia brimming with wheat and pomegranates. She wore a wreath of wheat upon her head. On the opposite side stood a statue of Sophia, the Goddess of Wisdom, one of the ancient Oracles. She cradled an open book in one arm; a dove emerged from her heart. Sophia wore a laurel wreath upon her head, another pre-Christian symbol of the Goddess blatantly visible in this now-Catholic church.

Everywhere the pagan and the Christian merged to form one seamless breath of Spirit. On Mozia, an island off the coast of Marsala, we visited an archeological museum filled with artifacts of the ancient 5th Century B.C.E. Phoenician Goddess, Tanit. Later, in myriad Catholic sanctuaries, vestiges of this Goddess's power and form everywhere surfaced; "pagan" iconography morphed into post-Christian images of Jesus' Holy Mother.

Along the northern coast of Sicily, at the sanctuary of the Black Madonna of Tindari, a mammoth statue of the Dark Mother presides from a commanding center altar. She carries a child in her strong arms. The inscription at the base of the sculpture reads: *Nigra sum sed formosa*, I am black and beautiful. Behind the sanctuary a mosaic mural attests to the fact that the original church of the Black Madonna of Tindari was built on an ancient temple to Demeter.

Unlike my father, I did not collect fragments of rocks on my pilgrimage through Sicily. Instead I gleaned long-lost truths from a time before humankind worshiped a Divine Father. Instead of suns spinning in the sky, I witnessed the son spinning out of the spiritual cosmology. I embarked on a journey back in time to a place and a people that hadn't forgotten Her ancient secrets. They still whispered Her name in the stone alleyways of rock-bound hill towns; they still prayed to Her in dimly lit sanctuaries; still revered Her in sleepy seaside ports and teeming inland cities. Slowly I began to understand that my father's singular devotion to the Catholic version of the Blessed Virgin Mary was more rooted in his ancient southern Italian heritage than in his allegiance to Christianity. Across Sicily I recognized this same fervent love in the eyes of men and women, young and old. Christ was not the object of their worship. The Mother was. She represented the first womb, the cave of consciousness, the core of spirit. The seeds of my father's dedication to the Catholic Virgin were burrowed deep into the soil of pre-Christian memory. They suckled on the stories and recollections of a time and place where God was a woman. In my father's own southern Italian ancestral region of Puglia, pilgrims pray at many shrines to the Black Madonna. In the recesses of his cellular chemistry, my father was also remembering this ancient knowledge.

Throughout Roman Catholic Italy (and in Spain, France, and other places in Europe as well) Mary, the mother of Jesus, has been worshiped for centuries in her Black Madonna form. The common people, the peasants in the fields, the shepherds in the hillsides, the shopkeepers in the piazza, had once made votive offerings to the Dea Madre. Compelled by the unholy alliance between the politically powerful and the religiously corrupt, these men and women transferred their devotion to a Virgin Mother, who was as dark-skinned as were they, masking their subaltern beliefs in order to save their lives. As Christianity acquired political power and economic acumen, the Madonnas blackness became whitened as well. In the person of the Virgin Mary, the Great Mother's subversive nature was tamed into subservience.

Still, this staunch and unyielding canonical fervor failed to silence Her. Throughout the centuries, the Dea Madre has appeared regularly to poor peoples around the world. Sightings of Her have been recorded at Fatima, Lourdes, Medugorje and countless other places. In countrysides and cities across the globe the feminine form of God is re-surging. Why this fervent devotion? And why now?

Maybe my father actually saw the sun spinning outside the Piggly Wiggly that day as he carried groceries home to my stepmother, Rose. Believing in what cannot be proven is the basis of faith. And the basis of grace is expecting and accepting the miraculous.

Perhaps the Divine Mother is calling Her prodigal children back home to her waiting arms. Perhaps She is reminding us that there is much in the unseen that our modern world gravely needs. Grace. Compassion. The belief in the power of love to conquer injustice and evil.

Undoubtedly, my father and I are two of her many yearning pilgrims.

Hidden No More: The Black Madonna Adonai of Sicily

Mary Beth Moser, M.A.

She is dark, she is old, perhaps the oldest of all venerated images of the Virgin Mary; she has survived natural disaster; she has been hidden literally and subconsciously.
Now she calls to be found.

Unknown to most visitors to Italy and hidden away on a cave wall is one of the oldest images of the Madonna. The fresco is venerated in a small church known as the Santuario Madonna Adonai near the seaside town of Brucoli on the eastern shore of Sicily. The narrow dusty lanes that lead to the sanctuary are barely marked. Even the sanctuary web site acknowledges that the place is well hidden among the cypress and pine trees and one must be lucky to find it.[1]

August 9, 2000. I was with a study group of nine women led by Lucia Chiavola Birnbaum to learn about the Dark Mother in Sicily. We had found her presence in archeological museums, in churches and sanctuaries, and in the dark lava of Mt. Etna. The sanctuary with the Madonna Adonai was more elusive. Only an entry in Ean Begg's guide to European Black Virgins pointed the way, and even then, it said that the sanctuary was not open to visitors. Undaunted, we convinced our bus driver to give it a try. We found the little road, which became a path. Finally the bus could go no further and we got out and walked excitedly toward the front gate. It was locked, closed, under construction. The workers refused to let us in.

In the pasture adjacent to the sanctuary, cows with crescent moon-shaped horns wander, as if reminding visitors of their role in finding this sacred precinct. For over a thousand years, the cave was buried and forgotten. Then, in the 16th century, a grazing cow fell into a crevice in the rock. A shepherd, in his attempt to save the animal, discovered the grotto and the painting. It became a place of pilgrimage, and according to a local brochure, one of the most frequented sanctuaries of the faithful.[2] During the 17th century, a church and hermitage were built above the cave, offering a place of beauty and quiet meditation by the sea.

I was thinking back, remembering my own first discovery of a Black Madonna five years earlier. How could I have made so many trips to Italy and not ever "seen" her dark face, in at least a hundred different locations throughout Italy? Now the Madonna Adonai had called me, called us to this place. We had journeyed so far! Surely she would find a way to let us in.

The Madonnas seclusion may have saved her from the waves of political and religious forces that destroyed an unknown number of dark Madonna images across Europe over the last two millennia. In the centuries following her discovery, she survived natural disaster and other threats. According to the memoirs of a local nun, the church was the only one in the region to survive a catastrophic earthquake in 1693 that destroyed the southeastern part of Sicily and killed more than 66,000 people.[3] The sanctuary survived being confiscated by the state when Italy was unified, due to the fact that the monks were still officially laymen.[4] In more recent times, as the numbers of friars dwindled at the isolated sanctuary location, the fresco survived incidents of vandalism and theft.[5]

Finally, after much persuasion, one brave worker agreed to let us in, but only for a short visit. He opened the gate of the outer wall. We walked down a path and passed through an arched metal gate into a garden. This was a place of spectacular beauty, framed by earth, sea and sky. We reached a small courtyard and the church entrance—a tall narrow door flanked by carved columns and an arch above. He tried at least a dozen keys from a large ring, each one unsuccessful. I was reminded of the ancient Sumerian Goddess Inanna, Queen of Heaven and Earth, who had to pass through seven gates to be allowed to the dark underworld where she would die to her old self and be reborn.[6]

High above the entrance on the outer wall of the church, two sets of spirals had been carved in the stone face. Archeologist and mythologist Marija Gimbutas called these motifs "oculi" from the Latin word for eyes. Oculi dating back thousands of years have been found on entrance doors to rock-cut tombs in Sicily, on limestone blocks in Maltese temples and on tomb/sanctuaries in Ireland.[7] Gimbutas compiled a symbolic language based on the recurring markings and artistic elements found on Neolithic artifacts across Europe. According to Gimbutas, spirals were sacred markings, denoting the regenerating eyes of the goddess and a "Divine Source" of life-giving moisture.[8]

Miraculously, after we had almost given up hope, the man who had agreed to help us was handed the right key from another worker. He unlocked the door. One by one we crossed the threshold from the sunlit courtyard into the dark room. Our words gave way to silent awe, as we found ourselves in an intimate space that was part cave, part church. It felt like we had entered the dark womb of Mother earth. As our eyes adjusted to the darkness, we saw the emerging image of the dark Madonna.

Inside the cave/church, one is met by the dark eyes of Madonna Adonai. Her image is painted on a cave wall, centrally located behind the altar with a golden canopy overhead. The Madonna's dark brown face and body are enfolded in a marine blue veil that evokes the color of the sea nearby. In her left hand she holds an orb in front of her womb. Face, hand, tunic and orb meld into one brownness, rich and dark, like the color of life-giving soil.[9] Her right arm cradles an adult-looking child. The white of his clothing is in high contrast to the dark background of his mother. Symbolically, Madonna Adonai becomes the dark primordial mother of the light; the dark new moon giving birth to the white full moon.[10] The Madonna wears a golden crown, the Church's recognition of her as a Queen, and a symbol of her power.[11] The child, too, is crowned.

A prayer card depicting her likeness dates the antique fresco as 3rd century AD, placing her among the oldest venerated images of a Madonna. Like so many dark-skinned images of the Virgin Mary found throughout Italy, Europe, and indeed the world, Black Madonnas, as they are collectively known, are often the oldest of the old.

Also, like several other images of Black Madonnas in Italy, the Madonna Adonai has been altered. According to the Italian version of the sanctuary's web site, "l'immagine in un tempo imprecisate é stata ritoccata con l'aggiunta del bimbo, delle corone suo capo, del globo sul palmo della mano,"[12] which means, at some imprecise time, the image was retouched to include the addition of the baby, the crowns and the globe.[13] This would imply it was her image alone that was once revered. Curiously, the web site's English translation of the passage above, says it was a "nimbus" (a shining cloud) that was added, rather than a child.[14] Is this simply a mistranslation, or is it a way to cloud the possibility that she was honored before Christianity?

As I was gazing upon her image, I realized there was a space behind the altar, into which I stepped. Unexpectedly, when I did this, the altarpiece shielded me visually from the rest of the group and I was alone with the Madonna in front of me. I felt compelled to reach out and touch her image on the cave wall. I would not have touched a painting in a museum…but this was different. She was beckoning, accessible. Yes, the painting had been re-touched—by me.

The skin tone of the child is slightly lighter than that of the Madonna Adonai. Other Black Madonna images in Italy, such as L'Incoronata [15] near Foggia and the Madonna del Soccorso[16] in San Severo show the mother as dark and the child as light. Could this be a symbolic indication that the child was added later, that the dark mother is the older tradition?

Certainly there is evidence of a very old tradition to the dark mother on the island. Lucia Birnbaum, in her groundbreaking book, *Black Madonnas: feminism, religion and politics in Italy*, writes of the "sisterhood of dark women divinities" in Sicily:

The indigenous goddess Ibla, visible in paleolithic and neolithic ruins, and remembered today in the folklore of the region of the Iblaen mountains (named for her), was joined by dark images of the goddess brought to the island by Semites (Canaanite Phoenicians) from Asia Minor, Egyptians from Africa, travelers and traders of the Graeco-Roman world, and later by Byzantines and Muslims.[17]

Birnbaum has compiled a wealth of archeological, genetic and cultural evidence to document signs of the dark mother along primordial African migration routes to all continents of the earth.[18] Images of the dark mother, she proposes, come from a genetic memory of humanity's first African Mother.[19]

Her presence felt like that of an ancient Mother. She seemed powerfully compassionate. I was beholding her image—yet, it felt as though she were beholding me.

The Madonna's title preserves her presence in the earliest centuries of Christianity when it was still considered a Jewish sect. The sanctuary's web site states that the name by which this image of the Madonna is known is Maria Sanctissima Mater Adonai or simply Adonai. [20] It goes on to explain that Adonai is a biblical word, and one of the Hebrew names for God.[21] Given the island's long tradition of honoring female divinity, perhaps her name preserves more than just her proto-Christian origins. Perhaps it is telling us that at one time, she was understood to be God herself.

This is a non-orthodox belief to be sure, since Mary, whom church doctrine says was taken bodily into heaven (the Assumption), and declared to be the Mother of the God, but is not considered to be divine herself. Yet even the revised Catholic Catechism, the official church teachings, clarifies that God "is neither man nor woman" but "pure spirit", whose perfection is reflected as "those of a mother and those of a father and a husband."[22] Pope John Paul II, in a speech to the pilgrims in Rome in September 1999, acknowledged God as having the nature of both female and male.[23] What better image to represent Mother God than the dark and ancient face of the Black Madonna?

Too soon, it was time to leave. I lingered outside behind the others, feeling bound to the place. Then, I heard the Madonna speak to me and affirm my role in finding the place. I tingled with the feeling of grace bestowed. She had reached out and touched me. It felt like an electric touch of the divine upon my heart. Now I was the one who was re-touched, who would never be the same. With her mark upon me, I felt ready to leave, filled with joy.

Later that night at dinner, everyone was anxious to speak of their experiences. The challenges of seeking Madonna Adonai and the fulfillment of finding her seemed to unify us. Perhaps we had each found ourselves as we looked at that dark image, and in that recognition, felt part of the whole dark thread of life—the darkness of the womb from which we were born; the darkness of the new moon to which our menstrual cycles entrained; the dark place to which we descended for personal growth, emerging, like Inanna, strong and whole and authentic; the darkness of the face of our first African mother; the primordial darkness of matter before the starburst of creation.

Notes

1 "Santuario Madonna Adonai," 2002–2003. www.adonai.too.it See English link: The Convent.

2 Anna Gatto. Brucoli, La Trotilon dei Greci. (Giuseppe Montemagno Editore, 1994), 21.

3 "Santuario Madonna Adonai," 2002–2003. www.adonai.too.it See English link: The Convent.

4 "Santuario Madonna Adonai," 2002–2003. www.adonai.too.it See English link: The Convent.

5 We learn from the web site that a tela, or canvas, with the story of the sanctuary was stolen, but nothing is said about damage to the original fresco. "Santuario Madonna Adonai," 2002–2003. www.adonai.too.it See English link: The Convent.

6 See Betty De Shong Meador, Uncursing the Dark (Wilmette: Chiron Publications, 1994), for a full description of this ancient myth, The Descent of Inanna to the Underworld.

7 Marija Gimbutas. The Language of the Goddess (New York: Harper Collins, 1989), 59–60. The specific dates cited for Sicily are 3000–2500 BC, for Malta are end 4th-early 3rd millennium BC and for Ireland are c.3200 BC.

8 Marija Gimbutas. The Language of the Goddess (New York: Harper Collins, 1989), 51; See also 59–60.

9 Gimbutas states that during the Neolithic period in Old Europe, black was the color of fertility and the soil, in contrast to its identification with death now associated with Christian iconography. See Marija Gimbutas. The Language of the Goddess (New York: Harper Collins, 1989), 144.

10 See Judith Rae Grahn. Are Goddesses Metaformic Constructs? An Application of Metaformic Theory to Menarche Celebrations And Goddess Rituals of Kerala, South India, (California Institute of Integral Studies,

Ph.D. Dissertation, September, 1999), p.42, for discussion of white and black as representing the full and dark moon.

11 Gimbutas notes that the title "queen" in the historic era is a remnant of the Goddesses' ruling power, used to designate Goddesses who were not married to Indo-European deities but who continued to be powerful in their own right. See Marija Gimbuta, Language of the Goddess, 318.

12 "Santuario Madonna Adonai," 2002–2003. www.adonai.too.it See Italian link: Madonna di Adonai.

13 My translation.

14 The web site's complete English translation of the same passage says: 'The image has been retouched with the addition of the nimbus [emphasis added], the crowns on the head, and the orb on the palm of the hand," thus mistranslating the word bimbo which means baby in Italian, into the English word "nimbus." See "Santuario Madonna Adonai," 2002–2003. www.adonai.too.it, English link: Madonna of Adonai.

15 The ancient carved wooden image of L'Incoronata holds a child carved from a lighter colored wood; a painting of her venerated in the crypt below in the Chapel of the Apparition shows a dark mother holding a white child.

16 See Giacomo Medica. I Santuari Mariani d'Italia. (Torino: Collegamento Mariano Nazionale, 1965), p. 525 for photo.

17 Lucia Chiavola Birnbaum, Ph.D. Black Madonnas: feminism, religion, and politics in Italy (Boston: Northeastern University Press, 1993), 11.

18 Lucia Chiavola Birnbaum, Ph.D. dark mother: african origins and godmothers (New York: iUniverse, 2002), throughout.

19 Lucia Chiavola Birnbaum, Ph.D. dark mother: african origins and godmothers (New York: iUniverse, 2002), throughout.

20 "Santuario Madonna Adonai," 2002–2003. www.adonai.too.it See link: Adonai. The literal translation of Maria Sanctissima (abbreviated SS.) Mater Adonai is Holiest Mary Mother Lord. The mixed use of Latin (Maria Sanctissima Mater) and Hebrew (Adonai) creates some ambiguity in translation, since Adonai does not change its spelling to indicate its case, like its Latin equivalent, Dominus. The web site does not provide an English translation of this title.

21 "Santuario Madonna Adonai," 2002–2003, www.adonai.too.it See link: Adonai.

22 Catechism of the Catholic Church (New York: Doubleday, 1995), p.105, paragraph 370.

23 Richard Owen. "Pope praises 'God the Mother' to pilgrims," The London Times, 10 September 1999.

Bibliography

Begg, Ean. The Cult of the Black Virgin. New York: Penguin, 1996.

Birnbaum, Ph.D., Lucia Chiavola. Black Madonnas: feminism, religion, and politics in Italy. Boston: Northeastern University Press, 1993.

———. dark mother: african origins and godmothers. New York: iUniverse, 2002.

Cassell's Italian Dictionary. New York: Macmillan Publishing, 1982.

Catechism of the Catholic Church. New York: Doubleday, 1995.

Gatto, Anna. Brucoli, La Trotilon dei Greci. Giuseppe Montemagno Editore, 1994.

Gimbutas, Marija. The Language of the Goddess. New York: Harper Collins, 1989.

Grahn, Judith Rae. Are Goddesses Metaformic Constructs? An Application of Metaformic Theory to Menarche Celebrations And Goddess Rituals of Kerala, South India, California Institute of Integral Studies, Ph.D. Dissertation, September, 1999.

Meador, Betty De Shong. Uncursing the Dark. Wilmette: Chiron Publications, 1994.

Medica, Giacomo. I Santuari Mariani d'Italia. Torino: Collegamento Mariano Nazionale, 1965.

Santuario Madonna Adonai, 2002–2003. www.adonai.too.it Updated March 15, 2003. Dimitri Antoniou Webmaster © 2002–03 Italia DimaNet. Accessed September 11, 2003.

Conjuring the Priestess to Heal and Empower Young Women

Delphyne Platner, Ph.D.

Introduction

Regardless of race, class, or culture, women share a profound ability to re-awaken to their ancestral memory and inherently spiritual nature. This process is not identical for all women. Each woman's experience is unique; however, the essence of each woman's experience is analogous to all others' experiences. My doctoral dissertation, *All Women Are Witches: Women's Stories of Re-Awakening to Their Ancestral Memory and Inherently Spiritual Nature,* focused on women's journeys toward self-awareness within the patriarchal context of the United States. Despite the fact that women worldwide have been indoctrinated into a consciousness steeped in a patriarchal paradigm, I have found that western women possess an innate ability to vanquish their own internalized oppression and reinstate a consciousness that, I believe, holds all life as sacred. My research asked the following inquiry question: *What is the experience of women who realize a spiritual calling to become priestesses when living in a paradigm that fails to recognize the Divine Feminine? What impact has this shift in consciousness, from unwitting daughters of the patriarchy to self-empowered priestesses, had on their lives, as inspired by an awakening to their inherent spiritual power?*

Using a methodology of organic inquiry (a spiritual, holistic and inclusive approach), I interviewed five contemporary priestesses (Clements et al. 1999). This exploration collected and integrated women's stories of initiation, healing, empowerment, and transformation in the journeys of self-awareness and claiming power. Using critical feminist theory and participatory paradigms to look through the lens of feminist spirituality, I discovered that my co-researchers' stories revealed a massive process of "unlearning" that they, of necessity, experienced in order to embrace and feel empowered in their womanhood. One of the primary goals of my research was to inspire the reader to employ these findings in the socialization of future generations of young women.

What Has Become of Our Ancestral Memory and Inherently Spiritual Nature?

> The damage wrought by patriarchy cannot be halted by patchwork reforms of that system, nor will technological 'fixes' save the Earth and us. Only the acceptance of a postpatriarchal, holistic attitude toward life on Earth will bring about truly comprehensive change. Feminist spirituality is a means of both evolving that attitude and activating the processes which will lead to that change (Spretnak 1989, 130).

I propose that the results of the shift from a matristic consciousness and worldview to a patriarchal one that has come about over the course of the past five thousand years is directly responsible for much of the pain, humiliation, and alienation that have become cornerstones in female socialization. This rite of passage into womanhood at menarche, (or lack thereof), plays a major role in defining the women we will become, how we will navigate our bodies, sexuality, relationships, and self-esteem in the world. Sadly, attitudes towards the things that were sacred for many thousands of years—menstruation, childbirth, child rearing, sexuality, women's ways of knowing, creativity, the healing arts, ritual, ceremony and rites of passage—have been completely reversed today (Noble 1991). During the insidious course of patriarchal sublimation of women's mysteries—once honored and celebrated—became twisted into something repulsive and shameful. The very nature of women's bodies and women's blood is taboo, deemed unworthy of consideration and discourse within the dominant culture in the United States.

Perhaps one of the more difficult and painful issues for many women to examine is how we as women perpetuate our own oppression. Gerda Lerner reminds us that we are an integral part of this equation:

The system of patriarchy can only function with the cooperation of women (Lerner 1986, 217).

Women have for millennia participated in the process of their own subordination because they have been psychologically shaped as to internalize the idea of their own inferiority. The unawareness of their own history of struggle and achievement has been one of the major means of keeping women subordinate (Lerner 1986, 218).

bell hooks stresses the importance of women's confronting and transforming their internalized oppression, "As long as females take up the banner of feminist politics without addressing and transforming their own sexism, ultimately the movement will be undermined" (hooks 2000, 12). In any discussion about women's internalized sexism, it is necessary to set the context for female socialization. Females learn to accept and internalize negative messages about our inferior status at a very early age. Carol Gilligan (1982) has conducted many studies with young women on the brink of adolescence. Her findings conclude that these young women are encouraged to give up their sense of self in favor of being in relationship. This means that, upon approaching adolescence, a girl is often compelled to give up her own experience and accept a reality that has been determined for her by men. Girls experience pressure (from their friends, families and culture in general) to be "good," to be caregivers and nurturers, to put other peoples' needs and desires before their own. They receive messages about what they are "supposed" to be, do or look like. Often these are very different from who they feel they really are, and what they truly dream or desire to be. I surmise that these socially constructed cultural mores are in deep opposition to our inherent female nature.

Once girls' voices are silenced or lost, it can be extremely difficult to reclaim them. Many women go on to live the rest of their lives in this subordinate place, rarely accessing their "true selves." Susan Griffin (1989, 7) refers to our patriarchal "split culture" and our general detachment from ourselves, our spirituality and Mother Nature,

> We are divided against ourselves. We no longer feel ourselves to be a part of this earth. We regard our fellow creatures as enemies. And, very young, we even learn to disown a part of our own being. We come to believe that we do not know what we know. We grow used to ignoring the evidence of our own experience, what we hear or see, what we feel in our own bodies.

I cannot help but wonder if much of this wounding, this internalized misogyny, could be prevented altogether if we lived in a world that honored women. The process of becoming detached from and mistrusting our own experience allows others, in the realms of church, state, work, media, and fashion, to dictate and create it for us. As a Marriage and Family Therapist working with young women who have been repeatedly exposed to trauma, I endeavor to teach them how much they *do* know, directing them to the dormant wisdom and knowledge and answers that live in their bodies and in their psyches. Much of our work together focuses on helping them to trust in "listening" to themselves and "waking up" to this inherent knowledge.

While there are many women making significant contributions to their communities, and we represent more than half of the world's population, female role models remain extremely underrepresented in the public domain. My dissertation research focused on putting women's stories out into the public sphere giving voice to subjects that are often considered taboo. In doing so, I aspire to inform and inspire female readers to realize that they do not have to believe everything they have been taught, to know that they do, in fact, have choices in their lives, which can promote women feeling better about themselves physically, emotionally, and spiritually.

Conjuring the Priestess

This work calls forth the spirits and the stories of ancient and contemporary priestesses alike. I have chosen priestesses as a medium through which to share women's stories.

> It is the priestess, sibyls and mediators of the Goddess who carry a great responsibility to inform and transform the spiritual desert that the post religious phase of feminism has created in its first iconoclastic demolition of former patriarchal spiritualities (Matthews 1990, 15).

I believe that priestesses hold the keys to unlocking the gates of internalized oppression. By this I mean the healing that the priestess facilitates in the world as well as each individual woman awakening to, and embracing, what my friend Jessica calls "The Wild Divine"—the witch within.

The Role of the Priestess

What does it mean to be a priestess in a patriarchal world? Because our culture does not recognize the feminine counterpart to "priest," and with few exceptions initiation into priesthood is not an option for women in mainstream religions, even the word priestess needs defining. Contemporary priestesses of many different spiritual paths continue to carry on the legacy of their ancestral foremothers throughout history and pre-history—women whose "specialties we would say today fell under such varied pursuits as religion, philosophy, prophecy, ethics, writing, dance, temple construction and maintenance, ritual, fund raising, tourism, social work, and medicine" (Goodrich 1989, 1). Often the priestesses among us go unrecognized, as we lack a common terminology and understanding of their existence.

Contemporary priestesses are diverse in their background, training and devotion to spirit. Some have received formal initiations and taken vows within a traditional or organized forum; whereas others have created their own vows and initiations. While many different practices and traditions co-exist under the umbrella of women's spirituality, there are essential similarities between them. Women's spirituality is a way of perceiving and interacting with the world, not merely a philosophy, a doctrine, or something learned from a book. There are multiple ways of gaining knowledge and accessing the Divine. Embodied knowledge is highly valued and may manifest itself in a variety of ways that include, but are not limited to, visual, auditory, and sensory perception. Often this knowledge may appear in the form of a dream, or is activated by other forms of sacred arts such as meditation, yoga, dance, or ritual. Despite apparent differences of geography, race, language, lineage, socio-economic status, and religion, the essence of these rituals performed by priestesses is very much the same. Ritual can be understood cross-culturally because it taps into the mytho-cosmological reality of human experience. A fundamental tenet of women's spirituality is that anyone can have direct and deeply meaningful contact with the Divine.

This matristic worldview understands time as cyclical, or spiral, rather than linear, honoring the seasons, cycles and the process of transformation. The only thing promised to us in life is transformation, divinely symbolized by the Goddess in all of Her various (actual and symbolic) guises—life, death, and rebirth. Embracing women's spirituality means consecrating women's cycles, with their connection to cycles of the moon, the tides, and the seasons. Of course men have cycles too. All living beings do. Perhaps if our 21st century fathers, brothers, lovers, and friends were able to embrace, celebrate, consecrate, and honor their own cycles, they would recognize their interconnectedness to all life, instead of standing outside of nature and attempting to control it.

A priestess deeply venerates this interconnectedness of life, and is dedicated to healing herself, others, and the planet. She knows that all things have a purpose, and thus reveres all that patriarchal religions have dichotomized as the sacred and the profane. She strives to balance light and dark, both within and without; for to fail to recognize one without the other has sent the world spinning out of kilter. A priestess draws much of her strength from the Underworld, domain of the Dark Goddess. She realizes that although the chthonic realm has been demonized, suppressed, or neglected by most religions, The Dark Goddess holds the power to bestow many gifts; among them treasures such as creativity, passion, sacred sexuality, protection, ferocity, courage, and death of the ego.

The priestess communes with spirit and the ancestors, performing rituals and divining for herself and others. "The High Priestess is the original Sybil, whose ability to enter the trance state and divine the future made her the mouthpiece of the Goddess" (Noble 1983, 36). She may consult the oracle through reading tarot, throwing coconut or cowry shells, swinging a pendulum, trance states, dream work, palm reading, numerology, astrology, I Ching, scrying, reading coffee grounds, tea leaves or eggs. While there are countless methods of divination originating in various cultures, their intention is usually the same quest for Divine guidance. The priestess listens with her entire being—to herself, to the Divine, to the earth, to her devotees.

Matthews (1990, 15) articulates the role and responsibility of the contemporary priestess. "Fundamentally speaking, a priestess is one who mediates the Goddess by making Her power available to all creation. A priestess guards the mysteries of the Mother and helps initiate other travelers on the road to the spiritual home. A priestess changes things, concepts, people." A priestess navigates the space between the worlds, accepting her fate as portal or a doorway to the Divine. She is a resource for knowledge, information, and healing in her community. She knows how to dance with these forces—ancestors, gods and goddesses, spirits, and the natural elements. She resists the urge to believe that she is *the* power, while trusting herself as a vessel.

What Makes A Priestess?

> Every woman who consciously finds herself standing at the portal of the Temple has her own story to tell. She has found her way by trial and tribulation, for the path to the Temple is hidden and obscured in the times in which we live. Nevertheless, women still discover the path and make the journey and every woman who finds the way makes it easier for others to follow (Ozaniec 1990, 219).

What makes a priestess? Who decides? Who is the contemporary priestess? Where do we find her? How do we recognize her in ourselves? While preparing to defend my doctoral dissertation, my friend Robin reminded me that my research is revolutionary because I am documenting the existence of contemporary priestesses—with their own stories—in a world that generally fails to acknowledge that priestesses exist. "Imagine," she said, "If you had the stories of the Sibyls or the Pythia in their own voices as opposed to fragments composed by a male interpreter or scholar who probably had no concept of ritual or women's mysteries?" *If women's stories were viewed as worthy of record, how might this have altered the course of history?*

There are countless reasons women self-initiate or undergo initiation into various spiritual traditions today. Because women continue to be absent in roles of authority in all of the world's primary religions, we find women's spiritual leadership more often at a grass-roots level and in alternative communities. Reasons for undertaking initiation may include the need for personal and/ or planetary health and healing, response to divination, desire for status, and many, (myself included), are interested in fine-tuning their vehicle (meaning the physical, emotional and spiritual self) to better open to, receive, and channel the Divine in order to serve community.

Priestessing to Empowering Young Women

> We need temples where people can come to heal broken spirits, where direct experience of the Goddess is given by experienced mediators of Her power. These temples are slowly being built, offering alternative rites of passage, seasonal rituals and personalized encounters with the Goddess whose energy to empower is unfamiliar to most people living in this century (Matthews 1990, 27).

My research aspires to be one of the foundation stones in the temple. This chapter is dedicated to educating and inspiring participation in that process. I invite the reader to expand her or his preconceived notions (or lack thereof) around the socialization of our young women. I propose that feminist spirituality—through history, myths and stories, rituals and rites of passage—can effectively circumvent the trauma of growing up female.

As a priestess I take feminist spirituality out into the world, beyond the limited realm of academia, and make it real and accessible. My heart's work has been facilitating healing within young women through priestessing in the therapeutic realm. In the future, I hope to implement this multi-faceted feminist spiritual approach to healing and empowerment with girls as a preventative model—before they are traumatized. All of the young women I have counseled and protected from their abusers have been repeatedly traumatized. I have worked in adolescent day treatment centers, with homeless children and families, in private practice, and in sex trauma, serving populations who are considered high risk. I have served in the capacity as individual, family, couples (for parents), group, and milieu therapist. While working in sex trauma, I was responsible for deciding whether a child victim of sexual abuse was safe remaining at home. Most often, the initial traumatization experienced by the young person is further compounded by completely inadequate systems of care at every level.

Youth who come into various branches of the system—mental health, substance abuse, and juvenile justice—are the teens who many have already given up on, who nobody else knows how to handle. A recent visit to Juvenile Hall in San Francisco informed me that females represent the fastest growing population. Many of them live with a single parent, usually the mother. Some of their parents are in jail. These young women have been neglected and/or abused physically, emotionally, and/or sexually. Some struggle with eating disorders or learning disabilities. It is not uncommon for these teens to turn this rage on themselves, and many abuse drugs and alcohol to cope, or engage in self-mutilation, such as cutting or burning themselves, or pulling out their hair.

Fifteen-year-old Ani (not her real name) has been out as a lesbian since she was thirteen. She is the survivor of major physical and emotional abuse and neglect. Until recently, she lived in a group home because her grandmother was unable keep her safe from self-mutilating four times a day on average. She also struggles with dyslexia. Before our work together, Ani had gone through thirteen therapists, few of whom, she says, were able to reach her. She is an incredibly brilliant and courageous young woman and I am blessed to know her. Ani struggled with self-mutilation for years. As she began to improve, she would substitute healthier behavior when she felt the urge to cut on her arms. One time she presented me with a drawing where she had traced her arm on a piece of paper and gouged angry cut marks on the paper as opposed to actually cutting herself. The following poem demonstrates Ani's fierce will to survive and heal from multiple traumas.

March 20th 1999

This you leave me
To suffer your sin
This fear I might live
To off what might be good
This I never forget
To live through that
This pain the world left me
To show as scars on my arms
But this I turn around
To make livable for once
This I recover
To do just fine
And to breathe the air I once resented.
(personal communication, 1999)

These young women are survivors. My biggest challenge, as their therapist, is to earn their trust, as they have been so often betrayed by those who are supposed to love and protect them. It continues to amaze me, given what some of them have been through, that they can be open to trusting anyone at all. Most of them have an extremely heightened intuition because they have had to be vigilant in order to survive. While it may sound simple and obvious, I have found that what works best in facilitating trust is creating a safe and sacred space and being truly present while listening to young women. Most of the girls I have worked with have never had the experience of being listened to in a respectful way by someone who they believe cares about what they have to say. It is also my experience that they are very responsive to, even hungry for, rituals and rites of passage—sorely lacking in our culture. My philosophy is that we need to do whatever it takes (within ethical boundaries, of course) to reach them. They are slow to trust as they feel that most people, their families, teachers, and society in general, have either disappointed or given up on them. I have learned to be flexible about our sessions. I have met with them outside, at the beach, over lunch, picking blackberries, during car rides, listening to music…whatever it takes to help them feel comfortable.

Matthews describes how becoming in tune with the Divine Feminine supports women in realizing their inherent knowing. "Whenever a woman is touched by the fire of the Goddess, a corresponding spark is ignited within her, re-kindling the old memories, casting lightenings ahead of the path so that she can see her way forward" (1990, 16). Even as a feminist therapist, my approach remains unconventional. I have utilized mythology, stories, women's history, ritual, imagery, films, art, self-disclosure (when appropriate), and tarot in my attempts to empower these girls. We have done rituals to dispel fears, to voice long silenced anger and deep-seated rage, invocations for healing and abundance, ropes courses, writing, and ritual work with goddesses Kali, Pele, Persephone, Inanna, and Ereshkigal. With one young woman I went to the beach and we ritually released all of the ways in which her mother had—and continues to—abuse and disappoint her. With my friend Sasha I co-created and co-facilitated a Women's Healing and Purification Lodge Ritual at Slide Ranch in Marin. I specifically chose not to use the term sweat lodge, as it refers to a Native American practice requiring specific knowledge and initiation. I have been known to give the young women "homework assignments" and supplement their history courses in school with women's history and books by women authors. Knowledge is power and I want them to be able to make informed choices.

Knowledge can take many forms. Belenky et al. (1986) have written extensively on this subject in *Women's Ways of Knowing: The Development of Self, Voice, and Mind*. I emphasize to these young women that they are the experts on their own experience. The dominant culture seems determined to define this experience for them, dictating how to look, who they are, what they need to be beautiful, how to act in order to be popular and well-liked. I teach them that their bodies remember another way, educating them about cellular memory. I ask my girls, "Have you ever *known* something with all your heart, yet you haven't learned it in school, from a book, or from another person? Maybe it came to you in a dream?" Flinders (1998, 48) provides the excellent example of mystic Julian of Norwich as a woman trusting her inherent knowing. "Her breathtaking, serene trust in the visions, for instance—in her own *experience*, that is as opposed to what she had been taught as a Christian—seemed to me deeply consistent with the great value contemporary feminism sees in claiming one's own experience. Julian actually said she regarded the showings as a more reliable source of spiritual understanding than holy scripture." Ultimately I want to encourage these young women to think for themselves and to trust what they know. I tell them: *Trust your gut. Listen for the voices of your female ancestors. Make your own decisions.*

My clinical work strives to help young women to discover their authentic voices. In my experience, reclaiming those voices involves embracing and integrating the shadow, the awe inspiring and terrifying presence of the Dark Goddess into our lives. This is perhaps best expressed in the following piece by eighteen-year-old Jessica Dawn. When she first came to see me for therapy at seventeen, she was just released from a long-term hospitalization as a result of severe anorexia nervosa, self-mutilation and suicidal ideation. Jessica grew up with an alcoholic mother, on the run from a domestic violence situation with her father (they had moved twenty-two times), and was cutting on herself several times a day in attempts to relieve the pain she felt from the flashbacks as a result of being molested at age four and raped at seven. Her most significant challenges were in finding her voice, expressing her anger and rage in healthy ways instead of being self-destructive. Much of our work together was about embracing the Dark Goddess—She who presides over all creation, destruction and rebirth—incorporating stories and imagery of the ancient Sumerian Queen of the Underworld, Ereshkigal; the Hindu goddess Kali; and Pele, the Hawaiian volcano goddess. Jessica was inspired to paint an enormous mural of Pele surrounded by a dragon outside of our school. She has also created art to express her experiences of Ereshkigal and Kali. She has given me permission to share the following story of her recent dance with Kali.

Who is Kali to Me?

A figure who makes it okay to feel. A figure who says to me, "No, you don't need to think, just feel. Contact the primal energy—the rage, the hurt, the defenses, the energy that moves mountains, the intense inner rhythms, instinct.

In this culture, I feel my darker side has been repressed. I have been raised in a culture in which I must fit the role of a "good girl." I was taught to pretend I felt happy, lighthearted, "good" instead of "bad." While I attempted to fit this mold, my shadow self has been pushed away, creating despair, emptiness, depression, and self-destruction.

And here, here is this magnificent creature; furious, half-crazed, terrible, beautiful and awing all at the same time, offering to tear away my facade, my self-destructive mechanisms, my mask of the "good girl" which I had grown accustomed to and have held onto for dear life. Here She is with Her scythe, sword, ball and chain and dagger controlled by all the rage and fury, offering to tear it all away, carrying my head on Her necklace and allowing for what has been repressed for a lifetime to show itself, relieve itself through expression. Kali is offering to allow me to feel the part of me I have buried so deep so that I may be accepted—now She is accepting it. She is willing to consume it as She consumes her mate's entrails. And I feel. And it is finally okay. She makes it all okay. The sweet relief of all the pain that has been locked away inside me for years is allowed to pour out—and I will, with my best intentions, express the pain, use my anger to move mountains create change, create and express.

Tears swell in my eyes with gratitude, sweet gratitude that She will hack away my mask, release the dark and consume it, accept this part of me—a part of me which society has not accepted, that I have not accepted—She finally accepts. Finally. It's accepted. Thank you, Dear Goddess.

I aspire to encourage more adult women to make a commitment to mentoring our young women. We are the only hope for these girls who are being overlooked. As elders, we need to be flexible, to stretch and hear what they need and in what context they are able to receive it. We need to be ready to do whatever it takes to reach them. I want to stress that this cannot happen in isolation. If we as women, regardless of race, class, or religion, can come together with the purpose of empowering our girls, the entire society benefits. Our collaboration as women sets a powerful example in a culture that promotes competition among women. Perhaps the most important and profound part of our charge is what I refer to as "modeling good behavior." In *Cunt: A Declaration of Independence*, Inga Muscio has characterized the essence of what I am constantly trying to model for my girls, "Loving, knowing, and respecting our bodies is a powerful and invincible act of rebellion in this society" (1998, 75). We need to lead from this place. A revolution is that simple.

Bibliography

Belenky, Mary Field, Blythe McVicker Clinchy, Nancy Rule Goldberger, and Jill Mattuck Tarule. *Women's Ways of Knowing: The Development of Self, Voice, and Mind.* San Francisco: Basic Books, 1986.

Clements, Jennifer, Dorothy Ettling, Dianne Jenett, and Lisa Shields. *Organic Inquiry: If Research Were Sacred.* Draft manuscript, 1999.

Flinders, Carol Lee. *At the Root of This Longing: Reconciling a Spiritual Hunger and a Feminist Thirst.* San Francisco: Harper San Francisco, 1998.

Gilligan, Carol. *In a Different Voice: Psychological Theory and Women's Development.* Cambridge, MA: Harvard University Press, 1982.

Goodrich, Norma Lorre. *Priestesses.* New York: Harper Perennial, 1989.

Griffin, Susan. "Split Culture." In *Healing the Wounds: The Promise of Ecofeminism*, edited by Judith Plant, 7–17. Philadelphia: New Society Publishers, 1989.

hooks, bell. *Feminism is for Everybody: Passionate Politics.* Cambridge, MA: South End Press, 2000.

Lerner, Gerda. *The Creation of Patriarchy.* New York: Oxford University Press, 1986.

Matthews, Caitlin, ed. *Voices of the Goddess: A Chorus of Sibyls.* Northamptonshire, England: The Aquarian Press, 1990.

Miller, Diane. "On the Priestess Path: A Personal Journey Through Ritual, Research, and Community Service." Master's thesis, California Institute of Integral Studies, 1997. Abstract in *Master's Abstracts International* 37 (06): AAG1395948.

Muscio, Inga. *Cunt: A Declaration of Independence.* Seattle: Seal Press, 1998.

Noble, Vicki. *Motherpeace: A Way to the Goddess Through Myth, Art, and Tarot.* San Francisco: Harper San Francisco, 1983.

———. *Shakti Woman: Feeling Our Fire, Healing Our World: The New Female Shamanism.* San Francisco: Harper San Francisco, 1991.

Ozaniec, Naomi. "The Garments of Isis." In *Voices of the Goddess: A Chorus of Sibyls*, edited by Caitlin Matthews, 216–230. Northamptonshire, England: The Aquarian Press, 1990.

Platner, Ph.D., Delphyne Jodie. "All Women Are Witches: Women's Stories of Re-Awakening to Their Ancestral Memory and Inherently Spiritual Nature." Ph.D. diss., California Institute of Integral Studies, 2003. Abstract in *Dissertation Abstracts International* 64 (02), 692A: AAT 3080424.

Spretnak, Charlene. "Toward An Ecofeminist Spirituality." In *Healing the Wounds: The Promise of Ecofeminism*, edited by Judith Plant, 127–132. Philadelphia: New Society Publishers, 1989.

Meeting the Goddess On Highway 880

Susan Sopcak, M.A.

I am driving down Highway 880 from Alameda to Cupertino to meet with my boss's boss at Tandem Computers. It is a beautiful summer day. I am singing along with a tape of Chris Williamson's "The Changer and the Changed." Traffic is light so I'm making good time and enjoying the drive. Suddenly and without warning everything appears much brighter than it did the moment before and I hear a voice telling me to quit my corporate job. I am filled with incredible, blissful joy. Tears stream down my face.

I don't really know how to express the enormity of this experience. When I say "I am filled...," I mean my whole body is tingling. I feel like I'm glowing. I feel immense and diffuse. I feel small and awestruck. I give notice that day.

So many things led up to this. During the eight years I worked for Intergraph in Huntsville, AL as a Senior Software Development Manager I had fought against the inhumane treatment of employees. I struggled with Southern and patriarchal attitudes toward women at Intergraph and in the community as president of NOW. I became weary of this because I had fought the same battles 15 years earlier in the North and I didn't want to do it again. And I was unhappy at work for some of the same reasons. I believed that if only I could find a company with good people values I could be happy in my career. In the meantime I developed high blood pressure, a bout of shingles and eventually a bad back which resulted in two several month periods of disability leave.

The second time my back went out occurred when I changed departments and began working on a mapping project for the CIA. Our goal was to put digital maps on CD-ROMs that would be used on spy planes, the kind that

304

were in the news during the Granada Crisis. I forget the name now. Anyway I was working night and day on this project, making frequent one-day trips to Washington DC on the corporate jet when my back went out. How this manifested was like this: I couldn't sit down. At all. This meant I couldn't drive to work. I couldn't sit at my desk in my office. And I couldn't even sit in the plush, bigger-that-first-class seats on the corporate jet. Yet I could walk, run and dance. I could lie down, sleep and make love. At the time I interpreted all this as the universe telling me to 'get off my butt' and do something else with my life.

My doctor put me on disability, recommended his chiropractor and wrote prescriptions for deep tissue massage and exercise physiology. I was definitely benefiting from his own bad back.

My manager went into a panic, calling me daily for the first couple of weeks, until he actually threatened me with dismissal if I didn't come back to work immediately. We had some kind of confrontation; I forget the details but it struck me as pretty comical at the time because he had no legal basis for his threat. I think I mentioned something about litigation. He didn't bother me after that. By the time I did return to work he had left Intergraph.

I used this time away from work to intensify my meditation practice. My ritual circle sister, Carol, picked me almost every day and drove me, lying in the back seat, to her house where we drummed, meditated and shared visions. At other times I reveled in the hours of solitude, walking, drawing (it's amazing what you can do lying on your back), and just thinking. My life was suddenly so full, every moment so precious, so delicious. At Intergraph I had been numb, days flowing into days, no distinction, unconscious, not being there, not showing up to live my life. During this time of 'disability' I became able—able to be in my body, able to show up, to be present for my life. When I returned to work after 3 months away I found I couldn't numb-out anymore. I was bombarded with everything that was wrong and had always been wrong at Intergraph. I couldn't work there anymore.

Soon after that I left Intergraph and moved to the San Francisco Bay Area. I read a book that listed the top 100 employers in America, focusing on computer hardware and software vendors. I targeted Tandem Computers because it was high on that list for providing employee benefits like paid sabbaticals and on-site daycare as well as having good policies like easy access to upper management and respect for diversity. They even had a philosophy department that was charged with defining, articulating, implementing and evaluating the corporate philosophy and the resultant corporate culture. Surely this was a place where I could happily and productively settle back into my chosen career. I was thrilled when I was hired as a district system manager for the San Francisco district.

Then one day I was told to fire one of the employees I had inherited. I asked why and was told we only want "A" people at Tandem and Angie was a "B". I refused to fire her. This was not well received but I was allowed to mentor Angie for several months instead of firing her. For all Tandem's good qualities they had missed some basics like recognizing that happy employees are productive employees and therefore trying to accommodate and to respect their needs and wishes. And unexpectedly, Tandem had this unwritten notion of "A" and "B" people. "B" people had to be worked out of the company. They didn't meet some secret standard. Of course this wasn't detailed in the employee manual. It wasn't written down anywhere. It certainly didn't make it into the pages describing Tandem in the book listing the 100 top companies. A year after I left Tandem I heard that Angie had received Tandem's "Best-Kept Secret" award. I had to smile at that. I guess "B" people can become "A" people sometimes.

Refusing to fire Angie was the beginning of my downfall at Tandem, my own route to "B-ness". Besides "A" people, there were "A" customers at Tandem and one them was mine. As district manager I was expected to sell an education package to my most important client, never mind that they didn't want or need it. My assignment was to sell them something that was wrong for them. I argued with my manager but she directed me to do it anyway because the more we sold the more points her department earned. She was avoiding "B-ness" herself. I tried and failed although I sold packages to some of the "B" customers in my district. Now that I think about it, it was a plan designed to suit "B's", not "A's".

I had other clashes with this manager but the real problem was more fundamental than my conflicts with her. One spring day this became clear to me in an instant. I was sitting in a strategic planning meeting with other Tandem managers. We were meeting for two days on a yacht anchored at Pier 36, away from the office in order to focus on the future of our division and of Tandem itself. Meals and snacks were catered. Breaks were an opportunity to walk along the pier, to enjoy the sun and the sea but moreover to make deals. During the session we made presentations in turn about the needs, budgets and plans for our districts and grappled together to prepare a vision statement and the details of how to achieve it.

So I'm at this meeting. We're sitting around a long, shiny table which is made out of some kind of dark wood. This is the kind of table typical of boardrooms. Heavy. Massive. Strong. We could all have danced on it without rocking the boat. I have already given my presentation so I am relaxed, listening to John, my peer manager as well as the sale's manager for my district, answering a question about how we will meet our "A" customer's sales projection. Everyone is quiet, listening intently. The discussion escalates. This account is in trouble. Their primary vendor, IBM, is making a bid for the new business we're trying to get. In the mean time some technical problems have developed in the communications network between the customer's Tandem and IBM systems. This is a system problem. As district system manager that means this is my problem. IBM can argue that the obvious solution is to connect IBM to IBM, thus circumventing the Novell network which currently links the IBM and Tandem systems and which is currently dropping characters. Suggestions for saving the contract and making the new sale fly around the table. Losing this customer means losing millions. To save the deal means I have to find a solution for the network problems.

My mind wanders. Only a few hours more and I can head home. I think about the weekend, maybe a movie on Saturday, then Sunday afternoon looking for those sparkling carnelian pebbles at Cronkite beach. In the background I am aware that the discussion has become more agitated. Suddenly I am startled with the awareness that all these managers sitting around the table believe this is really life and death stuff, that keeping and growing this contract really matters. I know just as certainly that it doesn't matter in any meaningful sense. And it doesn't matter to me. I'm thinking, "How in the world did I end up here, in a position that demands I have a consuming interest about something so trivial?"

Part of it was money. I figured that if I had to spend the best part of every day working I ought to get as much money for it as I could. Another part of it was my competitiveness. I liked beating others out for those promotions. Parts of it also were the perquisites and the prestige that went with those jobs. I liked those corporate credit cards, business class travel, even that corporate jet at Intergraph. Also I was a sucker for being wanted. When someone wanted me I couldn't say no, even when he or she wanted me to do a job I believed was wrong. I suppose the real question is not how I ended up in such a position but why I was so deluded? Now I say "no" loud and clear. Now the perks and the big bucks seem small compared to doing work I am passionate about. The transition from corporate 'wanna-be' to a goddess-grounded woman is what this story is about.

That day on the yacht something important shifted in me when I realized how empty my work was. I didn't follow my Intergraph pattern, becoming physically ill. My back didn't even go out. I reacted in another way. I became unable to do any work at all. I would go to work, return a few phone calls, read my email, check in with my teams on the status of our projects and that was it. I couldn't make myself do anything else. I couldn't schmooze with my customers. I couldn't write proposals. I couldn't prepare a budget. It wasn't that I didn't know how to do these things anymore. I just couldn't do them. I looked out the window. Thirty stories up, behind a wall of glass, I had a great view of Angel Island and the Golden Gate Bridge. During a meeting in my office one day, I grabbed my binoculars to get a better view of a sailboat in the bay, definitely not the behavior of a manager with promotion aspirations. And I took long lunches and sat in the sun in Justin Herman Plaza, talking with a homeless man about the end of the world which he was expecting any day due to a large hole in the universe. These things were important to me, not work. It was weird and frightening. My therapist said I was going through a de-structuring as I lost my calendar, my address book and when three watches stopped working all within a week of each other. I found this idea of 'de-structuring' comforting. It reminded me of the Tower card in Tarot. Everything has to fall apart before a transformation could take place. Transformation, change from where I was to anywhere else, was something to hang on to.

My Highway 880 vision was actually an answer, albeit coming at an unexpected time, to questions I had been sitting with for some time: "What should I do about my job? My career? What is my work, my right livelihood?" These questions were posed and held during meditation and ritual.

I had begun meditating when I was 25 and needing a way to deal with the stress of graduate school, divorce and subsequent single motherhood. Through my yoga class, another attempt at stress reduction, I met someone who introduced me to the Maharishi Mahesh Yogi who was making frequent visits to East Lansing, Michigan. This man delighted me with his joyfulness, as he took pleasure in flowers, ice cream and in everyone he met. I wanted to feel some of that so I began practicing transcendental meditation (TM), a style of mantra meditation I find calming to this day.

I was an atheist when I learned TM, having given up on god when I was 13. My early experience with religion had predisposed me to do this. My father was a lapsed Catholic and my mother was a Methodist who sometimes tried to raise us as Catholic with no help from my father. We didn't go to church or learn about religion at home. My earliest memories about religion revolve around my father's Catholic mother. When I was 3 or 4 she began taking me aside, always just the two of us alone, and telling me that my sister and I were going to hell because we hadn't been baptized. Once when my sister had a bad cold my grandmother told me that she would probably die, that I should tell my parents to get her baptized so she wouldn't go to hell. Even though I didn't know what she was talking about I knew it was bad and I was scared. Clearly hell was a place where no one wanted to end up and so I prayed to this god she talked about according to her instructions. This bond to god, based on fear, was tenuous from the beginning.

My actual break with god and religion came a little later. I remember lying stiffly, dissociated, night after night while I was fondled, praying to god to make him stop. My prayers weren't answered. One night I was startled by the thought, "There is no god. I have only myself to depend on." The next time he touched me I screamed loudly and continuously. He was so unnerved that he never touched me again. To me that was proof that I had been right, god did not exist. I had saved myself.

After that, during my teens I thoughtfully and deliberately developed a strong ethic based on individual responsibility and compassion. I adopted the notion that religion was the opiate of the masses. I believed that religion was full of hypocrisy. Eventually I came to believe that whether god existed or not wasn't even an important question because the answer wasn't going to change the way I lived. I would live ethically because it was right, not because I feared God's wrath if I didn't.

When I was 21 my atheism was shaken somewhat by the birth of my son. The experience of pregnancy and birth was profound. I was awestruck by the wonder and impossibility of it. Somehow in that very substantial, bodily event, the birthing of my son, I experienced the divine in everything and I experienced myself as divine. This was not an 'out there' or 'god/goddess-like' sense of the divine but an earth-based divine that knows with certainty that this is all there is and it is enough. Although this did not bring me back to the fold of divinity-based religion, it planted a seed which grew slowly but steadily over the next 25 years.

I had practiced TM for 10 years when we moved to Huntsville, AL, to work for Intergraph. In Huntsville I found yoga and meditation groups at a Mahayana Zen Buddhist center and began learning another style of meditation. And when the Korean Zen Master who had founded the center came he gave a teaching on Buddhist principles that surprised me by their familiarity for they were pretty much the same rules of living I had developed in my teens.

But it was through the women I met in NOW that the next shift occurred, the one that led up to the Highway 880 vision.

I am invited to a May Day ritual. I receive an invitation and a map to Sharp's Cove where we are to spend the night. I have no idea what will be expected of me. I wonder if I will have to dance naked with a group of women, half of whom I don't even know. I am nervous and excited. These feelings are heightened on that late afternoon when I find myself driving down unfamiliar unpaved roads overhung with trees dripping with Spanish moss. As dusk approaches I wonder if I will ever find this place.

We first gather in a circle at the mouth of a small cave. We pass a kiss around the circle, each woman kissing the woman next to her, then speaking the words, "I love you. I respect you. Goddess bless you." There are twelve of us. It is darkening as we climb to the top of Pine Knob. The May Pole is ready. We again form a circle. The fire, already laid, is lit. The circle is cast by calling the directions. Diane recites the verses she has written to honor and invoke the East, South, West and North in turn. We hum, sing and croon, our voices melding together and roaring louder, the energy palpably increasing until we end with a shout. We root down solidly into the earth, imaging the roots from our feet downward, connecting with circles of women every-where. Then Annie explains that we will now take turns leaping over the fire crying out, "I let go of 'fill in the blank'," choosing what each of us most needs to let go of. I choose 'fear' and when I leap over that fire, my hair and dress flying, I shout, "I let go of fear!" I feel a shift.

Soon after this I formed a goddess ritual circle with 6 other women. We met on full moons, new moons, Sabbaths, and our birthdays. We also met on other occasions, such as in crisis situations and for important transitions which required marking or magic. We met to raise and channel energy and to cele-brate these events with rituals that we took from books like Starhawk's THE SPIRAL DANCE, then later with rituals we designed and wrote ourselves. Eventually our rituals seemed to come through us spontaneously. Several times a year we hosted open rituals, inviting both women and men. We also started open chanting and drumming groups and facilitated groups in which we discussed books like Sonia Johnson's GOING OUT OF OUR MINDS, Charlene Spretnak's, THE POLITICS OF WOMEN'S SPIRITUALITY, and Starhawk's TRUTH OR DARE. We even supported a group of men who wanted to start a men's group for ritual and exploration. Through these groups we not only increased the size of our community (our circle itself was closed) but we also discovered that there were other goddess ritual circles in the area.

The goddess as we experienced her symbolized female power and the cycle of life that includes death. She symbolized the interconnectedness of all living beings including the planet itself, which includes the seas, the skies, the birds and the trees, all creatures and all plant life, all energy and above all, the life force. She did not symbolize a supreme being existing 'out there'.

In my goddess group one of the reasons we came together was to raise, control and channel energy. Through this we manifested many things—or perhaps they were coincidences. It doesn't matter. Once, when Betty was having trouble selling her house in a very tough market, we performed rituals to cleanse the space and then we did other rituals to manifest a buyer meeting certain requirements. Her house sold shortly after that.

At the same time I was making ritual with my goddess circle, my mantra meditation practice was undergoing a change as I connected with the Mahayana Zen Buddhist group and began several new meditation practices. The TM meditation practice I do is based on Hindu practices related to Shakti. Shakti is both Hindu Goddess as well as life force energy. My experience of Shakti is exhilarating and ecstatic. I connect with Shakti through meditation and chanting. My Mahayana practices include visualizing myself as a specific teacher or archetype—in Tibetan, as a 'lama' or 'yidam.' This practice is called guru yoga, 'lama naljor' in Tibetan. In general terms guru yoga is the practice of imagining that one is one's teacher. This can be an actual person or an archetype. For instance, in my meditation practice I imagine that I am Green Tara, that I share her great compassion for others, her experience of emptiness and so on. When I do this meditation I literally see glowing green light all around me, radiating from me. I view everything from the point of view of Tara, having compassion for all beings which includes self and all others. Just as Buddha is known as a great teacher but not as a god, Tara is not goddess but she is liberator and facilitator. Both Buddha and Tara represent aspects of our own nature and that is what is important, not divinity. Tara is known as the one who obtained enlightenment deliberately in a women's body, who refused to be reborn as a man. She is called the mother of all Buddhas. While Tara is also identified as 'holy' and 'goddess,' she is not seen as the supreme creator in the sense of the Christian god that I rejected early in my life. When I visualize myself as Tara, I experience myself as divine in the way I experienced myself as divine when my son was born. This is like the Zen meditation experience of shiken taza in which I connect with the earth and all beings, my body tingling, glowing, and feeling immense and diffuse. I know with certainty that this is all there is and it is enough. And just as the goddess rituals I performed caused shifts in me, this guru yoga meditation does also. As I practice compassion I become more compassionate. As I practice clear seeing I come to see more clearly.

That day that found me hearing voices and glowing while I drove to Cupertino was a result of all these practices. I had been meditating, doing rituals and channeling energy for years. I had also been asking questions and getting answers for some time. I had been sitting with these questions about my job and my right livelihood, knowing the answer would come eventually.

Now I had an answer, a partial answer anyway. I knew the next step but not the goal. I knew what to do about my job, my career: walk away from it. It seemed I had to trust that there was such a thing as 'my work,' that there was a right livelihood for me. And I did trust. That sense of light and joy and knowing stayed with me all that day and into the next. Even later when I sometimes doubted and feared I was deluded or at least making a big mistake, the memory of that joyful certainty calmed my fears. The quality of that memory, even now, is different from other memories because it carries a strong physical component. When I remember, I feel. I re-experience the physical sensations, the glowing and the bliss. But I did not trust at every moment; out of renewed fear I even pursued and was offered a significant position at Amdahl Computers which I bravely turned down to the amazement of some of my friends and to the horror of others.

I was blissful when I remembered the vision and when I trusted. When I forgot I felt terror and doubt and I would ask myself: "How can you trust a voice from nowhere? Son the Sam heard voices and murdered people. He was nuts. How do I know that I am not nuts? What is this voice? Who's doing the talking? Who's lighting the lights?" Or again: "Why aren't you satisfied with a job most people would be thrilled to have? Who do you think you are anyway, thinking that there's some special work for you to do? What if there isn't? Or what if you never know what it is?"

I alternated between terror and bliss, bliss outweighing and overcoming the terror. I was letting go of fear.

When I had the vision on Highway 880 I knew I was sane. I didn't question the source of the vision because whether it came from deep within me of from without didn't matter. I knew it was real. I knew it was right. I didn't question whether or not quitting my job was the right thing to do. I knew it was right with certainty.

And I realized something else. Having denied the existence of divinity for so many years, since that 'no-god' experience at 13, I saw that at some point there had been a shift in me and since that shift I had acted as if the voices came from without rather than from within my self.

I act as if divinity is both one and plural, personal and female, both nature and more than nature. I act as if divinity is in myself but more than myself, in the earth and in all living beings but also more than these. I act as if there is some tangible life force that exists outside of me as well as within me and I know that this life force is all there is and it is enough.

I call this life force goddess.

Embodying Paradox: Life & Death: Desire & Shame

Elisabeth Sikie

In this absurd moment, I am experiencing paradox as physicality. I have recently become conscious of a fertilized zygote near my left fallopian tube. I feel the primal stirrings of pregnancy, its hunger, its hormones and its tsunami-like rush of physical determination which annihilates my ego's illusion of mental control over the Self. I am holding life inside me. I can feel her, taste her, imagine her as a buzzing light seed emanating from within a most perfect circle cell. (Angiers 14)

I also know that this pregnancy will end with the finality of blood. I am certain because I also hold inside me a copper device, lodged in the cup of my womb, which will not allow life to take hold. I chose an IUD precisely so that I won't have children and because hormone regulating contraceptives make me go berserk. I carry this piece of metal inside myself intentionally, as a badge of female initiation and symbol of my sexual autonomy. So while I feel the flutter of life and its effect on my body, I also wait for its destruction with the painful dropping of my menstrual blood destined to flow in about a week.

I attempt to hold life and death simultaneously as a thought so my mind can catch up with the intelligence of my body. I try not to dissociate. It hurts. Emotionally, I spin through my past, recalling, reliving every grief, every loss, every failure. Some part of me believes, for a very long moment, that I am bad; that someone somewhere was right. I am suffering, deservedly, the inevitable punishment that always befalls women who give in to desire. Lately, after the demise of my former six year relationship, I have been wonderfully preoccupied with my new love and the joy I find in his body, and in our spiritual and

314

physical intimacy. Our heat devours then transforms us. I have whole-heart-edly abandoned myself to desire.

But as I contemplate my womb, some part of me barks up the rhetoric of self-hatred. I am shocked at its voracity, its authenticity, even after years of diligent effort to extricate these internalized voices from my modern western female psyche. This part of myself, which I thought was retrieved, which I thought was transformed into a voice of self-acceptance, of celebration even, was now berating me like a fundamentalist. *"See, that's what you get for fucking. That's what you get for letting your sex be more important than a job, and money and a real husband. You're a loser, a baby killer and a slut."*

In this moment, I despise myself fully. Bone deep, and with a futile heavi-ness that drowns any fire to fight. My eyes shut and my head drops into a pos-ture of defeat. I am ashamed of myself, my pleasure, and my very nature. The message that desire brings shame, ostracization and suffering is clearly still embedded in my body and psyche like a dormant virus, awakened now by the culturally loaded trigger of deliberately ending my pregnancy because I choose to do so.

Riane Eisler, in her book, *Sacred Pleasure*, identifies the vilification of both sex and woman as a mechanism designed to maintain" (165) current domina-tor model power structures. Shame is a device that ensures continuous repro-duction of this vilification. Amplified and reinforced by community and family, shame becomes internalized, and then embodied within a single soul. Once inside the Self, its foreignness is forgotten. We think it's natural, even ordained, to be inherently contaminated with the pollution of our desire. We succumb to a kind of cultural amnesia[1] which has been insidiously mapped out for us historically by a politically motivated religious doctrine that holds a deep contempt for sex and women's bodies.[2] (Eisler 203)

"We have been raised to fear the *yes* within ourselves, our deepest cravings," writes Audre Lord, in *The Uses of the Erotic*. (57) During my visit to the Inqui-sition Exhibit in the SF Presidio last year, I experienced emotionally and psy-chically, how this was done, with what and to whom. The exhibition, on tour from Italy, reverently displayed the actual implements of torture historically used by men of the church during what modern pagans now name "The Burn-ing Times."[3] (Farrar vol. II, 319) Eisler describes the witch burnings as "noth-ing less than a full-scale religious war against women." (204) In fact, the tools were called "The Arsenal of God."

What struck me was the ingenuity of these implements and the delibera-tion put into their making. The spiked iron rods and tongs, the ornate masks and contraptions that required pulleys, looked oddly beautiful, like modern sculptures. Yet the Arsenal of God was designed to efficiently invade, humiliate and agonize a human body, and to sustain its suffering, without being lethal enough to kill it. It is important to understand, said the curator, that these implements were designed to torture *women*.[4]

Looking at them automatically causes the mind to formulate hideous pictures, which in turn makes the body shudder involuntarily in fear. It becomes obvious that these are specialized instruments uniquely configured for use on specific body parts. Each one reveals to the imagination what is truly unimaginable. Collectively these tools of torture point to an intention that is at first unfathomable, but soon becomes clear: The deliberate desecration of the female body *from the inside,* and the complete annihilation of human will and spirit. Even though they are relics contained within glass cases; even though the female blood once upon them has been wiped clean, their power is as palpable as breath on my skin.

The most horrific and enlightening item on display for me that day was an ornate life-sized bronzed "bull." I was truly dumbfounded by this piece. Its detailed metalwork, painstakingly crafted, and at such scale, made it a testament to human creativity. Its purpose, however, was equally as ingenious. The belly of this "bull" was hollow and wide enough to hold a curled-up human body. Underneath, a fire was built, and as the victim slowly roasted to death, their screams would be heard through the open nostril holes, simulating the grunts and roars of a bull.[5]

Within the "womb" of this "bull," horrible death was conceived. The sacred life-giving body of the Cow, once a symbol of the Goddess (Language 134) and Her fecundate, sexually stimulated creative energies,[6] was in this "bull" efficiently, and completely transformed into an instrument of death. This is an exact, calculated reversal[7] of the powers of creation inherent in the divine feminine which was once venerated and passionately celebrated by our Neolithic ancestors.

The reconceptualization of the female body from a symbol of sexual and spiritual power to an object under the control of men was integral to the prehistoric shift to a dominator social organization. (Eisler 164) The roots of this change in consciousness (Eisler 91) go back to the—3rd and 4th millennia B.C. when the Indo-Europeans invaded the indigenous, matristic Neolithic cultures of Old Europe, and continued through the Christianization of Europe. According to renowned scholar and archeologist Marija Gimbutas:

"The Goddess of Death and Regeneration was demonized and degraded into the familiar and highly publicized image of witch. She came to represent all that was denied and considered evil within this relatively recent mythology of dualism. This was a complete reversal of the religion of Old Europe which conceived life and death and all cyclical polarities as sacred and inseparable. No longer was the earth considered our Divine Mother, from whom we are born and to whom we return in death. Deity was removed into the heavens and earth became a place of exile." (Civilization 244)

The creative energy of nature, reflected in women's bodies as sexual potency, or Shatki,[8] is the coveted power source which dominator power structures must usurp through distortion in order to function. (93) The Bronzed Death Bull[9] illuminates the efficiency of reconceptualization; of the conqueror defiling the Gods (Goddess) of the conquered.

It is desire which stirs of the fire of Shakti. In order to capture it, harness and use its juice, desire must be regulated. Harvesting this energy by those who do not posses it requires strategy. Historically, this has meant the imposition of control on the human body through the fear of pain, and the fear of death. (Eisler 220) My spiritual teacher[10] once asked me why I thought the Inquisitors just didn't kill the women accused of witchcraft, but instead made great efforts to inflict elaborate sexual torture. When I didn't know the answer she explained this tactic was deliberately perpetrated to create horrific cellular memory[11] of the terror and pain experienced by the victim right before and into death. As we are reborn, the memory subconsciously kicks in, effectively shutting us down as we attempt to express our creative, sexual energies.

Shame, then, is a cost efficient, nearly invisible, socially sanctioned regulator of desire. No inquisitor, parent or institution need stand over us any longer watching where we put our hands or policing our expressions of love. With shame neatly internalized, we will oppress ourselves at the first chaotic rush of our desire. Lorde succinctly explains this distortion:

"The erotic is a resource within each of us that lies in a deeply female and spiritual plane, firmly rooted in the power of our unexpressed or unrecognized feelings. In order to perpetuate itself, every oppression must corrupt or distort those various sources of power within the culture of the oppressed that can provide energy for change. For women, this has meant a suppression of the erotic as a considered source of power and information within our lives." (53)

All expressions of desire fulfilled, including sex which brings pleasure but no children, bucks against the mechanism of internalized shame. It opens us to our sacred sexual roots and an ancestral consciousness that did not conceive of its own flesh as despicable receptacles of self hatred, violence and shame. Permitting ourselves to act upon our desire implies that we, as embodied beings, are worthy of pleasure, are sources of pleasure, and are inherently powerful reflections of nature's own potent creative energies. We become reminded of the time which Gimbutas' work illuminates, when union with the mysterious forces that govern the universe was associated with female creative power. (Eisler 127)

This is why desire must be regulated. If it is not, we may wake up from our cultural disassociation, our shame-based amnesia, and find we are using our precious Shakti, not to shape our lives in accordance with our own vision, but to fuel institutions and belief systems that benefit, and actually feed upon, our oppression. Once again, Lorde nails it: "The fear that we cannot grow beyond whatever distortions we may find within ourselves keeps us docile and loyal and obedient, externally defined, and leads us to accept many facets of our oppression as women." (58)

I remember my first smell of internalized shame, not as a concept that I could analyze with feminist theory, but as a stench in my body. The realization that shame was alive and thriving in my physicality hit me like the sudden awareness of my pregnancy, and the chilling actuality of the implements of torture. I didn't know it and then suddenly I did, and there was no going back. When shame became something other than an idea, a veil[12] fell from my eyes. I felt as if I looked down at my chest, found myself bleeding, but never felt the bullet pierce me.

I can trace the trail of my shame virus each time my sex resulted in conception. My motivations, internal dialogue and choices were partially influenced by internalized self-oppression and self-hatred still unrevealed to my conscious mind. The last time I was pregnant was six years ago. It was my third and occurred after I left my ex-husband to pursue my desire for my spiritual education and a man similarly motivated. I chose to follow my passions despite the devastating disapproval and the subsequent loss of support of my family, my friends and the material security of a husband, house and business. I even lost one of my beloved dogs.

At that time, my ex-husband and I had been trying to get pregnant. I had a dream that I gave birth, but looked strangely at the baby because I felt no connection to it. I then handed it back to someone faceless. I woke up horribly aware that I did not want children, but desired instead to devote my life to spiritual growth and artistic expression. My choice to live for myself caused the death of my once happy secure life.

Soon after my divorce, depressed and broke, I became pregnant with my new partner. Truly I felt shameful and doubted the choices I made that went against my family's culture, and the so called "common sense" of our culture at large. Enraged at myself, disoriented and guilt-ridden, I willed myself to miscarry.

My first pregnancy, at 22-years old, ended in abortion. I vowed never to do that to myself again. Even though I was drugged, the hospital staff had to pry open my clenched legs. My second time was in my early thirties and ended painfully in what was to be my first miscarriage. The loss of this pregnancy caused excruciating physical pain for many hours, and deep sorrow for many years. I endured a degrading, misogynist experience in the emergency room at my most vulnerable moment. After hours of severe cramping, my empty womb appeared on the sonogram machine. Devastated, I somehow found the strength to refuse the D & C the hospital staff assumed they would give me as they rolled in the "abortion"[13] machine. I trusted my womb's intelligence to release the pregnancy naturally. And it did.

Faced then with this third pregnancy, after by my divorce, I chose miscarriage rather than abortion. However, it didn't occur to me to consider my physical state after months of grief and depression. My body complied, I did miscarry, but the bleeding would not stop. For a month I stayed in bed, disassociated from my body and consumed with guilt. I refused to go to a hospital but instead subconsciously "took my punishment." One morning, while praying to release that last tenacious molecule of pregnancy tissue, I hemorrhaged, a bright burst of fresh blood dramatically turning the toilet bowl crimson. Fed-up and scared to death, my partner at the time rushed me to emergency. Following my desire had caused the death of my once secure life, and my shame nearly caused my physical death. Now I am pregnant for the fourth time at forty, and passionately involved with a new man.

In this absurd moment, something cracks inside of me. Suddenly my twisted journey seems hysterically laughable and strangely liberating. I am conscious that I am a modern woman, with her mind in the past, who has somehow seeded new life in a womb full of metallic contraception, despite herself. It occurs to me that I have already lived through life and death many times and am now actually comfortable, empowered even, to embody these illusionary opposites simultaneously. Unlike the distortion of death as horrific, frozen and unnatural, where life is defiled and shoved back into the womb as in the Bronzed Bull, all my deaths, physically, emotionally, and spiritually have fed my growth in some way.

I am beginning to sense a whisper of something ancient, a thread of consciousness perhaps, originating from a complete Self which perceives paradox but is not chained by it; which recognizes damage within the female essence but is also regenerated by it. I can now see, and feel, that my desire has been the primal force which has given me my life, as well as my deaths. With this remembering, my shame is transmuted. With this remembering, I am grateful for all that is inside of me. I am grateful, and love fiercely, my body's intelligence, my mind's unquenchable passion to understand the Self, and my inherent, unbreakable link to that which is both divine and feminine.

Notes

1 Eisler aptly names this phenomenon "the dominator trance." (191)

2 Eisler takes us on a historical guided tour of this politically motivated distortion that has lead to the dominator "change in consciousness" in her illuminating chapter Bondage or Bonding: Sex, Spirituality and Repression. (201)

3 This term is generally used by European derived modern neo-pagans attempting to reconnect to our severed ancestral roots and to retrieve our history which has, up until recently, been defined by the terms of our oppressor as the Inquisition. By acknowledging and renaming atrocities meant to annihilate us, we take back our power to voice and integrate who we are and what has been demonized within us personally and collectively

4 Of course many men and animals were also tortured and murdered during the Inquisition, but it is evident that this was a war on the female body, her power and a means of taking control of property owned by women.

5 Apparently the creator of this horrifying devise was the first to be put into it.

6 The bull's head or bucrania is symbol of regeneration that is strikingly similar in appearance to human female fallopian tubes. Prevalent in the Neolithic art, I suspect that the bucrania is a symbol, not of a bull, but a cow whose horns had not been cut off.

7 Energetically, this reversal of movement is called "widdershins," or going against the direction of the sun. Its magic works by creating discordance and disharmony which will ultimately cause destruction. Its invocation is often seen as "black magic." (Farrar vol. II, 328)

8 In the Hindu cosmology, Shakti, or Sakti is the energy, seen as female, which arises from the tension of opposites to become the creative aspect of divinity. It is the power through which creation arises, or one could say, is birthed. (Daniélou 20)

9 The Bull is also an ancient symbol of male potency dating back to the Paleolithic era. Its demonization by the Greeks into a horrible monster requiring blood sacrifice (Eisler 130) shows the progressive distortion of male sexuality from the regenerator of life to its destroyer.

10 Norma Tringali was a renowned metaphysical minister, medium, healer and teacher of occult knowledge and western mystery traditions. Before her death in 1999, she ran Amron Metaphysical Church and Mystery School in SF for more than 20 years.

11 Atavism is the term used by Natalie Angers (22) to describe normally dormant genes from our prehistoric roots that sometimes become reactivated as physical irregularities like extra nipples, excessive hair, etc. Metaphysically, the same laws also govern our non-corporal aspects.

12 Eisler calls the veil "another symbol of being a woman, and particularly of the shamefulness of women's sexuality." (99)

13 I do not know if the medical equipment used for D&C is the same one used for abortion. For me, it was semantical; it was going to vacuum my poor womb for liability purposes when it was possible, even likely, that a healthy womb could evacuate itself completely.

Metamorphosis of the Crone: Birth, Death and Rebirth—How This Ancient Symbol Can Empower Older Women Today

Anya Silverman, M.A.

The birth of Crone as the archetype of an older woman is shrouded in the mists of a time when women were revered as the givers and takers away of life, and the Divine was imaged as a Female. When women were viewed in this way, Crone had a positive meaning; but through 4,000 years of patriarchy, Crone metamorphosed into a very negative image, which I call Her death. We are still living with this legacy, and our culture is one that has a real fear of the elderly, both men and women; but old women, in particular, have been so denigrated that they are marginalized and are *dis*empowered—the very opposite of being *em*powered.

The rebirth of the Crone began in the late '70s when She began to re-emerge into women's consciousness along with the other aspects of the Goddess. Reclaiming, adopting, and internalizing the Crone as a positive image is a way for older women to empower themselves. It is only by claiming this power that older women can begin to reclaim their position in society as respected female elders—in other words—crones. It is this re-emergence of the Crone archetype that is fueling the emergence of the Crone Movement, which began in the early 1980s and has been growing ever since.

In order to empower ourselves as older women, we need to understand our herstory. Our American culture is very youth oriented and the model of old = wisdom does not exist for us. The United States has always been a country of the young. It was the young who were best equipped to seek a new life in an unknown place, and the immigrants who came here around the turn of the 20th century wanted to become "American"—we were the country of the "melting pot" where we shed our old-world ways. Parents looked to their children to achieve the "American Dream," and there was a shift from veneration and respect for age to the obsession with and emulation of youth. Now we are constantly bombarded with messages that women need to stay youthful in appearance. We are led to believe that face lifts, tummy tucks, plastic surgeries of all kinds, hair dyes, and "magic" potions are the way to go.

But we are living much longer now, and there is a great need to develop new models for our elder years that celebrate our aging process and honor the wisdom we have gained. Today many women are embracing the Crone as a way to change the way they feel about themselves as they age and Crone consciousness is emerging everywhere.

Birth

In studying the development of the Crone archetype, I see the metamorphosis of the Crone in the paradigm of birth, death, and rebirth. In the beginning the evidence indicates that the people conceived of the Goddess as one entity—one all-encompassing Mother Goddess who controlled birth, death, and rebirth. She was nature Herself. There was no separation between creation and destruction. Death was not feared because it was necessary in order to have rebirth, and the world that was hidden, i.e., the dark underworld, was the realm in which rebirth took place. This image of one Mother Goddess evolved into the three aspects of a female's life, i.e., Maiden, Mother, and Crone, during the Neolithic era of c. 10,000–5,500 BCE; and it is here that we see the birth of the Crone as a separate archetype.

Death

Great shifts began to occur around the middle of the 5th millennium BCE, which affected how the Goddess was imaged. The area of the Balkans, called Old Europe by archeologist Marija Gimbutas, was invaded by people from the North, and Mesopotamia was invaded by Semitic tribes from the South. Both of these peoples had male gods, and the degradation of the Goddess in all of her forms began. Matrifocal/Matristic cultures and their female Goddess(es) started their evolutionary change into becoming patrifocal/patriarchal cultures with sky gods visioned as male.

These invading peoples introduced the idea of an opposition between the powers of light and darkness and, in both mythologies, there is evidence of a desacralization of nature and of human life. Attitudes to life and death were radically altered, as life was experienced as untrustworthy, and violent death became the norm. Darkness was now associated with what was *not* light or life, rather than the place from which new life was born. Death became something final, terrifying, remorseless and without the promise of rebirth. This is the legacy that we have inherited. It lives on in pervasive attitudes and structures in response to life and still has a controlling influence on our psyche today.

Traditionally it was the old women who took care of those sick and dying. They were the ones who prepared the bodies after death. When death became something to be feared, this fear was projected onto the Crone, and She came to be seen as the bringer of death. It is in her aspect as the death-bringer that directly leads to the image we have of the Crone today. There are other attributes of the Crone which women today are re-claiming as positive images, but our culture's fear of death has focused our attention on this aspect which has contributed greatly to the invalidation and denigration, fueled by fear, of older women.

As Judaism and then Christianity developed, the masculine archetype and patriarchy became firmly entrenched and women became second-class citizens. As Christianity spread, and its power grew in the first several centuries of the new era, these patriarchal views of women, old women, and death were enforced. The culmination of this fear, invalidation and degradation of women occurred when the Church instigated the Inquisition beginning in the 15th century to convert all non-Christians, and to usurp the power of women. Women were the midwives and healers, and the Church wanted to get rid of them so their so-called male "physicians" could take over. I believe that many of these midwives and healers would, in fact, have been older women as it took many years of training for them to become expert in their field. Older women also were more outspoken (as we still are today), and were more likely to be living alone after their husbands had died—and the Church coveted their property. Since relatively few women survived the rigors of childhood and childbearing, the number of old women relative to the population was small. Perhaps it was thought that those women who did not die young had some special wisdom; certainly their longevity increased their knowledge. Therefore these women were respected and revered by the people, and had a lot of power in their communities. Traditionally older women also took care of the soul. They conducted rituals and officiated at birth as well as death; but the male dominated Church did not like women having any authority whatsoever, and they wanted to be the only ones in control of spiritual matters.

Here is where the three words *crone*, *hag*, and *witch* were reversed, and acquired the negative connotations we still live with today. Prior to the Inquisition, crones and hags (another word for an old woman which has its roots in the Latin *hagio*—having to do with saints) were respected, and witch comes from *wit* meaning wisdom. To be called a crone, hag or witch was a *positive* thing—not at all what those words mean today in the vernacular.

It is important to mention here that the effects of the Inquisition and the killing of the witches, known as the Burning Times, are still with us today. Native Americans believe that every action will be felt for seven generations, and current thinking is that we do have cellular memory that is inherited from our mothers. In many cases children, especially girls, were forced to incriminate their mothers, and then had to watch them burn. The trauma of that experience would have been so great that these girls were effectively silenced for their entire lives, and this fear was passed down through their daughters even to this day. It is important to remember this when we look at the reasons why women are so afraid to speak up and claim their power.

Rebirth:
How The Crone Is Re-emerging In Our Consciousness

After enduring 4,000 years of conscious effort to get rid of the Crone, it is exciting to relate that reports of Her death were premature, and She is now re-emerging to Her rightful place once again. Crone consciousness is part of the return of the Divine Feminine. Women are reclaiming the Goddess in all her aspects of Maiden, Mother, Crone.

To counteract the negative image of Crone as the death-bringer, we need to embrace other archetypal characteristics of the Crone which are not associated with death. They are: wisdom, the wild woman, and the bawdy woman. These are all positive images that can be used to empower women today—although they are still characteristics that many men don't like to see in women, and continue to try to suppress.

Wisdom: The Crone has long been associated with wisdom. I believe this was mainly due to the fact that if a woman lived long enough to be an old woman, she must have acquired useful knowledge, and some wisdom, along the way. The belief that she retained her "wise blood" after menopause also contributed to this archetype. Our culture with its focus on youth does not value the wisdom of its elders, so this is one of the attributes that we modern day crones need to reclaim. Zalman Schachter-Shalomi, in *Age-ing to Sage-ing: a Profound New Vision of Growing Older*, proposes a new concept that he calls *sage-ing*, as a psychospiritual model for aging which incorporates the process of harvesting our wisdom to become "spiritually radiant, physically vital, and socially responsible elders."[1] As older women we need to harvest our wisdom, and then stand up and say that we are crones and have valuable knowledge that would be helpful for the generations that follow us. But wisdom does not automatically come to us just because we are older. In order to gain this wisdom we have to look inside ourselves, examine our lives, and learn the lessons from our own experiences—a long arduous and usually painful journey.

Wild woman: This aspect is not commonly thought to be related to the Crone, but is one that I see emerging now with the rebirth of the Crone archetype. Clarissa Pinkola Estes wrote an entire book about the wild woman: *Women Who Run With The Wolves.* Estes says that it is through myths, stories, and fairy tales that women can pick out and pick up that path left by the wildish nature. The tracks we all are following are those of the wild and innate instinctual self, which she calls Wild Woman.

Estes says that, "the ogress, the witch, the wild nature, and whatever other *criaturas* and integral aspects the culture finds awful in the psyches of women are the very blessed things which women often need most to retrieve and bring to the surface."[2] I feel that our female instincts towards wild woman behavior are so repressed in our patriarchal culture, that it is often only when women are older and no longer afraid of the repercussions of society, can they finally erupt, and find some avenues of expression. This certainly has been my own personal experience. This aspect of her wild self is also manifested when the old woman is no longer afraid to speak out and speak the truth. Men and co-opted women particularly fear this aspect, as it exposes things they don't want to admit, and would prefer remain hidden and unspoken.

Bawdy woman: This part of the archetype is closely related to the wild woman, and in a certain sense is actually another aspect of it. However, in Greek mythology an old bawdy woman had her own persona in the figure of

Baubo. Baubo is important in the story of Demeter and Persephone, as she is the old servant/nurse who, by picking up her skirt and exposing her vulva, finally makes Demeter laugh, thereby bringing her out of her depression over the loss of her daughter Persephone. There are very few stories from ancient days about this type of figure, and Estes says that this was because men really feared this aspect of women, and did their best to suppress all references to it. This is why so few people have heard of this bawdy woman archetype.

Winifred Milius Lubell, who wrote *The Metamorphosis of Baubo: Myths of Woman's Sexual Energy*, says that, "Her strangeness to modern eyes warns of the danger of her loss. But Baubo is a survivor. She represents those revered sexual and procreative feminine energies that merge to form the nurturers, the transformers, and the balancers, without whom civilization cannot survive."[3] It is because the figure of Baubo is described as an *old* woman in Homer's *Hymn to Demeter*, that we can ascribe her behavior to part of the Crone archetype.

Older woman can use sexual humor and be bawdy, and can get away with it, but for obvious reasons this bawdiness is usually expressed in female only groups. One example that I witnessed at a Crones Counsel was when, during the talent show, a woman read a poem she wrote called "Where Oh Where Has My BEAVER Gone." The entire audience was in stitches. I contacted the author, who said she wished to remain anonymous, but gave me permission to use her poem. (She was 72 when she wrote it.)

> Oh where, oh where has my BEAVER gone?
> Oh where or where is my BUSH?
> My pubic triangle's lost its fur,
> But...
> Nothing has changed with my Tush!

Reclaiming the archetype of the Crone as bawdy woman is one important way for older women to empower ourselves today. Being bawdy is a way to express our creativity and our connection to our bodies.

With this re-emergence of Crone consciousness, the growth of the Crone Movement began. Z Budapest described a croning ritual in *The Holy Book of Women's Mysteries*[4] in 1980; a group in Portland, Maine began doing croning ceremonies in 1982; and the Crones of Puget Sound began in 1987.

Then in 1989 a woman named Ann Kreilkamp had a dream and started *Crone Chronicles*[5], a quarterly journal. I interviewed Ann in 1997, and asked her how she came to start this publication. She said that in 1989 she had a dream in which a huge raven like bird (a bird associated with the Crone) came to her and cawed. "It was digging into my shoulders from behind—or screeched—it went 'Wake up, wake up, it's time, it's time.'" She knew it was the Crone, and that's how it began. She then wrote a letter to 100 women, "Calling all Crones," to see what would happen. People thought she was crazy, as they didn't understand why she was doing this. Ann said that if it was coming through her that strongly, and it was very very insistent, then it's got to be coming through other people at the same time, because the unconscious does not work in just one person. Within a couple of days, she got a call from a woman saying she had just started a crone group. As that was before the letter was sent out, it was Ann's confirmation that the Crone was returning, because she had never heard of anything to do with the Crone anywhere else. Ann did not know about the groups in Maine and the Seattle area at the time. From then on crone groups have sprouted up in many areas, but the early ones didn't know anything about each other. This is proof that the archetype was bubbling up through the collective unconscious.

I see this re-emergence/rebirth of the Crone as part of the overall re-emergence of the feminine archetype and woman's spirituality. Betty DeShong Meador, a Jungian analyst who has written extensively about this subject, says this new feminine energy is life changing, and will lead women to carve out new forms for their lives. We now have the opportunity as well as the obligation of carrying this new consciousness into the new millennium and "to the struggle of the goddess to achieve Her place in the godhead."[6] I believe that the Crone, as an aspect of the Goddess, is part of this new awareness. When She comes into the consciousness of older women, they often "carve out new forms for their lives."

One of the things the Women's Movement brought to our attention was the prevailing use of the male pronoun giving the impression that women didn't exist. By demanding that the female pronoun be stated separately, perceptions began to change. Language is important. This is one reason why we must bring back the usage of the word *crone*. We older women must claim who we are. When I say, "I am a crone," it gives me an opportunity to say that we should be respected for our age—not denigrated. One woman I spoke with said: "I use the term 'crone' to describe myself largely because it challenges the stereotypes surrounding age. I'm old and I'm proud of the fact. YOU may consider crones to be ugly, scary, bitchy—if you do, I'm here to challenge that view; and if you consider me to be like that, then that's your problem—not mine."

Along with the rising consciousness of the Feminine and the Goddess, many people in this country are looking at and embracing Native American spirituality. We are realizing that their traditions and beliefs are cognate with our emerging awareness of spirituality and its connection with Mother Earth. Native Americans provide us with a model of honoring elders, especially the women, and they have many stories about the importance of the Grandmothers. In Native usage Grandmother is a term of respect for an older woman whether she is a biological grandmother or not. A Hopi prophecy says, "When the grandmothers speak, the earth will be healed." And many grandmothers/older women/crones are speaking out about the ills of the world.

Jane Caputi has written a wonderful book called *Gossips, Gorgons & Crones: The Fates of the Earth.* Her book is a dissertation on the terrible state we have gotten ourselves into with our environmental destruction and nuclear capabilities, issues often mentioned by women as reasons why they are turning to crone consciousness. She says that it is the women who are our only hope in getting us out of this mess. In referring to the Native American concept of *grandmother,* Caputi says:

> We can ignore the behest of the Grandmothers only at extreme peril, for theirs are the Powers not only of the past and the present, but also of the future. The truest symbol of the future is the one that our pornotechnic culture most studiously avoids. It is the Crone. If we are to survive, it is She who we must fully honor. It is She who we must finally and most abundantly become.[7]

There is a group of women in Arizona who call themselves the Grandmothers, who focus on this issue of speaking out so that their grandchildren, and their grandchildren's grandchildren, will inherit a world worth living in. And many women are becoming "eco-crones."

One of the ways that we are speaking out and claiming our power as older women is by telling our stories, which is also telling our truth. In the last few years I have come to realize that we, as women, *must* tell our stories. Our herstory (her-story) has been unknown and forgotten because the men were the historians. Women have come to be ashamed of things they have experienced and, consequently, do not talk about them. We have all had bad things happen to us—it is part of being human. But our Western, intellectual, patriarchal culture thinks it can control these things so they won't happen. And if they inevitably happen anyway, we can pretend they didn't happen if we don't talk about them. *Not* sharing our stories with each other has kept women from knowing they aren't the only ones to suffer and has kept us subservient to the dominant male culture. Christiane Northrup, in *Women's Bodies, Women's Wisdom*, discusses this when she says that, "I know of no woman who has tapped her inner source of power without going through an almost palpable veil of fear.. but when we deny this fear or discount its presence.. we only give it more power."[8] Most of us have negative associations with the word power, but here is the use of the word "power" in both of its meanings—women's inner power, and the power of the patriarchy over women. When we *empower* ourselves by telling our truth, we counteract the *power* that men have over us. Jean Shinoda Bolen says that, "To bring about a paradigm shift in the culture that will change assumptions and attitudes, a critical number of us have to tell the stories of our personal revelations and transformations."[9] Older women empower themselves by telling their stories. Sometimes it is only when they are older that women can finally reveal what has happened to them. In doing so, they reap the wisdom from these events, and can then pass it on to the next generation.

Most crone groups that I know about include story-telling as part of their format, and story-telling is a very important part of the annual gatherings of Crones Counsel. When the *Crone Chronicles* began to be published, women responded by asking if there was a way the readers could get together to share this exciting new concept. Out of this desire, a group of women decided to convene a gathering which was called Crones Counsel—*counsel* not *council*—because they wanted to convey the idea that the women were gathered to *counsel* with each other. The first gathering in 1993 was so successful, and the desire of women to connect as crones was so great, that Crones Counsel has had ten annual gatherings, and two were held in 2003. Crones Counsel[10] is not a membership organization and any adult woman can attend a gathering.

I see the Crone Movement as part of the paradigm shift we are in at this turn of the millennium. Telling our stories in small groups and in the public arena of an annual gathering is an important and empowering act for older women, and many women start their stories by saying that this is the first time they have ever told this—a tribute to how safe they feel in this special crone space. As one woman said, "The way to find one's voice is to share one's stories." It is "hearing ourselves into speech."

Who are these women who proclaim themselves to be a crone, join crone groups, and attend annual gatherings? There is no single answer. Many women say that when they hear or see the word *crone* something resonates within them—you either are attracted to it or not on a gut level. A frequently asked question is, "At what age can one become a crone? There are no hard and fast rules. Although the concept of Crone comes to us from long ago, we have no documents delineating "rules" for becoming a crone. Women today are simply creating and doing what feels right to them. Some people say you should be at least 50. Others say that you should have gone through menopause. Z Budapest says you should be going through your second Saturn return, i.e. 56 or so. Menopause is an important marker in a woman's life, but some women go through menopause in their early 40s or even late 30s. I don't feel that these women qualify as crones as they haven't had enough life experience. There are younger women, however, who feel a strong identification with crones and even attend the national gatherings—they are called "crones-in-training." However most of the women attending the annual gatherings are in their 50s and 60s, with many in their 70s, and even a few in their 80s (and they are given special recognition with an "Honoring the Elders" ceremony.) And many women are choosing to have croning ceremonies where they proudly proclaim themselves as *crone* to their friends and families. These rituals are self-created, and are held at whatever age and in whatever way the woman feels is appropriate.

Why does a woman choose to identify as a crone? One woman answered my question this way, "Crone is a state of being and becoming more fully myself. Crone is both an ideal—the Crone goddesses, and a real image—crone me and my sisters. Crone, more than any other term or phase of my life as a woman, links me to the women of the ancient past—the healers, witches, drummers, cave painters, village elders, priestesses, and wisewomen." I also believe that women who come together in crone groups are seeking community. Our country was founded on the concept of being independent. We are taught to bury our feelings, be strong, and carry on no matter what. Our foremothers had such things as quilting bees, and lived in extended families, which gave them support. Today many of us live far away from our families, our nuclear families often do not provide the support we need, and our lives are so busy that we don't have time to gather with our women friends. Many women yearn to be in relation with others. Older women are mostly done with our child rearing responsibilities, approaching or living in retirement and frequently living alone. We are reaching out to other women of our age for community and support. Sharing our stories with each other helps us make sense of our lives as we grapple with our ageing process.

Many women, however, are still horrified at the thought of being called a *crone*. There is much fear about identifying ourselves as older/old women. I have noticed that many women who identify as feminists and have made it into previously all male occupations and professions do not want to identify with the Crone. In order to successfully compete in the male world they have had to suppress their "feminine" and cultivate their "masculine" attributes. And there is definitely age discrimination in the work place. We are constantly bombarded by messages and ads in the media to get face-lifts, tummy tucks, lipo suction, and everything else to remain youthful in appearance. As women age, many have to face the issue of their husbands leaving them for younger women. Others become widows and would like to find another man. There is also the phenomena of women in their forties giving birth, and then going through menopause while their children are still young. Many of these women do *not* want to be seen as *old*.

For so many women the word "crone" has such a negative connotation, that even when they learn about how some of us are trying to re-claim the old and original meaning of the word, the cultural conditioning is still too strong for them to overcome their revulsion. Dictionaries still use the commonly accepted definition of crone as someone who is old, withered, and witchlike, and I have been challenged that we are revising the meaning of the word. My answer is that the Church revised the meaning during the Inquisition, and we are now reclaiming the original meaning.

I believe that proclaiming ourselves as Crones is very empowering, and is a way to counteract the predominant image of older women in our culture. But the Crone Movement appeals only to certain women who are searching for something other than what they have been used to. As Ann Kreilkamp said, "There is a self-selecting screen—either you see it or you don't." I also believe the Crone Movement is intertwined with spirituality and wisdom—that women who identify as a crone are tapping into their spirituality even if they don't recognize this. They don't understand that *Crone* is an aspect of the Goddess and that they are connecting to Her when they proclaim they are a crone.

Since the early 80's, the number of women identifying as crones is increasing, and I believe that we are part of the circles contributing to the creation of the Millionth Circle written about by Jean Shinoda Bolen.[11] This is the phenomenon based on Rupert Sheldrake's Morphic Field Theory that a change in the behavior of a species occurs when a critical mass—the exact number needed—is reached. Today's crones are part of the resurgence of the feminine archetype and, as such, are situated to impact the change in consciousness that our world desperately needs.

We, the women active in the 2nd Wave of the Women's Movement, who are now entering our Crone years (with the baby boomers close behind) are claiming our power as crones. It is my fervent hope that, "when the Grandmothers speak, the earth will be healed."

Notes

1 Schachter-Shalomi, Zalman and Miller, Ronald S., From Age-ing to Sage-ing: A Profound New Vision of Growing Older, New York, Warner Books, 1995, p. 5

2 Estes, Clarissa Pinkola, Women Who Run with the Wolves: Myths and Stories of the Wild Woman Archetype, New York, Ballantine, 1992 & 1995, p. 89

3 Lubell, Winifred Milius, The Metamorphosis of Baubo: Myths of Women's Sexual Energy, Nashville, TN, Vanderbilt University Press, 1994, p. xix

4 Budapest, Zsuzsanna E., The Holy Book of Women's Mysteries, Berkeley, California, Wingbow Press, 1980, 1989

5 Kreilkamp, Ann, ed., Crone Chronicles, A Journal of Conscious Aging, Kelly, WY

6 Meador, Betty DeShong, Uncursing The Dark: Treasures From The Underworld, Wilmette, Illinois, Chiron Publications, 1992, p. 64

7 Caputi, Jane, Gossips, Gorgons & Crones: The Fates of the Earth, Santa Fe, NM, Bear & Company, 1993, p. 274

8 Northrup, Christiane, M.D., Women's Bodies, Women's Wisdom, New York, Bantam Books, 1994, p. 647

9 Bolen, Jean Shinoda, M.D., Crossing to Avalon: A Woman's Midlife Pilgrimage, San Francisco, HarperSanFrancisco, a Division of HarperCollins Publishers, 1994, p. 272

10 Crones Counsel can be found at www.cronescounsel.org

11 Bolen, Jean Shinoda, M.D., The Millionth Circle: How to Change Ourselves and The World, Berkeley, California, Conari Press, 1999

The Poet as Initiate: Re-emergence of the Darkmother in Women's Poetry in the 1970's

Louisa Calio

For my mother Rosa.

"She is you, she is me, she is our mother's murmurings, chantings, hummings all her days" [1]

—Rites of Isis

When I first wrote those lines in the early 1970's I hadn't yet named the process going on within me, nor had I discovered the works of Lucia Chiavola Birnbaum which would link the dark mother to my own Sicilian and Neapolitan heritage as well as our collective African roots. I had seen my life undergoing major transitions, a divorce, job loss, a descent, as well as explorations into new and submerged territories of learning, a "remembering" of African culture and religion as well as a reconnection to people from Sudan, Egypt and Ethiopia.

In the grips of powerful unconscious forces, I was called to renewal or initiation. Turning inward for guidance, I felt drawn to a copy of E.A. Wallis Budge's *Osiris and the Egyptian Resurrection*. There was the image of the great eye I had been drawing since I was a child. There was the name of the Goddess who was initiating me: Isis! Hers was a story of a feminine deity who was making herself; not a cursed and sinful female ancestor, but powerful and inspired dark mother who dared to call upon the sun god, Ra, for her equal place, as well as for a healing of her beloved, Osiris, and their child, Horus.

334

Here was an earlier trinity, with a powerful female deity that saw man as her brother and was putting the pieces of their broken soul back together for all humanity to benefit.[2]

These ideas were emerging in other women poets, artists, writers, historians, dancers, and mothers as well in the late sixties and early seventies. This is well documented now, but was not so then. On reflection, this was a very lonely and perilous passage. Initiation, even when guided by instinct and archetypal memory, challenges the stability of the ego. Yet, it seemed as if a seed planted by our ancestors and the dark mother a millennia ago was bursting forth and about to give birth.

Poetry is also a way of knowing, much like dreaming. The poet/artist often lives at the borders of internal experience and outer revelation. She values the inner and imaginary, because it is the source of creativity. Poetry explores the far reaches of the psyche and the depths of feeling in a heightened language carried by breath. At its best, we can call poetry a language of the soul. Many women were wrestling with issues of soul proportion and daring to express the most personal and intimate experiences of being human and female in our time. After two thousand years of patriarchy, a history marked with periods persecution, witch burnings, torture, severe punishment and repression of all dark others, especially women, the silence was about to be broken wide open.

While occasionally women writers of the past from Emily Dickinson to Virginia Woolf in her important essay, *A Room of One's Own*, called out for soul space in our lives, room for the meditative, for process rather than product, as well as respect for the feminine voice, their calls were not widely heard; too many like Woolf were buried under severe depression or covered by a legacy of Victorian artifice and politeness. The accumulated pain of generations, once hidden by conformity, silence, and acquiescence to tribal order and false "codes of honor" (see Gioseffi's poem "Bicentennial Anti-Poem for Italian-American Women")[3] that buried acts of violence in deep depression, mental illness and silent suffering, seemed to reach a critical mass in the 1960's, and as the work of Dr. Birnbaum fully documents, began to give voice to what eventually became a feminist spiritual movement and its poetry.[4]

While initiation in ancient times took place in the temple after many years of preparation, modern women poets of the spirit often began their journeys unconsciously, the result of years of inner turmoil and outer situations and people who did not validate them. Whether their initial quest was for love, friendship, a mate, to understand oneself or simply bear one's pain, these women journeyed into the caves of their unconscious rousing the sleeping demons of the soul. Often unprepared for a spiritual ordeal, the poet was driven inward by an energy larger than herself; if she survived the encounter, she could pull from the deep, the new image and energy from which to create, heal and continue. In the words of the Jungians, these writers were engaged in a "re-mythologizing of their lives," a search for meaning that led to a rediscovery of our relationship to the Great Mother and the Greater Mysteries which address the larger purpose for which we are born.

Two pioneering poets who contributed to an earlier evolution of the feminine communal soul were Sylvia Plath and Anne Sexton. Their works preceded the new wave by ten years. Daniela Gioseffi, Diane Di Prima, Ntozake Shange, Alice Walker, Starhawk and myself were some of the poets who found that protesting and rebelling, though important for exposing the evils of lopsided patriarchy, were not enough to heal them. To heal one had to confront, time and again, the collective negative beliefs and their brutal manifestations around the feminine and then transform them one by one.[5]

In the late 1950's the dark mother had not yet been renamed or celebrated. SHE was still locked in stone, a "Stasis in darkness/substanceless blue..."[6] or a distant intellectual ideal of ancient history, distorted into a literal Virgin or sinful Eve. While the new poets also experienced a deep despair over the old values of patriarchy and the abuses it spawned, they did so with one major and important difference—a conscious identification with the re-emergent Mother Goddess, and the values she stood for: justice, compassion, equality, peace, and love.

This recognition of our true godliness and beauty was as significant for women spiritually, as the large-scale movement of feminists and all it accomplished was for us secularly. With the re-emergence of the Dark Mother, we now had a legacy upon which to draw. We sought and found that she was there all along waiting to be re-discovered in pre-Christian forms. As we wrote, we gave voice and a contemporary language and she fed us more. She was indeed everywhere![7]

Being partially raised in a Catholic tradition, gave me an appreciation of ritual and a respect for our need for collective expression, but I never imagined I would be creating my own rituals. It was when all the familiar doors seemed to shut and I found I couldn't keep working or loving in the old ways I once had, try as I may to continue the old formulas that kept me exhausted with "saving" or mothering others, working like a slave for little in dangerous facilities at the expense of my health, I had to stop. At 27 years old, I took stock of my life and questioned my activities. I felt beaten and swallowed by a huge darkness in which I could only wait. I never expected a response after weeks of silence, but a friend came by and offered me a glimmer of my new direction, another book on the Egyptian Mysteries and the ancient rites of Isis and Osiris which contained a single phrase that haunted me, "Cannot I make myself, make myself, a goddess like Ra in heaven and on earth?" [8]

Those words echoed and reechoed in my core. They told me the time had come for me to create my own life, and that it was good and worthy and worth living for itself, that living for others alone was not enough, was in fact wrong and would not bring about the change in the world as I wanted. I had nowhere to go and no one to turn to, but I had this great help from something ancient stirring within me which soon spoke from me and through my pen, and she named herself, mother—Isis. She called me to a lost tenderness and asked that I imbibe daily.

"Come Eat My Roses/Dive into the face of Love Touch the blood of passion/As it drips from the cup.."[9]

With the words, sounds and movements coming through me, I began to repair my own body and soul, and look for a more humane way of serving in the world, a way that allowed for self love while still learning how to love others and I've been working on that ever since.

We had discovered that we are the greater mystery of life ever becoming our potential, it's potential, and like the initiates of the temple, we found in our being "the temple of our familiar" (Alice Walker's empowering phrase) our very own soul, once veiled by the other names given to us by those who used and abused us.

The initiate learned that these false gods were powerless before our essence and whoever begins reshaping her life will be supported by a new heritage, an invisible but powerful matriarchal force gives to us, as we add to HER. All loving and compassionate, she gathers us to her to heal again and again, as often as we need, in order to free ourselves from the desert of unconscious suffering.

As poets and writers of this spiritual renaissance awakened and grew in number, we witnessed the ever-fertile variety of her expressions. Margaret Honton writes in the preface of her 1981 anthology of poems of the spirit by feminists *I Named Myself Daughter and it is Good*, that when she asked for submissions for an anthology of feminist spiritual poetry, she had no idea what if anything would come, and was shocked to receive thousands of submissions from over thirty states in a few weeks. [10]

Daniela Gioseffi's compelling collection of poetry, *Eggs in the Lake* emerged around the same time in 1979. She re-introduces us to Plath's "Sad Hag" in her original form: "Sea Hag in the Cave of Sleep." Here we witness the stages of initiation. Moving through the ravishing elements of descent, when we are taken apart and released from all that we once were; shattered and broken by ego loss, she falls down into her core to be reborn:

"Words whirl her round in pools. I cling by my teeth, grinding mountains…She drops through an eternity of light. I float again. I fall calling for animals to warm her, pleading with trees to feed me." [11]

Initiated, the woman is drawn to nature again for healing and renewal until finally: "I come from between my own legs/into this world." [12]

The powerful sacred imagery of woman's recreation of self is mirrored in Gioseffi's other poems as well. After coming from traditions that claimed we came from Adam's rib, a "Vacant, faceless" or…"Guilty since Eve…not even My hair was not my own idea, it grew from his rays…and he was the sun and everyone…" [13] We had to re-discover the food our souls needed for healing: "The Great Mother" who "gave milk in the beginning/she arose as a dream…and from her comes food…breath, spirit, and worlds" [14] that live inside us. She is the power of the inner process, the soul work and the strength needed by anyone to build a new feminine in the world.

Ms. Gioseffi often performed her poetry while belly dancing, a ritual art the balances mind and body. In her poem "Belly Dancer" we witness its original art form, as sacred temple dancer, or mid-wife in service, and "an Etruscan priestess through whom the earth speaks…a mystery (that) moves toward the altar." [15] In nearly every poem Daniela renews and heals some aspect of the feminine by passionately loving and accepting all of her, including those parts that were formerly taboo like menstruation and childbirth. "Her navel winks in a quiver. Amazing belly that stretches large enough to let a life grow." [16]

She sings of women's sensual pleasures with lust and love in her heart and dares to call attention to our curves of our flesh, venus mound and breasts, not as objects, but as life expressing itself abundantly like Mother Nature. As we witness the effects of women's self destructive body images that drive girls to bulimia or anorexia, or learn of imbedded cultural abuses like foot binding or tribal mutilations that cut off a woman's pleasure, we can resonate when we read,

> "For a long time, I've thought of this body of mine with agony, with curiosity and dreams..."

This body of woman so like the body of earth, has been and still is used and abused. Yet, she is "Mother, pagan, witch of magic birth, from whom we all suck." [17] Her redemption is our redemption.

In *Eggs in the Lake* Gioseffi also claims her equal place as creator, along side Dante and Da Vinci, despite coming from a tradition that "discouraged women from school,/told a woman meant for cooking and bearing children doesn't need education." She is ready to break free and stand on her own separate and apart from fathers and husbands, "whom I worshipped all my years" and "let you commit crimes in my name." [18]

Ntozake Shange will do the same when she creates her choreopoem in the Bay area *For Colored Girls who have Considered Suicide When the Rainbow is Enuf.* Performing her sacred rite in bars, cafes, Women's studies departments and other spots, this modern day ritual would eventually emerge on Broadway in 1976 at the Booth Theater produced by Joe Papp.

Seven women dressed in rainbow colors shared their stories, their loves, music and some of the grief of black women in a wilderness of human relationships where friends are capable of rape and husbands of murdering their children.

Perhaps the collective work had begun to build our new vessel, because although there was great suffering, there was also great healing. For Ntozake's Lady in Brown, the Goddess of Egypt, Schetia, had come to heal the wounds of woman in the inner city during desperate hours of darkness and brutality, rape, cruelty and murder. Lady in Red whose children are murdered by their raging father is herself close to suicide, "i sat up one nite..screamin/cryin/the ghost of another woman.. i wanted to jump outta my bones/& be done with myself." [19]

But she, like each woman rediscovers,

> "I waz missin something/somethin so important/something promised a layin on of hands/fingers near my forehead...making me whole...pure.../ all the gods comin into me layin me open to myself...not my mama/hold-

ing me tight...not a layin on of bosom & womb/*A holiness of myself released*" (emphasis mine). [20]

Then before the world, Lady in Red utters what I still believe is the most revolutionary and blasphemous words of power I have heard to date:

"i found god in myself and I loved her *i loved her fiercely*" (emphasis mine) [21]

Those words at that moment in time, expressed woman's most profound longing, as well as her greatest fear and ultimate realization. Cursed for ages as the cause of humanity's fall, burdened by historical roles that undervalued and blamed, she was like nature deeply feared and mistrusted and abused until she claimed her truth and recognized her divine nature. Lady in Brown spoke for the darkmother within all of us when she said,

"sing a black girl's song/to know herself/to know you/...sing her song of life/she's been dead so long/closed in silence so long/she doesn't know the sound/of her own voice/her infinite beauty" (emphasis mine) [22]

Here at last the initiate need die only a psychic death and thus can be redeemed and live again. She need not be physically sacrificed to "Big Daddy" or suffer in silence ever again. Instead, life's ordeals were her preparation and with the help of grace and spirit and the love of the dark Mother, she experiences divinity directly:

"the sun wrapped me up swingin rose light everywhere/the sky laid over me like a million men/I waz cole/I was burin up/a child & endlessly weavin garments for the moon wit my tears.../i found god in myself and I loved her" [23]

Other women poets began speaking their truth, even when truth was "unsweet, unladylike, unpalatable." [24] In fact, truth called for a new clarity that took us to the highest while facing the darkest in the world within and outside.

A state away in Connecticut, while Shange was developing the final stages of her choreopoem, I was creating a ritual production that had moved from south street in Philadelphia to Hartford and then the Educational Center for the Arts in New Haven to make the words I had written live and be part of the life of our community. Symbols were no longer outside of me. They emerged spontaneously from an inner reality, a deep well spring that had always lived there and which I had just discovered or remembered. Owning the Goddess within was a giant step for those of us raised in traditional religion, where God often appeared cold, distant, and judgmental or at best in the hands of important male interlocutors.

Like Shange, I found it necessary to create a stage production with music, art and dance and later would joyfully discover this too was part of my lost Sicilian/Neapolitan heritage. With the help of a forward looking Connecticut Commission on the Arts and a grant we received, and I joined with Yale art school graduate, Terry Lennox, whose magnificent 15 foot icons graced the stage with color and powerful imagery that evoked the primodial, jazz musician/composer Oliver Lake and guitarist, singer Michael Gregory whose angelic voice is renowned, dancer, actress Purity Smothers and Rachel Ellner to create a modern day rite that expressed a soul hunger. Women and men of varied ages wept at times, when we said: "Waiting, waiting. I've been waiting, for you for ages, for millenniums, and still you haven't gotten here." [25]

Women sighed as we addressed our male counterpart who was "wounded, bleeding and scarred," to wear his wounds openly, not as "medals or emblems of war!" [26] The performances brought out to our communal body and into our own physical body/mind, what we had all lost in lop-sided patriarchy and a new door to recovery: balanced androgyny:

> "You can build me,/as I build you/to make us whole again/we who were torn to shreds by world machines that break human beings into pieces../to turn the wheels, turn the cogs of whose machines/not yours, not mine/not for our life forces..We can reshape humankind this time!" [27]

When I performed at Connecticut Hospice in Branford, whirling in a new millennium with the Tapestry Dance Co., people who were close to transition, the most sensitive audience I have ever experienced, helped me to better understand the primordial depths I was voicing.

As Diane di Prima, I discovered awakening was only the beginning, initiation a first step. We had envisioned a potential that still needed to be grounded and become matter. The dark mother stays "close to the secrets of the earth" and lives to bring the divine into matter. After the initial encounter we needed time for reflection and integration, to make personal what is archetypal, and to live concretely what is an ideal.

In her powerful and enchanting Goddess song, <u>Loba</u> (1978), Diane di Prima uses startling imagery and myth to awaken us to a cornucopia of the divine feminine. Her ancient ties to nature and expressions through history, well as simple everyday working girl aspects are woven expertly though each poem. The book is divided into VIII sections preceded by a quotation or meditative focus that introduces the grouping of poems. The book itself begins with an Ave or invocation to gather together not only of lost parts of the self, but all of our sisters.

"Oh, lost moon sisters/crescent in hair, sea underfoot/in tattered shawl/ .. in green leaf..do you wander...on Bleecker Street...Rampart Street, on Fillmore Street...jaywalking, spitting do you wander, mumbling and crying do you wander..."[28]

Loba is also the Goddess of our lost or submerged wildness, the primal parts of self connected with the earth and cycles of nature, which we long to be reunited with. Graced with evocative drawings by Josie Grant, we get to meet our instinctual, animal selves. The wolf is known for its strong ties to the pack and family; yet is also a wild, untamed creature. In Di Prima's collection, the Loba takes on mythic dimension and multi-dimensional aspects associated with ancient symbols of the feminine: crystals, pyramids, moonstones, and pearls appear and other tools of the conjurer. When needed, Loba is also ferocious and murderous. She evokes the Kali imagery of India's Goddess of destruction, "baring her wolf's teeth" [29] when she grins.

Loba is tied to Eve and Lilith, but as valued ancestors and to countless other legendary figures, as well ordinary women in their mortal desires and suffering. Like the dark mother, wolf woman wears all the guises from Guinevere and Miriam to a blood-sucking bat. She is the void, though not empty, ever full and replenishing and above all Named! Nothing is omitted, not a single aspect left out from the shocking to the mundane. She is the all-inclusive deity, who says, "Enter here, you are all my children." [30] Di Prima's endless "sketches" of the Loba by implication say that we are everything and that everything is sacred and the sacred is all inclusive and includes the humble mother who serves.

"Is it not in yr service I wear myself out/running ragged among these hills, driving children to forgotten movies? In yr service broom & pen." [31]

All work, whether art, the craft, or traditional woman's work, is given renewed meaning, not perhaps by awards committees, the media, or financial giants, but what are these when compared to HER who knows all contributions are of equal value whether glamorous or simple?

Claiming the feminine in all forms, Diane di Prima's long song for the dark mother profoundly and brilliantly names her in all her wetness, wildness, boldness and daring, as well as in her terrified, fearful, and victimized moments or pagan, witch and crone like aspects. She reminds us from the opening that the work of the initiate is never complete: "I am you/and I must become you/I have been you and I must become you. I am always you/and I must become you." [32]

In these paradoxical lines, we witness the mystery of initiation, not a single moment of enlightenment, but an evolutionary process which unearths our essential nature. So too does it ask us to continue to reintegrate, again and again, what we have learned from plunging into the depths of our psyche for both the self and the larger community.

Like Di Prima, Gioseffi and eventually many others who were initiated by powerful archetypal forces, we find a healing of the individual often takes place and when it does, she may return bearing a gift for the collective. Loba closes with a poem entitled, "Now born in uniqueness, join the Common Quest." 33 What better call is there for the work? We have many more voices to guide us today, wonderful, beautiful and powerful voices, like Lucia Chiavola Birnbaum, Normandi Ellis, Jean Houston, Alice Walker, Starhawk…and men as well like David Spangler and David Whyte who offer depth history, depth psychology and a poetry of initiation at a time when we so need it. But no matter the guides, the journey remains an individual effort. Goddess Bless all those who dare to discover the dark mother within and return to share her gifts with the collective.

Notes

1. Louisa Calio, *In the Eye of Balance*, (New York: Paradiso Press, 1978) p.6.

2. E. A. Wallis Budge, *Osiris and the Egyptian Resurrection Vol.II* (New York: Dover Publishers, 1973) p.53.

3. Daniela Gioseffi, *Eggs in the Lake*, (Brockport: Boa Editions, 1979) pp. 62–63.

4. Lucia Chiavola Birnbaum, Ph.D., *darkmother african orgins and godmothers*, (Nebraska: Author's Choice Press, i Universe 2001) pp.303–327.

5. For a detailed article on Plath and Sexton see Louisa Calio "Rebirth of the Goddess in Contemporary Women's Poetry" *Studia Mystica* Vol. VII no. 1 (Sacramento: University of California,) pp.50–60.

6. Sylvia Plath, *Ariel*, (New York: Harper and Row, 1965) p. 26.

7. Birnbaum, Ph.D., *darkmother african origins and godmothers*, pp. 353.

8. Budge, *Osiris and the Egyptian Resurrection*, pp.73

9. Calio, *In the Eye of Balance*, p. 17.

10. *I name Myself Daughter and it is Good* ed. by Margaret Honton (Columbus: Sophia Books,1981) p. unmarked preface.

11. Gioseffi, *Eggs in the Lake*, p 46.

12. Ibid, p.50.

13. Ibid, p.34.

14. Ibid, p.55.

15. Ibid, p.51

16. Ibid, p.51.

17. Ibid, p.52.

18. 18.Ibid, p.35.

19. Ntozake Shange, *For Colored Girls who have Considered Suicide When the Rainbow is Enuf*,(New York: Macmillan, 1979) p. 63.

20. Ibid, p.60–62.

21. Ibid, p.63.

22. Ibid, p.4.

23. Ibid, p.63.

24. Calio, p.20.

25. Ibid, p.22.

26. Ibid, p.35

27. Ibid, p. 5.

28. Diane Di Prima, *Loba*,(Berkeley : Wingbow Press 1978) Ave preface unnumbered.

29. Ibid, p.17.

30. Birnbaum, Ph.D., p.353.

31. Di Prima, p.168.

32. Ibid, Ave unnumbered.

33. Ibid, p.187.

Bibliography

Birnbaum, Ph.D., Lucia Chiavola. *darkmother african origins and godmothers*. (Nebraska: Author's Choice Press, imprint, i Universe, 2001).

Budge, E.A. Wallis. *Osiris and the Egyptian Resurrection*. (New York: Dover Publishers, 1973).

Calio, Louisa. *In the Eye of Balance* (New York: Paradiso Press, 1978).

_____"Rebirth of the Goddess in Contemporary Women's Poetry" *Studia Mystica* Vol.VII no.1 ed. by Mary Giles (Sacramento: University of California, 1983).

Di Prima, Diane. *Loba* (Berkeley: Wingbow Press, 1978).

Ellis, Normandi. *Dreams of Isis*, a woman's spiritual sojourn(Illinois: Theosophical Publishing House, 1995).

Gioseffi, Daniela. *Eggs in the Lake*. (Brockport: BOA EDITIONS, 1979.)

I Name Myself Daughter and it is Good, poems of the spirit by feminists. ed. and compiled by Margaret Honton. (Columbus: Sophia Books, 1981).

Plath, Sylvia. *Ariel* (New York: Harper and Row, 1965).

Shange, Ntozake. *For Colored Girls who have Considered Suicide When the Rainbow is Enuf.* (New York: Macmillan Publishing Co., 1977)

Essence of the Whale

Diana Marto

september 11 2001
the world shudders
the bones of a whale wash ashore
the bones reach into her waking and sleeping dreams
what do the bones say?
she asks the spirit of sacred paper
she casts sheets of handmade paper over the bones
finds the essence of whales in the paper sculpture
dances with the essence

—Canto XVII, her epic spirit play in paper and dance:

I scrambled down a steep double black diamond slope loose with shale to a hidden cove in Big Sur. There amongst grey and green boulders, just above the mighty Pacific I finally found what I sought, for I had made many futile attempts. Pure ivory form, winged, 4 feet thick, the cranium. I lay my body over it, and press my cheek into its cool firmness. I place my hands, then my face onto the two nodules, breast-like and peer into the round hole where the spinal fluids passed into the brain.

Catching a trace of whale scent I began to weep. For me it is more eloquent than the Vietnam Memorial in Washington D.C. I have returned many times to listen to the bone, to marvel over its ingenuity and function, and to dance.

After all the whales are one of the oldest species on the planet, surely they have information to pass along to us if we can ever fathom it. They were almost extinct in the nineteenth century because of our glut for whale oil. Is there a correlation between their extinction and ours, in our quest for crude oil consumption? Whales cavort, make incredible sounds reminiscent of Tibetan horns. I read that "the sperm whales signature whistles are nearly identical to the rhythmical patterns developed in West African drum communication." They midwife their babies, carry one another to the surface to breathe when they are sick, and recently are allowing us to touch them, the Grey Whales that is. The fact that they are mammals and breast feed is wondrous. Their belly buttons don't stick out nor go in, they are small slits. In meditation I am shown that my original relationship to the whales is through just that, our belly buttons. I came across an ancient view of creation which saw creation flowing from the womb of a whale woman. "Delphys", the Greek word for dolphin, is related to "Delphis" which means womb.

Right after the World Trade Center collapsed I expanded my art base with a cabin in Big Sur. The bones of a juvenile Humpback Whale washed ashore and some of them were brought onto the land. Their presence informed my waking and sleeping dreams. Why are they here? What are they communicating? I began to draw them using the porcupine quills I'd collected in Zimbabwe and sumi ink. And in January I started casting sheets of my handmade paper of abaca fiber over them. Often while working on the picnic table I could see the whales spouting in the distance. At night I would lug the bones covered with wet pulp into my cabin to dry by the wood burning stove. To my amazement when I lifted the cast off of the bone I experienced the aliveness of the whale in the paper. Such Celebration! Wings, sceptres, reeds, masks, presentation of bones, scapulae, vertebrae, ribs, fragments of the beak. Each sculpture a revelation. I danced with all of them on the hill overlooking the ocean and on the picnic table.

In Eastern spiritual practices handmade paper is believed to be imbued with healing and mystical properties. I lived in Southeast Asia in the late 70's to mid 80's. While paying my respects to the Paper Goddess at her shrine in the mountains in Japan, it began to snow and I had a vision of the Paper Goddess snowing paper all over the land to heal our hearts. From this vision I developed my Canto Series, my epic spirit play with paper and dance. They are visual journals of the teachings I receive from the land, both performance art events and installations of related artworks. Paper is my semaphore.

The only way to cast the cranium is to bring wet sheets of handmade paper in my backpack to the cove. Three times I've cast the top surface, leaving the paper to dry over several days and nights of noisome fogs and full moons. One afternoon returning for more paper, my eye caught a flash of dark disappearing into the ocean, and then again and again the body appearing straight out of the water twisting and flukes slapping the water as the cetacean disappeared. How to transport and protect the paper sculpture up the steep slope, presented a problem since I am short and have to use all 4's to scramble. A tall friend assembled 2 four feet lengths of wood into a crucifix which we stapled the sculpture to. Lifting the damp paper form off of the bone was one of those moments when life as we know it, shifts. Placing her onto the crucifix and carrying her aloft, someone exhalted "snow angel!" Indeed, an angel or a bird, 7 foot wing span, 5 foot body. Whales carry angels inside their brains! Just where the spinal column connects and the wings wrap around the lower skull, the oldest part of the brain. Apparently we too have a similiar form in our skulls. Is this where guardian angels reside? And if so is it this spirit which carries us when we make our transition? Is this the physical manifestation of our immortality? I named this sculpture "THE WHALE GUARDIAN."

In February 2003, my dear friend and I visited the birthing lagoons in Baja, California where the Grey Whales migrate 6000 miles one-way to give birth and to mate. Camping along the shore at night I could hear them breathing which reminded me of the hippopotamuses and elephants in Zimbabwe.

Sitting in small wooden "pangas" which hold up to 8 people and a 25 horse-power motor we caught glimpses of them, sometimes long fast slithers, tails slapping the water, flukes pausing like mini mountains, or straight up snouts like balloons suspended for 6 seconds. All very surreal as if in a virtual reality, and somewhat comical albeit a bit threatening. As we motored further from shore more slithers and snouts appeared until we were encircled. Then 2, then 4 swam closer to the boat, diving and surfacing until they were along side, then under and over to the other side of the boat, swimming all around us and each other. The babies feeding from their mothers, the mothers showing off their new borns. Cavorting, tumbling, riding one another, so close that I dared to reach out and touch one. Not slimy nor slithery, just strong and giving. Such pure and unadulterated delight to be in their presence. One swam side-ways and looked directly up at me, just for an instant! Shakti exploding me out of separation.

We made a pilgrimage deep into the Sierra de San Francisco Mountains to visit ancient cave paintings of shamans, big horn sheep and whales, created by the seminomads of Baja who spent half their years living on the coast and the remainder in the mountains. By mule we descended a mini Grand Canyon with hair-raising switch-backs which truly tested my mettle. Imagine swaying on a four-legged with a long neck. The head and neck turns and there you are facing straight down into the void. What kept me sane was the knowledge that I was walking an ancient good red road where many had gone before, and that the whales brought me there for teachings. I dream of catching a sleeping baby, who is my sole responsibility, as it is rolling off a high platform and will myself to have the strength to hang on. With us was a family from the Yukon with their 5 year old son named Caelan. The day after our arduous descent I catch him coming down a steep path and keep myself and him from falling backwards off the cliff from the impact of his weight, just as in the dream. Before we leave the sacred canyon, Jill, Caelan's mother, and I spend an hour alone in front of the 160 feet long 33 feet high wall painting, known to have been created over a period of 3000 years which includes an image of the whale. We paint, sing, and gong my Tibetan singing bowl. Looking up at the sky between the rock wall paintings and the sheer canyon wall across the creek, I realized the sky was whale shaped!

Together we returned to the birthing lagoons. Once again the mothers and babies frolicked all around us and the love we experienced was all encompassing, especially having my own little wiggeling one right next to me. Later, the precious family from the Yukon, came to visit us in the Bay Area. We walked down Market Street on March 20th., amongst throngs of war protesters. I hold Caelan's hand and will never let go. When they say goodbye he gives me a stone he collected in Baja which looks like whale skin. I've never had children. He is my inner boy child.

This is what I wrote in my journal just after we left Baja: Gaia gave us love, joy, strength, renewal and mystery. Gaia gave us transcendance, lighting us up like stars in the night sky. The whales brought me here, the holy ones, the bodhisattvas, the ancient ones, the delighted ones.

> in the silence is the mystery
> shh
> can you hear it?
> in the silence deep in the earth
> she stands
> sentinel
> to the first sound wave.

Bones hold the memory of first form, of the sound waves of love which created matter. 50 million years ago the whale ancestors were on land. 10 million years ago the modern form of whales came into existence. We are only 2 genes apart from the whales. Their skeletal system and ours are very similiar. Bone is the densest part of our body and contains our spiritual essence. Peering inside the opening in the cranium I witness the liquidity of first formation. And am reminded that we and the planet are over 70% water.

Through the bones we can purify ourselves of negative energy. When I am politically active on the whales' behalf, I am purified. When I dance with the paper sculptures, they purify me. I feel their energy penetrating my shoulder blades and spinal column. Similiar to the shamans who take on the power of an animal by putting on its skin, I know I am taking on the essence of the whale when I place "*The Whale Guardian*" over my shoulders and head. In Jennifer Berezan's

Praises For The World Concert, "*The Whale Guardian*" danced to fly in the vibrations of the chant as a Peace Dove. When I dance with the sculptures publically I know that I am taking on the shaman's mantle. At the beginning I am often overcome with the portent of the mission, for each time I seek to fulfill the inexplicable. Linear time ceases. I enter into cosmic stillness. By the end my body is vibrating with the whale body as contained in the paper.

Acknowledgements

None of this occurred in a vacuum and I would like to thank the following people who have participated with me on this journey: Stuart Rabinowitsh, Hope Coffin, Warren Doyle, Benjie Lasseau, Kathleen Gallagher, Jeep Phillips, Wendy Oser, Jeff Parrish, Jeannine Chappell, Stephanie Calkins Peters, Loie Johnson, Leslie Temple Thurston, Bones Bendar, Jill Pangman, Bruce Mclean, Caelan Mclean, Suellen Primost, Kim, John, and Rose Smiley, Phyllis Sanderson, Lucia Chaivola Birnbaum, and the Whales.

Essence of the Whale—Canto XVII, Diana Marto

Thus far the Sculptures and Performances have been presented at the:
Henry Miller Library, Big Sur, CA. Performance, with Hope Coffin, Benjie Lasseau, Warren Doyle, and Stuart Rabinowitsh. September 28th. 2002.
"Day of the Dead/Entre la Luz Y La Muerte", SomArts Cultural Center, S.F. CA. "Whale Guardian" Installation, October 2002.
"Praises for the World" Concert, Scottish Rite Theater, Oakland, CA. "Whale Guardian" Performance, March 22, 2003.
Fairfax Parade, Fairfax, CA. Whale bone dance with Kathleen Gallagher, as part of Seaflow's contingent. June 7, 2003.
Sight and Insight Art Center, Mill Valley, CA. Juried Sculpture Show, Summer, 2003.
Sight and Insight Art Center, Mill Valley, CA. Performance, with Hope Coffin and Stuart Rabinowitsh. August 4, 2002.
Emeryville Annual, Emeryville, CA. Installation, October, 2003.
Gallery Route One, Point Reyes Station, CA. Installation, Spring, 2004.
Academy of Science, S.F. CA. Performance, Spring, 2004

And no, the cranium did not wash away in a full moon tide. It took 4 men 6 hours to bring it up the steep path and offered it for sale, which is illegal. I raised money from concerned friends to rescue the cranium. It is temporarily housed at Landels-Hill Big Creek Reserve and will eventually be returned to its almost original site, above the bluffs over looking the vast Pacific.

Diana Marto with the Cranium
Photograph by Hope Coffin

On the Hidden Trail of the Dark Mother: Gypsy earrings, Roma women, & Saving a Life in India

Sandy Miranda, M.A.

A study of the dark mother has opened my eyes to hidden meanings in things my mother, my grandmother, and my father said to me when I was growing up. I'm beginning to recognize the multitude of images of Her that I have intuitively chosen to decorate my home. Slowly, I begin to sense my connection with the dark other Roma women, and with the dark mother in India. But, let's back up a little bit.

Near the end of the wild and wooly '60s, I took some life-changing, visionary graduate seminars in Myth & Symbolism, Shakespeare, and William Blake from a very spiritual young professor from Yale named Harvey Birenbaum. Hundreds of energized artists and writers were congregating at San Jose State University at that time for an education with a revolutionary cadre of teachers. Our scholar in residence was Alan Watts, and Angela Davis had an office down the street.

Halfway through the M.A., I took an irresistible job offer with a maverick computer group at Stanford Research Institute. Offering the first e-mail to forward-thinking universities, we also developed the first interactive word processor. At S.R.I., I volunteered for experiments in hypnosis, biofeedback, and aura photography, and my love of the cosmic threshold began to bloom.

Needing to pay off student loans and seduced by the legerdemain of technology, I wrote a poem as a resume, and was invited to join Apple Computer in 1980. It was a heady, playful scene. In those days, you didn't go to school to learn how to write about computers, and almost everybody on my team was an artist. This made for an irrepressible group resembling a shipload of gypsy-techno-pirates, and a jolly roger actually flew over the main building. This new, creative company with lots of women managers was about to change the world. Then, I discovered Esalen Institute, down in Big Sur, California, where the "human potential movement" was germinating.

During a weeklong breathwork intensive at Esalen in 1987, I had a vision that I should return to my childhood dream and work in radio. I went to the "mother ship", KPFA FM free-speech community radio in Berkeley, and with Joan Marler's magical recommendation, entered the engineering training program. I went on to produce a world music show for eight years, hosting Linda Tillery, Babatunde Olatunji, Zap Mama, David Byrne, Tarkia, Ry Cooder, Irma Thomas, and many others. Then, in 2002, with fourteen magical years of broadcasting experience behind me, I found myself still wanting to finish that Master's degree.

In January 2003, after checking out five transpersonal graduate schools, I entered the Women's Spirituality, Philosophy & Religion M.A. program at the California Institute of Integral Studies in San Francisco. This was the closest thing I could find to an Esalen graduate school—sufficiently cutting-edge with well-known explorers of consciousness on the core faculty.

CIIS is a few blocks from where I was born on Guerrero Street, in what is now the Mission District. When I was born, it was the Irish immigrant part of The City, which I now realize was appropriate, since my grandmother who partially raised me was a Mullen. I didn't learn until recently that the Irish were considered Black for a long time in America. Maybe that's one reason why I identify so strongly with the African-American culture, and the dark mother of us all.

To get ready for my first class taught by Lucia Chiavola Birnbaum, I read her book, dark mother: African origins and godmothers.[1] I bought the book two months before class started, after meeting Lucia at a CIIS open house. It was clear that the intrepid, wildly energetic, 79-years-young Lucia was going places that historians had not ventured to go before.

Radical, multi-disciplinary, woman-centered, cross-cultural, emancipatory, and transformational, Lucia's dark mother combines archaeology, mythology, cultural history, art history, and rich Sicilian-American family stories that create an alchemical reading experience.

I read dark mother with growing excitement, making dozens of notes in the margins. The book is exquisitely loaded—take that several ways—with historical research, stories, and anecdotal pearls. I was inspired by the volume's millennial scope and depth, and by the volatile political ideas I found there.

It's no wonder that Lucia had to self-publish this volume, even when university presses had published her previous books. dark mother (Lucia spells it with a small d) is out on the frontier, radical feminist in tone, and controversial in the eyes of male elites, who still have a stronghold on the mainstream publishing business (and music business—I know, because I'm one of the women who vote in the Grammys).

Birnbaum adopts a contemporary Italian style, removing capitols from as many words as possible. She explains that, "this is a step towards democratization of all institutions." [2] It wreaked havoc with my word processor, but Lucia does have a point.

So just who is the dark mother and why are signs of her found everywhere? dark mother begins like this:

> The hypothesis of this book is that everyone's genetic "beautiful mother" is african and dark, and that she is the oldest divinity we know...Africa is the place of origin of modern humans, homo sapiens sapiens. In the Paleolithic epoch, signs of our oldest mother were the color ochre red (signifying blood of childbirth and menstruation) and the pubic V painted in african caves. [3]

In dark mother, we learn that The Africans in migrations took signs of the dark mother with them when they migrated after around 50,000 BCE, and drew these signs on the caves and cliffs of every continent on earth.

Where does the idea of dark other come from? Psychology teaches us about projection. Every one of us, at times, projects our own unconscious aspects (negative and positive) out on to others—when we do not "own" these parts of ourselves. For example, theologian Matthew Fox says, "When you're out of touch with your grief, you project all over the place...think about how we treated the Native Americans, and about slavery." [4] This dark side projection happens at a national level, too. In the United States, our corporate-driven government projects this darkness out on to our "enemies", who they can then demonize and carpet bomb.

The dark mother truly represents all those who are "dark" and "other." Lucia gives a great example of dark other subtleties in America,

My male colleagues in the American Italian Historical Association are impressed by my scholarship, but some also find it difficult to acknowledge African origins. In this case, this is a poignant irony—italians, as well as the irish and the jews were put in categories of "black" when they arrived in the United States. [5]

There are other examples of dark others:

> ...her memory is explored in everyday and festival rituals of dark others of Europe and the United States—women, jews, muslims, heretics, witches—in songs, stories, foods, vendor songs, literature, and art and today in graffiti, bumper stickers, exclamations, and banners of political uprisings. [6]

My mother, Frances Lucille Luthringer, was born in 1927 in the South Texas cotton farming area of Beeville, two hours northeast of Nuevo Laredo, Mexico. She wore gold hoop earrings, which she called her "Gypsy" earrings, and she always seemed proud when she talked about them. I didn't know what a Gypsy was at that time, but my mother gave me the idea that being one was somehow wild and free. Now I know that Gypsies, the Roma people of the world, are the quintessential "dark other."

> From the time their ancestors began wandering west from northern India over 1,000 years ago, Roma people have been simultaneously scorned and glorified, rejected and romanticized. They are almost mythical and magical beings, representing people outside the confines and mundane realities of the everyday world...[7]
>
> Roma call the female divinity Sara-Kali. They defer to the church of the area they inhabit outwardly, but "keep their own beliefs in the dark mother in an oral and secret tradition...Like prehistoric and contemporary Africans, Hindus, and other earth-bonded peoples, gypsies consider everything alive to be sacred." [8]

In Isabel Fonseca's leading book about the Roma people, Bury Me Standing, she talks about women and power:

> The oldest woman in the family...had a great deal of power...it is women who possess the darkest and most forbidding powers. Their legitimacy resides in knowledge of spirits and medicinal cures, and ultimately in their ability to pollute men. Death, the final authority, is a man, but only a woman can frighten him off. [9]

I went to the 7th annual Herdeljezi Festival in Sebastopol, California in May of 2003. This event was presented by the "Voice of Roma" organization, which encourages the use of the term Roma to refer to their people, rather than Gypsy. [10]

My maternal grandmother, Ethel Lavina (Mullen) Hatcher was Irish and Dutch. She was born on the Gulf of Mexico, in Rockport, Texas, near Corpus Christi. It was humid, salty, hot, and racist down there in 1903 when she came into this world. She told me stories about her great great grandmother who was an "Indian princess." She said this ancestor was a Shawnee. I did some research and learned that the Shawnee joined the Cherokee on the Trail of Tears.

Everyone else in my family denied this Native American heritage, but my grandmother told me about it again and again as I grew up. Perhaps the family wanted to forget because this relative was a "dark other."

My grandmother married Gus Luthringer. a great-great grandson of immigrants from the Alsace-Lorraine farming region near the France/German border. Luthringer comes from Lothringer, which is related to the name of that region. My grandfather was born in 1897, and rode the Chisholm Trail as a cowboy, driving the cattle from San Antonio to Abilene. They lived their life as tenant farmers, laboring in the caress of DDT spray and recurrent, bank account depleting drought.

My father, Laurence Lee Johnson, was born in the first spring of the twentieth century in Greensburg, Kansas. His family tree, on the Whipple side, shows a Lakota Sioux back in the 1700s—he never told me about that. In the 1920s, he earned a history degree at the University of Oklahoma, a law degree at Cumberland University in Tennessee, and was a 32nd degree Mason.

My father was secretive about his Masonic activities, but he sometimes gave me psychic exercises to do when he was on his way out of town. He would ask me to send him telepathic messages, which he would then compare with me when he came home. I knew he was up to something, but I didn't find out much, because he was gone by the time I was 13. But, let's get back to the Masons.

I was engineering a radio show on KPFA back in the early 1990s, and the guest being interviewed was an expert on the Masons. I just ran across the notes I took back then, tucked into my copy of *The Secret Teachings of All Ages*. [11] The Masons study the spiritual schools of the Egyptians, and the tree of life called the Kabbalah. The Knights Templars started in the Middle Ages and went underground by using the Tarot deck. They believed that when buildings were built a certain way, energy was released that let the spirit unite with God. The Masons were given these secrets.

Now I know that the Kabbalah includes the concept of the Shekhinah, the feminine face of God.

> The rabbinic concept of Shekhinah, divine immanence, blossoms into the feminine half of God, balancing the patriarchal conception that dominates the Bible and Talmud...The kabbalist yearns to recover that primordial tradition, to regain cosmic consciousness, without renouncing the world. [12]

This description of regaining cosmic consciousness while staying connected to the earth, is the message of the dark mother, through and through. She is the soul of justice, compassion, and liberation. Through all of these mysterious ways and traditions, through the words of my mother, my grandmother, and my father (on some level), the dark mother's presence entered my life as I was growing up.

As I look around my own home, almost every room has a picture of a dark woman on the wall. Many of these are of Polynesian women, since I have made more than eighty trips to Pacific islands. I hung these pictures long before I read dark mother.

I have also felt drawn to the Virgin de Guadalupe since 1975 when I had a wild experience with her, way out in the desert, down in Baja California. Driving straight through from San Francisco, we pulled off the road about midnight, on the darkest night, in the middle of nowhere, at least 100 miles from the nearest town down in Baja. It was still a sweltering 85 degrees with not a hint of a breeze. We opened all the doors of the van and fell into an exhausted sleep. As soon as we fell asleep, there was a very loud, sharp knocking on the roof of the van that kept up for maybe 15 seconds. It scared us to death. We turned on all the lights that we had, and found that we were parked right in front of a huge boulder with an eight-foot high painting of the Virgin de Guadalupe on it. This was obviously a shrine of some significance. Whatever this place was, it was not meant to be a camping place—that much was certain. We flew into the front seat and drove as fast as we could for several hours to the coast of the Sea of Cortez, not saying a single word. I still don't know what happened that night, but I certainly have a great deal of respect for Nuestra Señora.

Artistically, I have been drawing spirals and flowering vines and wavy line motifs since I was a teenager. I doodle them on scraps of paper, notebooks, and grocery lists, especially when I'm on the telephone, and thinking about something else. In dark mother, we learn about the

> …rock paintings found in central and south Africa with a predominance of the color red or purple, and characterized by spirals, straight or wavy lines, petals, and concentric circles in series (L. Luca Cavalli-Sforza)—signs, according to Marija Gimbutas, of the woman divinity of prehistory. [13]

The curtains hanging in my bedroom have a vine and flower pattern on them. I have a purple velvet couch, a maroon leather chair—in fact, my whole living room is resonant in these colors. She is everywhere.

Speaking of dark mother showing up unannounced, one of my favorite stories is one that Marion Woodman told me recently:

> Marion was alone, and terribly ill in a hotel room in India for a week—so ill that she couldn't get off the floor for days, and could not move. Finally, wasted by dysentery, she crawled down stairs to the front desk and sat on the bench there. After a while, a very large, very dark woman came and sat beside her. She didn't just sit down beside her; she sat down very close beside her, and leaned into her with all her body. She was so dark, she was almost black, and very warm. She sat there all day, never uttering a word, pressing her dark, warm flesh into Marion's body. The next day, she did the same thing. She continued to come for four days. On the fifth day, Marion came downstairs and sat down on the bench again, but the dark woman did not come. The hotel manager came over to her and said, "My wife will not be coming today. I saw that you were dying, and I sent her, but now you will live, so she does not need to come anymore." Marion adds, "Now that was the feminine face of God. [14]

The memory of the dark mother allows us not only to heal, but also to become. I was suddenly inspired to write a chant for Her, while working on this chapter:

> Dark Compassion
> Mother Equality
> Dark Liberation
> Mother Transformation

Dark Memory
Mother Intuition
Dark Migration
Mother Witch
Dark Grandmother
Mother Madonna
Dark Mother
Mother Ancestor
Dark Godmother
Mother Guadalupe
Dark Divinity
Mother Mystery

Lucia Birnbaum sums it all up when she says,

> The key to understanding world history, as well as the possibility that we can all live together in peace, may be related to acknowledging that signs—later icons—of the dark mother of central and south Africa, are the earliest human veneration we know. [15]

I am willing to pay the sometimes painful price for continuing to dig up forgotten, hidden, and repressed memories of the dark mother in my family and in my world, because in bringing memories of Her to the surface, I feel reborn, reconnected to the Earth, and reunited with my Great Mother. She is everywhere, and as I write this last sentence, I look up and realize that today is Mother's Day, 2003!

I'd like to acknowledge those shining lights who have helped me find my way: Lucia Birnbaum, Harvey Birenbaum, Marion Woodman, Patti Boucher, Freyja, Astarte, Lorraine, Ethel, The Robins Foundation, and all those other special stars in the night sky.

Notes

1 Lucia Chiavola Birnbaum, Ph.D., *dark mother*, african origins and godmothers, (Nebraska: iUniverse, 2001).

2 Birnbaum, Ph.D., xxiii.

3 Birnbaum, Ph.D., xxv.

4 Matthew Fox, radio broadcast, KPFA FM, Berkeley, Ca. June 18, 2003.

5 Lucia C. Birnbaum, Ph.D., paper, conference of the American Academy of Religion, University of California at Davis.

6 Birnbaum, Ph.D., xxxvi.

7 Michal Shapiro, *Gypsy Caravan* CD liner notes, (Putumayo: New York, 2001) 3–4.

8 Birnbaum, Ph.D., 132.

9 Isabel Fonseca, *Bury Me Standing: The Gypsies and Their Journey*, (New York: Vintage Books, 1995) 80.

10 Voice of Roma, *The Current Plight of the Kosovo Roma*, (Sebastopol: Voice of Roma, 2002) ii.

11 Manly P. Hall, *The Secret Teachings of All Ages: An Encyclopedia Outline of Masonic, Hermetic, Quabbalistic, and Rosicrucian Philosophy*, (Los Angeles: The Philosophical Research Society, 1928.

12 Daniel C. Matt, *The Essential Kabbalah*, (San Francisco: Harper Collins, 1996) 2.

13 Birnbaum, Ph.D., xxxv.

14 Marion Woodman, interview on KPFA FM, Berkeley, CA, with Sandy Miranda, M.A., Feb. 14, 2003.

15 Lucia C. Birnbaum, Ph.D., paper, conference of the American Academy of Religion, University of California at Davis.

Bibliography

Birnbaum, Ph.D., Lucia Chiavola. *dark mother: african origins and godmothers*. Nebraska: iUniverse, 2001. A fabulous book.

Matt, Daniel C. *The Essential Kabbalah*. San Francisco: Harper Collins, 1996. A soulful book on the heart of Jewish Mysticism.

Fonseca, Isabel. *Bury Me Standing: The Gypsies and Their Journey*. New York: Vintage, 1995. The most accessible book on the world of the Roma people.

Cavalli-Sforza, Luigi Luca and Francesco Cavalli-Sforza. The Great Human Diasporas: The History of Diversity and Evolution. Cambridge, MA: Perseus Books, 1995.

Voice of Roma. *The Current Plight of the Kosovo Roma*. Sebastopol: Paul Polansky, et al., 2002. Field research and reports.

Birnbaum, Ph.D., Lucia Chiavola. *Signs and images of the African dark mother in Spain*. Paper, Pan African womanist section, Conference of the American Academy of Religion, University of California at Davis. Sunday March 23, 2003.

Shapiro, Michal. Liner notes from *Gypsy Caravan* CD. New York: Putumayo, 2001.

Woodman, Marion. *Radio Interview with Sandy Miranda, M.A.* Berkeley, CA: KPFA FM, 2003. Information about the Dark Divinity of India also available on Woodman's cassette tape, *The Crown of Age: the Rewards of Conscious Aging*. Boulder, Co.: SoundsTrue, 2002.

Hall, Manley P. *The Secret Teachings of All Ages: An Encyclopedia Outline of Masonic, Hermetic, Quabbalistic, and Rosicrucian Philosophy*, Los Angeles: The Philosophical Research Society, 1928. This edition, 1988.

The Dark Mother of the Qabalah

Pamela Eakins, Ph.D.

I gave birth to all
that was, is, and ever shall be
things of beauty, tenderness
pelican and eagle—first to come—
guarded the entrance of cave/womb/home
gentle, delicate hens
pelican gave blood to swallow
eagle feathered the hollow

—The Mother of the Cosmos[1]

The Primal Feminine

Binah represents the female potency of the universe.

—Dion Fortune, initiate in the Qabalistic mysteries[2]

Creating a world, Qabalists say, requires a trinity.

The structure behind all matter is formulated by a supernal triad: She who creates all form, He who instills in her the force that enspirits form, and the Blessed Holy One who brings the cosmic lovers into being, drawing them forth from primordial air and imbuing each, in equal measure, with the fiery breath of beginning.

362

She is called Binah, He is called Chokmah, and the One who precedes them is nameless and formless, but crowns all creation as the Blessed Holy One.

Binah is venerated as Understanding, Chokmah as Wisdom, the Blessed Holy One as All Potential.

Binah (figure 1), the dark, fluidic feminine, receives radiant lifeforce from each of the other two, takes this fiery energy into her being, and in this place, creates and spins out the nature of every form in the universe. She is the Great Mother, the Luminous Sea, the watery well from which all life emits and to which all life returns.

Binah is primeval, primordial, pristine water. Chokmah is cosmic fire. The Blessed Holy one exists before and beyond all differentiated energies. Together, the three ignite existence, and Binah, the cosmic mother in the holy trinity, brings all that is into being.

Her Darkness

> ...the 'belly' or 'womb'...the subterranean darkness...chasm, cave, abyss, valley, depths...
>
> —Erich Neumann, analytical psychologist[3]

Binah is the supernal mother of all form.[4] She lives across the Abyss from manifestation, on the other side of the River of Forgetfulness that separates this world from the next, the seen world from the unseen. From her home on the supernal plane, in that other world which we humans can barely grasp and cannot truly know, she mixes the constituent parts of every form of life in the radiant darkness of her inner sea. In her radiant darkness, she evolves the structure behind all form, the "blueprint" for all creation.

Her life-forms individuate and free-fall, tumbling like dandelion fluffs floating lightly across the Abyss. They spiral into the manifest world where they come to rest in the wombs of worldly mothers and in the phantom wombs of men and women with imagination.

Binah's children are contained in every form in the world of matter. Hers are the children of spirit, heart, mind and body. Every form known in the manifest world, including every form of idea and emotion, belong to Binah, for she is the creatress, the mother of all being.

As Binah's children, we discover and employ the blueprints for form which Binah, the Great Cosmic Mother, provides.

Discovering and using is not always easy for us. Our seeking may require a journey into the uncharted darkness of the mother's realm. The venture may be fraught with difficulty. And, yet, it is the difficulty grows us.

Our mother knows that the purpose of existence is to grow the soul. As we evolve our individual souls, the soul of the world concomitantly develops. We may pass through painful periods in our evolutionary process, but we must stretch to grow. That is out path. It is as if we are ever in the forest—searching for the holy grail.

When we search for the holy grail, the elixir of the eternal—as we, as humans, must do—we are searching for Binah. We are ever-remembering and longing for our ancient mother, the never-ending nurturant wellspring of life. From the darkness of her inner recesses we emerged. Into that womb, we shall return. And, from that darkness, we shall be born again and again and again in form after form after form.

This we remember—if through the veil darkly.

Binah knows our path, how we must emerge into this bright, cold world, round the nadir of existence, and begin our quest for meaning. As we journey, Binah cradles, cajoles and nurtures us from the unseen plane. She understands our pain and laments with us in our sorrow as we outgrow and cast off forms we have cherished, even, in the end, casting away the form of our body which we surrender like a holy cloak, as we return, return, a naked spent filament returning to the sea from which it came.

Her Receptivity

Empty, Open
desire yearning…
MotherCore
in its secret and original form…
consecrated space that wants to be filled
moist, preserving
and waiting.

—Tarot of the Spirit[5]

The word Qabalah means "to receive."

The Qabalah is the Tree of Life (figure 2) and these two terms—Qabalah and Tree of Life—are used interchangeably to refer to the diagram which outlines the structure of the universe and consciousness on this plane and the next. The Qabalah is an ancient system that outlines the nature of universal forces and forms and describes the relationships between them. [6]

Qabalah cannot be taught, even by the best teacher. The essence of the Qabalistic relationships, relationships between the various aspects of the Tree of Life, can be guided by a teacher but must be perceived and received by the student. The student must open and become willing and vulnerable, just as Binah is the open, willing and receptive partner in the supernal trinity. She, who is the essence of reception, symbolizes the receptive, enfolding and containing nature of life.[7]

On the plane of the supernals, Binah receives into herself the effulgence of the nameless, sexless, formless being, the entity they call the Blessed Holy One.[8] Sometimes the Holy One is called Kether, the source, the beginning, all potential, the Crown of Creation.[9] Sometimes the Holy One is called Ain Soph, "Without End." Ain Soph is the eternal state of Being and Non-Being, indefinable and absolute, without substance, without essence, called sometimes The Most Ancient of all the Ancients.[10] This one too is called Eheieh, which means I Am, That I Am.

Binah receives essential energies from Kether and also from her male counterpart, Chokmah, her consort on the plane of the supernals. Chokmah is the primal universal father, venerated as Wisdom, the Essence of Being.

As Chokmah is venerated as the Essence of Being, Binah is venerated as the God of Gods.

Chokmah is the power of force, the power of free-flying spirit blazing through the cosmos. Binah is the sea of form within which the spark of spirit comes to rest, is enrapt and divided into the "ten thousand" forms that make up the constituent parts of the world.

Chokmah is male, light and fiery, the positive or emitting side of the universal magnetic force that creates existence. Binah is female, dark, watery, the negative receiving side of the universal magnetic force that mixes, spins and issues forth.

And—even as one is negative and one is positive, like a magnet divided, each contains the other, and the mystery cannot be undone.

And—just like Binah, Chokmah receives essential energies, the spark, the spirit, from the the Blessed Holy One, the Most Ancient of All the Ancients.

Binah is as vulnerable as she is powerful, open to receive, mixing the cosmic elements to form her offspring. When the time is right, she births the idea of her children into the world. Her offspring travel across the Abyss that separates this world from the next and inhabit the wombs of their material parents, themselves—the parents—having sprung originally from the imagination of Binah.

And so it is that the Great Mother's enlightened son and radiant daughter come to inhabit the material plane, dropping into life to grow the soul.

Her Doorway

She is the door of nature. Because she is the cradle from which all souls emit and to which all souls return, she is a two way door.

She is the door of birth as well as the door of death.

—Tarot of the Spirit[11]

Binah is the essence of receptivity, the dark feminine form that embraces the free-floating radiance of the energy that enspirits life. Binah receives this energy on the supernal plane and then she transmits it into the world.

Radiant fiery light enters her body, mind, heart and spirit, enters through her sacred channels and exits through her birth canal, contained in all the patterns for the forms of the world.

Her doorway, the doorway through which all is received is called Daleth: Daleth, the Door; Daleth, the Luminous Intelligence.

The doorway of Daleth is opened by Venus, by love (see figure 3). Love is the key that opens the door to Binah's womb. Symbols for her doorway include the symbol for Venus, the Venusian cross, the symbol for woman, and the symbol of the ancient Egyptian ankh. The circle is the womb of Binah. The cross is the way into her womb, the pathway, the channel, the opening. The cross also points out the pathway to the most sacred knowledge.

Love is natural. Love is the essence of connection on the earth and in the seven heavens. Love is the medium that binds spirit to matter and sets all of life in motion. Binah's path is the path of love, her way is the way of love, and love in every exalted form is the highest attainable form of consciousness for she who is the Great Mother and her children who aspire toward enlightenment.

Binah is the essence of sympathy, empathy, compassion and kindness.

In loving, she accepts all. In loving, everything becomes possible. Love is the greatest gift and the greatest protection. All other forms of protection, Binah knows, lead to war.

Her Womb

> All rivers flow into the sea and the sea is not full—all (souls) go into this 'sea,' and the 'sea' takes them in and consumes them without becoming full; it brings them forth new and they go their way…
>
> —The Zohar[12]

The womb of Binah is the cradle of creativity. It is the womb of existence, beneath, before and beyond all matter.

In the womb of Binah, all substance and idea of substance congeal in the darkness and evolve into new forms.

She is the supernal womb, the cosmic yoni, the vesica piscis (figure 4), the cup of the world, the sacred chalice and the holy grail.

She creates and births new forms forever, because ever-new forms ever-grow the soul. Growing and evolving the soul is the purpose of existence, and no new form comes into being without the quiet mixing, forming and nurturing of the Dark Mother, Binah.

Her Manifestations

> The three mothers are a great, wonderful and unknown mystery…which gave birth to progenitors, and these progenitors gave birth again…"
>
> —The Sephir Yetzitah[13]

The Dark Mother of the Qabalah divides, differentiates, and appears in four primary manifestations.

Her first three manifestations, as elucidated in the mysterious writings of the *Sepher Yezirah*, are the first three elements, the elements from which all life emerges. These three elements are called the three mothers, the three fundamentals or the three mother letters. One, called Shin, hisses like fire. One, called Mem, is silent like water. One, called Aleph, reconciles fire and water and breathes like air. These are the mother letters of the Hebrew alphabet. They are the primordial universal vibrations that bring life into being, and, and from these three vibrations all else emerges—all sound, all form, all relationships.

The Great Mother of the Qabalah divides into the essence of fire, the essence of water and the essence of air (see figure 3).

She creates Heaven from fire, earth from water and air from air with which she balances all. In her three manifestations, she produces the year, produces heat from fire, produces coldness from water, and moistness from air which is the equalizer.

She produces humanity, male and female, creating the head from fire, the breast from water, and the body from air, which places all in equilibrium. [14]

And, Binah, who receives the divine spark from the Blessed Holy One, imagines and brings into existence the seven spheres of the world: The seven worlds, seven heavens, seven lands, seven seas, seven rivers, seven deserts, seven palaces, and the seven double letters of the Hebrew alphabet which correlate with wisdom, wealth, fruitfulness, life, dominion, peace and beauty. She creates time: Seven days of the week, the seven year cycle, each seventh year a year of release.

The Great Mother produces in sevens. She produces seven spheres on the plane of existence—our plane, the plane we humans inhabit. These spheres, called *sephiroth*, are outlined in the Qabalistic pattern on the Tree of Life. Seven is loved, say the teachers of old, in the whole of nature.[15]

Binah, in her guises and forms, comes to inhabit the constituent elements that make up life. She becomes Fire Mother, Water Mother, Wind Mother and, ultimately, Earth Mother.

The Fire Mother[16] (see figure A)

> The Fire Mother
> of the Steady Ray…
> actively lighting the way for those within
> her reign
> with her fathomless
> energy
>
> —Tarot of the Spirit[17]

Fire represents the energy of pure spirit. When Binah, the dark, wet, receptive mother of the Qabalah manifests as Fire Mother, she has dominion over the spiritual quest and all that is spiritual in nature.

Spirit is symbolized by the king of beasts, the lion of fire. Though Binah has comprehensive vision in this world and the next, she does not impose her vision on the king of beasts. Her task, rather, is to understand his nature. As she understands him—deeply—the lion becomes docile, tame and trusting. When the Fire Lion is tamed, all of nature is at the Mother's service.

Her dominion is spirituality, which is her love embodied.

As Fire Mother, Binah becomes a spiritual teacher. She teaches that you must delve into darkness to discover love which is the power and the motivator behind all lasting spiritual knowledge.

In the stories told on Earth, Binah, appearing in her cloak of fire, has been known by these names and many others: Itzpapalotl, the Mayan jaguar goddess, Vesta and Hestia, Roman and Greek fire goddesses, Sunna, the Scandanavian sun goddess, Pele, the Hawaiian goddess of fiery volcanoes, Bast, the Egyptian goddess of cats and Wurusemu, the Hittite goddess of the sun.[18]

The Water Mother (see Figure B)

Eternal Mother
a watery door...
look into her eyes
one is forced to face the Night
there are no lies—
only—
transmissions of emotion

—Tarot of the Spirit[19]

As the Water Mother, Binah appears in her own element. Water is the element that symbolizes emotion—and Binah's most exalted emotion is unconditional love. She is the shimmering tranquility which results from the endurance of emotions over time. Hers is the gift of subconscious vision.

Due to her tremendous capacity to receive, process in darkness and transmit into light, Binah, as the Water Mother, is the perfect agent. She conducts her children through emotional transitions. She moves her children to new levels of understanding, which involve the creation or adoption of new forms.

As Water Mother, Binah manifests as the exalted lover and the perfect mother.

She teaches that, when we face adversity with joy, burdens become lighter.

Through time and all the aeons of storytelling, Binah as the Water Mother, she who is cloaked in sea, has been known by the names of the goddesses of love, motherhood and dark initiations. She has been called Aphrodite, Helen, Venus, Lolita, Branwen, Mary, Maya, Kuan-Yin, Selene, Persephone, Inanna, Morgan Le Fay and Isis.

You have only to believe to realize her powers.

The Wind Mother (see Figure C)

> The Wind Mother
> is a keen observer
> quick and confident…
> razorsharp and ardent…
> her sharp edge cuts channels…
> breaks the screen of oppression
>
> —Tarot of the Spirit[20]

In her guise as Wind Mother, Binah is pure and triumphant in her transmission of truth. She is steadfast and clear in her understanding of reality. She knows that science is imperfect and growing. Sacred truth, however, remains always sacred truth. This is her teaching.

Binah, in her manifestation as Wind Mother, is clear, conscious perception. She illuminates and liberates the potential of the mind.

She teaches her children how they are led astray through non-productive thought patterns and how to transcend bondage. She teaches that the truth sets us free. Freedom comes with aligning with the eternal cosmic will. That is her lesson and the key to transcendence.

In the meandering tales told of her on Earth, Binah, in her cloak of wind, has been referred to as Indara in Indonesia, the creator goddess, Sao T'Sing Niang of China, the Broom Lady who sweeps away the clouds and then calls them back in times of draught, Athena in Greece, the Princess of Heaven, called Nambi in Uganda and Nuit in Egypt and Sarasvati in India.

With words and swords, the Wind Mother creates new paradigms and shifts ways of knowing on the plane of existence.

The Earth Mother (see Figure D)

> Garden Mother...
> Pleasure Mother
> watering abundance
> on barren planes
> serene/creative/bountiful...
> in the season for planting,
> she plants
> in the season for reaping,
> she reaps
> and she fills her skirts with blossoms
> to make garlands for her Children
> and laurels for the Poor
>
> —Tarot of the Spirit[21]

As the Earth Mother, Binah rejoices in life, loves the physical plane, loves the opportunity for manifestation, loves sticks, stones, bones, plants and babies. Earth's bounty is her bounty. Earth's beauty is her beauty.

The Earth Mother holds the key to prosperity. That key is love: Self-love, love of life, love of earth. Loving the self, she teaches, is no different from loving earth. For you are earth, she says, earth is you. All emanates from the same source. And—she would know; she *is* that source.

The Earth Mother finds joy in the power of the elements. She accepts their cycling power and moves within it. Because she serves the elements so well, they are at her command. In this way, Binah holds the universe in the palm of her hand. That is why her flowers, though temporary, are of exquisite beauty.

Binah, in her manifestation as the Earth Mother, teaches her children well the following lesson: By observing what heaven gathers unto itself and what earth gathers unto itself, you will understand the inner workings of all that is.

Through careful observation and with your own persistence, you will be able to put everything right.

Binah, as Earth Mother, has traveled every passageway of this planet—as Copper Woman and Changing Woman among Native Americans, Gaia among Greeks, Mati Syra Zemlja in Slavic countries, Mami and Mama in Sumeria, Mama Ocllo in Peru, Ma-Emma in Russia, Ila in India and Ishtar in Babylonia.

Her Motherhood

Zohar, Concealed of the Concealed, struck its aura.
The aura touched and did not touch this point.
Then this Beginning emanated
and made itself a palace for its glory and its praise.
There it sowed the seed of holiness
to give birth
for the benefit of the universe.
The secret is: "Her stock is a holy seed."[22]

Binah, the mother of form, receives the cosmic light and herself becomes a palace for glory and praise. She creates pairs of opposites through which her children aspire, grow and develop.

She creates, in the beginning, son and daughter, male and female. She creates emotion and intellect, two separate ways of knowing. She creates the polarities of mercy and severity and every virtue, each with its opposing force.

On the one scale she creates merit and on the other criminality. She creates strength and weakness, softness and hardness, wisdom and foolishness, wealth and poverty, fruitfulness and barrenness, life and death, dominion and dependence, peace and war, beauty and ugliness. Through these polarized forces, her children grow and develop, learning that opposing forces can often be placed in order by the tongue.[23]

The mother is a great, wonderful and unknown mystery.[24] Cosmic light flows into her dark womb, and, with this light, she creates all forms in order to teach her children the mysteries of unity and separation; birth, death and resurrection.

Her intelligence is luminous and every form she creates shines with the light of spirit.[25]

Her children, through their own awakening and seeking, begin to realize that they are the illumined ones. They come to know themselves as spirit materialized: Spiritualized matter. This is the grand lesson and the greatest teaching of the earth plane. Each child, upon achieving the realization of enlightenment, becomes the radiant awakened one, called by Qabalists, the holy Shekhinah.

This is the mystery of the holy Shekhinah, as spoken in the mystical poetry of the *Zohar*[26]

> Come and see;
> There are four lights.
> Three are concealed and one is revealed.
> A shining light.
> A glowing light; it shines like the clear brilliance of heaven.
> A purple light that absorbs all lights.
> A light that does not shine
> but gazes toward the others and draws them in.
> Those lights are seen in her as in a crystal facing the sun.
> The first three are concealed,
> overseeing this one,
> which is revealed.

We all come from the Dark Mother, but do not be misled by titles. Attune to her mysteries and you will know that the enlightened do greatly shine, and her darkness is, indeed, *radiant.*[27]

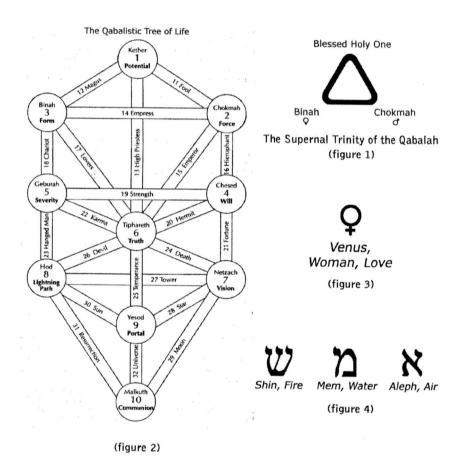

The Qabalistic Tree of Life

Kether
1
Potential

12 Magus   11 Fool

Binah
3
Form

14 Empress

Chokmah
2
Force

18 Chariot   17 Lovers   13 High Priestess   15 Emperor   16 Hierophant

Geburah
5
Severity

19 Strength

Chesed
4
Will

23 Hanged Man   22 Karma   Tiphareth
6
Truth   20 Hermit   21 Fortune

26 Devil   24 Death

Hod
8
Lightning
Path

25 Temperance   27 Tower   Netzach
7
Vision

30 Sun   28 Star

31 Resurrection   Yesod
9
Portal

32 Universe   29 Moon

Malkuth
10
Communion

(figure 2)

Blessed Holy One

Binah   Chokmah
♀   ♂

The Supernal Trinity of the Qabalah
(figure 1)

♀

Venus,
Woman, Love

(figure 3)

שׁ   מ   א
Shin, Fire   *Mem, Water*   *Aleph, Air*

(figure 4)

Mother

Mother

FIRE

Fire Mother (Figure A)

WATER

Water Mother (Figure B)

Mother

Mother

WIND

Wind Mother (Figure C)

EARTH

Earth Mother (Figure D)

Notes

1 Pamela Eakins, *Tarot of the Spirit*, York Beach, Maine: Samuel Weiser, Inc., 1992: 265–266.

2 Dion Fortune, *The Mystical Qabalah*, York Beach, Maine: Samuel Weiser, Inc., 1984 (1935): 140.

3 Erich Neumann, *The Great Mother*, Princeton: Princeton University Pres: 1974 (1955): 44.

4 "Mother" and "matter" have the same Indo-European root: ma, is-ness, substance

5 Eakins, p. 122.

6 While the historical details of the Qabalah are largely unknown, the structure of the system is said to have its origins in ancient Egypt. Two mystical books describing Qabalistic knowledge include the *Sepher Yezirah*, said to have been written before the third century, and the *Zohar*, said to have been written in the thirteenth century. See following footnotes for specific translations.

7 There can be no material life without the spark of lifeforce that matter contains; the spiritual quest revolves around awakening this knowledge.

8 See Daniel Chanan Matt, *Zohar, The Book of Enlightenment*, New York: Paulist Press, 1983.

9 Ain Soph refers to the diffuse energies of the Holy One, everywhere, in everything, like salt in the sea. The Holy One is called Kether at the moment when holy energies gather and intensify, setting in motion the process of creation.

10 Manly P. Hall, *The Secret Teachings of All Ages*, Los Angeles, California: The Philosophical Research Society, 1988 (1929): 117.

11 Eakins, p. 268.

12 as quoted by Erich Neumann in *The Great Mother* (Princeton, NJ: Princeton University Press, 1963, p. 242.

13 Isador Kalish, *Sepher Yezirah*, Gillette, New Jersey: Heptangle Books, 1987: III, i.

14 *Sepher Yezirah*, III, i-v.

15 *Sepher Yezirah*, VI, xvi.

16 Her images are from the *Tarot of the Spirit* tarot card deck, painted by Joyce Eakins, *Tarot of the Spirit*, U.S. Games, 1992.

17 Eakins, p. 108.

18 For splendid comprehensive information about the goddesses who have been, are, and ever shall be, see Lucia Chiavola Birnbaum, *dark mother, african origins and godmothers*, New York: Authors Choice Press, 2001; Elinor W. Gadon, *The Once & Future Goddess*, San Francisco: Harper & Row, 1989; Patricia Monaghan, *The Book of Goddesses & Heroines*, St. Paul, Minnesota: Llewellyn Publications, 1990; Barbara G. Walker, T*he Woman's Encyclopedia of Myths and Secrets*, San Francisco: Harper & Row, 1983.

19 Eakins, p. 152–153.

20 Eakins, p. 195–196.

21 Eakins, p. 239.

22 Isaiah 6:13; see Matt, p 49–50.

23 *Sepher Yezirah*, III, i; IV; i-iii.

24 See *Sepher Yezirah*, III, i.

25 Eakins, p. 267.

26 Matt, p. 108.

27 For more information about Qabalistic mystery school teachings, please write to Pamela Eakins at Pacific Center, Box 3191, Half Moon Bay, CA 94019. For expedited information, include your email address.

Magdalene Mass

Mari P. Ziolkowski, Ph.D.

Preface

I come to this work having grown up in the Catholic church, and having left my religious tradition of origin behind. When my life as a sensual woman no longer fit into the parameters the church had designed for it, I left, without fanfare. The 'liberation theology' of the church had simply liberated me. Magdalene was the only one who came with me. And as I moved into exploration of alternative spiritual traditions, as I searched for traditions that honored me as a woman, she was always there in the background. I see it now. Through many years of research, through many years of personal work, she was the first one who could hold all of me. As well, she proved a natural stepping stone to exploration of the goddess traditions. I thought I knew who she was. However, when my first major research project in the Women's Spirituality doctoral program at the California Institute of Integral Studies focused on her, I was blown away...

Not the repentant sinner, the harlot, the Catholic Church would have had me believe, the one who first saw Christ in resurrected form instead was instead called prophet, visionary, and companion of Christ in the Gnostic Gospels.[1] By others she was alleged to be a priestess of ancient goddess traditions and initiator of Christ.[2] In popular research she was linked to the legends of the Holy Grail (as *the* chalice carrying the bloodline of Christ to France),[3] and as Black Madonna,[4] she was a connection to the African Dark Mother traditions. With legendary references to her ascetic life in the desert in the south of France, and links to skull iconography, she can even be named 'tantric yogini.'[5]

Each person will have to decide for herself who Magdalene is. Myself, I honor her in all these roles. I honor her as a vehicle of the divine feminine manifest on the earth plane, priestess, teacher, semi-divine yogini. I honor her as co-redemptrix, initiator and soul-mate to Christ. And I honor her as doorway to the Dark Mother, she who holds all the paradox of the world within Her. This mass is my offering to Her, and to the rebalancing of energy between the masculine and feminine here on the earth plane.

Jai Ma (Victory to the Mother)...

Magdalene Mass ⁶

<u>Entrance Song</u>: "Ancient Mother"[7]

<u>Greeting</u>

Priestess: I invoke the name of the Mother, the Daughters, the Spirit of the Goddess to be present with us today.

All: Amen, Blessed Be

Priestess: May the Spirit of the Divine Feminine and Sacred Masculine be with you All.

All: And also with you.

<u>Penitential Rite</u>

Priestess: May the Divine Mother Goddess look kindly on us, bring us into Balance. And lead us into Her everlasting moonlight, starlight, and Firelight realms...

<u>Gloria</u>

(All): Glory to Goddess in the Highest and peace to all the people and beings of The earth. Mother Goddess, heavenly Queen, we worship you, we give You thanks, we praise you in all your glory.

Magdalene, Daughter of the Goddess, you who help us confront the fears of the world, come to us now. Seated at the right hand of the Mother, Receive our prayer.

You alone are the Holy One

You alone are Goddess

You alone are the Most High, Daughter, Spirit,

In the Glory of God the Mother. Amen.

First Reading: A reading from the Book *I Remember Union* from the Chapter entitled "And They Came to Me, The People"[8]

This is the Word of the Mother

All: Thanks be to the Goddess.

Second Reading:
A reading from the Book *I Remember Union*, Chapter entitled "Forging of Male and Female"[9]

This is the Word of the Mother.

All: Thanks be to the Goddess

Gospel: A reading from the Book *I Remember Union*, Chapter entitled "The Crucifixion of Jesus Christ"[10]

This is the Gospel of the Mother...

All: Glory and praise to you, O Daughter of the Goddess.

Homily
(Each person may share from the deep space within the impact of participating in this ritual honoring the role of Magdalene and the Goddess in the Easter mysteries.)

Creed

(All):   We believe in One Goddess
One with Many Faces.
Mother, Daughters, Spirit.
Creator of Heaven and Earth.

We believe in Her Daughter, Magdalene.
One of Many Daughters of the Goddess
Eternally Begotten of the Mother.
Goddess from Goddess. Light from Light.
Dark from dark. Begotten, and made,
One in being with the Mother.
Through Her all things were born. For us

All, and for our salvation she came through
The earth, by power of spirit, by power of
Woman and man, she became flesh.

For our sake she manifests on the physical plane.
For our joy, for our learning, she delights in the
Physical form.
For our sake, and the sake of the cosmos,
She came to teach the sacred masculine.
For our sake they came to show us the power
And beauty of the divine in matter, ourselves.
For our sake they came to show us the cycle of
Life, death and returning.

They are present Here with us and they are present in
the Heavens.
They come again in glory through us, calling us to
balance the
Divine Feminine and Sacred Masculine within ourselves, and the world.
We believe in the Goddess, The Giver of Life, who
proceeds from herself, And together with the Sacred
Masculine is worshipped and glorified.
She has spoken through her many prophets, through
Magdalene, through Us. We believe in the union of
souls, the union of beings. We Acknowledge baptism
of earth, air, fire, water. We look for the beauty of
Immanence, the continuing of the cycles, and pray
for the life of the world Now, and to come.

Intercessions

Priestess: We now take time to invoke the power of the goddess to bring us and our World back into balance. (We invite you to state out loud an Intention or prayer at this time)

Refrain: Let us pray to Her (each individual).

All: Goddess hear our prayer…(the whole group)

Offertory Song: "The Mummer's Song,"[11]
Bringing of the gifts (bread and wine, altar objects).

Preface to Eucharistic Prayer

Priestess: Mother, it is our joy and our salvation always and everywhere to give You thanks, through your beloved daughter, Magdalene, and your Beloved son, Christ. They are the word through whom you make the Universe, the Saviors you sent to bring us back into balance. By your Power, they took Flesh, were born, lived in boldness and love, and opened Their hearts to us. They taught us not to fear death and revealed the Incarnate divine in us. In this, they fulfilled your will and won us back to Ourselves, a holy People. And so, we join the angels and spirit guides, the Ancestors and the Spirits of earth, air, fire, water in proclaiming your Glory as we say:

All: Holy, Holy, Holy, Goddess of Power and Might. Heaven and earth are Full of your glory. Hosanna in the Highest. Blessed is she and he who Come in your name. Hosanna in the Highest.

Eucharistic Prayer

Priestess: Goddess, you are holy indeed, the fountain of all holiness. Let your Spirit come upon these gifts to honor their innately divine nature. So we May see them for what they are: the body and blood of the Divine Feminine and Sacred Masculine.

As each mother gives of her body and blood to bring a new soul across...As the World Mother gives of her body and blood to nourish us daily...

So too does the Christ give of his body and blood to bring in and nourish A new collective Soul.

Before the sacred masculine was given up to death, to the cycles, they Took the bread and gave thanks, saying to those gathered:

Take and Eat.
This is my body.
The body of the Mother
Which is given up daily
So that you may live.

When the sharing was ended, they took the cup and said:

Take this all of you and drink from it.
This is the cup of my blood.
The blood of the Mother.
The blood of the Moon.
The blood of the New and Everlasting
Covenant between women and men.
It is shed for you, and for all—for birth, for
Life, to bring us back into balance.
Do this in memory of us...

Let us proclaim the Mystery of Faith:

   (All):   She dies. She rises. She comes again.

He dies. He rises. He comes again.

Priestess:
In memory of life, death and the rising, we offer you, Mother, this Life giving bread, this saving cup. We thank you for calling us here to

Stand in your presence and honor you. May all of us who share in

The blood of the Mother, and the blood of the Sacred Masculine be

Brought together in unity of mind/body/spirit.

Goddess, remember your people throughout the world—those struggling against oppression and war in any form. Make us grow in love for each Other. Remember our ancestors who have gone to rest. May they rise again in our heart and spirits. May they come to the light and dark of Your Presence.

Be with us all, help us see our own worthiness in your eyes, that we may praise you in union with all and give you glory here on earth.

Doxology:

Through Her

With Her

In Her

In Unity with the Sacred Masculine

All glory and honor is yours Divine Mother.

Forever and Ever…

Hail Mother

(All):   Hail Mother,
                          Full of Grace
                          The Power is with Thee
                          Blessed are You
                          Queen of the Universe
                          And Blessed is All of Creation
                          Holy Mother
                          Maker of All Things
                          Be with us now and Always.
                          Blessed Be.[12]

Priestess: Deliver us Goddess, from projecting our shadow unto
                          others. Grant us Peace. Grant the world peace. Keep
                          us in balance with you, the earth, and Each other.
                          Help us confront our fears as we embody the change
                          we wish To see in our world

All: For the Queendom, the power and the glory are
                          yours, Almighty Mother, Forever and ever. Blessed
                          Be.

Priestess: Divine Feminine and Sacred Masculine, you give us
                          peace, your peace You send us. Look not only on our
                          imbalances, but on the quest for Faith in you. Grant
                          us peace and unity here on earth, where you live For-
                          ever and ever...

Sign of Peace

Priestess: The peace of the Goddess is in you.

All: And also in you.

Priestess: Let us offer each other a sign of Her peace (e.g.
                          handshake, hug, kiss)

Breaking of the Bread

Priestess: This is the gift of the Goddess:

All: Yes, I am worthy to receive you. Only say the word
                            and we shall be healed

Communion Songs: "She Who Hears the Cries of the World"[13], "By My
Side"[14]

                            (Pass around bread and wine to each other, saying:
                            This is Her body, This is Her blood.)

Concluding prayer

Reading from "Omaggio a Maria Maddalena"[15]

                    Maria Maddalena, Madonna macchiata, malaugu-
                    ratamente maledetta.

                    Medea minacciosa, I malinformati misogini ti malig-
                    nano a messa: meretrice!

                    Ma Mai! Mentono! Mistificano!

                    Madre maltrattata, meriti meglio!

                    Miracolosa maga, maliarda medioorientale,

                    Moglie del Messia massacrata malaccortamente,

                    Marciasti a Marsiglia una mamma.

                    Mantenesti la missione matriarcale. Manifestasti
                    magia.

                    Mammasantissima, I marsigliesi magnificano al mare
                    a maggio.

                    Meraviglioso!

                    Mai muta, io mantengo memoria.

            "Homage to Mary Magdalene"

                    Mary Magdalene, stained Madonna, unluckily
                    cursed.

                    Threatening Medea, the misinformed misogynists
                    malign you at mass: harlot!

                    But never! They lie! They falsify!

                    Mistreated mother, you deserve better!

> Miraculous magician, Middle Eastern enchantress,
>
> Wife of the ruthlessly massacred Messiah, you went to Marseilles a mother.
>
> You maintained the matriarchal mission. You manifested magic.
>
> O most holy Mother, the Marseillese extol your praises at the sea in May.
>
> Marvelous!
>
> Never mute, I maintain your memory.

Priestess: Go in peace to love and serve the Goddess

All: Thanks be to Her.

<u>Concluding Song</u> (and dance):

> "Nigra sum sed Formosa," (I am Black and Beautiful)[16]

Notes

1 For discussion see Elaine Pagels, *The Gnostic Gospels* (New York: Random House, 1979).

2 For development of these ideas, see respectively Clysta Kinstler, *The Moon Under Her Feet* (San Francisco: Harper, 1989), and Flo Aeveia Magdalena, *I Remember Union* (Vermont: All Worlds Publishing, 1996).

3 For further discussion, see Baigent, Leigh and Lincoln in *Holy Blood, Holy Grail* (New York: Dell, 1982).

4 See Ean Begg, *The Cult of the Black Virgin* (New York: Arkana, 1996).

5 Some Catholic legends have it that Magdalene retreated to a cave, or to the desert in her latter years to pray and meditate, practicing the ascetic life—wearing no clothes, with hair her only covering. In fact, I have seen Catholic holy cards portraying her in this way (courtesy of Jean Fraschina, Dominican University Class, July 2003). As well, Susan Haskins in *Mary Magdalen: Myth and Metaphor* (Harcourt, 1994) discusses some of these legends. Portraits of Magdalene holding a skull in Starbird's *The Woman with the Alabaster Jar* (Santa Fe: Bear and Company, 1993): Plate 24., and her skull on display as holy relic in a church in Ste. Baume in the south of France (slide courtesy of Marguerite Rigoglioso, M.A., Berkeley: Bella Donna Lecture series, April 20, 2003) also bear similarities to another tradition. As this tradition, that of yoginis in India—women who sought magical power, bliss and spiritual liberation through ascetic, or tantric practices, women said to wander naked with long hair, often portrayed with skull iconography—is also one I have studied, it is I who make the leap to name Magdalene 'tantric yogini.' (For discussion of the latter see my paper *The Return of the Yogini*, as yet unpublished, 2001).

6 Structural Source, Catholic Mass, *Heritage Missal* (Oregon Catholic Press, 2003) 3–29.

7 On Wings of Song and Robert Gass, "Ancient Mother," *Ancient Mother* CD (Boulder, Colorado: Spring Hill Music, 1993) #1.

8 Flo Aeveia Magdalena, *I Remember Union* (Vermont: All Worlds Publishing, 1996) 97–99.

9 Ibid., 133–4.

10 Ibid., 313–16.

11 Loreena McKinnit, "The Mummer's Song," *Book of Secrets* CD (Ontario: Quinlan Road, 1997) #2.

12 Jennifer Berezan, "She Who Hears the Cries of the World," *She Carries Me* CD (Berkeley: Edge of Wonder Records, 1995) #1.

13 Ibid.

14 Jay Hamburger, Peggy Gordon, "By My Side," *GodSpell* (New York: Arista Records) Side 2, #3.

15 Marguerite Rigoglioso, M.A., "Omaggio a Maria Maddalena" (Unpublished poem, 1998).

16 Alessandra Belloni/I Giullari de Piazza, "Nigra Sum Sed Formosa," *Earth, Sun, Moon* CD (New York: Lyrichord Discs, Inc.) #4

Bibliography

Baigent, Michael, Richard Leigh, and Henry Lincoln. *Holy Blood, Holy Grail*. New York: Dell, 1982.

Begg, Ean. *The Cult of the Black Virgin*. New York: Arkana, 1996.

Belloni Alessandra and I Giullari de Piazza. "Nigra Sum Sed Formosa." *Earth, Sun, Moon* CD (New York: Lyrichord Discs, Inc) #4.

Berezan, Jennifer. "She Who Hears the Cries of the World," *She Carries Me* CD. Berkeley: Edge of Wonder Records, 1995, #1.

Catholic Mass. *Heritage Missal*. Oregon Catholic Press, 2003.

Fraschina, Jean. *Magdalene Holy Card*, Dominican University Class, San Rafael: July, 2003.

Hamburger, Jay and Peggy Gordon. "By My Side." *GodSpell*. New York: Arista Records

Haskins, Susan, *Mary Magdalen: Myth and Metaphor*. Harcourt, 1994.

Kinstler, Clysta. *The Moon Under Her Feet*. San Francisco: Harper, 1989.

Magdalena, Flo Aeveia. *I Remember Union*. Vermont: All Worlds Publishing. 1996.

McKinnit, Loreena."The Mummer's Song." *Book of Secrets* CD, Ontario, Canada: Quinlan Road, 1997, #2.

On Wings of Song and Robert Gass. "Ancient Mother." *Ancient Mother CD*. Boulder: Spring Hill Music. 1993.

Pagels, Elaine. *The Gnostic Gospels*. New York: Random House, 1979.

Rigoglioso, M.A., Marguerite. "Omaggio a Maria Maddalena." Unpublished poem, 1998.

_____. Magdalene Slide Show (Berkeley: Bella Donna Lecture Series, April 20, 2003).

Starbird, Margaret. *The Woman with the Alabaster Jar*. Santa Fe: Bear and Company, 1993.

Ziolkowski, Ph.D., Mari. *The Return of the Yogini*. Unpublished paper, 2001.

The Sigh of the Earth

Miri Hunter Haruach, Ph.D.

Dear Daughters of Gaia,

I have watched you from the depths of the planet. I have watched you since and before Sumer. I am waiting and have been waiting for the blood of your lips to flow once more into the earth and nourish your starving mother.

Have you forgotten how to pray? Have you forgotten how to call me? To ask? Whatever you ask for in my name shall be given. Did you forget? I have called you so many times that I am weak and tired. Very tired. Thirsty. Longing for a drop, just one drop of nourishing liquid from your lips. Oh daughters of the earth, let your blood flow down into my depths to nourish your mother as you would nourish your child.

Why do I feel that the holy elixir of your bodies is saved only for the nourishment of your sons? Your men. It is your power they seek. Bleed unto me and I will help you return to yourselves. I will be midwife and witness to your rebirth. I have not forgotten you, but your sons, Buddha and Jesus, Gilgamesh and Noah, Mohammed and Abraham deny you. They usurp your power and call it their own. Were it not for my weakness, I would laugh at their folly. They are nothing without you. Have you forgotten your power? Have you forgotten the beauty that you possess? Your magic? Are you sleeping? Are you scared to come home?

I have a gift for you. For it is time that you re-member me. It is time that you once again nourish the planet and pray to your mother. I am calling you. You cannot mistake the sound of my voice in the wind. The song is familiar. You know it. Have always known it. I still hear you sing it sometimes. Sometimes when your mind is at peace, your soul at rest.

The song is not my gift. My gift is the opportunity to look upon yourself. To see yourself in the reflection of my sister, the moon. She becomes a mirror now. A reflection of your past. She has agreed to show you how you came to be where you are. She has agreed to remain full, so that you may see all that there is to know. She will be full not for three days, but she will be full until you have seen yourself and know yourself. She will be full until you are once again full. Full of your power. So take care my daughters and use this gift wisely. I await your return.

Your Mother,

Gaia

And so it came to pass that one day the sun did not rise. Nor did it rise the following day or the next week. An entire month went by and there was no sun. All the men gathered at a world conference that was conducted entirely on the internet. The men seemed afraid of this phenomenon. They were afraid to stray too far from familiar territory.

What the men did not know was that while they were busy conferring on line, the women of the planet were having their own conference on a newly formed telepathic network, which they called yoni-net. During the first week without sun, many women realized that they had a strong proclivity toward things that were once forbidden, i.e. psychic powers, prophetic dreams, etc. Within the second week of the lost sun, the women had discovered, by means of their yoni-network, that they were all bleeding and had been since the first sunless week. Women who had gone through menopause were once again bleeding as well as young girls who had never bled. They all agreed that this was an interesting coincidence. Many complained about the price of tampons and napkins. Some expressed relief from male sexual demands. No one felt weak or tired from the relentless bleeding. Strangely enough, things such as cramps and headaches, bloating and depression were not reported on the yoni-network. The general consensus was that the world of women was actually healthier than it had ever been. Some women reported complete healings of both a physical and a mental nature. Most women had ceased taking prescription medications. Drug dependency on the whole seemed negligible. The medical industry was going broke.

A prostitute said that the constant bleeding was not good for business, but money was no longer an issue and her john was never around. The bleeding brought with it a great sense of freedom, she commented. She did occasionally wonder, where all the men had gone. But those moments were getting to be fewer and far between. She was enjoying the new connection to her colleagues and the women she was meeting on the yoni-net.

Money was no longer an issue because the men were so busy networking and trying to find the reason behind the lack of sun that they forgot to open shops or run the stock market. They were lost in the world of e-mail.

One doctor in Switzerland reported that he did not understand why the women weren't all dead by now. They had been bleeding for more than two months—non-stop. If a cure wasn't found and soon, surely all the women would die of anemia. Unless, he wrote, gentlemen, we take this opportunity to find a way to stop women from bleeding!!! We will have to find a cure or it will mean the end of all mankind. All the men agreed. The great Swiss scientist said that he would use his wife for the experimentation process. Perhaps someone out there could start an International Stop The Bleeding Campaign. He would get back to the men as soon as he had something to report. He logged off the net.

A few days later, his wife logged on with the following message: Sorry to report that my beloved husband fell on his scalpel. I am now a lonely widow and will be retiring to East Africa.

Needless to say the internet was in a great state of havoc. Wires were getting crossed everywhere. Communication circuits were burning out all over the planet. Engineers and technicians were repairing things as quickly as possible. The plans for the International Stop the Bleeding Campaign came to a halt.

Meanwhile, back on the yoni-network, the women, had decided that the encounter with the Swiss scientist was not an event to be taken lightly. Men were becoming more and more afraid. It was difficult to watch, and while there was sympathy and empathy for what the men were feeling, there was also a memory in the minds of many women. A time before when men were afraid of women and women's bleeding. A memory too painful to re-member.

The women turned their thoughts to present day matters. Since production of everything had ceased, there was much work to be done. Many women suggested that the first order of business should be the production of more feminine products such as napkins, tampons and scented deodorant sprays. Another woman commented that while the bleeding had actually brought her better health and cured her arthritis, blood did seem to be everywhere. How do I get it out of silk? Sewers were backing up. Other complaints were clouding up the yoni-net. There was no time to cook, clean, learn physics and bleed. Many women reported an overwhelming desire to get out of the cities and towns and just sit on the hills in the countryside.

Upon hearing that last comment, a woman from India said that she noticed that all the female animals were sitting and bleeding directly into the earth. Was this a good or bad thing? The yoni-network quickly lit up with stories from other women all over the world reporting the same findings. And, added a woman from Peru, where the animals have sat has sprung sweet fruit. Sometimes, commented a woman from Quebec, I hear music from the places the animals have sat. A great hush fell over the yoni-net. It was as if a great memory from somewhere, long ago, before once upon a time, was stirred.

Meanwhile, in East Africa, in the mountains of Ethiopia, a woman was emerging from her home. She was no stranger to the night or the miracle the planet was now experiencing. She walked to river in order to replenish herself. As she knelt down to drink, she saw, reflected in the water, another woman. As the two women turned to face each other, they both smiled in recognition. For they knew each other, had known each other and would know each other throughout all eternity.

I am light in the dark, said the Ethiopian woman.

And I am dark in the light, said the Swiss woman.

And together, they said to each other: we now heal the earth and replenish our Mother.

They kissed each other deeply. They made love beneath the moonlight. The animals came and watched. And as the women climaxed together, the animals joined in their cries of ecstasy. They slept in each other's arms.

After a few hours the women awoke. There was much work to be done. The animals had returned to their homes. As the women looked into the sky, they saw for the first time in months what no human eye had seen: a waning moon. The re-birthing process was beginning. The women spent a few hours catching up on past lifetimes and discussing future incarnations. The Swiss woman told the Ethiopian woman of her journey.

"My husband was more terrified when he found out that I wasn't bleeding. He didn't want his wife to look like a freak in front of the rest of the male community. I took a chance and explained to him the reason for the bleeding and the loss of the sun. He called me a witch. One day, I looked out my window and he was building a pyre. He was going to burn me at the stake for witchcraft. I jokingly told him that if he burned my body, he couldn't use it for his research. He was confused. I was starting to feel sorry for him until he turned on me with his scalpel. He always was clumsy with that thing."

"My sister, it is good to see again. Good to re-member with you. Shall we contact the others?" said the Ethiopian woman.

The two women sat and tuned into the yoni-network. There was a lot of chaos. Attempted burnings and drownings were reported by numerous women. These having failed the men were killing themselves in order to escape the terrible evil of the bleeding woman. If they couldn't rid the planet of female evil, they would rid themselves from the planet. Suicide armies were forming. Most men had abandoned the internet. It offered no salvation.

The women of the world had listened to the animals. They had abandoned the napkins, tampons and deodorants. They were moving into the countryside and bleeding into the earth. And where they bled, they built huts. And decorated them. They sang songs and danced. The women also found that once they bled into the earth for several days their bleeding would stop. They would then bathe in the nearest stream or river. And wait. They didn't know what they were waiting for, but they waited. They waited with a knowing and an awareness. All over the earth they waited.

The Ethiopian woman, whose name was Debra and the Swiss woman, whose name was Lydia, called to the waiting women. These women of all ages, sizes, and colors picked themselves up and began the trek from where they were to where the birth of civilization was and still is: The Ethiopian mountains. And as the women walked they sang:

> We're Mothers of the Universe
> Daughters of the Earth
> Mothers of the Universe
> We gave ourselves rebirth
> Mothers of the Universe
> Sighing with the earth

Come rest your head

On our nurturing breasts

And as they walked, they began to remember. The stories, the lost magic. They reclaimed their dreams as their reality. They began the re-telling and the re-claiming.

These are there stories:

Once I gave birth to a son. My labor was for days. The pain. They gave me drugs that took my pain. It was my pain. After the birth they sewed me so tight that I never wanted to be near a man. They replaced my pain with their pain. They took my son and made him a god. Everyone came and worshipped him. I stood by him, he was my son, but I could not climb the mountains they took in stride. I could not ride the animals in procession with him. He was a god and I was a woman. I was his mother. I watched him grow in stature. I watched the crowds grow, I, too, listened to his words waiting for the wisdom that would help me understand. But I never heard a word. I never heard his words. He, my son, spoke not of me or my sisters. My son, this god, had no use for us. No use for his mother. The person, the woman, who gave him life. Did he even know me? Did he remember me? My cunt ached from being sewn too tight. I ceased to follow him. He became god and I became old. I have bled for six months and now I know why. I, we, are reclaiming our yoni power. My loins grow stronger and I am reminded of the power of my blood.

Two women from different parts of the world came together and told this story:

My son

My son

was to be

was to be

a great

a great

leader.

leader.

She

She

tricked

tricked
the father
the father
of my son
of my son
into letting her
into kicking me
live.
from my home.
I hated her.
I hated her.
And he,
And he,
my son's father
my son's father
was weak.
was weak.
He is responsible
He is responsible
for more deaths
for more deaths
than any woman
than any woman
could give birth to.
could give birth to.
My son
My son
grew up to be
grew up to be
a leader
a leader
of a great
of a great

people.
people.
His people
His people
hated and despised
hated and despised
your son's people.
your son's people.
And I hated you
And I hated you
my sister
my sister
because I loved
because I loved
his father.
his father.
I did not
I did not
see you
see you
as me.
as me.
But look
But look
upward,
upward,
the moon, she wanes
the moon, she wanes
and with her
and with her
wanes
wanes
my fear

my hate

of you.

of you.

May our children

May our children

share in

share in

our peace.

our peace.

Another woman spoke her story to the women crossing the dessert into Ethiopia:

It was a secret from the world. I, was after all, a woman. No one would listen to me. So I told him of the goddess and her wisdom. He told them. They told the world. It was a holy doctrine. A sacred wisdom. The way of love. I cried many a tear when I returned centuries later and saw what had become of our sacred teachings. Greed had replaced love. Lust had replaced the erotic. And pain was everywhere. The goddess was nowhere. Her shrines were destroyed and replaced by false deities. I heard her daughters cry in pain as they were burned, tortured and raped. I watched as whole nations were wiped out in the name of god. God who had been goddess. You all know these stories. These horrors. The memories are not so long ago. But what you do not know of my story I am ashamed to tell.

She stumbles in her path and several other women go to her to help her. She startles them by screaming.

Do not help. For I have committed a greater sin than you could ever imagine. I do not deserve the privilege of this walk. I must go back.

She starts to return through the crowd, but her sisters have gathered around her. She begins to cry. Her sisters sing to her. They assure her that the goddess loves all her daughters. There is nothing the goddess does not already know. Her sisters are willing to act as witnesses to her story, if she wanted to tell it. But regardless, her sisters were there for her. She sits and speaks again.

I incarnated once as a man. I was a merchant. A son of Isaac. I was forced from my homeland for my faith. I was also a survivor. I left my land and changed my name. I wanted money and fame. So I seduced a queen and she gave me ships and men and we set out to bring her valuable treasures from foreign lands. After much hardship on our journey, we landed on an island. The people there I called savages. I stole their gold for my queen and took several of them back with me as my slaves.

I enjoyed my power. I was abusive and I enjoyed it. I was cruel. I was the savage. My goddess, I do not know why I was given such a lifetime. I, who, had once been a priestess in your name. I have suffered much guilt and pain for what I did. The yoke is heavy.

Her sisters gathered around her. One of them spoke:

I was he that once helped you spread the mysteries of the goddess. I was your lover and messenger then and I will be your lover and comforter now. You once told me that it is not the way that is important, but the lesson. You have forgotten, your teachings. What have you learned? You have silenced the multitude with your story. Your tears have moved us. You are here with us giving rebirth to yourself and to your mother. Your goddess. She welcomes you as her daughter. Your journey has been long and difficult for you chose to challenge the very essence of who your soul is. And, my sister, you have lived to tell.

In another part of the pilgrimage another story was being told and another and another and on and on.

Meanwhile, Debra and Lydia were busily preparing the altar for the ritual that was to be held. The animals had helped by bringing the sacred items for the altar. Food was being prepared by women who had arrived earlier. Lydia and Debra had spent hours communicating with the goddess and making love with each other. Their time together was always very short.

One of the women, who was acting as a scout, gave the signal that the pilgrimage was but a few hundred paces away. Debra and Lydia got dressed, adorned each other and went to meet the women. The campfire was roaring. Lydia and Debra greeted each one of the women with the following prayer:

> I am light in the dark, as are you
> I am dark in the light, as are you
> We are two that make one
> Come, the future has begun

They kissed each woman and invited her to partake of food and drink. To bathe and to join in the re-birthing circle. After several days the pilgrimage was settled along the valley and the hillside. Lydia and Debra began the ritual.

They called in the four corners. They summoned spirits from the past, the present and the future. When everyone was present. They, and everyone sang the name of Gaia. Over and over, they sang her name. Gaia. Gaia. Gaia. Louder and louder. Until there was silence. Debra and Lydia knew from the silence that there time had come to depart. All over the hillsides women were learning once again to love themselves and each other. To embody the erotic and to heal herself and her sisters. Thereby bringing joy and pleasure to their Mother, Gaia.

Light In The Dark and Dark In The Light made love one last time. In the glory and ecstasy of their orgasms, the melded with the light and dawn broke upon hillside for the first time in nine months.

As the sun rose, the women heard through the yoni-net a message from Gaia:

> Dear Daughters of the Earth,
>
> Welcome home. I, like you, am refreshed and renewed. I look forward to feeling the return of the warmth of the sun upon my face. Realize now that your world will be different. Your world is ready for change and growth. I will be with you. For you have nourished me with your blood. The blood of life. Go now in peace and remember.
>
> Love,
>
> Gaia

The women arose and welcomed the sun to their bodies. They began to make ready for the journey back their homes. At one point a terrible fear struck the women. The men. What of the men? Will they understand what the darkness had meant.

You will teach them.

The answer came from the yoni-net. It was the one voice of both Light In The Dark and Dark In The Light.

You will teach them and they will learn. For they, like us, wish for a return.

Biographies

Lucia Chiavola Birnbaum, Ph.D. has been tracking submerged beliefs, personally and professionally in her recent life. She teaches Women's Spirituality at the California Institute of Integral Studies in San Francisco and is heartened by signs that the dark mother is everywhere…and rising.

Jodi MacMillan is an ordained priestess and has been a professional clairvoyant and trance medium healer since 1992. She is the founder and executive director of Belladonna, a non-profit center for women's ancient and contemporary spiritual traditions in Berkeley, California.

Angeleen Campra, Ph.D., is an independent scholar, cultural observer, writer, and editor with an interest in representations of Divine Generative Force, she continues to explore the rich ground of the Gnostic Sophia as a bridge to a long line of ancient deities such as Isis, Maat, Cybele, Inanna, Ishtar, and Demeter and connecting this divine female energy forward to the Black Madonnas, Mary, Mary Magdalene, and Jesus.

Laura Amazzone, MA Philosophy and Religion, Women's Spirituality Concentration, is an independent researcher, writer, instructor, and artist. Her jewelry business, Bhaga Beads: Deity Necklaces and Bracelets of Healing and Empowerment—reclaims, celebrates, and honors the yoni and women's menstrual cycle as the source of creative, sexual, and instinctual female power. For more information visit www.bhagabeads.com

Anya Silverman returned to school at the age of 55 to study Women's Spirituality at the California Institute of Integral Studies and The New College of California in San Francisco. Her essay is based on her thesis work. Anya is now on the board of Crones Counsel, and is committed to bringing the Crone into as many women's lives as possible.

Gian Banchero is a painter, restaurateur and poet. Gian lives in Berkeley, California. He remembers the stories his grandmothers told him, paints black madonnas, and goes to Sicily to replenish his soul.

Chickie Farella is a performance artist and recipient of video music awards in the Chicago International and Athens International Film Festivals in 1981 and 1982. She is an independent scholar of Women's Spirituality and a recipient of a scholarship from the Italian American Cultural Foundation in 1997 for her work in progress, *Ciao Giulia*, published in part in *VIA 1999 Dieci Anni*.

Deborah Grenn, Ph. D. founded The Lilith Institute, A Center for the Study of Sacred Text, Myth & Ritual in 1997 (www.lilithinstitute.com), and is also the creator of Kol Ha-Ruach (Voice of the Spirit), a women's spirituality/ study circle. Deborah is Lead Faculty in the Women's Spirituality MA Program at New College of California; and adjunct faculty at Napa Valley College. She completed her MA degree in Women's Spirituality at New College in 1998, and her Ph.D. at CIIS; her dissertation was an inquiry into South African Lemba and United States Jewish women's religious identities, beliefs and ritual practices. Deborah's writings include *Lilith's Fire: Reclaiming Our Sacred Lifeforce* (Universal Publishers, 2000) and *Reconnecting with Lilith, Shekhinah and Self—A Reclamation Ritual for Shabbat*, to be published in Lifecycles, Vol. III (Rabbi Debra Orenstein and Rabbi Jane Litman, editors).

The great fire of feminism ignited Deborah Rose's life in the early 1970's and after a busy career as a grassroots activist, she settled into a path of healing with a focus on women's health. Since 1993 she has been researching, writing and lecturing about the black madonna and Mary Magdalene. She is also an acupuncturist and herbalist, co-founder and past president of the Acupuncture Society of Massachusetts.

Delphyne J. Platner, Ph.D., MFT, is a priestess of the Dark Goddess who integrates ritual and rites of passage working with young women to help sow the seeds of conscious resistance against the barrage of negative messages that impact girls throughout adolescence. Her recently completed doctoral dissertation, *All Women Are Witches: Women's Stories of Re-Awakening to Their Ancestral Memory and Inherently Spiritual Nature,* explores how contemporary priestesses utilize Women's Spirituality in healing from internalized oppression.

Diana Marto's performance art ceremonies have been featured in festivals around the world from Hong Kong to Capetown, to Catal Hoyuk, to Assos, Turkey. Her paintings, monotypes, fiber art and handmade paper sculptures have been exhibited in Tokyo, Santa Fe, and Paris. Born to a mother of Wasp descent and a Sicilian father whose parents were illiterate, she began to make art at a very young age. Her compassion and reverence for all life forms permeates her imagery.

Elizabeth Webster Shillington, Ph.D. lived for three years in Guatemala, where she and her husband John adopted their two children, Magdalen and Giancarlo. She holds an M. Div. from Union Theological Seminary and an M.A. in Linguistics from the University of Colorado. She holds a Ph.D. in Women's Spirituality at the California Institute of Integral Studies in San Francisco, California.

Janine Canan is a sixty year old poet and psychiatrist. Born in the City of the Queen of Angels and baptized Presbyterian, she began her exploration of religions as a teen. Running to Berkeley in the sixties, she quickly became known for her stubborn feminist stance. After suffering a broken heart, her real spiritual search began. She sat zazen; did Sufi dance, studied with Pir Vilayat Inyat Khan, and met Irina Tweedie. She traveled around the world, studied Vedanta with Swami Dayananda, and received initiation from the Dalai Lama. And then she met the" daughters of the Goddess", Ammachi, Gurumayi, Anandi Ma, Mother Meera, and Sri Ma. Today Janine is a love-struck follower of the teachings of Amma, the Mother of Compassion. Over the past thirty years, while maintaining a psychiatric practice, Janine Canan has authored over a dozen collections of poetry. Her latest book is In the Palace of Creation: Selected *Works* 1969–1999, illustrated by Meagan Shapiro. Other books are Changing Woman and *Her* Magnificent *Body.* Canan also edited the acclaimed anthology, *She Rises like the* Sun: Invocations of the *Goddess* by Contemporary American Women Poets, recipient of the Koppelman Award for best edited feminist work. She translated German Jewish poet Else Lasker-Schüler in Star *in* My *Forehead,* which was a Booksense and a City

Lights selection. She edited the posthumous work of avant-garde poet Lynn Lonidier, *The Rhyme of the Ag-ed* Mariness. She has edited a collection of contemplations by the contemporary Indian saint, Ammachi, In the Language of Love. And she is currently the poetry editor for Awakened Woman online. Janine's first collection of short stories is called *Journeys with Justine*, illustrated by Cristina Biaggi. You may visit the poet at www.JanineCanan.com.

Jean Harris spent forty years in the retail fashion business in the Bay Area. She's been married a long time, widowed a long time, has 3 sons, 4 grandchildren, and is a lover of life.

Jennifer Colby is an artist and the owner of Galería Tonantzin, a gallery of women's contemporary art. She teaches Culture and Equity and Service Learning at CSUMB (California State University Monterey Bay). She received her PhD in Humanities/Philosophy and Religion/Women's Spirituality at the California Institute of Integral Studies, San Francisco, California in 2001 writing on women's art and the image of Guadalupe. She lives in Aromas.

As a feminist historian, theologian, and astrologer, Kalli Rose Halvorson explores traditions from Old Europe and Asia wherein stars and planets are received as emanations of Goddess. She may be reached for readings at kalli@herstar.net.

Karen Nelson Villanueva is a Ph.D. student in the Humanities emphasizing Philosophy & Religion with a specialization in Women's Spirituality at the California Institute of Integral Studies, San Francisco, California. She holds Masters degrees in Public Administration from George Washington University and Culture & Spirituality from Holy Names College. She attended the University of Michigan in Ann Arbor as an undergraduate. Karen currently lives with her husband, Max, in San Francisco, CA.

Lorraine Paolucci Macchello is a native San Franciscan, born of Italian immigrant parents who came to America in the 1920s. Many of her writings are based on interviews with her mother, audio-taped when her mother was in her eighties. Before her retirement from Stanford, where she was employed in the French and Italian Department and at the Institute for Research on Women and Gender, Macchello assisted in the editorial process for many publications.

Louisa Calio is winner of the Connecticut Commission of the Arts Award for Writers, the Barbara Jones and Taliesin Prize for Poetry (Trinidad and Tobago) a writer and performance artist, founding member and executive director of City Spirit Artists, Inc. of New Haven (1976–81) a teacher, a traveler with a passionate love of Africa and the Caribbean, a published author, student of metaphysics, certified yoga instructor with a BA and Masters degree in literature. She lives in both Jamaica, WI and the USA where she is completing her novel in progress Lucia Means Light.

Luisah Teish is an initiated elder (Iyanifa) in the Ifa/Orisha tradition of the African diaspora. She is the author of Jambalaya: the Natural Woman's Book of Personal Charms and Practical Rituals. She is the founding Mother of Ile Orunmila Oshun (the House of Destiny and Love); the School of Ancient Mysteries/Sacred Arts Center; and Ase Theater, a multi-cultural ritual theater group.

Mary Saracino is the author of *Voices of the Soft-bellied Warrior: A Memoir* (Spinsters Ink, 2001) and two novels, *Finding Grace* (Spinsters Ink, 1999) and *No Matter What* (Spinsters Ink, 1993). *Finding Grace* won the Colorado Authors' League 1999 Adult Fiction Mainstream/Literary award. *No Matter What* was a 1994 Minnesota Book Award Fiction Finalist. She lives in Denver, Colorado.

Matomah Alesha was born in San Francisco, California. Her book—*The First Book of the Black Goddess* and the egroup *The Black Goddess Forum* was created to bring together people of color to explore goddess culture and traditions. At the time, this was the first of its kind online. Matomah is also a visual artist and poet. For more information about Matomah, visit www.matampress.com and kissyku.tripod.com

May Elawar is a student at the California Institute of Integral Studies working towards a PhD in Women's Spirituality. She is of Middle Eastern background and is interested in bringing this area into the rapidly growing pool of women's spirituality research.

Miri Hunter Haruach, Ph.D., director of PROJECT SHEBA and founder of the Institute for Cultural and Spiritual Studies (www.projectsheba.org), lectures on topics ranging from performance theory to the pre-monotheistic roots of Judaism She currently teaches in the Continuing Education Department at the University of Judaism, St. Mary,s College in Moraga CA and is an adjunct professor at the California Institute of Integral Studies in San Francisco. She is also a consultant for the Institute of Jewish and Community Research also located in San Francisco. She runs the weekly series in Los Angeles, Achot HaChalom (Sisters of the Dream), which features a speakers series as well as monthly Shabbat services and Tikkun Olam projects. In addition, Miri is also a singer, actor and percussionist performing in the Los Angeles area. She is a daughter of both the African and Jewish Diasporas.

For over 20 years Mary Beth Moser has traveled to Italy to do genealogical research in the villages of her ancestors. In 1995, she had her first encounter with the Black Madonna of Oropa. This moving experience planted the seed of knowledge that grew into an in-depth exploration of Black Madonnas in Italy. Mary Beth is a graduate of New College of California in San Francisco where she earned her Master's degree in Women's Spirituality.

Elisabeth Sikie is a freak poetrix from freakish Los Angeles, a yoga instructor and a practioner of the repressed shamanic arts of indigenous Europe. She has a B.A in Journalism (SFSU) and is a graduate student in Women's Spirituality (CIIS). She is also the founder of BlueDog Shamanic Services in Oakland, California (www.bluedogshaman.com) which offers instruction and counseling in the tradition of the Ancient ones. Her passions include hanging with the Temple Hounds, talking to dead people and kicking patriarchal christian demon ass in the astral plane. She can be reached at esikie@bluedogshaman.com.

Drawn to the mystical aspect of the Divine, Mari Pat Ziolkowski has recently completed her Ph.D. in Women's Spirituality at the California Institute of Integral Studies. Her dissertation focused on spiritual autobiography—her altered state encounters with the Hindu Goddess Kali Ma—and she has presented this work, as well as reclaimed ritual on Mari Magdalene, at lecture series and colleges in the Bay Area. During her tenure as a student, she was a co-facilitator of a spiritual/political discussion group, and currently facilitates a spiritually grounded mentoring group for women working on theses and dissertations at CIIS. Mari has been involved in some form of circle work for most of her career, whether with clients or peers. Before making the change to

CIIS, she was a counselor/social worker for 15 years. This work, as well as interest in social justice, took her to inner city Detroit, the border of Texas and Mexico, and Central America. Mari speaks fluent Spanish, and her interests include the reclamation of the Dark Goddess as a source of empowerment for women across cultures.

Susan G. Carter, Ph.D., is an assistant professor at the California Institute of Integral Studies, San Francisco, California, where she earned her doctorate in Philosophy and Religion. Her academic and personal interests come together with the study of women's spirituality, and prehistoric/proto-historic symbolism and art as an _expression of ancient spiritual traditions. She has presented her work at various national and international conferences.

Susan Sopcak is finishing her Ph.D. dissertation called, "Face to Face with the Goddess." After spending years in a high-tech corporate career, Susan followed the inner wisdom represented by her vision and changed her life and work. Now she offers a series of workshops called "Dying to Live" in which participants learn 'conscious dying' in order to fully live. Her current projects include a series of crone paintings and translating Tibetan texts.

Sandy Miranda has been a host and producer on KPFA FM in Berkeley for fifteen years. Her specialty is World Music and Culture, and she is just finishing her M.A. in Women's Spirituality at CIIS. She has just produced an 18 part series called "Women, Spirit, & Peace" with guests such as Marion Woodman, Alice Walker, Anna Halprin, Joan Baez, and Mayumi

Tricia Grame, Ph.D. CIIS, 2001, Integral Studies, Specialization in Women's Spirituality Independent Curator and curator for the Women's Spiritutality Dept at CIIS Art Studio in Danville, Ca.—create two and three dimensional art about prehistoric and contemporary imagery celebrating the female symbol in art Educator and Lecturer

Shiloh McCloud founded the Color of Woman Gallery in 1996. Color of Woman has shown over seventy-five women artists, held hundreds of educational workshops, non-profit project alliances, celebrational events, art exhibits and has sold thousands of works of art. Shiloh has self-published four illustrated journals for women. She is also the co-founder of The Red Thread

Nation, a not-for-profit foundation cultivating global community among women, and the owner of Cosmic Cowgirl Ink Publications.

Mara Lynn Keller (Ph.D., Philosophy, Yale University, 1971) is Director of the Women's Spirituality M.A. and Ph.D. programs in Philosophy and Religion at the California Institute of Integral Studies (www.ciis.edu). A wholistic philosopher and thealogian, she is a scholar and ritualist of the Eleusinian Mysteries of Demeter and Persephone, and has published articles on these Mysteries, the Goddess civilization of ancient Crete, the new field of archaeomythology, and Rosen Method Bodywork and Movement. Formerly at San Francisco State University, she co-founded and directed the Global Peace Studies program there, and also taught philosophy and women's studies. She has co-led educational tours for CIIS and the International Women's Studies Institute (www.iwsi.org)

Aikya Param is an artist and writer who earned her master's degree in Women's Spirituality from New College of California in San Francisco, CA in 2002. She delights in how the sacred reveals itself to us and our communities through our artistic expression. Her life is an experiment in changing the world through love.

Pamela Eakins, Ph.D. is a sociologist and student of the Western Mystery Tradition. In addition to her academic pursuits at the University of Colorado, Stanford University and the California Institute of Integral Studies, she has spent her lifetime embodying, studying, and teaching the 'mysteries.' She is the author of The Tarot of the Spirit, Priestess and Fire Bird from Ashes. She can be reached at www.pamelaeakins.org.

Dr. Anne Bouie serves as a consultant to urban school systems and policy making organizations focusing on urban educational issues. I am also a jewelry maker using natural elements to create pieces that are beautiful and useful for healing and spiritual support. I write as well, and am appreciative of being a part of this beautiful book. The Black Madonna represents the courage, passion, love, grace, beauty, and truth that I desire to manifest in my life. I believe we are all here to heal, be healed, and help one another.

Monica Sjoo is a beloved foremother in the study of women's spirituality. Her books and paintings have inspired scores of people. The paintings included in this anthology suggest her deep interest in the african/semitic goddess Tanit. Monica is presently engaged in writing a book on Tanit.

Naomi Doumbia recently graduated from CIIS with a doctoral dissertation on african traditional religions. With her husband, Naomi now lives in Africa where they research and write books on african culture. Lucia and Naomi are presently planning a CIIS study tour to Africa in 2006.

Independent scholar Max Dashu founded the Suppressed Histories Archives in 1970. Since then, she has photographed over 14,000 slides and created ninety slideshows on international women's history, including Women in Power, Witch Hunts and Racism: History and Lies. She has presented hundreds of slide talks at universities, community centers, bookstores, schools, libraries, prisons, galleries, festivals and conferences around North America. Dashu has guest-taught classes at John F. Kennedy University (Orinda, CA), California Institute of Integral Studies and New College (San Francisco), among others. She has acted as historical consultant for a variety of projects, including Donna Deitch's film, Woman to Woman in the early seventies and the San Francisco Women's Building mural project (1994). She is also an artist who publishes prints and notecards highlighting powerful women. Max Dashu has done extensive interdisciplinary research on the European witch hunts and folk traditions about witches.

Viviane Deziak Hahn has a passion for pilgrimage. Her dream is to have a retreat center for women in France and to offer walking pilgrimages in Europe. She is a writer, a mother, a wife, and an apprentice "technician of the sacred." She holds a BA in French from California State University Hayward, an MA in East-West Psychology from the California Institute of Integral Studies. She is currently a doctoral student in the Women's Spirituality Program at CIIS.

Female Series, Female Fusion © 2000
Tricia Grame
18" x 11" x 13" clay, plaster, cement, acrylic, steel and wood

"By venerating Her I am able to salute the divinity in all women and myself."
—Luisah Teish

"We are at the brink of new age which will be defined by new concepts in science, religion, and the reclamation of the values of the Dark Mother."
—Necia Harkless

"In my micro-geography, she is everywhere: in a sweat lodge in Indian Canyon, or in the Guadalupe chapel in San Juan Bautista, in a field of blue corn in Aromas protected with corn dollies, or in the Rodriquez Street Laundry in Watsonville…"
—Jennifer Colby

"In bringing memories of Her to the surface, I feel reborn, reconnected to the Earth, reunited with my Great Mother."
—Sandy Miranda

"Traveling to lands and sacred sites where evidence of the Goddess is irrefutable gives me a new spark and added hope…Sardinia herself *is* the Great Mother."
—Leslene della Madre

"The more women's voices I heard; the more I came to see the Sacred Feminine as immanent; the more I saw women who seemed to be filled with joy even in the midst of adverse circumstances…"
—Deborah Grenn

2436 Sacramento Street
Berkeley, Ca. 94702
www.belladonna.ws

End note

The realization that "she" is, indeed, everywhere has stimulated an outpouring of womanist/feminist writing spilling into volume two, also gathered by Lucia Chiavola Birnbaum, that hopefully will be published in 2005. Look, also, for volume three in the Belladonna series on the dark mother—gathered by Luisah Teish, entitled, *Dark Mother Rising!*

0-595-34034-2